INSIGHT GUIDE

MALAYSIA

D0069698

Discovery
CHANNEL

APA PUBLICATIONS
Part of the Langenscheidt Publishing Group

ABOUT THIS BOOK

Editorial

Editor
Francis Dorai
Editorial Director
Brian Bell

Distribution

UK & Ireland
GeoCenter International Ltd
The Viables Centre, Harrow Way
Basingstoke, Hants RG22 4BJ
Fax: (44) 1256-817988

United States
Langenscheidt Publishers, Inc.
46–35 54th Road, Maspeth, NY 11378
Fax: (718) 784-0640

Canada
Prologue Inc.
1650 Lionel Bertrand Blvd., Boisbriand
Québec, Canada J7H 1N7
Tel: (450) 434-0306; Fax: (450) 434-2627

Australia & New Zealand
Hema Maps Pty. Ltd.
24 Allgas Street, Slacks Creek 4127
Brisbane, Australia
Tel: (61) 7 3290 0322; Fax: (61) 7 3290 0478

Worldwide
**Apa Publications GmbH & Co.
Verlag KG (Singapore branch)**
38 Joo Koon Road, Singapore 628990
Tel: (65) 865-1600; Fax: (65) 861-6438

Printing

Insight Print Services (Pte) Ltd
38 Joo Koon Road, Singapore 628990
Tel: (65) 865-1600; Fax: (65) 861-6438

©2000 Apa Publications GmbH & Co.
Verlag KG (Singapore branch)
All Rights Reserved
First Edition 1972
Eighteenth Edition 2000

CONTACTING THE EDITORS
Although every effort is made to
provide accurate information in
this publication, we live in a
fast-changing world and would
appreciate it if readers would
call our attention to any errors or
outdated information that may
occur by writing to us at:
**Insight Guides, P.O. Box 7910,
London SE1 1WE, England.
Fax: (44 171) 403 0290.**
e-mail:
insight@apaguide.demon.co.uk

This guidebook combines the
interests and enthusiasms of
two of the world's best known
information providers: Insight
Guides, whose titles have set the
standard for visual travel guides
since 1970, and Discovery Channel, the world's premier source of
nonfiction television programming.

The editors of Insight Guides
provide both practical advice and a general under-
standing about a place's
history, culture, institutions and people. Discov-
ery Channel and its
comprehensive web site,
www. discovery.com, help
millions of viewers explore the
world from the comfort of their
homes, and also encourage them
to explore it firsthand.

How to use this book

The book is carefully structured
to convey an understanding of
Malaysia and its culture, and to
guide readers through its sights
and attractions:

◆ The **Features** section,
with a yellow colour bar,
covers the country's
history and culture in
authoritative essays.
◆ The main **Places**
section, with a blue

EXPLORE YOUR WORLD
Discovery CHANNEL

Map Legend

▬ ▪▪	International Boundary
▬ ▬ ▬ ▬	State Boundary
⊖	Border Crossing
▪	National Park/Reserve
▬ ▬ ▬ ▬	Ferry Route
✈ ✦	Airport: International/Regional
🚌	Bus Station
P	Parking
ⓘ	Tourist Information
✉	Post Office
✝ ✝ ⛪	Church/Ruins
✝	Monastery
☪	Mosque
✡	Synagogue
⛫ 🏛	Castle/Ruins
∴	Archaeological Site
∩	Cave
𝟏	Statue/Monument
★	Place of Interest

The main places of interest in the Places section are coordinated by number with a full-colour map (e.g. ❶), and a symbol at the top of every right-hand page tells you where to find the map.

bar, is a complete guide to all the sights and areas worth visiting. Places of special interest are cross-referenced by numbers or letters to specially commissioned full-colour maps.

◆ The **Travel Tips** listings, with an orange bar, provides information on travel, hotels, restaurants and other practical aspects of the country. Information can be located using the index printed on the back cover flap, which also serves as a bookmark.

The contributors

Apart from the usual tourist stomping grounds, this new 18th edition covers exciting new sights in both Peninsular Malaysia and the Borneo states of Sarawak and Sabah. Supervised by Singapore-based managing editor **Francis Dorai**, the book was completely restructured, building on the earlier edition put together by **Jessamym Cheam-Gwynne**.

Updating the history chapters and writing new essays on contemporary politics and religion was **Desmond Tate**, author of several books on Malaysian history. Malaysian Nature Society managing editor **Gail Saari** was a natural choice for revising the environment chapter. Practising architect **Puvan J. Selvaratnam** wrote the piece on architecture. The Insight On picture stories were largely the work of **Wendy Moore**, who also penned the arts and crafts essay.

The Places section was essentially the labour of two people: Peninsular Malaysia was updated by Kuala Lumpur-based freelance journalist **Siew-Lyn Wong**, who also found time to write the piece on adventure sports and the new Travel Tips section. Sabah and Sarawak were handled by veteran photojournalist **Jill Gocher**, a frequent traveller to Borneo.

New photography was provided by **HBL Network**, **Arthur Teng**, **R. Mohd Noh** and **Jill Gocher**.

This edition retains material from previous editions, largely the work of writers **Star Black**, **Harold Stephens**, **Sharifah Hamzah**, **Marcus Brooke**, **Susan Amy**, **Joseph Yogerst** and **Jeremy Cheam**.

The copy was edited in London by **Tim Harrison** and indexed by **Hilary Cooper**.

INSIGHT GUIDE
Malaysia

CONTENTS

Maps

Lush tea plantations of Cameron Highlands in the morning light

Travel Tips

◆ **Full Travel Tips index is on page 345**

Places

A PALETTE OF IMAGES

*Blending millennia-old rainforests with high-tech skyscrapers,
Malaysia will astound the most jaded of travellers*

Selamat Datang ke Malaysia – "Welcome to Malaysia" – is perhaps the first sign you'll see walking past the cool steel and glass corridors of the gleaming Kuala Lumpur International Airport (KLIA). It is a sentiment that will be warmly echoed by the smiling Malay, Indian or Chinese taxi driver who takes you from the airport into the booming capital of Kuala Lumpur. Even if you enter Malaysia by road and arrive first at a small Malay *kampung* (village), this same friendly greeting will be warmly offered.

Over the centuries, Malaysia has been open to millions of visitors from all over the globe, and its people have changed, absorbed and adapted customs and traditions from far-flung countries to suit the Malaysian way of life.

What is the most accurate image of the country? Travel brochures romantically depict a land of beaches with coconut palms, lost idyllic islands and amazing coral reefs. Somerset Maugham's short stories paint vivid pictures of colonial bungalows set in rubber plantations, while naturalist Alfred Russell Wallace's *Malay Archipelago* conjures up pictures of ancient jungles, screaming with monkeys and orang-utans, and brimming with butterflies. Yet, given the publicity Malaysia has enjoyed in recent years (thanks partly to the vociferous proclamations of its prime minister, Dr Mahathir Mohammad), the media would have us believe that the country is grooming itself to become the next Asian metropolis with big-ticket projects like the Petronas Twin Towers, the world's tallest pair of buildings, and the Multimedia Super Corridor IT project. These images are far from contradictory; indeed, Malaysia combines, album-like, every one of these visions – and more.

In Malaysia, you may find yourself in many incongruously different scenarios: from jiving at a ritzy Kuala Lumpur nightclub and visiting Malay *kampung* on the east coast to tramping millennia-old rainforests of Pahang and visiting tribes once known for their headhunting exploits in Borneo.

Some of the country's secrets will be unlocked from the pages of this guide; others are waiting to be discovered. You will find those idyllic beaches and islands, those rubber plantations (with the *punkah wallah* replaced by air-conditioning) and you will, if you venture out, find yourself in age-old jungles. But, no matter how strange the sights are to you, there is an innate sense of being in a land that welcomes you to explore it – Malaysia beckons, as it has done for countless centuries. ❑

PRECEDING PAGES: a *gasing*, or top spinner from Kelantan; ancient burial poles of Sarawak; Malaysian boys in their traditional finery; patriotic Malaysians at the opening of the 1998 Commonwealth Games.
LEFT: KL's Petronas Towers lays claim to fame as the world's tallest building.

Decisive Dates

THE EARLY CENTURIES

c.38,000 BC Remains of people found recently in Sarawak, on Borneo, date back 400 centuries.

c.2,500 BC Proto-Malays spread south from Yunnan area in China.

c.300 BC Earliest signs of Bronze and Iron Age cultures in Malaysia.

c.200 BC Start of trade with India and China.

100 BC–AD 200 Emergence of trading kingdoms in the Isthmus of Kra.

AD 500–1000 Development of local trading polities

with Hindu-Buddhist orientation on Bujang Valley and in northern Perak.

1290 First Muslim states begin to develop in northern Sumatra.

THE RISE OF MELAKA

c.1400 Founding of Melaka.

1409 Chinese Admiral Cheng Ho arrives in Melaka.

1411 Ming Emperor of China recognises Melaka's sovereignty and Parameswara's right as ruler.

1446 Melaka becomes a sultanate.

c.1450 Beginning of Melaka's expansion into an empire in Southeast Asia.

1509 The first Portuguese arrive at Melaka.

1511 Melaka falls to the Portuguese.

1512–1699 Empire of Johor comes under the control of Melaka.

1528 Sultan Muzaffar Syah establishes the Perak Kingdom.

1641 The Dutch take Melaka from the Portuguese; start of Dutch dominance in the area.

1699 Assassination of Sultan Mahmud of Johor at Kota Tinggi.

1699–1819 Empire of Johor, mostly at Riau, under Bendahara line.

1699–1784 Period of Minangkabu-Bugis struggle for domination of the Straits of Melaka.

1726 First sultan of Terengganu Kingdom installed.

1784 Death of Raja Haji at Melaka; Dutch break Bugis power in area.

1786 The British occupy Penang.

1812 Death of Sultan Mahmud Syah, last ruler of united Johor-Riau Kingdom.

COLONIAL MALAYA

1819 British occupy Singapore.

1824 Anglo-Dutch Treaty; Melaka is peacefully ceded to the British.

1826 British treaty with Bangkok limits the spread of Thai influence on the Malay Peninsula.

1831–32 The Naning War.

1840s The importance of tin increases, bringing an influx of Chinese tin miners to the western coast.

1841 James Brooke established as Rajah of Sarawak.

1846 British annex the island of Labuan.

1858–68 Civil war in Pahang.

1867–74 Selangor civil war.

1874 Start of British intervention and control in Perak, Selangor and Sungei Ujung.

1875–76 The Perak War.

1881 British North Borneo Chartered Company establishes a centre in North Borneo (what is known as present-day Sabah).

1891–95 Pahang Rebellion.

1895–1905 Mat Salleh Rebellion. The introduction of new taxes had earlier created general discontent, and Mat Salleh gathers many supporters in his revolt against the North Borneo Company. (Today, he is still regarded as one of Sabah's most famous heroes.)

1896 Treaty of Federation – the Federated Malay States (FMS) are created.

1909 Treaty of Bangkok transfers four northern Malay states from Thai to British control.

1914 Johor brought under British control.

1914–18 World War I.

1920–41 British adopt decentralisation policy in FMS; early signs of a Malay nationalism against British rule begin to surface.

MALAYA, MERDEKA, MALAYSIA

1941–45 Japanese conquest and occupation.

1945 British reoccupy Malaysia.

1946 Malayan Union scheme introduced but is opposed; formation of United Malay National Organisation (UMNO); Sarawak and British North Borneo become Crown colonies.

1948 Malayan Union scheme abandoned; Federation of Malaya inaugurated.

1948–60 Communist uprising – The Emergency.

1952 First municipal elections in Kuala Lumpur; UMNO and Malayan Chinese Association (MCA) parties cooperate.

1953 Alliance coalition comprising UMNO, MCA and Malayan Indian Congress (MIC) formed.

1955 First general elections in the peninsula; landslide win for the Alliance.

1956 Tunku Abdul Rahman leads Merdeka Mission to London to negotiate for independence.

1957 Malaya becomes independent, and the Union Jack is lowered for the last time.

1960 The state of emergency ends.

POST-INDEPENDENCE

1960 Formation of the Association of Southeast Asia (ASA) with the Philippines and Thailand.

1961 Tunku proposes a political association – called Malaysia – that would include Malaya, Singapore, North Borneo, Sarawak and Brunei.

1963 Creation of Malaysia.

1963–66 Confrontation with Indonesia, which intensifies its "Crush Malaysia" campaign. In 1966, Sukarno is ousted from power in Indonesia; the new Indonesian government, led by Suharto, is not keen to continue the confrontation, and a peace agreement brings the conflict to an end. The Philippines drops its claim on Sabah and recognises Malaysia.

1965 Singapore leaves Malaysia and becomes an independent nation.

1969 Riots in the wake of the general elections on 13 May are the result of simmering racial tension between Malays and Chinese. Violent outbreaks, mainly in Kuala Lumpur, kill hundreds of people and destroy a considerable amount of property.

1970 Start of the New Economic Policy (NEP), established to encourage a fairer distribution of wealth among the races.

1981 Malaysia's fourth prime minister, Dato' Seri Dr Mahathir Mohamad, takes office.

LEFT: Sultan Abu Bakar of Johor. **RIGHT:** an early 1990s portrait of Dato' Seri Dr Mahathir Mohamad, Malaysia's Prime Minister for almost two decades.

1983 Constitutional crisis involving the position of Malaysia's hereditary rulers.

1987 UMNO racked by power struggle between Mahathir Mohamad and Tengku Razaleigh Hamzah; "Operation Lallang" carried out by the Mahathir administration results in the detention of prominent opposition politicians, trade unionists, educators, environmentalists and church/community leaders.

1988 Deregistration of UMNO; formation of UMNO *Baru* (New UMNO) by Mahathir Mohamad.

1989 Semangat '46, led by Tengku Razaleigh Hamzah, registered as a new political party. The Communist Party of Malaysia abandons its 41-year armed struggle to overthrow the Malaysian government.

1990 General elections – the ruling coalition retains its two-third majority in Parliament.

1990s National car project, Proton, leads the move to transform Malaysia into fully-developed nation.

1996 Malaysia launches its first satellite.

1997 Petronas Towers, the world's tallest buildings, open. Economic downturn ensues; ringgit plummets and currency control laws are imposed to stop its free fall.

1998 Kuala Lumpur is the first Asian city to host the Commonwealth Games. Dismissal of Anwar Ibrahim from office as Deputy Prime Minister and subsequent arrest creates unprecedented political crisis.

1999 Anwar Ibrahim is given a six-year jail term for corruption and is further tried for sodomy. The economy shows positive signs of recovery. ❏

BEGINNINGS

Malaysia's ancient history is shrouded in myth, but its ideal position as a port
brought rapid development. And with trade came mighty empires

Gentle, young and growing – Malaysia is all this. But peel away the surface layer of modernity, and the kaleidoscope of Malaysia's history unfolds. The beginnings of human settlement go back at least as far as 35,000 years, with a motley cast of Malays, Ibans and Bidayuhs, Kadazandusuns and Muruts, Chinese, Indians, Europeans and other races. And the land's rich architectural history has borne an abundance of megaliths, ancient inscriptions, traces of Buddhist temples, abandoned forts, medieval mosques, and neo-classical colonial buildings.

Prehistoric Malaysia

The story of human habitation in Malaysia is enveloped in shadows as deep as those cast by the equatorial rainforest. What we know is pieced together from archaeological discoveries and ancient Indian, Chinese and Arab texts. However, these origins are still rife with unexplained mysteries.

A *Homo sapiens* skull discovered in Sarawak's Niah Caves, and believed to date from 35,000 BC, provides the earliest evidence of human life in Malaysia. In the Malay peninsula itself, the earliest archaeological remains so far excavated are at least 10,000 years old, indicating that these people were Mesolithic (Middle Stone Age) hunters and shifting cultivators. They lived in rock shelters and caves in the limestone hills of the peninsula and used stone implements for cutting and grinding, as well as for hunting wild animals. A typical tool was the hand axe, made by chipping a round pebble until a cutting edge was formed on one side. These people may have been the ancestors of the Negrito aborigines (Orang Asli) or of their successors, the Senoi.

Around 2,500 BC, the Proto-Malays, spreading south from Yunnan in China, made their way to the Malay peninsula and the islands beyond. These were the New Stone Age people,

their implements more sophisticated than those of the Negritos or Senoi. As well as hunters, they were also cultivators and sailors and thus lived a more settled life. Eventually they forced the Negritos and Senoi into the hills and jungles of the interior of the peninsula.

Much later, around 300 BC, a new wave of

immigrants, also of Malay stock pushed the Proto-Malays inland. Called Deutero-Malays by anthropologists, these were Iron Age and Bronze Age people, who used metal for their weapons and tools. The Deutero-Malays are in fact the direct ancestors of today's Malays in the peninsula and the archipelago.

Through trade, the early inhabitants of the Malay peninsula were exposed to older civilisations. The peninsula's location (including the Isthmus of Kra above it) interrupted direct sailing on the main sea route between east and west and the area was affected by nature's arrangement of alternating monsoons – southwesterly followed by northeasterly. These factors made

LEFT: ancient megaliths at Negeri Sembilan.
RIGHT: Orang Asli family, the original inhabitants.

it the natural meeting point for Indian and Chinese traders to exchange their wares. These foreign traders also came to buy the produce of the region itself, such as gold – the Malay peninsula was known to early geographers as "the Golden Chersonese" – aromatic woods, spices, and as far as the Chinese were concerned, birds' nests, highly prized for making revitalising soups.

The first of these Indian and Chinese trading voyages are believed to have taken place in prehistoric times and by the beginning of the Christian era, the trade routes were already well established. Convenient ports of call soon

The Indian period

Some settlements eventually grew to become kingdoms in which various features of Indian culture were adopted. The local rulers were known as *rajah*, and Brahmin rituals dominated royal courts. Even today, this early Indian influence can still be seen. Many Malay words are derived from Sanskrit, and some Malay social customs, especially wedding rites, reflect Hindu customs. So deep was this impact on local Malay society that the 1,500 years of Malaysian history between the arrival of the first Indians and the coming of Islam is called the Hindu or Indian period.

sprung up, which would later become the nuclei for other minor states.

Trade with China was as valuable as that with India. But the Chinese traders kept to themselves largely and were more interested in trade, thereby making little impression on local Malay culture. But a good number of the Indian traders settled down and integrated with the local inhabitants. As a result, many of the settlements along the straits were influenced by Indian ideas and resulted in many local Malays becoming Hindus or Buddhists. These new converts built temples, traces of which are still visible in the Bujang Valley of the state of Kedah and elsewhere.

The fame and fortunes of the Indianised kingdoms of the region depended entirely on their success in dominating the trade routes passing by their shores. Monopoly was the name of the game, and the port-kingdom which could secure the widest control over international and local trade by attracting foreign traders to its harbour was the winner, and thereby evolved into a maritime empire.

The first of these empires was Funan, based on the Mekong Delta. Next was Sri Vijaya, which from its base at Palembang in Sumatra, dominated the trade of the Straits of Melaka for the best part of a thousand years. In the 14th century, it was the turn of the great Javanese empire of Majapahit to control the trade of the region. Then at the dawn of the 15th century came Melaka, the first maritime power to be based on the Malay peninsula itself. It is with Melaka that the story of Malaysia truly begins.

The *Sejarah Melayu* or *Malay Annals*, was written in the early 1600s. Part historical fact and part legend, the text traces the transformation of a small coastal village into this famous trading empire. According to the *Malay Annals*, it all began on the island of Tumasek (now Singapore) at the tip of the

RAPID DEVELOPMENT

Parameswara founded Melaka with just a handful of followers; within just two years, the population had reached 2,000.

Taking a cue from this good omen, Parameswara decided to build a settlement on the site. As he happened to be standing near a melaka tree, he decided that the settlement should bear the name of that tree. The great port and kingdom of Melaka (or Malacca) came into being.

Parameswara and his followers cleared the land around it, planted rice and orchards, and exploited the rich tin deposits inland. News of the settlement's wealth spread, which soon began to attract passing traders.

Malay peninsula, which at the time was ruled by a Palembang prince with the Hindu title of *Parameswara*. When Javanese forces attacked Tumasek, Parameswara and his followers were compelled to flee northward to Muar in Johor on the peninsula.

One day, when Parameswara was out hunting near the coast, one of his hounds was kicked by a white mousedeer. The king, always appreciative of valour, exclaimed, "This is a good place! Even the mousedeer are full of fight!"

LEFT: 9th-century Hindu temple in the Bujang Valley, Kedah, reflects the influence of Indian traders.
ABOVE: Melaka was once a bustling trading port.

Chinese protection

At this time, the Ming Emperor of China was sending out large fleets of ships to expand trade with Southeast Asia and beyond. In 1409, one of his most famous admirals, Cheng Ho, called at Melaka. He recognised Parameswara as its legitimate ruler, and at Parameswara's request, placed the new port under China's protection. In 1411, Cheng Ho took Parameswara back with him to China – a trip which confirmed Parameswara's status as a sovereign ruler owing fealty to China alone. These moves were very important for Melaka's survival, for the new port-state was under constant threat of Siamese attack.

Melaka was ideally placed as a port and emporium. It had an ideal position on the Straits of Melaka, astride the great east-west maritime trade route. It also had a fine harbour free of mangrove swamps and deep enough for the ships of the day, with waters sheltered from storms by the island of Sumatra.

Melaka's harbour soon became crowded with ships of all kinds, the streets of the city alive with merchants from all parts of Asia. Its bazaar was crammed with exotic goods: silks, brocades,

ARABIC ARRIVAL

Muslim traders brought Arabic script to Melaka – the Malay version is called *Jawi* – which replaced the ancient Indian script Melakans had used before.

and porcelain from China; cloth, glassware and jewels from India; jade and diamonds from Burma; pepper, sandalwood, ebony and rice from the islands of the Malaysian/Indonesian archipelago, and tin, gold and other produce from Melaka's own hinterland.

An important reason for Melaka's success was its ability to ensure the safety of the traders who called there. Melaka's rulers commanded the allegiance of the Orang Laut, or sea gypsies, who managed to curb the pirate menace in the Straits of Melaka. In Melaka itself, *shahbandars* or harbourmasters, were appointed, each representing a particular community of traders. He watched over the daily affairs as well as settling disagreements among the sailors and merchants in his group.

The first Muslims in Southeast Asia were Arab traders, who can be traced back as early as the 11th century. Marco Polo, the great Italian traveller, discovered a Muslim kingdom in North Sumatra at the end of the 13th century. From North Sumatra, Islam was introduced into Melaka which by the middle of the 15th century had become a fully-fledged Muslim sultanate. Muslim Indian traders played a major role in this conversion and it was through trade that Islam spread to the other parts of the Malaysian/Indonesian world. At the same time, Islam became established wherever Melaka's own power as a maritime empire expanded. By the end of the 15th century, Melaka's empire included all the states of the Malay peninsula and those on the east coast of Sumatra.

The other states' conversion to Islam was a total revolution for the Malays. Islam brought with it new ideas about government and encouraged literacy by reading the Koran and other Islamic texts. Being a missionary religion with a message for each individual, Islam gradually had a great impact on the values and outlook of ordinary people. At the same time, however, the Malays managed to retain or merge much of their pre-Islamic customs with the new religion.

Mighty power

Over a period of some 20 years, Melaka rose from obscurity to become one of the most powerful states in Southeast Asia. Its population at the zenith of its might was 40,000 – mainly Malays, but also including a large number of Javanese and other settlers from the region, as well as Indian and Chinese traders.

The city was located at the mouth of a river and was divided into two halves. The sultan's palace and the Malay *kampung* were south of the river, while on the north bank the houses and stores of the merchants provided the cosmopolitan bustle of the city. The two halves were linked by a bridge, on which, like the bridges of many medieval European cities, a number of merchants built their shops.

The palace was the centre of life. Peasants, traders and noblemen had the right to present their petitions to the sultans, in his *balai*, or audience hall. The sultan would sit on a raised platform, surrounded by richly embroidered cushions and flanked by his ministers, two or three steps below him.

The ruler's power was, in theory, absolute and the biggest crime was *derhaka* or disloyalty to him. This concept is well illustrated by the famous tale of Hang Tuah and Hang Jebat, two of the Sultan's most famous warriors, who were also good friends of one another. In an act of treachery intended to please a capricious sultan, Hang Tuah murdered his old friend Hang Jebat. The killer was regarded at the time to have acted correctly; loyalty to the ruler, right

Shapers of Melaka

Parameswara died in 1414, leaving behind him a prosperous trading port. When his grandson, Sri Maharaja, died in 1444, there was a power struggle in the court between Malay chiefs and their supporters who defended Hindu tradition, and a rival group of Malay chiefs who, with the backing of Indian Muslim merchants, favoured Islam. It centred on two rivals as heirs to the throne. In the end the Muslim party won.

Muzaffar Shah, the new ruler, declared Islam the state religion. An able man remembered for his code of laws, his reign saw the emergence of Tun Perak, who was to become the leading

or wrong, came above all else. The *Sejarah Melayu* is full of tales of Melakans who would sooner have killed their friends or relatives, or suffered in silence, than to have shown disloyalty to the sultan.

In his administration, the ruler was assisted by a *bendahara* (chief minister), a *temenggung* (chief of police), and a *laksamana* (admiral). Below them were the various titled nobles. The royalty, common people and traders abided by this system. Apparently, it worked for Melaka.

LEFT: Indian Muslim traders played a crucial role in the expansion of Islam.
ABOVE: a Dutch-built bridge over the Melaka River.

ROYAL PREROGATIVE

The power of the sultan and the royal family was emphasised by a series of special privileges and prohibitions. No commoner could wear yellow, the colour of royalty. White umbrellas were to be used only by rulers, and yellow umbrellas only by princes. And only royalty was allowed to wear gold anklets.

There were also strict rules on language, with special words reserved for royalty and denied to commoners. For example, the everyday Malay word for "to eat" was *makan*; the act of taking sustenance became *santap* when applied to royalty. And while commoners would merely sleep (*tidor*), a tired royal would regally *beradu*.

figure in Melakan politics for 42 years. He became the new *bendahara* in 1456, and in that year repelled a Siamese invasion.

During the reign of Sultan Mansor Shah, who succeeded Muzaffar Shah, Melaka reached the peak of its glory. Its expansion is largely attributed to Tun Perak's efforts, who built a formidable fighting force. He also honoured brave warriors with the title of *Hang*, or captain, including the bearers of such famous names in Melaka's history as Hang Tuah and Hang Jebat. Tun Perak's expeditions led to the conquest of most of the peninsular states as well as those on the Sumatran shore opposite.

Sultan Mansur Shah was succeeded by Sultan Alauddin Riayat Shah. He was probably the strongest and most efficient of Melaka's rulers and took a direct and active part in the administration, including – so the *Sejarah Melayu* tells us – walking the streets at night to check the enforcement of law and order. But his direct methods upset some of his high officials who felt that their own powers were being undermined, and made him many jealous enemies. After a reign of only 12 years, he died in mysterious circumstances, probably poisoned. Alauddin's successor, Sultan Mahmud, was a man of different mould. He was destined to lose Melaka to the Portuguese.

The invasion of the "Franks"

The 15th century was Portugal's age of discovery. The Portuguese had two basic reasons for their voyages of expansion to the far corners of the world. One was to continue their crusade against Islam, for had they not just liberated their own homeland from the Muslims? The second was to grab a slice of the lucrative trade in spices from Southeast Asia. Since that trade was virtually monopolised by Muslims, their two objectives conveniently merged into one. And there was also the fabled Christian kingdom of Prester John, believed to lie in Abyssinia which, if found, could prove a useful ally.

Spices were the most important commodity in the trade between Europe and Asia. Portugal wanted to divert the trade route via the Red Sea and the Mediterranean, which was monopolised by Muslim traders, to a new route around Africa's Cape of Good Hope. Melaka was one of their targets, as it was the collecting point for spices from the Moluccas (the Spice Islands). As the Portuguese writer, Barbosa, put it, "Whoever is Lord in Melaka has his hand on the throat of Venice", which was the European terminal and mart for spices at the time.

The Portuguese first arrived in Melaka in 1509. They sought permission to establish a trading post, but were rebuffed by Tun Mutahir, the *bendahara*, who – backed by the Indian Muslim traders – attempted to seize the Portuguese and their vessels. Warned by a Melakan woman, the Portuguese – whom the Malays had nicknamed the "Franks" – escaped, leaving 20 of their number behind. These men were taken prisoners, giving the Portuguese a good excuse to return in force. This took place in 1511, when a large Portuguese fleet, led by Alfonso D'Albuquerque, the architect of Portuguese expansion in Asia, attacked Melaka. The Portuguese concentrated their onslaught on the bridge over the river, where the Melakan defenders put up a courageous resistance. Even Sultan Mahmud and his son were in the thick of battle, riding on caparisoned elephants. Most foreign traders, however, were either apathetic or supported the Portuguese.

On 24 August 1511, Melaka fell and the sultan and his followers fled into the country. Melaka had lost its independence, and under a string of foreign rulers, it never regained its former days of glory.

D'Albuquerque set up a Portuguese administration and built a fort, calling it *A Famosa* ("The Famous"). Within its formidable walls, a medieval Portuguese-style city developed, with a town hall, offices and homes for the Portuguese civil servants, while locals and other workers lived outside the walls of the town.

The Portuguese set about restoring Melaka to its former status as the leading emporium in the region, a title it formerly enjoyed under its Malay rulers. They also tried to make Melaka a great centre for Catholic missionary

FORMIDABLE FORTRESS

The *A Famosa* fort, built by D'Albuquerque in the early 1500s, was so solidly constructed that no enemy managed to breach its walls for over 130 years.

fending off attacks from their Malay neighbours on all sides. In many cases, *A Famosa* proved to be the only saving factor. As for the attempts to proselytise, Catholicism did not appeal to the local population – least of all to the Muslims – and the Europeans' arrogance did not go down particularly well either.

Meanwhile, following his flight from Melaka, Sultan Mahmud had settled in Bintang in the Riau Archipelago. He made two unsuccessful attacks on Melaka, and died in 1528. His elder

work among the local population. St Francis Xavier, the well-known Catholic missionary, stayed in Melaka three times whilst spreading the Christian gospel.

But the Portuguese did not succeed in either direction. They attempted to obtain a monopoly of the spice trade by requiring all ships using the straits to obtain passes from them, and by imposing arbitrary duties at the port of Melaka. But such actions aroused strong anti-Portuguese feelings, and they found themselves

LEFT: the Portuguese first arrived in Melaka in 1509.
ABOVE: Alfonso D'Albuquerque led the Portuguese conquest of Melaka in 1511.

son established himself in Perak, while his younger son started a new sultanate in Johor, from where he too continued to harass Melaka periodically. Meanwhile, in North Sumatra, Aceh, with a growing monopoly over pepper, became an important local power. It launched attacks on its main rivals in the area – Melaka, Johor and other Malay states. This three-cornered contest for control over the trade of the Straits of Melaka dragged on throughout most the 16th century.

Later developments in Europe led to the arrival of the Dutch and the English in Southeast Asian waters. In 1594, the port of Lisbon, now the spice mart of Europe, was closed to

Dutch and English merchants, compelling them to go direct to the source of the spices and collect them for themselves. The Dutch trading companies combined to form the United East India Company (VOC) in 1602. The VOC's interests were primarily focused on the Moluccas. However, they considered control of Melaka necessary to complete their own monopoly over the spice and local trade of the region,

In 1640, after blockading the port of Melaka and bombarding *A Famosa*, the Dutch encircled the town. As the siege continued, the Portuguese garrison and the people trapped in the fort began to starve and were forced to eat

whatever came into sight – rats, dogs, cats and snakes. It was reported that a mother even ate her dead child. The acute hunger was aggravated by diseases such as malaria, typhoid and cholera. Finally, in 1641, after a seven-month siege, the Dutch forces stormed into *A Famosa* and fought on to victory.

The Dutch were much more powerful and efficient than the Portuguese and were able to establish a much more effective monopoly over the trade of the region, particularly in spices, which they rigidly enforced. Since they made Batavia (now Jakarta) their headquarters, Melaka declined in importance as a trading centre. But it was useful as a base from which to control the local trade (such as tin and pepper) of the Straits of Melaka.

The Malay world

Meanwhile, Johore and the other Malay states of the peninsula continued very much as they had always done, in spite of the Portuguese and then the Dutch presence in Melaka. The main effect of the European presence was to reduce the scope of their trade. The Dutch capture of Melaka put paid to the triangular contest for control of the straits between the Portuguese, the Acehnese and the Johoreans, because the trade of both Aceh and Johore suffered as a result of the Dutch monopoly. Johore was further weakened by a disastrous war with Jambi, one of its former vassals in Sumatra in the 1670s, and at the end of the century, the last of its rulers directly descended from the sultans of Melaka was assassinated.

The pattern of a triangular contest to control the trade of the Straits of Melaka was repeated during the 18th century, but the players were newcomers – the Bugis, traditional seafarers and mercenary warriors from Celebes; the Minangkabau, based on the Sumatran state of Siak; and the Dutch themselves in Melaka.

By the 1780s the Dutch had come out on top, but by this time Bugis "underkings" were in effective control of the Johor sultanate and had established an independent sultanate of their own in Selangor. The Minangkabau settlers in the hinterland of Melaka had also established an independent state of their own in the form of a federation called Negeri Sembilan (The Nine States). Of the rest of the peninsula states, Perak, Terengganu and Pahang still owed allegiance to the sultans of Johor but in practice ran their own affairs. In the north, Kelantan and Kedah had fallen within the orbit of the Thais of Bangkok.

As for what is today Malaysian Borneo, Sarawak was a province of the sultanate of Brunei, while Sabah was divided between Brunei and the Sultanate of Sulu, which dominated the northeastern part of the domain.

Such was the state of affairs when the British appeared on the scene in the form of Francis Light and founded a settlement on Penang Island in 1786. ❏

LEFT: *A Famosa* fort in Melaka still stands today.
RIGHT: a 17th-century Italian map of the peninsula.

SIAM

PRETTO DI MALLA

LFO DI SIAM

ISOLA DI SALAN

Cornaie
Along
Clai
Ligor
Bondelon
Wanting
Pendaon
P. Boulon
Keidab
P. Iado
Queda
o Vechio
P. Pisang
Torano
P. Sorga
Bazuas
Soengei
Boros
Salom
Pendaon
Lago di Diamanti
delli Olandesi
P. Sambila
P. Iara
P. Aru
Soengei
Pao
Perrac
Solongor F.
Pulo
Bracelar
Pulo Cara
Pulo Panjag
Pulo Ubi
I. Ligor
Singor
Cabo Potane
Patane
F. Secco
F. Kalantan
Poncian
Banan
Kedaor
F. Bessot
F. Dongon
F. Palang
Pontigaran
Tingaran
Pahang
I. Coffin
Tuaro
S. P. Rou
Pinaca
Pulo Ridang
Pulo Capes
P. Barbala
P. Verella
P. Timon
P. Pisang
P. Laor
P. Tingi
C. Romania

MALACCA

Gori
Pairi
Casang
Brama
Porto Besar
Col. di Loque
Col. di S. Anna
Behacl I.
Utiel I.
Col. di
Tempesta
Cincel
Boere
Pita
Cincon
Balahan
Sickerban
P. Boby
P. Batou
I. del
Aqua
P. Medano
I. Pedrus
I. Pisang
I. Naos
Brancalis
I. Pantou
Siagua
Campar
C. Rachardo
Malacca
Prado
Baccalia
Quicil
Tantan Boori
Tantan Biggi
Orco Quercio
Passir
Djohor
Sincapoera
Senausu
Carimon
Saban
Stretto di Sincaporea
Bintan
Domines

Equina

Lingen
Gelgote
Sojo
Fratelli
Liz
Passaman
Aron
Priaman
Cafatenga
Padang
Jellekan
Manacabo
Saleda
I. Cocos
I. Willens
Indrapo
Remtapou
Bantal
Mothomocho
Lomanta
Nasson I.
Mosquiten I.
I. Tartaruga
I. Bassa
Batauira
Drop
Andragari
Taoje
Olandesi
Lamby
Speriam
Baros
Telombuan
Salecar
Palambam
Lamang
Cattoan
Ipce
Bencolen
Monte Sillebar
Sillebar
Jonjon Tiande
Pongon
Fort
Martebour
met Recif
Pietra di Guvin
Petten I.
Madona Formosa
Monte
Manapihi
Qualagung
La 1.ª
Punta
La 2.ª Punta
La P.ma Punta
F. Giouan
F. S. Clara
F. Dolce
Dampin
Cabo Tristo
Goudan
ISOLA BANC
Beraio

ISOLE

Engano I.
Pisang I.
Pongon
Massomahi
Montali
Zollok
Bouton
Sfaliamento

COLONIAL MALAYA

Malaya's position as a trading nation continued to attract the attentions

of Europe's imperial powers, eager to exploit its wealth

The British first arrived in Southeast Asia in the early 17th century. But finding their trading opportunities stymied by their more powerful Dutch trading rivals, the British had concentrated their efforts on India instead.

The English East India Company (EIC) had, by parliamentary charter, been granted monopoly rights over all British trade with India and beyond. In the 200 years since their first unsuccessful forays into the region, the EIC had developed a very profitable trade with China, exchanging Bengal opium for Chinese tea. A base along the way would protect the trade and serve as collecting centre for straits produce.

Doing deals

The first step in the formation of the Straits Settlements occurred in 1785 when the Sultan of Kedah allowed the EIC to establish a base on the island of Penang. The sultan saw this as his chance to obtain protection against Siam, his northern enemy, and was prepared to grant trading rights to the British in exchange.

Francis Light, who had negotiated the agreement on behalf of the EIC, landed in Penang in 1786 and raised the Union Jack on the sparsely populated, jungle-smothered island. But Light's agreement with the Sultan of Kedah was based on false pretences. The sultan wanted British protection against his enemies but it soon became obvious that the EIC had no intention of providing this. The angry sultan assembled his ships to recapture Penang, but Light attacked first and destroyed the fleet. The resulting treaty guaranteed the sultan $6,000 a year, in return for which the EIC got Penang.

Penang was declared a free port, attracting merchant vessels from all over the east-west trade route. The population grew rapidly and Light followed the Malay and Dutch practice of appointing several *kapitan* – community leaders with authority to hear all minor crimes committed by members of their representative

communities. For major crimes, Light himself tried offenders with his rough and ready sense of justice. Penang prospered, but not as greatly as the EIC had hoped, for it proved to be a little too far up the Straits of Melaka to be a focal point of regional trade.

The second of the British settlements in the

straits was Singapore, occupied when the EIC's representative, Stamford Raffles, landed there in 1819. Raffles was a great imperialist and champion of free trade – which suited British commercial interests – and he was alarmed at Dutch attempts to restore their monopoly over regional trade. So Singapore was designed as a regional bastion of free trade, as well as a useful port of call on the China trade route. The territory was fully secured by treaty in 1824.

The last of the three main British settlements in the straits was Melaka itself. The British had already occupied Dutch-controlled Melaka on two occasions during the French Revolutionary and Napoleonic wars. The French had occu-

LEFT: James Brooke, first "White Rajah" of Sarawak.
RIGHT: Francis Light monument in Penang.

pied Holland, and the British were concerned that Melaka too might fall to them. The onset of peace saw the Dutch returning to Melaka in 1816, but only for a few years. In 1824, under the terms of the Anglo-Dutch Treaty of that year, which settled conflicting British and Dutch interests in the region, the British acquired Melaka in exchange for their Sumatran settlement of Bencoolen.

In 1826 Penang, Singapore and Melaka came together under one administration based in Singapore, and given the collective name of the Straits Settlements (SS). Singapore soon emerged as the most important. With its free port status and strategic position, Singapore became the new emporium, its harbour crowded with ships of all nations. By the 1850s, it was the leading port in the region and its trade further increased after the opening of the Suez Canal in 1869. Singapore soon became one of the greatest ports in the world.

Strictly speaking, the SS were concerned only with trade, and the British tried to stay out of the peninsula's other affairs. But this official policy of non-intervention was broken on a few occasions, generally in order to protect British trade from Thai interference in the northern Malay states.

British intervention

But there were murmurs of dissent from the merchants of the Straits Settlements. Many were growing restless with the policy of non-intervention. The Chinese had started to plant pepper in the neighbouring Malay states of Johor, and tapioca in Melaka and Negeri Sembilan. Prosperous straits merchants wanted similar opportunities for investment. But the biggest attraction was tin.

The Malay peninsula had always been rich in tin, its ore mined and traded for centuries. In the mid-19th century, with the rise of the canning industry, demand for the metal shot up. SS merchants with money invested in the new mines of Selangor, Perak and Negeri Sembilan now campaigned for British intervention in these states to safeguard their interests.

The tin rush brought with it widespread unrest. Malay chiefs blessed with rich tin deposits in their domains became rich and powerful magnates whom the sultans could no longer control. Conflicting ambitions led to disputes and civil war. Even the Chinese miners who flocked into the tin districts were themselves divided between rival secret societies that constantly fought one

nese miners of Larut on his ship off Pangkor Island. This resulted, in January 1874, in the signing of the Pangkor engagement, which settled a dispute over the throne of Perak, and imposed a British "Resident" on the new sultan whose advice had to "be asked and acted upon on all questions other than those touching Malay religion and custom". By August, Clarke had made a similar agreement with Selangor, and soon after that with Sungai Ujong, the largest of the Negeri Sembilan states.

another. These uncertainties threatened investments, and caused a drop in tin exports just as world demand began to exceed supply. The troubles also threatened to overflow into the SS. Meanwhile, British officials feared that if they did not intervene in these states, investors would seek assistance from a rival imperialist power, such as France or Germany.

A new governor, Andrew Clarke, was sent to sort out the situation. First, he met the Malay chiefs of Perak and the leaders of the rival Chi-

FAR LEFT: Stamford Raffles, founder of Singapore.
LEFT: painting of early 19th-century Penang.
ABOVE: British officials pose for the camera.

The residential system

Under the new system in these states, British residents were appointed only "to advise" the rulers on how to improve the administration of their states. However, control would ultimately rest with the resident, and the success of the system very much depended on how each resident exercised his power.

J. W. W. Birch was the first resident in Perak. Intolerant and tactless, with little regard for local customs and impatient for change, his proposed reforms of taxation and the banning of debt slavery threatened to undermine the social fabric of the state. The reforms were naturally opposed by the Perak chiefs and by the sultan himself. In response, in 1875 the governor ordered the state to be placed under the direct rule of British officials. Birch's attempt to put this new command into effect cost him his life. He was killed at Pasir Salak, a village on the Perak River.

Birch's eventual successor was Hugh Low, who took a different approach and laid the foundations for the effective working of the residential system. One of his innovations was the setting up of a state council. Its members included the

THE BIG PAYBACK

Debt slavery – mortgaging yourself to your creditors in return for financial help – was common practice in 19th-century Malaya. In bad times, it was the only way a peasant could raise finances.

port of the *Yam Tuan Besar* or head of the Negeri Sembilan federation and resorted to arms, but were easily defeated by superior British musketry. In the end the progress brought about by the residential system in Sungai Ujong finally won over the Yam Tuan and the heads of the other states of the Negeri Sembilan Federation. In 1895, they were joined by Sungai Ujong in one reunited state with a British resident and the Yam Tuan as their head.

Exaggerated reports of great mineral wealth

resident, the sultan, major chiefs and one or two Chinese leaders who discussed the government's policies. The council provided a useful sounding board for public opinion, but the resident was the real policy maker. The format of the Perak State Council was adopted by the other states which came under the residential system. Low also succeeded in ending debt slavery in Perak, but by gradual means which avoided hardship.

Residential progress

In Selangor, things went a little more smoothly. In Sungai Ujong, the Malays were divided. Those who opposed British rule got the sup-

in Pahang awakened British interest in the state. In 1887, Pahang's ruler, Sultan Ahmad, was persuaded to accept a British agent, but the first agent, Hugh Clifford, found the sultan and his chiefs unwilling to relinquish their rights. The atmosphere grew tense, and when the following year a British subject was murdered in Pekan, the state capital, the British used this as an excuse to force the sultan to accept a British resident. But many of the Pahang chiefs resented the new regime because of their loss of power and income. In 1891, a number of them rebelled against the British presence, led by Dato' Bahaman of Semantan (Temerloh). Though the British were far too strong to be defeated, the rebellion took four years to quell.

In 1896, Selangor, Perak, Negeri Sembilan and Pahang were brought together as the Federated Malay states (FMS), with its capital at Kuala Lumpur. A British resident-general was appointed with jurisdiction over the four states. The purpose of this move was to ensure uniformity in administration, promote faster economic development, and to help the richer members (i.e. Perak and Selangor) assist the poorer ones, especially Pahang. The creation of the FMS made for more efficient government and served the business and commercial interests of the colonial regime.

and Perlis in the north of the Malay peninsula recognised the general overlordship of Siam. This was demonstrated by the sending of the *Bunga Mas* (golden flowers) to Bangkok.

British strike deal with Siam

However, Thai power over these states was vague and fluctuating. In 1909, the British made a treaty with Siam. This gave to Britain whatever rights and power Siam possessed in these states, so that they now became British protectorates under British advisors with similar status to the British residents in the FMS.

This change was made without consulting

The rulers agreed to the federation thinking that, by joining together, they would exercise more control over the residents and regain their lost authority. Unfortunately, this did not happen. Instead, the resident-general now exercised real power, which he used without reference to the residents or the rulers. In effect, "federation" centralised power in the hands of British officials, who ran the show almost by themselves.

Meanwhile, Kelantan, Terengganu, Kedah

the Malay rulers concerned, which caused a lot of resentment. In fact, these states had run their own affairs quite satisfactorily, and British interference was unpopular. In Kedah, a treaty defining the role of the British advisor was not signed until 1923 because of the hard bargaining to win Malay acceptance of the British presence. In Kelantan (1916) and Trengganu (1928), there were popular anti-British uprisings which were put down by force. Finally, in the south, Johor – the most progressive of all the Malay states – was pressured into accepting a British advisor in 1914. British control was complete, and the Malay peninsula was divided into three separate parts – the Straits

FAR LEFT: Hugh Low, who laid the foundations of the Residential System. **LEFT:** Sultan Abdullah of Perak. **ABOVE:** Frank Swettenham, the Resident of Selangor. **RIGHT:** *Bunga Mas* tribute to appease the Siamese.

Settlements (SS), Federated Malay States (FMS) and the Non-Federated Malay States (FMS).

The Malay peninsula had just undergone rapid change. Meanwhile, the territory of Sabah (called British North Borneo) and the "White Rajah" state of Sarawak, had been enjoying developments of their own.

The first "White Rajah" of Sarawak, James Brooke, was an Englishman born in India. As a young man, he had served with the East India Company's army in Burma and when his father died in 1835, leaving

BUOYANT EXPORT

By 1920, the rubber tree was the mainstay of Malaya's economy – the country provided over 50 percent of the world's rubber.

crushed and in return for Brooke's help, Rajah Muda Hashim awarded him control of the province. In 1841, Brooke, aged 38, was installed as Rajah of Sarawak.

With the help of local chiefs, Brooke set out to establish law and order. This meant overcoming Iban and Malay warriors who lived by piracy. He won, because he had the help of British warships against which Iban and Malay *perahu* (boats) were helpless. Brooke did not introduce new laws, but used existing customs and consulted with the chiefs.

Brooke a sum of money, he used it to buy a schooner and organise an expedition to explore Borneo and the Celebes.

Brooke's lucky break

Stopping off at Singapore on his way, Brooke was asked by the governor to deliver a message to the Malay governor of Sarawak, a province of Brunei confined to the area around Kuching. When Brooke arrived in Kuching in 1839, he found the Rajah Muda Hashim, a relative of the Sultan of Brunei, trying to put down a rebellion against Sarawak's governor. On returning a year later, Brooke decided to help the Rajah Muda Hashim. The rebellion was

Brooke was always short of money, but he refused to introduce foreign capital; he believed that government should be in the interests of the Sarawakians, and not of outside business interests. Under his rule, more territories were brought under Sarawak's control. In 1857, a Chinese revolt nearly overthrew him, but it was quickly suppressed. In 1863, he retired to England where he died five years later.

Brooke's nephew, Charles Brooke, became the second rajah. A better administrator than his uncle, he brought Sarawak out of debt, reduced head-hunting, expanded trade, and brought greater prosperity. He died, at the age of 87, in 1917.

Meanwhile, sovereignty over North Borneo (present-day Sabah) was acquired from the sultans of Brunei and Sulu in 1877 by Overbeck, the Austrian consul-general in Hong Kong, and Alfred and Edward Dent, prominent Hong Kong businessmen. In 1881, Overbeck withdrew and the Dents formed the British North Borneo Company under a royal charter.

The North Borneo Company, like the Brookes in Sarawak, faced considerable opposition to the imposition of its rule. The most serious resistance came from Mat Salleh, a Sulu chief, who rose up in revolt in 1895. The introduction of new taxes had created general discontent, and Mat Salleh gathered many supporters. In 1900, Mat Salleh was killed, but the rebellion was not quelled until five years later.

Material wealth

Throughout the entire colonial period, tin and rubber were Malaysia's main exports. It was these that engendered the development and great social changes that the region enjoyed.

Tin rose in importance in the mid 19th century because of the invention of the tin can, the rise of the canning industry and other new uses for tin plate. This created an ever-increasing demand for Malayan tin on the world market. By 1904, the peninsula was producing more than half the world's tin supply. Besides the political repercussions on the Malay States, this also led to a huge influx of Chinese immigrants.

Until the 1900s, tin mining was mainly in Chinese hands. The introduction of tin-dredging in 1912 enabled Europeans to gain an upper hand in the industry, as they had the technology and capital which the Chinese did not.

Rubber arrived in Malaya as a foreign plant but grew to become the mainstay of its economy. Rubber seeds were transported from Brazil to London's Kew Gardens for experimentation as an Asian crop in the 1870s. Some of the seeds were sent to Malaya where they were planted in Singapore and elsewhere. The millions of rubber trees in Malaysia today all stem from these original seedlings.

However, no one took rubber seriously until H.N. Ridley became director of the Singapore Botanical Gardens in 1888. Ridley had no doubts about the future of rubber but his attempts to persuade coffee planters to experiment with this strange new crop were initially unsuccessful. However, at the end of the 19th century, the price of coffee collapsed. The birth of the motor-car industry and the consequent demand for rubber tyres triggered the rush to farm the plant. Many fortunes were made in the great rubber-boom which followed.

Migrant Indian labour was brought in to work the rubber estates, while many Malays became smallholders. The industry went through gluts and slumps, but remained the mainstay of the Malaysian economy right up to the 1970s.

Revenue from tin and rubber was used to build up the country's infrastructure and social amenities. Attention was focused on the tin mines and rubber estates at the expense of the less profitable areas, which remained neglected. In particular, development and social change were noticeably slower in Sabah and Sarawak, although rubber was still very important to both their economies. As the tin and rubber industries boomed, Malaysia's plural society developed. By the 1930s, the population of Malaya (excluding Singapore) was about 4 million, comprising 49 percent Malays, 34 percent Chinese and smaller groups of Indians, European expatriates and other races. ❑

LEFT: Sarawak's Ibans with their *perahu*, or small boats, were no match for the British warships.
RIGHT: tapping latex, the raw material of rubber.

قشمهوران کمرديکاءن

دڠن نام الله يڠ مها موراه لاݢي مڠاسيهاني، سݢالا ڤوجي باݢي الله يڠ مها برکواس

دان صلوات دان سلام اتس سکلين رسولڽ

بهاواساڽ اوله کران تله تيبا ماسڽ باݢي اومة ملايو اين منچاڤاي طرف سواتو بڠسا يڠ مرديکا لاݢي بردولة اينامڤستيمبيلكي دود کڤد دغن شکل سلوره دنيا

دان بهاواساڽ اوله کران دڠن ڤرجنجين يڠ دماتري ممان ... تاهون 1957

دان بهاواساڽ اوله کران تله برستوجوءولاه برستو ... تاهون 1948

دان بهاواساڽ اوله کران دولي ... ملايو لوکس ڤرسکوتوان تانه ملايو تاهون 1957

دان بهاواساڽ اوله کران سبواه ڤرلمباݢاءن باݢي کراجاءن ڤرسکوتوان

دان بهاواساڽ اوله کران ڤرلمباݢاءن ڤرسکوتوان ... تاهون 1957

مک دڠن نام الله يڠ مها موراه لاݢي مڠاسيهاني ... ڤرتنرين المرحوم سلطان عبد الحميد

محمد رجيم مرزا
ڤردانا منتري

کوالا لمڤور
31 هاريبولن أوكسس تاهون 1957

MALAYA, MERDEKA, MALAYSIA

After a period of peace and prosperity, World War II shattered the colonial calm.
For good or bad, Malaysia would never be the same again

Between 1900 and 1941, British rule in Malaya was stable, their subject peoples contented, and the economy basically sound and expanding. In many ways, British Malaya was a showcase of benevolent imperialism. The British referred to Malaya during this period as a land without politics.

This, of course, was not quite true. The British had brought into being a multi-racial society, the contradictions of which were steadily mounting – even if they had not yet reached crisis point. Issues which would one day have to be faced, included the rights of the Malays and other indigenous peoples in their own country, and the position of the Chinese and Indians, the two major immigrant groups, who were beginning to regard Malaya as their permanent home. British policy was to stick to the principle that Malaya was the land of the Malays, and that Sabah and Sarawak were also the lands of their indigenous peoples. This was acceptable when there were no pressures, economic or political. But rising nationalism, the threat of international communism, and the impact of the Great Depression of 1929–33 increasingly threatened the Pax Britannica.

The Japanese Occupation

But what finally ended the deceptive calm was the sudden extension of World War II – raging in Europe since 1939 – to Southeast Asia. In December 1941, Japan launched her attack on the Western colonial powers which she believed were out to strangle her. Within 9 weeks, Japanese forces had overrun the whole of Malaya. Their victory destroyed the comfortable colonial world and ended for ever the unchallenged supremacy of British rule. Things could never be the same again.

The writing on the wall had come in 1931 when the Japanese army unilaterally annexed Manchuria, and became the dominant force in

LEFT: the Malay Proclamation of Independence, 1957.
RIGHT: a Japanese Occupation newspaper reports on Japan's successful invasion,1943.

Tokyo. The next move came in 1937, with the attempt to bring China under Japanese control. But China proved unconquerable, and the growing Japanese need for strategic raw materials such as oil and rubber made Southeast Asia the target, especially the British and Dutch possessions where these materials abounded

but were denied them by the Western powers. In early 1941, the Japanese took advantage of France's defeat to occupy French Indo-China. It was clear that Malaya would be next.

Among the many reasons advanced for Britain's humiliating failure to defend Malaya – poor strategies, untrained troops, guns pointing in the wrong direction, etc. – the most telling is British weakness in the air. Effective airpower would have crippled the Japanese invasion. Instead, it was Japanese airpower that triumphed; by sinking two capital British warships in the first week of the invasion, the British were crippled.

The Japanese Occupation caused great hardship among the peoples of Malaya. The Japanese arrived with persuasive propaganda about a "Co-prosperity Sphere" and "Asia for Asians". But they had won a great battle, not the war, so were unable to put these promises into effect. Instead, they were obliged to rule with an iron fist to control the resentment of a population suffering from shortages of food and essential goods, high inflation and low incomes.

The Japanese were especially wary of the Chinese, most of whom were hostile towards

NEW NATIONALISM

The end of World War II saw conspicuous growth in political self-determinism, now summed up by the fashionable slogan: *Malaysia Boleh*! (Malaysia Can Do It!)

ority before the white man. Those working in the administration, in public utilities and wherever else assumed the responsibilities once held by their European masters, and gained a new self-confidence and self-respect. This was the beginning of the spirit of *Malaysia Boleh*! (*see page 47*). As a result, when the Japanese were finally defeated by the Western powers, Malayans had a new attitude and new outlook. They were no longer prepared to go back to the way things were before World War II.

them because of "the China incident". The brunt of Japanese brutality was directed against the Chinese, tens of thousands of whom were executed or imprisoned. Europeans (except for nationalities who were neutral or Japanese allies in the war) ended up living under atrocious conditions in detention camps. Some were sent, along with thousands of Indian labourers and a good many Malays, to work on the notorious "Death Railway" – constructed to provide a rail link between Thailand and Burma. Conditions there were even worse, and many died.

Despite the terrible suffering, the Japanese Occupation did have an important plus side. It liberated Malayans from their sense of inferi-

Peace and a fresh start

The Japanese Occupation ended as swiftly as it had begun with the dropping of atomic bombs on the Japanese cities of Hiroshima and Nagasaki in early August 1945. The war finally ended in Malaya in September, when British and Australian forces landed in Malaya and Borneo – in fact the liberation of Borneo had already begun – and re-established British authority. The British received a warm welcome; their return promised relief from the hardships of the Japanese occupation. But everyone agreed, including the British themselves, that the political situation had changed and that British rule could not last for ever.

In fact, the British had already decided to form the FMS, the non-FMS, Penang and Melaka – but not Singapore – into a single state to be called the Malayan Union. The union would have a central government headed by a (British) governor and the former Malay States would cease to exist, their rulers simply remaining as heads of Islam.

At the same time a common citizenship was created, including long-term Chinese and Indian residents as well as the Malays. In short, Malay sovereignty was to be transferred to the British Crown, turning Malaya into a colony and destroying Malay political pre-eminence. A British envoy came to Malaya, and after using a lot of pressure, got all the Malay rulers to accept the scheme.

However, this proposal was strongly opposed, especially by the Malays, who felt that they were being sold down the river. In March 1946, representatives of 41 Malay associations met in Kuala Lumpur to form a national movement to oppose it. This led to the birth of the United Malay National Organisation (UMNO) led by Dato' Onn Jaafar. UMNO demanded the repeal of the union. Although the British inaugurated the union in 1946, Malay opposition was so strong that after negotiations with the Malay rulers and UMNO it was replaced by the Federation of Malaya, which included all the Malay States and Penang and Melaka as members. The new federation came into being on 1 February 1948.

The Malays accepted the federation because it preserved the sovereignty of the rulers and restored state rights. Because the citizenship terms for Chinese and Indian Malaysians were not so generous as before, it was more grudgingly accepted by those communities.

Meanwhile, in 1946, Sarawak and North Borneo became crown colonies. The cost of post-war reconstruction was beyond the resources of the Brooke government and of the British North Borneo Company. In Sabah, the change was accepted without protest, but in Sarawak there was serious opposition, particularly from the Malays who feared they would lose their privileged position without the Brookes. The climax of this opposition came in 1949 when the new British governor was

assassinated in Sibu. This action was too extreme for most Malays, and the movement gradually lost momentum and faded away.

The Emergency

During the Japanese occupation, guerrilla groups which were mainly Chinese, lived in the jungles and organised resistance against the invaders. The most important group was the Malayan Communist Party (MCP) whose guerrillas called themselves the Malayan Peoples' Anti-Japanese Army (MPAJA). Their aim, once the war was over, was to expel the British and set up a communist republic in Malaya.

When the MPAJA was disbanded after the war, the MCP believed that they could overthrow British rule by stirring up mass unrest, particularly through the trade union movement. Communists began infiltrating the unions and succeeded in organising a series of strikes among dockworkers, tin miners and rubber plantation labourers demanding better living conditions. This alarmed the colonial authorities and laws were passed to bring the trade unions under stricter control. This was probably the main reason for the MCP's decision in 1948 to abandon its non-violent strategy and to resort to armed insurrection instead. Under its new leader, Chin Peng, the MCP was reorganised and

LEFT: Japanese leaders surrender their swords in 1945.
RIGHT: a Communist caricature.

all its activities moved underground. After a spate of attacks on European miners and planters, the government proclaimed a national state of emergency in June 1948. "The Emergency" became the official name for the communist insurrection which lasted 12 years, so called, it is said, to escape inconvenient insurance requirements connected with acts of rebellion – a matter of some importance to rubber and tin companies whose property was being attacked and destroyed by the insurgents.

From their secret jungle bases, the communists caused widespread confusion. They would also coerce food and supplies from Chinese

squatters in remote areas, and attempt to indoctrinate them. But clamping down on guerrilla activity was made especially hard by the lack of coordination between the various security forces. However, the tide began to turn with the appointment of General Sir Harold Briggs as Director of Operations in 1949. Briggs, a veteran of the World War II Burma campaign against the Japanese, was responsible for the basic strategies which overcame the MCP revolt. He set up war executive committees which coordinated military and civil operations, and created 500 new villages to re-house squatters in less remote areas. This cut off the main source of the communists' food supply. As anticipated, the insurgents attacked the new settlements, but the security forces, now fighting on their own ground, were too strong for them. These forces were soon able to concentrate on jungle operations to destroy the communists and their camps.

In 1953, areas from which the communists had been eliminated were declared "white areas". Food restrictions and curfews in them were relaxed, inducing fuller local co-operation with the government. By 1954, a large number of the communist guerrillas had been eliminated. Many more surrendered later, and the few remaining guerrillas retreated deep into the jungle. The state of emergency officially ended on 31 July 1960.

Malayan nationalism

A major factor that enabled the quelling of the communist revolt was that it was largely a Chinese affair – few Malays or Indians were involved. At the same time, the British saw the need to meet the growing demand for national independence. If they had not done this, many Malayan nationalists might have made common cause with the rebels to oust the British.

Stirrings of a Malayan nationalism were felt throughout the country soon after World War II. The problem was how to unite the three main races in the peninsula in a common struggle for independence from the British. The first step was taken in 1951, when the Malayan Chinese Association (MCA) formed a political partnership with UMNO. The Malayan Indian Congress (MIC) followed suit in 1954, and the political coalition called the Alliance came into being, which played a major role in the struggle for independence.

COMMUNIST TACTICS

For a guerrilla army, the Communist Malayan Peoples' Anti-British Army (MPABA) was a well-organised fighting force. They grouped themselves into regiments and lived in jungle camps. These camps, well-screened from the air, with effective escape routes and well-organised living quarters, could often accommodate 300 men. From these bases, the communists would attack rubber estates and tin mines in order to disrupt the colonial economy. High wire fences were put up around tin mines and rubber estates to keep the communists out, but travel was particularly risky because of the danger of ambush lurking at every corner.

Elections were held for the Federal Legislative Council for the first time in 1955, and the Alliance won 80 percent of the votes cast. Tunku Abdul Rahman, UMNO's leader, became Malaya's first chief minister. The Tunku was a district officer in Kedah before the war. In the 1950s he took a law degree and soon after entered politics. He took over the leadership of UMNO in 1951.

POLITICAL PEDIGREE

It could be argued that Tunku Abdul Rahman, Malaya's first chief minister, was born to lead – his father was Sultan of Kedah.

In 1955, the Alliance government offered an amnesty to the MCP and invited Chin Peng to Baling, Kedah, for talks to end the Emergency.

based on a memorandum submitted by the Alliance, was accepted by the Malay rulers, and the British and Malayan governments.

Malaya became a constitutional monarchy, with the king selected from among the nine Malay rulers every five years. Parliament consisted of a fully elected lower house and a senate of nominated members. Executive power lay mainly in the hands of the lower house. Each state had its own fully-elected state assembly. Malaya became an independent state at midnight on 30 August 1957.

The talks failed and Chin Peng went back into the jungle. The Alliance now concentrated on bringing about national unity in Malaya's multiracial society. One move was the creation of a national system of education which catered for the needs of Malays, Chinese and Indians alike.

In 1956, Tunku led a delegation to London to negotiate the terms for independence. As a result, a commission of Commonwealth legal experts, headed by Lord Reid, was appointed to draw up a constitution. The draft document,

LEFT: a British jungle patrol to flush out communists.
ABOVE: Tunku Abdul Rahman gives the *Merdeka* salute, declaring Independence in 1957.

The formation of Malaysia

In 1961, Tunku proposed the formation of Malaysia, a wider federation which would include the territories of Malaya, Singapore, British North Borneo (Sabah), Sarawak and Brunei. In Singapore, opinion was sharply divided over the merits of the plan; Brunei decided in the end to stay away. A commission of Malayan and British members investigated the reaction of the inhabitants of Sabah and Sarawak and found that the majority of people there were in favour of the plan. Therefore, the British and Malayan governments set 31 August 1963 as the date on which Malaysia would be established.

But Indonesia condemned the whole scheme as a neo-colonialist plot, and in January 1963 announced a policy of "Confrontation" against Malaysia. Meanwhile, the Philippines also opposed the creation of Malaysia, claiming that North Borneo belonged to them. Confrontation took the form of armed Indonesian incursions across the borders of Sarawak and North Borneo. Indonesia and the Philippines both repudiated a United Nations survey which confirmed that the Borneo territories wanted to be a part of Malaysia.

EARTHY ORIGINS

In local dialect, the Malay people have traditionally been referred to as *Bumiputras*, which translated means "sons of the soil".

Meanwhile, political differences had surfaced between Malaysia and Singapore. On 9 August 1965, Singapore left the Federation and became an independent state.

When Malaysia was formed, its population stood at 10.4 million – Malays forming 47 percent; Chinese 34 percent; Indians, 9 percent; Dayaks, 4 percent; Kadazans, 2 percent; other indigenous groups, 3 percent and foreign immigrants, 2 percent. Turning this medley of peoples into one nation was not an easy feat. Under colonial rule, economic roles tended to

Territorial disputes

When the Federation of Malaysia was officially inaugurated on 16 September 1963, Indonesia and the Philippines severed diplomatic ties with Malaysia; Indonesia intensified its attacks along the borders of Sarawak and British North Borneo (now renamed Sabah) and Indonesian troops made landings in Peninsular Malaysia to carry out acts of sabotage. But they were quickly foiled by the security forces.

In 1966, Sukarno was ousted from power and the new Indonesian regime wanted to end confrontation – negotiations settled the conflict. The Philippines also dropped its claim on Sabah and recognised Malaysia.

be identified with specific ethnic groups. In particular, the Chinese resented the Malays' greater political power, while the Malays feared the greater economic strength of the Chinese. The simmering racial tension erupted on 13 May 1969 in the wake of the general elections. Communal riots broke out, mainly in the capital, Kuala Lumpur, killing hundreds of people and destroying a considerable amount of property. As a result, the constitution was suspended and a Department of National Unity was set up to formulate a national ideology and social programmes. Finally, a statement of ideological principles, the *Rukunegara*, was produced to guide the national polity.

The 13 May incident represented a watershed in Malaysian politics, as the government was forced to formulate new economic and political strategies to restore long-term national stability. The riots would also spawn the New Economic Policy (NEP) and the formation of the Barisan Nasional (BN) or National Front.

The BN was the work of Tun Abdul Razak, successor to Tunku Abdul Rahman who resigned a month after the riots. Tun Razak reorganised the Alliance, incorporating every political party except the Democratic Action Party (DAP) and some smaller parties. In 1974, the BN won a landslide majority, and won again in 1978.

Economic policy

Although the nation's new constitution gave the Malays considerable political power, their participation in the country's trade and commerce was minimal. Despite accounting for over half of the country's population, the Malays owned only 2 percent of corporate equity. The Chinese, on the other hand, practically ran the economy, holding prominent positions as bankers, brokers and businessmen.

In 1970, the New Economic Policy (NEP) was launched to encourage a fairer distribution of wealth among the races. This involved setting up corporations and share-ownership schemes to elicit greater Malay participation in the economy. Racial quotas, scholarships and subsidies were introduced to raise the Malay stake in the economy to 30 percent. However, the plan was to achieve this by increasing the size of the pie, and not at the expense of the non-Malays. Therefore, everybody would benefit.

The NEP was inevitably deemed unfair by many non-Malay critics who felt that the Malays already had too many privileges and that "positive" discrimination on the basis of race and not merit would seriously undermine the economic, political and cultural position of non-Malays in Malaysian society.

In any event, the business acumen of the Chinese has kept them prosperous. Twenty years later, however, the Malay, or *bumiputra* stake has reached only 20 percent, the majority of which is owned by big *bumiputra* investment

companies. In 1991, the old policy was replaced by the New Development Policy (NDP), a more liberal strategy which uses incentives rather than quotas, and sets no deadline for the 30 percent *bumiputra* ownership target.

The boom years

When Malaya became independent in 1957, the economy was almost completely dependent on exports of tin, rubber, palm oil and tea. Therefore, in the early 1970s, the government launched an ambitious crusade to transform Malaysia from its agro-mining foundation to a mixed economy with a strong manufacturing

sector. By the end of the 1970s, substantial progress had been made. Light industries had been formed and were now saturating the local market. The country was poised to make an industrial leap to becoming an exporter of manufactured goods and in concentrating on heavier industry. The 1970s also witnessed the harvesting of newly-found offshore oil and natural gas reserves in the South China Sea, giving a spectacular boost to the economy.

This impressive economic performance was brought about by a series of Malaysian Five-Year Plans. However, much of the credit for the country's rapid economic progress since 1981 must go to one man: Dr Mahathir Mohamad. ❑

LEFT: Tun Razak (with cane) succeeded Tengku Abdul Rahman as PM. **RIGHT:** Islam figures strongly in Malaysian politics; prayer time in KL's Jame Mosque.

THE MAHATHIR ERA

Under the leadership of Dr Mahathir Mohamad, Malaysia has become one of the stronger economies of Asia. But at what price to political freedom?

The appointment of Mahathir Mohamad as Malaysia's fourth prime minister in 1981 marked the start of a new era in the nation's politics. Nearly 20 years later, its end may be in sight but it is not yet over. However, the stamp of the Mahathir years, for good or ill, is already indelible.

The Mahathir era marks a break with the past. Unlike his three predecessors, Mahathir is not only a commoner, but is also the first Malaysian prime minister to have received all of his education locally and not in Britain. He was also much younger on taking office, a member of the post-World War II generation of students who were actively involved in the struggle for national independence.

Right from the start, Mahathir was a stormy petrel in UMNO politics. Although he was sitting on its Supreme Council by 1965, he was expelled from the party four years later for criticising what he saw as the failure of the then prime minister, Tunku Abdul Rahman, to protect Malay political interests.

Mahathir's political comeback began in the 1970s. Re-admitted into UMNO, in 1974 he took his first ministerial post (Education) and the following year was re-elected to the Supreme Council to became the party's vice-president. In 1978, he was appointed Deputy Prime Minister under Hussein Onn.

Radical reforms

Anyone who knew Mahathir also knew that things would change under him. One of his first acts on assuming office in 1981 was to make all government servants clock in for work, – a harbinger of the no-nonsense style of government he aimed to promote.

Since that day, there has hardly been a dull moment. Mahathir's initial priorities were to shake the Malaysian, and more particularly, the Malay mindset out of its colonial mould, to make Malaysians more self-reliant, and to raise their self-esteem. He also wanted to put Malaysia on the world map, to establish the country as a power to be noticed and taken heed of. All this is conveniently summed up by the now fashionable slogan, *Malaysia Boleh!* (Malaysia Can Do It!).

To achieve these aims Mahathir resorted to shock tactics. One of them has been to jolt Malaysians out of their reverential attitude towards all things Western, and particularly British, by attacking these icons. In 1982 came his "Buy British Last" campaign. This was ostensibly in retaliation for the British Government's action in raising university fees for foreign students, but in reality it was designed as a slap in the face for Malaysians brought up to believe that "British is Best." He also urged Malaysians to adopt a "Look East" policy, and singled out Japan, the villain of World War II, as a role model of hardwork and efficiency that Malaysians should emulate.

LEFT: Malaysia's hosting of the 1998 Commonwealth Games was a high point. **RIGHT:** much of its economic success is due to its manufacturing expertise.

Mahathir has also commissioned numerous civil engineering projects, building roads, bridges, and, most spectacularly, skyscrapers. While each has its own merits, these high-profile schemes also serve collectively to demonstrate to the world what can be done when a Malaysian puts his mind to something.

In the same vein, Mahathir has encouraged Malaysians to make their mark in the world arena as individuals, by going in for world-class exploits. By now Malaysians have climbed Mount Everest, taken part in international safaris, and parachuted onto the North Pole and crossed the Artic polar cap. At the time of writing, a Malaysian is sailing solo round the world. The successful hosting of the Commonwealth Games in Kuala Lumpur in 1998, a triumph of individual and collective Malaysian effort, seems to have marked the apogee of Mahathir's mega-schemes.

Another of Mahathir's efforts on the global stage has been to project himself as a world leader, at least in the eyes of his countrymen. He has certainly succeeded in making Malaysia heard as a champion of the Third World and as cheerleader for the countries of the undeveloped "South" in their attempts to secure a better deal from the wealthy industrialised

ENGINEER OF SUCCESS

Mahathir's almost obsessive love of ambitious mega-projects has seen Malaysia trumping the world in many aspects of civil engineering. The 7-km (4½-mile) long bridge linking Penang Island to the mainland is Asia's longest; Kuala Lumpur Tower was the world's third-highest when built, and the Petronas Twin Towers, completed in 1998, is currently the world's tallest building. Kuala Lumpur also lays claim, bizarrely, to the world's highest flagpole, at Merdeka Square. Most recently, the country saw the construction of one of the most sophisticated airports in the world, Kuala Lumpur International Airport (KLIA). More projects are in the offing.

"North". Mahathir's strident criticism of Western values and policies has been good for Malaysian pride, however much it has irritated people in the West.

Mahathiresque economics

Nevertheless, the most important of Mahathir's initiatives have lain in the realm of economic policy and affairs.

After only a couple of years in power, the Mahathir administration was confronted with a major global trade recession; but it proved able to ride the storm. Assimilating the new trend away from government control over national economies towards liberalisation and the free market, Mahathir launched a thoroughgoing privatisation programme of his own, tagging it with another catchy slogan, "Malaysia Inc." – i.e. the nation as a commercial enterprise involving everybody. Since early in 1983, when this programme was proclaimed, a whole series of government institutions and agencies have been privatised, including power and water supplies, telecommunications, postal services, the railway, the national airline, and the construction of toll highways.

BOUNCING BACK

Among its many economic achievements, Malaysia is the largest producer of condoms and surgical rubber gloves in the world.

creation of a local automobile manufacturing industry which in 1985 produced the Proton Saga, the first locally manufactured car and the first to be made and designed in Southeast Asia (with a little help from Mitsubishi of Japan). Today, the Saga not only dominates the domestic market but is exported to more than a dozen countries. This, and ventures into iron and steel manufacture, are projects instigated by the Heavy Industries Corporation of Malaysia (HICOM), established in 1980 to identify and promote such projects.

Boom time

Privatisation proved highly successful; the country was brought out of recession, and the government divested much of its heavy burden of expenditure on basic services. Foreign capital poured in, business boomed, the property market expanded, and the stock market soared.

At the same time, another major thrust with image-building implications has been the fostering of heavy industry along with a massive broadening of the infrastructure. First came the

LEFT: KL's National Stadium was erected for the 1998 Commonwealth Games. **ABOVE:** Symbols of success, Malaysian-built Proton car and country flag.

Other giant infrastructural projects have included the 848-km long (527 miles) North-South Expressway (NSE); ocean ports at Pasir Gudang, Port Klang and Lumut – in competition with Singapore; the huge Liquefied Natural Gas plant at Bintulu and the controversial Bakun Dam, both in Sarawak. Most ambitious of all, is the attempt to catch the wave of the future by making Malaysia a frontrunner in the new world of information technology through its Multimedia Super Corridor, a new international hub of IT centred in the Klang Valley where the capital sits. Low labour costs have also enabled Malaysia to become a world leader in electronic goods and microchips.

By the early 1990s, locally manufactured products had become the country's greatest export earner, leaving the traditional export of raw materials far behind. Malaysia had also become one of the fastest growing economies in Asia, with one of the highest GDPs in the region.

Much of the credit for Malaysia's success must go to the innovative thinking and bold entrepreneurial moves that Mahathir promoted. But providence has played its part, not least the discovery in the 1960s of substantial natural gas and oil reserves off Malaysian shores, which came onstream in the 1970s and has provided a lifebelt to the economy.

The new prosperity has been reflected in the rash of high-rise office blocks and condominiums in the larger towns, and in the many golf courses which have greened the land.

Vision 2020 and the future

All this material progress found philosophic expression in another typical Mahathir contribution. "Vision 2020" (*Wawasan 2020*) is a statement setting out the targets that the nation should achieve by the year 2020. Though primarily economic – i.e. the achievement of Newly Industrialised Country (NIC) status by that date – the "vision" also incorporates the

POLITICS IN SABAH AND SARAWAK

In Sarawak, the ruling coalition – led by the Parti Pesaka Bumiputera Bersatu Sarawak (PBB) – has been in power for the past 25 years. In Sabah, the Malay/Muslim ruling coalition is dominated by UMNO (of Peninsular Malaysia) – a result of political developments in the 1990s.

Politics in Sabah and Sarawak have little relevance to the peninsula, and vice versa. However, Sabah's and Sarawak's support for the Barisan National (BN), the ruling coalition in the federal parliament, is vital. Without it, the BN could lose its majority and its control over constitutional change. So the federal government's policy towards these political parties has been highly flexible, subject to their

unquestionable loyalty to the BN. Kuala Lumpur has never tolerated any chief minister in either state showing signs of independence. Hence, the ousting of Kalong Ningkan, Sarawak's first chief minister, in 1966; the eclipse of Dato Mustapha Harun, Sabah's first head of state, in 1976; and the downfall of Pairin Kitingan, the chief minister of Sarawak, in 1992. The BN hasn't yet found the need to establish a presence in Sarawak, but the strong opposition to federal influences in Sabah resulted in UMNO making a base there in 1992. With Kuala Lumpur's financial backing and carefully redrawn constituency boundaries, UMNO and its local allies have ruled the roost ever since.

goals of creating a common and unified Malaysian identity to replace the various communal identities – Chinese, Indian, Malay and so on – that stand for "Malaysian" today. Mahathir also hopes to establish a well-educated society based on spiritual values.

However, the "vision" and the achievements of the Mahathir era were suddenly placed in serious jeopardy by the Asian financial crisis which broke in early 1997. Over the next 18 months, the Kuala Lumpur stock market index fell by 80 percent, precipitating a political crisis on top of economic problems, the repercussions of which are still being keenly felt.

Benevolent dictator?

The political crisis centred on the sudden dismissal in September 1998 of Anwar Ibrahim, the deputy prime minister (Mahathir's fourth) and his subsequent arrest, trial and imprisonment on charges of corruption and homosexuality. The vicious manner in which this was carried out and the perceived unfairness of the court proceedings evoked an outburst of popular protest, especially amongst the Malays, on a scale not witnessed since independence. More than anything else, these events put in high relief the most prominent political trend manifest during the Mahathir era – the steady growth of authoritarian government.

Mahathir's long tenure of office (since 1981) shows that he is a shrewd political operator, but his success has been largely achieved by gathering power into his own hands and using it to maintain his own position. Since 1981 the constitution has been amended almost beyond recognition, the fundamental rights which it enshrines strangled by escape clauses and qualifications. The prerogatives of the monarchy have been reduced – in a manner that merely enhances the power of the prime minister. Amendments to parliamentary procedure have robbed the legislature of much of its authority. The independence of the judiciary has been emasculated, a process begun in 1988 with the removal – by devious means – of its head. Draconian legislation (the Internal Security Act) allows detention without trial, muzzles the press and restricts access to official information. And as anyone who has watched

Malaysian TV or read the national dailies will tell you, these are basically little more than organs for orchestrated official propaganda.

Nevertheless, despite these obvious dictatorial trends, the Barisan Nasional (BN), the name of the ruling coalition, has romped home in each of the last three general elections, all held during this period. A deep-rooted desire for security and stability, and fear of communal unrest and disorder form the glue which binds many Malaysians to the present regime – feelings more firmly entrenched amongst the Chinese and Indians in the peninsula than amongst the Malays. Another major factor in favour of

the regime is the improbability of the opposition parties ever being able to form an effective alternative government, fundamentally divided as they are by communal and religious issues. The politics of Sabah and Sarawak, however, is another thing. (*see box opposite*).

Against this background of economic and political disarray, and Mahathir's increasing signs of frailty (he is now in his 70s), the political scene in Malaysia has become unpredictable. A younger generation of Malaysians is beginning to make itself heard, and their values and views may not coincide with those of their elders. This could be a matter of some hope for the country's future. Only time will tell. ❑

LEFT: PM Dr Mahathir at an official signing ceremony.
RIGHT: On his way to court, ex-DPM Anwar Ibrahim.

THE LIVING WORLD

From lush rainforests to the coral reefs that fringe its shores, Malaysia has some of the most important – and fragile – environments on earth

The Indo-Malayan rainforests are the oldest in the world, making those in Africa and South America seem adolescent in comparison. While creeping icecaps were swelling and shrinking across the northern hemisphere, the Indo-Malayan jungles lay undisturbed – for an estimated 130 million years. As a result many diverse species of animal and plant life evolved, with a large number of these occurring nowhere else in the world.

Amazing biodiversity

Rainforests on the Malaysian peninsula and in the Malaysian states of Sabah and Sarawak on the island of Borneo continue to excite a great deal of scientific interest. But those visiting for only a few days, or even weeks, will miss most of the rare flora and fauna; scientists can spend entire lifetimes at work here. Optimists believe that the plants and animals yet to be investigated may hold cures for many human diseases.

The biodiversity is truly staggering. It is estimated that over 15,000 flowering plant species (9 percent of the world's total) and 185,000 animal species (16 percent of the world's total) are found in Malaysia. The flowering plants include some 2,000 types of trees, including 200 different palms, and 3,000 species of orchids, the most exotic of flowers. The 50-hectare (125-acre) Forest Research Institute of Malaysia (FRIM) contains more tree species than exist in the whole of North America. The world's largest flower, the *Rafflesia*, is unique to the region (*see box right*). Carnivorous pitcher plants can be seen, most abundantly on the slopes of Mount Kinabalu in Sabah but also on the peninsula, waiting for careless insects to drop in and drown. Another record-breaker is the towering *Tualang tree*, tallest of all tropical trees. It can reach up to 80 metres (260 ft) in height and over 3 metres (10 ft) in girth.

The rainforests also hold hundreds of thousands of animal species, many of which are unique to the region. Almost 300 species of mammals live here including tigers, elephants, rhinoceros (though sadly their numbers are greatly diminished), black and white tapirs, civet cats (*musang*), leopards, honey bears, and

RAFFLESIA

The *Rafflesia* sp. is the largest flower in the world, measuring up to 1 metre (3½ ft) in diameter when in full bloom. Rafflesia can be found in forests on the Main Range in Peninsular Malaysia as well as in Sabah and Sarawak. There are seven species altogether, *R. arnoldii* being the largest.

A parasite by nature, the plant lives by infecting the roots of a woody climber, *Tetrastigma* sp. The flower takes many months to develop, and the open bloom – which lasts for only a few days – looks like dead meat, crawling with maggots when it starts to rot. It emits a similar odour, thereby attracting flies for pollination.

PRECEDING PAGES: *Rafflesia*, the world's largest flower. **LEFT:** orang-utan, or "man of the forest" in Malay, hanging onto the jungles of Borneo. **RIGHT:** one of Malaysia's myriad butterflies rests on a hibiscus.

two kinds of deer – the *sambar*, and the barking deer (*kijang*) with its dog-like call. Malaysia is also home to the cat-sized mousedeer (*kancil*), which is technically not a deer at all, the scaly anteater (*pangolin*), the badger-like *binturong* with its prehensile tail, and many kinds of gibbons and monkeys including the quaint loris with its sad eyes and lethargic manner. Borneo is also home to the extraordinary orang-utan ("forest man" in Malay).

Whether you venture into the jungle or not, you are sure to see some of the estimated 736 species of birds (11 of which are endemic) and quite a few of the 150,000 species of invertebrates. Alfred Russel Wallace, the celebrated Victorian naturalist who spent more than ten years in the Malay Archipelago, had a particular fondness for insects of all sorts and often described himself as "trembling with excitement" upon the discovery of a new type. The country is also home to over 1,000 species of butterfly, and an estimated 12,000 different species of moth.

Shades of green

About three-quarters of Malaysia is covered in trees (about 50 percent forest and 25 percent plantation). The green cover begins at the edge

ORANG-UTAN

Orang-utan means "man of the forest" in Malay, a name given to the primate by the indigenous people of Borneo, probably because its appearance and behaviour is similar to that of humans. Orang-utan are found only in Borneo and are a protected species. They prefer to live in swamp forests, and forests near the coast and along the sides of rivers. Though strong, they are peaceful animals.

Orang-utan are normally quiet and difficult to spot in the wild. It's easier to see them at the Lanjak-Entimau Wildlife Sanctuary in Sarawak and the Sepilok Orang-utan Centre in eastern Sabah, which rehabilitates young orphans and re-introduces them into the wild.

of the sea and climbs to the highest mountain peaks. Along the coastline, there are extensive areas of mud swamps, peat swamps, and mangroves. Behind the mangroves are lowland dipterocarp forests, which extend to an altitude of 600 metres (2,000 ft) and where some forest giants attain heights of 80 metres (262 ft), with the first branches 20 metres (65 ft) above ground. The lowland forest is important as a source of timber for the nation's sawmills. Timber is becoming Malaysia's main export, comprising 10 percent of the nation's total export earnings, and efforts are being made to control logging so that the country's fertile jungle will assure the industry a green future.

The next level of forest is mostly oak and chestnut. Above 1,500 metres (5,000 ft) it becomes a kind of never-never land with elfin woodlands of small gnarled trees covered in folds of hanging mosses and lichen.

With growing awareness of the importance of conservation, the government has set aside 12.5 million hectares (30 million acres) as Permanent Forest Estate, to be managed sustainably, and an additional 1.2 million hectares (3 million acres) as National Parks, Game Reserves and Wildlife Sanctuaries. There is room for hope that the Malaysian jungle will be allowed to flourish and retain some of its great biodiversity.

In this regard, the Wildlife Department has evolved from an office that mostly oversaw the issuance of hunting licences, into an organisation that actively enforces preservation of wildlife and habitats, though at present the department remains handicapped by a lack of resources and manpower. Poaching is still a problem, as there are markets both locally and abroad for the parts of wild animals, especially as traditional remedies and aphrodisiacs.

Lush vegetation

A smooth highway unrolls through green hills. Rubber trees flash by in never-ending even rows, and tin mines appear where plantations leave off. Freshly-planted oil palms cover the land in a patchwork of deep green against cleared red earth. In northern and coastal areas, fields are rich with stalks of golden rice.

As far as the eye can see the lush green vegetation of the tropics smothers the landscape. Yet, contrary to its looks, Malaysia is not suited to intensive agriculture. Unlike the Nile River Basin or the Ganges Valley, where seasonal rains flooding the land bring new fertile soil, the torrential downpours in Malaysia wash away the thin but valuable topsoil, leaving only red mud and filling the rivers with silt.

Erosion is one of Malaysia's oldest problems. Geologists believe that the Malay peninsula and Borneo were once a single rugged landmass running the length of the Indonesian and Malay archipelago. Over millennia the sun, wind and torrential rains have reduced the mountains to hillocks and outcrops. Precious soils were washed into the sea, and land became cut off by subsidence and erosion.

Despite the shifting landscape and annual monsoon rain, Malaysia's early settlers were basically food growers. As far back as AD 500, crops such as sugar cane, bananas, pepper and coconuts were grown for export, while rice was introduced over 1,000 years ago. Traditionally both men and women were involved in rice cultivation – the staple food and prime

MALAYSIAN MAJESTY

The beautiful Rajah Brooke's Birdwing, with its emerald markings on jet-black wings, is Malaysia's national butterfly.

source of income for rural Malaysians. The tempo of kampung life has quickened with the introduction of double cropping, using hybrids which yield a second crop every year. What stands out in Malaysia is a plant that comes from Brazil – the rubber tree – that was initially viewed with great scepticism, and even some scorn, by the planters.

The man inspired to bring the rubber tree to Malaysia was H. N. Ridley, director of the botanical gardens in Singapore, where some of the first trees were planted. "Rubber Ridley", as the planters called him, was convinced that his crop had great possibilities and he journeyed around the country with seeds in his pockets,

LEFT: the sculptural form of the strangling fig.
RIGHT: buffaloes working the rice fields.

looking for anyone he could convince to plant them. It was a farsighted and lonely crusade until John Dunlop invented the tyre and Henry Ford put the automobile on the assembly line.

Agricultural expansion

To this day the rubber tapper continues to set out before dawn to collect the cups of latex that make up nearly half of the world's rubber supply, but he stops short of the old estate boundaries to view a field planted with oil palms.

The Malaysian government encourages farmers to diversify their crops by growing coconut, coffee, tea, fruits, nuts, spices – and oil palm.

pled with the discovery of large tin deposits in the early 19th century, led to new settlements springing up from a few prospector's shacks and growing into large cities like Kuala Lumpur. The industry gave the British the revenue to build roads and railways through the jungle, and it also introduced Chinese settlers to Malaysian soil.

The all-male mining townships were rough and risky. Malaria and cholera thrived in the intense heat and wiped out thousands. Those who survived did so under a constant threat of tiger attacks, recorded at one time as a daily occurrence. Thousands more perished in

The first commercial planting of oil palm started in Malaysia in 1917, but development was slow until the 1950s, when the government embarked on a massive commodities diversification programme. Many estates replaced rubber with oil palm and opened up new land for its cultivation. The area planted with oil palm increased from 54,000 hectares (130,000 acres) in 1960 to almost 2 million hectares (4.9 million acres) in 1990. Today, Malaysia is easily the world's largest producer of palm oil, accounting for 54 percent of world output.

For over a century, tin and rubber were the two main pillars of the Malaysian economy. The growth in industrial demand for tin, cou-

Chinese secret-society feuds. Others made fortunes; for decades, the Chinese held a virtual monopoly on the tin-mining industry.

By 1883, Malaysia had become the largest producer of tin in the world, and by the end of the 19th century, it was supplying about 55 percent of the world's tin supply. Today, it is still a significant player, contributing about 30 percent of the world's output.

Tides upon the sea

For three months of the year, fishing people on Malaysia's east coast store away their nets, dock and repair their boats, move their fishing huts far up the beach and settle down in the shelter of their wooden houses to wait for the winds to change. During the rainy season, time is spent in more leisurely pursuits: repairing fishing nets, making a trip to the city or even embarking on a pilgrimage to Mecca if the year's trade has been prosperous. When the winds drop, they will again venture out to sea in search of the wide variety of fish and other seafood for the nation's markets. This pattern of life has characterised Malaysia's eastern shore for centuries.

TRADING CENTRE

Business in 16th-century Melaka was conducted in 84 languages. Small wonder that Malay contains words adopted from Arabic, Chinese, Sanskrit, Persian, Portuguese, Dutch and English.

Four hundred years ago, spices were literally worth their weight in gold, and it was the Moluccas, with their cherished aromatic produce, that set Asian maritime kingdoms against one another and sparked off the European Age of Discovery in the 15th and 16th century. In time, the spice trade to Europe became so lucrative that a vessel loaded to the gunwhales with spices from the Far East could make enough profit to pay the cost of the voyage, including the value of the ship, 10 times over.

Almost entirely surrounded by water, Malaysia has always been where the monsoons meet, where the tides of the Indian Ocean and the South China Sea flow together into the Straits of Melaka. Seafaring merchants, explorers, adventurers and pirates stopped along the coasts to wait for the tradewinds to blow their way and carry them onward on their journey. As Malaysia was midway between China, India and the Moluccas (Spice Islands), it became a major entrepot.

LEFT: the rubber industry is a significant contributor to the economy. **ABOVE:** cruising around the islands that dot Malaysia's coast.

"Melaka is the richest seaport in the world with the greatest number of merchants and abundance of shipping that can be found in the whole world," wrote one Portuguese sailor in the 16th century.

Ocean bounty

Piracy was once widespread and for centuries sailors trembled at the thought of passing unarmed through Malaysian waters. The most formidable pirate bands were the Lunans from Mindanao in Philippines who would sometimes recruit Borneo head-hunting warriors. While the captains pillaged the cargoes, the crew collected war trophies. Today, piracy has been largely eradicated, although there are still sporadic episodes, especially in the seas off Sabah.

Above water, a steady stream of oil tankers and cargo vessels ply the Straits of Melaka, transporting oil (Malaysia produced 4 billion barrels of crude oil in 1997) and tin instead of silks, spices and porcelain. The recent increase in offshore oil exploration and mining has greatly enhanced the value of sea territory with the result that the nations of the region are involved in a number of sovereignty disputes.

On the other hand, progress has been made among ASEAN nations to address cross-boundary problems, including pollution of the Straits – the beautiful and varied marine life of the Malaysian waters. Much of the coast is surrounded by coral reefs, and Malaysia is known for its great diversity of coral species, and for the marine life that inhabits them.

To protect these unique and biologically important ecosystems, Malaysia has gazetted 38 of its coral islands as protected areas. Some of the more important are Perhentian, Redang, Kapas, and Tioman on the east coast of the peninsula, and Langkawi, Pangkor and Sembilan on the west. The Semporna islands, Turtle islands and Tunku Abdul Rahman Park in Malaysian Borneo are also worth visiting.

of Melaka and air pollution from forest fires. It is hoped that these efforts and a growing awareness of its uniquely rich environmental heritage will enable Malaysia and its neighbours to manage their natural resources wisely.

Underwater treasures

Malaysian seas today hold untold riches from ships wrecked by storms or plundered by pirates. Rumours still circulate of hidden treasures buried in caves on islands off the east coast of the peninsula.

Whether or not there are secret treasure troves loaded with gold and precious jewels, there are certainly other underwater treasures Four species of giant sea turtles, including the endangered Leatherback, lay their eggs on Malaysian shores, while offshore the *dugong*, or sea-cow, can occasionally be found.

Until recently, the seas were thought of only as a source of food, but today there is a growing interest in underwater discovery, and numerous scuba-diving and marine clubs are springing up. Malaysia is reaping new profits from its long stretches of beach and coral-fringed islands as tourists flock to coconut-sheltered beach huts or luxury resorts. ❏

ABOVE: Good visibility and a thriving underwater life make for some excellent diving in Malaysia.

An Environment in Danger

Malaysia is one of the world's 12 mega diversity areas. Many plants and animals are found nowhere else in the world and the majority most likely have yet to be identified and named. Tropical forests, the most biologically diverse ecosystems on earth, cover approximately 46 percent of the land. In addition, Malaysia is blessed with a variety of other ecosystem types, including mangrove and peat swamps, mountain ranges, coral reefs, limestone habitats, and caves.

Whether Malaysia can maintain its unique natural heritage will depend on its ability to balance environmental conservation with economic development and a fast-growing population. Malaysia's population has doubled in the past 30 years and is expected to double again by 2025, with some major urban areas experiencing up to 5 percent growth annually. Squatter settlements have mushroomed and in many cases intruded into forested reserves. As such illegal settlements are not usually serviced by the cities' infrastructure, this leads to open burning or dumping of wastes into rivers.

As the country has progressed, there has been competition for land use for agriculture, mining, industry, timber and development. Decisions about land conversion are based exclusively on economic rates of return on investment. This contributed to massive deforestation for tin mining in the early 1900s, for agriculture and land development schemes in the 1960s and 1970s, and for urban and industrial development in the 1980s and 1990s. Rubber and oil palm are two major cash crops, occupying 15 percent and 12 percent, respectively, of the total land area in Peninsular Malaysia. Oil palm cultivation is the main reason for the loss of lowland forests, and the amount of land under oil palm cultivation was increased by 10 percent annually from 1970 to 1992.

Another major money earner is timber. In response to international consumer pressure, there is a declared objective to implement sustainable-yield harvesting, and Malaysia's furniture-making industry is being promoted so that more money can be made from fewer logs. Nevertheless, the authorities find it difficult to police the

vast, densely-forested areas involved, so excessive logging continues.

As Malaysia makes the transition from an economy based on commodities to an industrialised one, future threats to the environment are likely to be from industrial pollution. During the early industrial phase of the 1970s, palm oil and rubber processing resulted in the discharge of large amounts of organic effluents into Malaysia's water. With growing industrialisation, the Department of Environment has identified the chemical, food and beverage, textile, metal finishing, and animal husbandry industries as additional contributors of pollution. Of 119 rivers monitored for water quality

in 1995, 14 were categorised as highly polluted and 53 as slightly polluted. Air pollution has also increased, with the Klang Valley regularly experiencing smog during the annual dry season.

Malaysians have recently suffered a series of environmental disasters, including months-long blankets of smoke from the burning of forests in neighbouring Indonesia, landslides, flooding and contagious-disease epidemics. These have begun to drive home the importance of nature's role in the preserving of the quality of human life. Changes in attitude and policy are clearly perceptible; one can only hope that Malaysians care enough to preserve their land and seas with all their lush beauty. ❑

RIGHT: lorries laden with tropical timber – sometimes illegally gotten – are a familiar sight on interior roads.

THE PEOPLE

Aborigines, Malays, Indians, Europeans, Chinese – these are just some of the many and diverse peoples that have given Malaysia its unique character

The traveller in Malaysia will be fascinated by the obvious multi-culturalism of the country: there are Malays, Chinese, Indians and Eurasians; as well as large tribal communities like the Kadazandusuns of Sabah and the Iban of Sarawak. And given the melting pot of ethnicities, a sizeable number of people of mixed race abound as well.

The population stands at 21.7 million today, with 83 percent living in Peninsular Malaysia, 9 percent in Sarawak and the remaining 8 percent in Sabah. The distribution of population is grossly unequal when one considers that most people are found in the peninsula, which at 131,587 sq km (50,800 sq miles) is considerably smaller than Sarawak (124,967 sq km/48,250 sq miles) and Sabah (72,500 sq km/27,900 sq miles) put together.

The original inhabitants of the peninsula, the Orang Asli, were followed by the Malays, who built upon traditions of the soil and ocean, and embraced influences from elsewhere as well. Due to its rich resources and strategic location, Malaysia attracted still others – the culturally-rich Indians, Chinese, and Europeans – resulting in rich yet culturally diverse traditions.

Orang Asli

The Malay term Orang Asli means "original people" and covers three more or less distinct groups and a score or more of separate tribes. Of the estimated 60,000 Orang Asli, 60 percent are jungle dwellers, while the other 40 percent live in the coastal villages. The British were perhaps the first to group the Orang Asli together, using the term *sakai* or debt-slave to define them. Their origins still remain something of a mystery; what is known is that the main groups vary from one another racially, culturally and linguistically.

Undoubtedly, the oldest inhabitants of the Malaysian peninsula are the Negritos, arriving

PRECEDING PAGES: snapshots on a longhouse wall.
LEFT: the new breed of high-tech workers.
RIGHT: inside a makeshift Orang Asli home.

in Malaya some 8,000 years ago. Making up the largest group of Orang Asli, the Negritos are mostly dark-skinned and frizzy-haired, their features, though unique, are similar to the peoples of Papua New Guinea or East Africa. The Negritos mostly inhabit the northeast and northwest of the peninsula, and are the only

truly nomadic of the Orang Asli tribes. Practising little or no cultivation, the Negrito tribes pride themselves on their mobility. Although some Negritos have left the protection of the forest and sought education and jobs in the city, the majority of the tribes have spurned the specially-built government villages.

The second largest group is the Senoi, thought to share a common ancestry with the hill peoples of northern Cambodia and Vietnam, arriving in Malaysia between 6,000 and 8,000 years ago. Most of the tribes are shifting cultivators, moving from a settlement when the land is exhausted. Many Senoi in the Cameron Highlands have become wage-earners, working on the highland tea estates. Others have headed for the bright city lights, getting jobs as varied as civil servants and taxi drivers.

The last group of Orang Asli, the Proto-Malays, were the last to arrive, around 4,000 years ago, from the Indonesian island of Sumatra. Many of this group also have a distinct resemblance to the Malays – modern Malays have a common ancestry with many of them.

Malays

The Malays, long linked to the land as *bumiputra*, or sons of the soil, are known for being generous and hospitable with an easy smile and

Rural Malays today still cherish the simplicity of the uncluttered, outdoor life, nurturing a provincial conformity laid down centuries ago. Malay *kampung* are peaceful enclaves, with wooden houses propped up on stilts above courtyards shaded by coconut palms, banana and papaya trees. The village mosque calls the faithful to prayer several times a day, often interrupting evening television programmes that are now a part of everyday family life.

Kampung youth and children may favour shorts and blue jeans but the daily dress code is still the comfortable cotton *sarung*. Rolled expertly at the waist, and topped off with either

a well-developed sense of humour – traits perhaps of a people who have had the good fortune to live peacefully in a land abundant year-round with food.

As a whole, Malays comprise 52 percent of Malaysia's population. Historically, as *bumiputra* or "sons of the soil", the Malays have always wielded political authority. However, when the status quo of the Malays was threatened in the 1969 elections, culminating in bloody racial riots, the New Economic Policy (NEP) was set in place to protect the interests of the *bumiputra*. Racial quotas, scholarships and business and housing subsidies were introduced to raise the Malay stake in the economy.

HOME CLEAN HOME

In Malay homes, be it a humble *kampung* dwelling or a high-rise condominium in the suburbs of Kuala Lumpur, traditional customs hold sway.

The most noticeable hallmark of a Malay home is cleanliness, a trait considered next to godliness. It is said that the brighter the house, the more blessings God will bestow upon those who dwell within its walls. In *kampung* homes, a basin of water is always placed at the bottom of the entrance stairs. This is to allow for the washing of feet before entering. As in practically all Asian cultures, to tread into someone's home wearing any form of footwear is absolutely unthinkable...

a batik shirt or T-shirt, this airy garment is especially indispensable among older Malays. On special occasions, the traditional and comfortable *baju kurung* is worn by women, while men don their *baju melayu* and *songkok*.

The inherent talents of the Malays, however, find outlets far from the countryside. Malay businessmen and civil servants in the cities wear Western-style clothes, drive cars, speak English fluently, and carry mobile phones. Urban youths pick up the latest in street fashion from the US and display their new togs in shopping malls. Despite a ban on men with long hair appearing on national television, many young men sport a popular straggly hairstyle. Hard rock and heavy metal is popular, as is the electric guitar. The amplified sounds of the instrument can even be heard blaring from isolated *kampung* houses.

Although the rift between the *kampung* and the city has widened over the years, it does not threaten the strong unity the Malays derive from a common faith. The laws of Islam immediately set a Malay apart from fellow Malaysians. Intermarriage between races is uncommon, though Muslim foreigners are accepted, keeping the Malay-Muslim cultural identity distinctly separate.

Muslim women, especially, stand out from other ethnic Malaysians mainly because of their dress codes. Recently, an increasing number of Malay women have chosen to wear the veil, or *tudung*, a garment of modesty. Despite this seemingly strict dress code and traditional Islamic laws (which, for example, allows polygymy), Muslim women in Malaysia are given an increasing amount of employment and property rights; many run their own businesses and have high-profile jobs.

Indians

Indians began visiting Malaysia 2,000 years ago, following rumours of fortune in a land their ancestors knew as Suvarnadvipa, the fabled "golden peninsula". Tamil blood even flows through the royal lineage dating back to 13th-century Melaka, where the first sultanate was found. But it was not until the 19th century that Indians arrived and stayed in large numbers, employed mainly as rubber tappers or other plantation labourers. Most came from south India, and about 80 percent were Tamil, with small numbers of Sikh, Bengali, Keralan, Telugu and Parsi. Malaysian Indians still maintain strong home ties with their former villages, sometimes even taking wives from there and bringing them to live in Malaysia.

Today, Indians (mostly concentrated in the states of Selangor, Perak and Penang) make

THE BIRTH OF ISLAM

The earliest record of Islam on the Malay peninsula is an inscription in Terengganu dating from 1303, prescribing penalties for those not observing the faith's moral code.

up less than 10 percent of the population of Malaysia, yet they own less than one percent of the country's corporate wealth. It has been estimated that four out of five Indians, mostly Tamils, are still manual labourers on plantations, a situation that has been explained as a legacy of colonial Malaysia.

However, as the country gains in economic prosperity, other Indian communities are increasingly well-represented in the various professions. Several programmes have been initiated to raise the Indian share of Malaysia's wealth but the general consensus is that the economic restructuring plans of the NEP have generally overlooked the Indians.

LEFT: friendly Malays, also known as *bumiputera* or sons of the soil. **RIGHT:** Indians are a minority race.

Indian Muslims are also a significant part of the Indian community. When they arrived in Malaysia, many opened restaurants, textile shops and other successful businesses, and some of them married Malay women.

Southern Indians have brought a rich cultural influence and colour to Malaysian life. Bright silk saris, fiery Indian cuisine, Tamil movies with their song-and-dance scenes, and the indomitable prevalence of the Hindu faith that continues to absorb change have all become part of Malaysia.

EARLY ARRIVALS

Chinese Ming admiral, Cheng Ho, first visited Melaka in 1403; many Chinese traders afterwards followed his example and set up warehouses for trade there.

It was for both fortune and adventure that the Chinese first headed for *Nanyang*, the South Seas. From the 13th century onwards, the Chinese were frequent traders in the Indonesian and Malay archipelago. However, the majority of the Chinese arrived in the 19th century during the Manchu dynasty when problems were rife in China. An edict was issued banning Chinese from travelling abroad, but a number risked their lives and escaped. These later Chinese immigrants were organised under clan

Chinese

The Chinese population makes up 30 percent of the country's total, yet their presence and control of major industries such as rubber and tin and the commercial sector would seem to make their numbers far greater. They can be found in any trading centre, from Kuala Lumpur to the smallest isolated shop far up the Rejang River in Sarawak. In 1794, Francis Light, founder of Georgetown, Penang, was so impressed by the hardy Chinese that he wrote: "The Chinese constitute the most valuable part of our inhabitants:... they are the only people from whom a revenue may be raised without expense and extraordinary effort by the government."

associations (*kongsi*) and secret societies, which often engaged in rival warfare. The new settlers took on many of the toughest jobs in tin mining, road and railway construction; but they also played as hard as they worked, and opium and gambling were popular pastimes.

Rather than integrating with Malay culture, the Chinese community has put its own traditional stamp on the land. Officially, all Chinese must learn Malay, but at home, Mandarin and local dialects are often spoken. Younger generations, however, are more caught up in modern Malaysian and Western lifestyles.

There is a strong belief in self-help and industriousness among the Chinese, but close family and clan ties are also priorities. The Chinese in Malaysia are defined by their history of hardship and pioneering, as well as the three important Chinese code of ethics: Confucianism, Taoism and Buddhism. Even if converted to Islam or Christianity, this background is deep-rooted and many of the associated festivals are regularly celebrated.

Even among modern Malaysian Chinese, the belief in symbolism is prevalent. Jade is worn by the majority of Malaysian Chinese for aesthetic reasons as well as for its evil-warding powers. *Feng shui* (literally, "wind, water") is the Chinese belief system based on geomantic omens. The numeral 8 is extremely coveted for house numbers and car licence plates, as it sounds like the Cantonese character for "prosper"; meanwhile, the number 4 is carefully avoided, as it sounds like "death".

Peranakans

The Peranakan culture was first established when Chinese trade missions established a port in Melaka in the early 1400s. Inter-cultural relationships and marriages were forged between traders and local Malay women, as well as between Melaka's sultans and the Chinese Ming emperors. In 1460, Sultan Mansor Shah married Ming Princess Hang Li Poh, who brought with her 500 "youths of noble birth", and many handmaidens and settled around Bukit Cina (Chinese Hill).

Subsequent generations of Chinese-Malays were known as Straits Chinese, or Peranakan, which in Malay means "born here". When the Dutch colonists moved out in the early 1800s, more Chinese immigrants moved in, thus diluting Malay blood in the Peranakans, so that later generations were almost completely Chinese. However, this did not alter the Straits Chinese identity, which combines the best of Malay and Chinese cultures. This colourful balance encompasses Malay dress such as the *sarung kebaya*, a unique bi-cultural cuisine, and a spoken language of mixed Malay, Chinese and some English colloquialisms.

Peranakan culture reached its height in the 19th century, and though Melaka was the Peranakan centre, large communities also flourished in Penang and Singapore. Today's Peranakans are proud of their heritage and consider themselves different from the other Chinese, although they are counted as part of the community.

Eurasians

When the Sultanate of Melaka fell to Portuguese invaders in 1511, the new rulers sought to establish control by encouraging Portuguese soldiers to marry local women. As can be expected, a strong Eurasian community grew up with loyalty to Portugal through its ties of blood and the Catholic religion.

Nearly 500 years after their arrival, there is still widespread evidence of the Portuguese legacy. Eurasians in Melaka, as well as in other towns in Malaysia, bear such Portuguese surnames as Sequiera, Aranjo, Pinto, Dias, D'Silva and D'Souza, and still cherish the traditions of their European lineage. They are proudly protective of their unique Eurasian cuisine, and some still continue to speak *Cristao*, a medieval dialect from southeastern Portugal. The language has long since died out in Europe, but is still used in some parts of Malaysia. Descendants of cross-cultural marriages in the 19th and 20th century are equally proud of their English or Dutch heritage.

LEFT: the Chinese are well known for their business acumen and industriousness. **RIGHT:** a Peranakan bride getting dressed for her big day.

The people of Sabah and Sarawak

The two easternmost states of Sabah and Sarawak, situated in the north of the island of Borneo, have the most diverse racial groups of all Malaysia. Most of them are of Mongoloid extract and moved here from Kalimantan (Indonesian Borneo).

In Sabah, the largest group comprises the Kadazandusun tribes, followed by the Murut, Bajau and Rungus, and Bisaya, Suluk, Lundayeh and Kedayan in smaller numbers.

In Sarawak there is an even greater diversity of peoples and languages: the Dayak include Ibans, who make up the majority of the Sarawak population, and the Bidayuh or land Dayaks. The Melanau are also a large community, and then there are many tribes lumped together under the name of Orang Ulu. This term, meaning "interior people", has become somewhat derogatory in the sense that it denotes a primitive and ignorant people – most tribes prefer to be known by their own names. The Orang Ulu group includes the nomadic Punan and Penan, the highly structured Kayan and Kenyah communities, and the Kajang, Kelabit, Lun Bawang and Bisaya. Even these names house several different tribes who have their own special names. ❑

MYTHS AND TRADITIONS

Borneo has been known as a land of head-hunters, a term which seems to conjure up a cruel and aggressive people. Contrary to this misconception, the people of Sarawak are a gentle, law-abiding people and in the days of head-hunting, taking the heads of one's enemies only occurred when the community suffered some plague. The heads of enemies were thought to bring protection from danger and sickness. Taking a head was also a way of proving one's manhood. Only the heads of warriors were coveted, and the women and children of the enemy eventually became integrated into the victor's community. Today, head-hunting is outlawed, and the skulls seen hanging in longhouses are those that have been inherited by families.

Tattoos are another cultural tradition in Borneo, and both men and women sport elaborate designs on their bodies. Worn both for protection and decoration, each tattoo is designed to suit the wearer. Many tribes also place long weights or simple wooden plugs in the ears of children in order to stretch the earlobe. Women, however, wear the heaviest ones so that their lobes may eventually stretch down to their chests. Such lobes are still considered a sign of great beauty by traditional tribespeople, although many young women are now snipping and stitching their long lobes for more modern "normal" lengths.

Festival Fever

Malaysia's multi-cultural population makes for a heady mix of festivals. Not only are all the major religious events celebrated but there are dozens of other happenings around the country, from kite-flying to Formula One racing.

Most religious festivals are calculated on the lunar calendar and their dates change each year, so check with a tourism office first.

If you don't know any locals, the big religious celebrations can be a non-event for tourists as most of the action happens in the home. If you get an invitation take it up, as it is the only way to really experience these events – and the home-cooking is superb. Enquire at tourism offices about "homestays" and families who invite tourists to participate in their celebrations.

Here are just a few of the major events:

January–March

● Chinese New Year culminates in the festival of *Chap Goh Mei* when houses and shops are decorated, lion dances are performed and temples are thronged with worshippers. To immerse yourself in the action, visit Kuala Lumpur's Petaling Street night market before the event.
● Thaipusam, a spectacular Hindu festival (banned in India), where penitents pierce their bodies with hooks and shoulder huge yokes, draws up to a million spectators at Kuala Lumpur's Batu Caves, and is also held in Penang.
● Le Tour de Langkawi, Malaysia's answer to the classic Tour de France, a gruelling pan-peninsula bike race.

April–June

● Hari Raya Haji, the finish of each year's pilgrimage to Mecca.
● The International Kite Festival, attracting the world's largest and weirdest kites, is held at Tumpat Beach in Kelantan.
● Sabah Fest is an annual 2-week get-together for the state's 30 colourful ethnic groups, showcasing Borneo's unique cultural heritage.
● Gawai, Sarawak's biggest event, is a celebration of the rice harvest, with dancing, feasting and bountiful toasting with *tuak* (rice wine).

LEFT: An Iban of Sarawak in traditional dress.
RIGHT: the Lion Dance is a vibrant highlight of the Chinese New Year celebrations.

July–September

● The International Towerathon sees marathon racers running up the KL Tower, one of the world's highest telecommunications towers.
● National Day, the commemoration of Independence, is held every 31 August with pomp and parades, in a different location each year.
● World Rainforest Music Festival, at the Sarawak Cultural Village, Damai, brings together the best of world music and indigenous beats.
● The Moon Cake Festival and the Lantern Festival mark an ancient Chinese peasant victory over Mongolian warlords. Special cakes are eaten and children celebrate with lantern processions.

October–December

● Deepavali, the Hindu Festival of Lights, is a family affair to celebrate the triumph of good over evil. Expect to see tiny oil lamps flickering all night in Hindu homes.
● Malaysian Grand Prix, at the state-of-the-art Sepang International Circuit in Selangor.
● Hari Raya celebrations at the end of the month-long Muslim fast of Ramadan include special food, prayers, and a month-long "open house" when families and friends visit each other and enjoy a spectacular array of cakes and snacks.
● Christmas is best enjoyed in Melaka, especially in the Portuguese Settlement, where the Eurasian Catholic minority celebrate in exuberant style. ❑

RELIGION

Malaysians have long enjoyed a harmonious atmosphere of religious tolerance.
But recent outpourings of Islamic extremism could presage future strife

For anyone wanting a crash course in comparative religion, Malaysia is the place to come. From animism to the latest revivalist movement, Malaysia is home to all the world's major beliefs and a host of minor ones besides. Religion is found everywhere – in mosques, temples and churches, in the perpetual round of religious festivals, in diverse rites of passage, and in a multitude of everyday sights and sounds.

Each faith tends to identify with a specific ethnic group. Every Malay is a Muslim, but there are also Indian Muslims, Sarawak Muslims (Melanau) and Sabah Muslims (Bajau and Orang Sungai), as well as small but significant groups of Chinese, Kadazandusun, Murut and other converts. Buddhism is allied to the Thais and the Chinese, while most Chinese who are not Buddhists are Confucians, Taoists and/or ancestor-worshippers. Hinduism is the preserve of the Hindus, and Sikhism of the Sikhs. Only Christianity is truly multi-ethnic, embracing small minorities of Indians and Chinese in the peninsula and rather larger groups of Ibans, Bidayuhs, Kedayans, Kadazandusuns and Muruts in Sarawak and Sabah. Folk religion holds sway among many in these Bornean states. In the interior of the peninsula, small clusters of Orang Asli (aborigines) still cling to their ancient animism.

Religious tolerance

This great variety of faiths within the compass of a small nation is hardly surprising, given the rich ethnic mix that Malaysia enjoys. What is more surprising is that the followers of these different creeds – some of whom are at daggers drawn with one another elsewhere – live here in relative peace and harmony.

Although Islam is the official religion and Muslims account for over half the total population, the constitution guarantees the free pursuit of all other beliefs. Religious friction rarely arises. If it does, it is easily controlled by a combination of effective monitoring by government, and of a lively awareness among people at large of its destructive and antisocial consequences. In any case, ethnic interaction, particularly in urban areas – at the workplace,

in shops and offices, in the arts, on the sportsfield, and on social occasions – contributes towards mutual understanding and tolerance.

One advantage of a land with many different creeds is a prolificacy of public holidays. All the major religious festivals are treated as national holidays, and a list of minor ones at state level adds to the score.

This happy state of affairs has given rise to the peculiarly Malaysian "open house". Guests don't have to be followers of the particular religion whose sacred feast is being celebrated. Operating at all social levels, at its pinnacle, the homes of royalty and political leaders are thrown open to everybody, including tourists.

PRECEDING PAGES: Kayan girls of Sarawak.
LEFT: Impish schoolgirls sporting *tudung* (Muslim headwrap). **RIGHT:** a more liberal Muslim sister.

Islamic Resurgence

Islamic resurgence in Malaysia forms part of a global Muslim phenomenon which has emerged since the end of World War II. In general, its proponents say that it is a movement to restore Islamic civilisation to its former prominence, and to re-establish an alternative world social order to the existing one dominated by the individualistic and materialistic values of the West. The ultimate goal of this re-ordering of Islamic society is the creation of Islamic polities, whose government and administration are based on the *Koran* and the *Sunnah*

(i.e. the words, deeds and actions of The Prophet).

Since the early 1970s, there has been a conscious attempt to establish an Islamic identity in law, medicine, education, economy, and ultimately to set up an Islamic state. From the purely religious point of view, this is all well and good. But in Malaysia's plural society, Islamic resurgence poses problems both for Muslims (especially the Malays) themselves, and for non-Muslims who make up almost half the country's population.

For the Malays, the growing trend of Islamic resurgence has deepened the rifts already existing between fundamentalists and moderate Muslims, politically expressed in the rivalry between the fundamentalist Pan-Malay(si)an Islamic Party

(PAS) and the United Malays National Organisation or UMNO, the party of the moderates. A foretaste of what life might be like in an Islamic state is provided by Kelantan, where PAS forms the state government and imposes strict regulations regarding the consumption of alcohol, dress codes and forms of entertainment, including traditional ones. However, the rights of non-Muslims in the state have been equally strictly respected.

Tensions caused by stricter interpretations of Islamic rules have been sharpened by UMNO's identification with a rising Malay middle class wed to the inequalities of capitalism and the shortcomings of urban living, as opposed to PAS's stand for a pristine Islam rooted in a rural society. For non-Muslims, the spectre of Islamic rule, with all the implications this holds, has reinforced their support for the ruling coalition, the Barisan Nasional (BN), of which UMNO itself is the leading member.

The successful Iranian Revolution of 1979, as the first successful Islamic revolution in modern times, gave an enormous fillip to Islamic resurgence everywhere and aggravated existing tensions between fundamentalists and moderates. The BN and its antecedents have been in power ever since independence in 1957, and so politically have had the upper hand. However, PAS has managed to collect an average of almost one-fifth of the total votes cast in most general elections.

Aware of the dangers of extremism in a multiracial society, BN has met mounting Islamic resurgence by a policy of adoption and assimilation. Existing Islamic institutions have been strengthened and new ones added, including Islamic banks, schools and colleges and an international Islamic university, a system of separate *shariah* courts with judicial autonomy, and greater media coverage has been given to Islamic issues.

These strategies proved quite successful in containing Islamic resurgence until very recently. However, the political repercussions of the summary dismissal in late 1998 of Anwar Ibrahim, the deputy prime minister, himself a prominent champion of Islamic values, have alienated many Malaysians, especially Malays, from their traditional support for the BN administration. The net result has been to give a new complexion to Malaysian politics and a further impetus to the Islamic resurgence movement, with consequences which no-one at present can predict. ❑

LEFT: Islamic not just in manner but in dress – Kelantan schoolboys in traditional garb.

The reward for queueing long hours to gain entry is the chance to greet the VIP in person and to partake of the fare always provided.

Another revelation for the visitor from abroad is the devoutness of the adherents of all faiths. Religion is a living force in Malaysia. At prayer times mosques and temples are packed and the large congregations in churches must be the envy of any parish priest in the West. Hindu and Chinese devotees perform their penance in their thousands. The faithful participate in

BEAUTY FATWA

Although Malaysia's Islamic law is generally moderate, in 1997 *ulamas* (muslim theologians) in Selangor placed a *fatwa* banning beauty contests in the state.

not make Malaysia an Islamic state, because government is not based on Islamic law. But it does mean that Islam has the full backing, financial and otherwise, of the state. Left to fend for themselves, other religions are all the more conscious of their dependence on their own efforts to survive and flourish.

As for the administration of Islam itself, each of the 9 Malay rulers is the religious as well as political head of his state, while in states not headed by Malay royalty – such as Sabah and Sarawak – the

ABOVE: Islamic calligraphy outside a KL mosque.

religious parades and processions in the tens of thousands. Religious devotions are observed with equal zeal at home.

Of course, not all Malaysians take their religion so seriously. But religious faith is real and palpable and forms an important element in determining public values to a degree rarely found in modern Western society.

The role of Islam

This great religious fervour is probably a consequence, at least in part, of Islam's position as the official religion. Islam's official status does

King of Malaysia fills the gap. Maintaining the Malay rulers in this traditional role – acting at federal level collectively through the Conference of Rulers, with the king as their chairman – helps solve a major dilemma; reconciling Islam's dogma of the unity of the religious and the secular with modern Western pragmatism, which keeps the two distinctly apart. The arrangement also facilitates the acceptance by the Muslim majority of secular laws for secular affairs, while domestic religious issues (such as property rights, marriage and divorce, etc.) remain under the jurisdiction of the Islamic *syariah* courts. By the same token, the Islamic courts hold no jurisdiction over non-Muslims, so that the system safeguards the interests of other creeds as well.

Despite its obvious pre-eminence today, Islam was a late arrival in Malaysia, long preceded by Hinduism, Buddhism and animism. The Malay conversion to Islam was only effectively completed some 500 years ago, during the days of the Melaka sultanate. Before that, Malays had been Hindus, Buddhists or animists (or all three rolled into one). But unlike the aristocratic forms of Hinduism and Buddhism which it replaced, Islam is a religion of the people, with a message of salvation for everyone. Propagated by generations of Arab and Indian-

sist of Malaysian Thais and smaller Burmese and Sinhalese groups.

The main difference between the two seems to be one of sophistication. The Theravada School is much simpler, more abstract and claims to be much closer to the original teachings and way of life of the Buddha. The Mahayana School, having absorbed other influences in the lands where it flourishes (such as in China itself) acknowledges a number of deities, the most famous in Malaysia being the Goddess Kuan Yin. The Mahayana School also has far more complicated rituals and observances.

Chinese Buddhists have been long established

Muslim missionaries, the new faith gained an unshakeable hold over the Malays. It is probably the single most important factor that saved Malay society from disintegration under the pressures of the industrial imperialism of the West in modern times.

Malaysian Buddhists

Next to Islam, in terms of numbers, comes Buddhism, forming just under a fifth of the total Malaysian population. Buddhists fall into one of two main schools, the Mahayana and Theravada (Hinayana). The Mahayana (Great Path) School is the Buddhism of the Chinese, while Theravada (Little Path) Buddhists con-

in Malaysia, being virtually synonymous with Chinese settlement in the country. Their earliest contact probably goes back to the days of the Sri Vijayan Empire during the 9th century AD, when its capital, Palembang in Sumatra, was a great centre for Buddhist studies. But Chinese Buddhism only achieved a permanent presence when the Chinese began to establish themselves as a community in Melaka. Most Chinese Buddhists today are the descendants of the droves of Chinese immigrants who arrived during the 19th century and the first half of the 20th.

Chinese Buddhists are far more numerous than their Thai counterparts. It has been reckoned – though no one has actually taken a count

– that there are at least 3,000 Chinese Buddhist temples, societies and organisations in Malaysia, all of which run their own affairs, although most are also members of the Malaysian Buddhist Association. Thai Buddhists arrived on the scene much later, namely during the late 18th century when their political influence penetrated deepest into the Malay peninsula. As a result, they are mostly concentrated in the peninsula's northern states where their legacy lies in some of the most beautiful temples to be found anywhere. Apart from the Thais, there is a community of Burmese Buddhists in Penang, and one of Sinhalese

pounded with traditional ancestor worship into an intricate web of ideas, beliefs and ritual that is best described simply as "Chinese Religion".

Wherever the Chinese went, they took their "religion" with them as an integral part of their culture. Today, Chinese religious traditions reveal themselves in ubiquitous household altars, in little shrines along the roadside, in giant joss sticks smouldering at temple thresholds, and in little prayer slips and red paper banners serving a multiplicity of purposes; keeping evil spirits at bay, seeking a cure for an illness, and paying respect to the dear departed.

As with Buddhist organisations, Chinese

Buddhists, whose impressive headquarters forms a prominent landmark in Kuala Lumpur.

Chinese religion

The line between Chinese philosophy and religion has always been a tenuous one. The thoughts of Confucius and the mysticism of the Taoists have been dominant influences in the evolution of the Chinese world view. Down the centuries, these influences have become com-

temples are run autonomously by local associations, although most of them also are members of the umbrella Buddhist, Confucian and Taoist Association of Malaysia. Altogether, about one tenth of all Malaysians come under the category of Chinese religion.

Hindus and Sikhs

Hinduism goes back to the dawn of history, when it came with the first Indian traders to Malaysian shores. The new religion created a cultural revolution. It transformed Malay headmen into kings who absorbed Hindu beliefs and cosmology and adopted Hindu traditions of government without losing their own identity as

FAR LEFT: a Chinese house altar with offerings.
LEFT: Thai-inspired image of the Buddha.
ABOVE: a Hindu devotee carrying sacrificial *kavadi* during the festival of Thaipusam.

Malays. This Hindu period, which lasted for 1,500 years before it was replaced by Islam, has left its traces in Malay language and literature, in Malay art forms such as the shadow play (*wayang kulit*) and in such traditions as the *bersanding* ceremony, when the bridal couple sit in state during a Malay wedding.

However, the Hinduism of the past has very little to do with today's Malaysian Hindus. Now numbering around one million, they are the descendants of Indian immigrants who over the last 200 years came to work as contract labourers, with a seasoning of English-educated clerks, apothecaries, shopkeepers and mer-

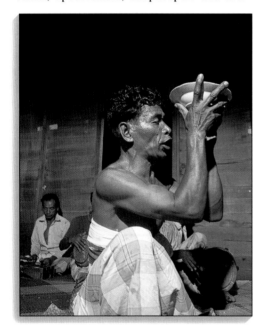

chants who laid the foundations of a modern Indian middle-class. Hindu temples in Malaysia are managed by local committees, following closely the traditions of their place of origin in India. Temples in the towns are more sophisticated affairs, supported by wealthier members of the community.

The 50,000 Sikhs in Malaysia are the representatives of a Hindu sect which became a religion. It was founded in 15th-century India by Guru Nanak who, influenced by Islam, converted his pantheist Hindu followers into monotheists. The Sikh presence in Malaysia is a direct result of British recruitment of members of this famous warrior community to provide the core of the new police forces in the country. Sikhs nowadays are prominent in business and the professions, and despite their small numbers, are found in all the main centres in the land, including Sarawak and Sabah.

Christianity

The first Christians in Malaysia were the Portuguese conquerors of Melaka in 1511, whose descendants from inter-marriage with local women still live there, forming a distinct group of their own. The Dutch, who followed a century later, made no attempt to convert their subjects and so the great period of Christian proselytisation came in the 19th century with the British. Official British policy was not to interfere with other people's beliefs, but Western Christian missionaries were given a free hand to spread their religion, which they did primarily by founding English-medium schools. Christian missionary activity got a second wind after World War II, led by small Christian revivalist churches, many from the USA.

Today, there are about one million Christians in Malaysia, two-thirds of them in Sabah and Sarawak. The three main Christian divisions are all present, but Orthodox Christians constitute only a handful. Roman Catholics, of whom the first were the Portuguese, form the largest group, about two-fifths of the whole. The Protestants are represented by Anglicans – a legacy of British colonialism – Methodists and Presbyterians, largely American-dominated, and smaller groups amongst which the Baptists are the most prominent. ❑

SPIRITS IN THE TREES

In traditional Malay society, the *bomoh* (witch doctor) is a respected spiritual expert, often called upon to use *ilmu* (magic) and herbal potions to heal illnesses, especially those caused by *hantu* (spirits). Primitive animism, which peoples every article of creation with resident spirits, is practised by a tiny, dwindling group of Orang Asli (aborigines), living in the remoter areas of the peninsula's interior.

The folk religions of the indigenous peoples of Sarawak and Sabah are more sophisticated, and feature ingenious theories about the origins of life. Their deities are often imbued with very human foibles.

LEFT: a *bomoh* seeking help from the spiritual world.
RIGHT: St. George's Church in Georgetown, Penang.

ARCHITECTURE

From traditional homes to the shining splendour of the world's tallest skyscraper,
Malaysia's buildings reflect both its colourful past and its hopes for the future

I t is said that the spirit of a society is embodied in its architecture, and Malaysia, a champion and torch-bearer for developing nations the world over, has taken this sentiment to heart. As a result, the evolution of vernacular and modern architecture on the Malay peninsula and in the Borneo states of Sabah and Sarawak ably documents not only the history of the land, but also the essence of its various indigenous and immigrant peoples.

The evolution has been guided by historical markers, the colours of which are strong even today: the first ocean-canoeing Polynesians from the Pacific; Indian and Arabic traders from the West; the era of the wealthy sultans; the European influence; imported Chinese and Indian cultures; the elation of Independence; and the path to globalisation.

City of dreams

The architectural journey begins at the US$6 billion-plus Kuala Lumpur International Airport (KLIA). When craning to view the skylights 40 metres (130 ft) above you, the grandeur of the project becomes apparent. As all architects agree, design is in the details, and KLIA bags the prize in every category: from the conical columns-cum-air-conditioning vents and returns; the inspired "forest-canopy" effect lighting and the highly contrived but suprisingly effective "forests" within the satellite building. International flights are usually routed through the satellite, involving a breakneck electric shuttle journey into the main terminal – leaving you suitably shaken for your encounter with Malaysian immigration.

The show continues along the 88-km (55-mile) journey as an autobahn-standard highway snakes its way into the capital. Kuala Lumpur rears into view, as any city sporting the world's tallest buildings might, with as much drama as surprise. The highway links directly with the

PRECEDING PAGES: Kuala Lumpur's National Stadium. **LEFT:** Minangkabau-inspired architecture, Negeri Sembilan. **RIGHT:** Kuala Lumpur International Airport.

inner ring-road and the Golden Triangle in the most built-up part of the city. Among a drab offering of 1970s international styles and post-modern aspirants, the elegant Tabung Haji (or Pilgrim's Fund) "hourglass" building draws the eye, but then, out of the concrete forest, rises the Petronas Twin Towers.

The towers bought Kuala Lumpur the kind of instant charisma once promised to puny boys in the advertisements at the back of comic-books – no more would this former tin-mining outpost have sand kicked in its face! For security reasons, the casual visitor to the towers is limited to an aesthetic appreciation of only the facade and the lower levels. Instead, you'll be encouraged to part with your foreign exchange in the vast shopping mall "podium" from which the monument rises. Also at the towers is the impressive home of the Malaysian Philharmonic Orchestra, the Dewan Filharmonik Petronas concert hall which, on a per-seat basis, is the most expensive ever constructed.

Colonial past

Stepping outside brings you back to the real Kuala Lumpur, with the standard architectural hang-ups of any insecure city. Eagle-eyes will spot many high-rises with pitched-roofs: a contemporary vernacular that captures domestic Malaysian sensibilities, and couples them with the country's reach-for-the-sky aspirations. Lower your view, and head toward the tallest flagpole in the world (it's even in the record books). Located in the *Padang*, upon which cricket is still played, the Malaysian flag flies over the centre of the former British administrative headquarters of Malaya. As with all colonial planning, the adage "God, King and Country" are literally represented by St Mary's Cathedral, the Sultan Abdul Samad Building and the Royal Selangor Club. Of the three, it is the club which has changed the most architecturally: its mock-Tudor facade has undergone numerous face-lifts and extensions over the years. On the other hand, the conspiratorial chattering of the lawyers who frequent its Long Bar has probably altered little since the distant days of Governor Swettenham.

The legacy of Victorian society can be seen along every trunk-road out of the city, in the form of estates of linked-terraced houses. These

THE MALAY KAMPUNG HOUSE

Once out of the urban centres, which are dominated by the ethnic Chinese, the *kampung* (villages) are characterised by a simplistic vernacular architecture representative of the ethnic Malay lifestyle. The basic elements are a single-level wooden structure, raised off the ground with wooden or bamboo walls and a thatched roof; these have evolved to incorporate many decorative influences from Indonesia and Thailand (in the south and north of the peninsula, respectively), and also from Indian and Arab traders.

There are four acknowledged styles of Malay house – Perak, Melaka, Kedah and East Coast. The styles are primarily differentiated by roof shapes, geometric patterning of the wall panels, fenestration and layout. Generally, the climate-friendly design accommodates a verandah, a sleeping area, the main living room and a kitchen at the back. The windows are shuttered and set at a low height to allow occupants to look out when seated. There are several practicalities to the design: the raised floor protects against floods and fauna, and also against heat gain from the ground by circulating air beneath the structure; the steep roofs shed water quickly, their deep eaves shade windows and the thatch dampens the sound of beating rain – while the high interior disperses warm air effectively.

have become the preferred dwelling-type of a burgeoning middle-class. Built to government order, such developments grow in strict regimen; you'll see various stages of completion in sequence on the same site. Sub-contractors move from ground-beams up, until the homes are completed.

An imaginary line joins the Twin Towers to the airport, known as the Multi-media Super-Corridor (MSC). Planned as a "global-gateway" for everything "cyber", the MSC has suffered from an over-liberal planning brief. The result is a mish-mash of architectural styles that spectacularly fails to match the political coherence of Malaysia's policy on new technologies. MEASAT (the Malaysian Satellite Broadcasting company) managed a low-rise brick-motif gesture with a Vegas-esque signboard, while Microsoft and all the others who took advantage of the everything-exempt sweeteners to take up space, are planning sheds that appear to import their aesthetic from Nebraska.

Ancient origins

An hour or so south of Kuala Lumpur sits Melaka, founded around 1400 by fleeing Sumatran Prince Parameswara. He laid the foundations for what was to become a centre of teaching and trade in the thriving Southeast Asia of the 15th century. The Melaka Cultural Museum is housed in an 1895 replica of the timber-framed palace of the third sultan, Mansur Shah, which was originally destroyed by the Portuguese during their 130-year rule. The Portuguese's architectural artefacts in Melaka are the most significant – including the formidable *A Famosa* fort of 1512.

In 1641, control of Melaka was wrested by the Dutch, who set about building a regional trade hub, the administration of which was housed within the Stadhuys. This 1650s town hall, together with the Christ Church of 1753 (the ceiling beams of which are formed from single trees with no joints), represent probably the most complete examples of 17th-century colonial Dutch architecture in the region.

Commerce with the Dutch saw the growth of Johor as an urban centre. However, the architectural character of the city was defined later, in the 17th and 18th century with the influx of

Minangkabau and Bugis immigrants from Sumatra and Sulawesi respectively. The ordered and highly artistic Minangkabau later headed north – their tall, sweeping roof-style is found throughout the state of Negeri Sembilan (adjacent to Melaka). The Bugis, however, a feared warrior race, stayed in Johor, establishing a distinctive vernacular of ornate timberwork and design. Modern Johor has suffered from its proximity to Singapore. Having assumed the role of a black-market bordertown, its grandiose "floating-city" schemes have resulted in urban erosion and negligible architectural worth.

THE STRAITS ECLECTIC STYLE

The favoured building-type in the Straits Settlements (from Penang down to Singapore) was the "shophouse", a double-storey unit with a lower level business floor and a verandah to keep pedestrians sheltered from the sun or rain, while upstairs the family maintained a residence. The style evolved from buildings favoured in mainland China, but Malay, Indian, Arab and Peranakan (Straits-born Chinese) flavourings have created lively and colourful variations on every street facade. This building-type has since matured into the most ubiquitous commercial architectural form on the peninsula – new shophouse developments climb six storeys or more.

LEFT: KL skyline with the green expanse of the *padang* as focus. **RIGHT:** Dutch architecture, Melaka

Island-life encounters along the east coast are far more inviting. Although the journey from Johor up to Terengganu takes in a number of vast hotel resorts, you'll also see scattered fishing communities with their beach-huts and stilt-raised shelters nestling in quiet coves and on the shore above the cobalt surf. The walls and roof are invariably a thatch of *Nipah* leaves – cooling and comfortably aesthetic.

Kampung life

Although not as dominant as the west coast colonial settlements, the east displays every evolutionary variant of the Malay *kampung*

(village) house. Over in the states of Sabah and Sarawak, 1,000 km (620 miles) over the South China Sea on the island of Borneo, the long-house (see *pages 294–5*) is the typical indigenous building. The basic construction follows the lines of a *kampung* house, but is extended to provide dwellings for many families – and sometimes an entire village. While the layout remains simple, including a "street" formed either between facing rows of living units or on their perimeter, the social organisation is highly complex; where, when and how units are allocated are based on hierarchy, and define cultural rituals of welcoming visitors, marriage, childbearing and security.

Crossing back from the east coast involves a trek over a highland spine featuring architecture both wholly indigenous and imported. Taman Negara National Park occupies tens of thousands of hectares between the coasts and is home to the Orang Asli, or "original people". Their transient settlements are driven by their nomadic lifestyle – simple shelters of bound leaves and flexible supports adjacent to a hearth for cooking and warmth, all built using materials from the jungle.

The cultivated contrast of the colonial Cameron Highlands hill resort offers the peculiar charm of an English country village surrounded by verdant tapestries of lush tea plantations. Die-hard archaeologists could circuitously route themselves via the state of Kedah in the northeast corner and find in the Bujang Valley remnants of the 6th-century *candi* (temples) of the Malay peninsula's Hindu-Buddhist period.

The quiet reflection of such an experience offers a delicate preamble to the bustling urban centre of Penang. Penang attracted the most dynamic influences of British and Chinese architecture. The British contribution is apparent in the urban planning, wide boulevards, sea esplanade and imposing administrative buildings; the East India Company literally ran the island from 1786 onwards, and a great deal of capital was invested in its power base. Building conventions and by-laws took root here which set a precedent for almost every other high-street in Malaya.

Travelling back to Kuala Lumpur via Ipoh reveals another important architectural phase fuelled by wealth (primarily from tin-mining) and independence in the 1960s. Self-determination brought with it an architectural self-actualisation that resulted in forms unmatched ever since in integrity or detail. The cantilevered free-forms of amoebic car-porches were perfectly in tune with the swinging culture that borrowed the very shiniest from the West and cultivated home-grown heroes such as the legendary actor P. Ramlee. In the light of contemporary attempts at seeking a distinct Malaysian architectural identity – the current common approach being to slap a suitably Islamic motif on a pre-packaged curtain wall system – the 1960s remain a beacon of light. ❏

LEFT: a Malay *kampung* house on stilts for ventilation.

Petronas Twin Towers

The Petronas Twin Towers stand 452 metres (1,480 ft) tall and are the focal point of the new Kuala Lumpur City Centre (KLIA) development. Although there was some contention when first commissioned, the towers currently enjoy the status of being the world's tallest buildings. However, such records are, inevitably, held only briefly.

A more pertinent attestation would be that a small developing country like Malaysia managed to muster enough global wealth, expertise and local confidence to not only conceptualise but also realise such a feat. Many may quibble on points of political motives, white elephants, Other People's Money and absolute irrelevance – but there is no denying the extraordinary power of such monumental architecture. On par with Gustav Eiffel's tower heralding the advantages of steel-construction, or the dramatic urban planning of Christopher Wren's St Paul's rising goliath-like over a shanty 17th-century London, the spirit of the Twin Towers is historic and "millennial". Considering that the local content (both in terms of expertise and materials) is minimal, the fact that they were built in Malaysia at all is testimony to the power of globalisation and how projects of any nature and size will be developed in years to come the world over.

Architecturally, the towers are practically faultless: the American architects delivered a Gothamesque vision shinily clad in about 85,000 sq metres (280,000 sq ft) of imported European stainless steel. Executed with the simple, almost fascistic clarity of vision of all great monuments, scores of imported consultants laboured for just under – a remarkably short – four years to deliver the Kuala Lumpur skyline an attention-wrenching silhouette. When pushed into providing a link with local sensibilities, some rather contrived sketches reveal an 8-pointed star superimposed on eight semi-circles which together yield a tenuous Islamic floorplate geometry, giving face to Asian Values.

The path to realisation was fraught with having to achieve as many "world-firsts" as possible – the Malaysian rally-cry that screams "*Malaysia Boleh!*" ("Malaysia can do it!") could permit an attitude of no less. Some of these include the blistering construction schedule of two daily 12-hour shifts util-

ising over 2,000 workers at any given time; the double-level skybridge on the 42nd level, which is one of the highest in the world at 170 metres (560 ft) and took 4 weeks to lift into place; and the highest number of "double-deck" lifts to be contained in a building ever, running at speeds of 5 metres (16 ft) per second – going from the basement to the top floor takes about a minute.

When completed, the record height was disputed by the incumbent Sears Tower in Chicago; the latter wasn't quite ready to step off its podium. However, Malaysians insisted that the towers were the final word on the matter. To cap it all, literally, and somewhat controversially, were the two 75-metre

(246-ft) stainless-steel spikes that sat atop the 88th level, which, arguably, gave the buildings the winning edge over Sears Tower. But such unbecoming squabbling was put to rest when Malaysia declared that it was never the original intention to construct the tallest buildings in the world – it was just a "happy coincidence".

Unfortunately, because the towers are held in semi-private hands as headquarters to the national petroleum company, excursions to anything above the 3rd floor are out of public reach.

Sean Connery and Caroline Zeta-Jones had access to the top when they filmed the movie *Entrapment*, but if you want to get to the higher floors, you had best ask the Prime Minister. ❏

RIGHT: the stunning Kuala Lumpur City Centre.

CUISINE

Malaysia's many peoples have retained their own culinary traditions. The result is a deliciously diverse national menu – and a playground for the tastebuds

Malaysia has been blessed with reliable weather and a lush landscape: tropical jungles, verdant rice paddies, endless coconut groves bending to meet teeming coral reefs submerged in emerald seas. These gifts of nature, and the ethnic complexity of Malaysia's population, combine to provide the country with flavours to thrill the palate.

This hedonistic encounter extends not only to multicultural tastes, aromas, colours and textures, but also to the vast spectrum of dining experiences available in Malaysia. Eating establishments range from dusty roadside stalls and noisy Chinese coffee shops, to smart air-conditioned restaurants and Western-style fast-food joints. The choices are infinite.

Village fare

For centuries, Malays lived in *kampung* (villages) close to rivers and coasts, enjoying the natural abundance of food. Traditional meals consisted of rice, fish, vegetables, and chilli sauces (*sambal*), while fresh herbs and coconut milk added fragrance and richness. However, until the 20th century, travel across the jungle-covered country was limited and regional styles of cooking prevailed. The northern states of Kedah, Kelantan, Perlis and Terengganu, for instance, have incorporated sour tamarind (*asam*), limes and fiery chillies in their cuisine because of the influence of neighbouring Thailand. One of the best known northern dishes is *nasi ulam*, a dish consisting of rice, finely sliced raw herbs and vegetables, a spicy chilli-coconut sauce, grilled fish and other cooked side dishes.

Indonesian influences are evident in various Malaysian states. In Johor in the far south, Javanese food was assimilated into Malay cooking over the past few centuries. In the central state of Negeri Sembilan, Minangkabau settlers from West Sumatra brought with them

their rich, spicy dishes cooked in coconut milk. A perfect example is *rendang* – a semi-dry coconut-based curry which needs hours of gentle simmering, melding beef with fresh herbs like lemon grass, turmeric and ginger, and spices such as coriander, nutmeg and cloves. The result is pure ambrosia.

SATAY

Satay is possibly the world's most popular Malay food, but whatever you've tasted in your own country, nothing can prepare you for the real thing. Marinated bite-sized pieces of beef, mutton or chicken (and pork if sold by Chinese) are skewered onto thin, bamboo sticks, and barbecued over a charcoal fire. The sizzling satay is served with thick, spicy peanut gravy, chunks of raw onion and cucumber, and *ketupat* – compressed squares of rice. Leave the remaining bamboo sticks on the table, as the "bill" is settled by counting the total number of sticks left. For the adventurous, there are even satay variations of tripe, intestines, or crispy chicken skin.

PRECEDING PAGES: rice is the focus in this spread of fiery but flavoursome Malay fare.
LEFT: local produce on sale at a Kota Bahru market.
RIGHT: charcoal-grilled *satay*.

Despite differing regional styles, Malay food is, in general, heavily seasoned. Chillies are an everyday pick-me-up, either in dishes or as a blended *sambal* side-dish. The key to almost any Malay dish, however, is the *rempah* – a pounded paste of onions, garlic, chillies, fresh turmeric, and galangal (*langkuas*). The rempah is stir-fried in hot oil in a *kuali* (Chinese wok) and patiently stirred to prevent sticking and to release its tantalising aromas; it is said that this process is the make or break of the whole dish. A subtle seafood flavour is often added in the form of dried shrimps, dried anchovies (*ikan bilis*) or a pungent shrimp paste (*belacan*).

Rice and noodles

Mouthwatering as they may sound, Malay recipes are lost without the simple, indispensable staple: rice (*nasi*). Rice dishes take many forms: *nasi minyak* (flavoured with spices like cardamom and cinnamon), *nasi tomato* (with tomatoes for a hint of sourness), *nasi goreng* (stir-fried with meat, eggs and chillies), and entire meals consisting of rice and side dishes: *nasi padang* (of Indonesian influence), *nasi kandar* (famous in Penang), and *nasi dagang* and *nasi ulam* (in Kelantan and Terrenganu). Another popular rice dish is *nasi lemak*. The name means "rich rice" – a savoury rice cooked

MILDER MALAYSIAN

The keynote of any Malaysian dish is chilli – and often lots of it. For milder tastes, the selection at hawker stalls and in Chinese coffee shops presents a mind-boggling selection. Among the more popular fare, **wantan mee** are thin, fresh egg noodles either served in a broth or tossed in a chilli and oil-and-soy-sauce dressing, and topped with roast pork slices and prawn and pork dumplings. Another popular noodle dish is **Ipoh kway teow**. As the name suggests, this soupy dish gained fame in the town of Ipoh, Perak. Smooth, translucent strips of rice noodles are served in a prawn and pork broth and garnished with bean sprouts, shredded chicken and prawns. Ipoh boasts the most

delicate *kway teow* and fattest bean sprouts, supposedly because of the soft water which flows down from the surrounding limestone hills.

Char kway teow is another classic Malaysian-Chinese noodle dish: stir-fried flat rice noodles, garlic, prawns, cockles, bean sprouts, eggs, chilli paste, and lashings of thick, dark soy sauce for a hint of sweetness. Finally there is **chicken rice**, which no gourmand should miss. There are several variations, but the most popular is the Hainanese style, where whole chickens are simmered in chicken stock so that each slice is moist and tender, and served with delicious rice cooked in chicken stock instead of water.

not in water, but gently steamed in coconut milk till every drop of the liquid richness has been absorbed. The rice is then served with a fiery *sambal*, cucumber for coolness, small crispy fried fish, and a fried egg or omelette.

When you tire of rice, try noodles. Chinese immigrants introduced noodles to Malay cuisine and they are now an indispensable part of Malay cuisine: *mee* (a spaghetti-like yellow wheat noodle), *kway teow* (flat strips of smooth rice noodle), and *mee hoon* (thin rice vermicelli) – all can either be stir-fried (*goreng*), served in a light soup, or in speciality dishes such as *mee siam* (mee hoon in a red, spicy, and sour soup), and *mee rebus* (mee in a thick, brown spicy gravy). Chinese immigrants also brought with them the cooking styles of their mainland regions; Cantonese, Hokkien, Teochew, Hakka, and Hainanese predominate.

You are what you eat

Symbolism plays an important part in Chinese cuisine. There is a belief that parts of the animal are supposed to strengthen the corresponding part in the human body. Hence, eating pig's brain soup will increase concentration and alertness, braised beef tendons will boost tired legs, and so on.

Symbolic meaning also comes from the names of foods. For example, a kind of seaweed that looks exactly like black hair is called *fatt choy*, meaning hair vegetable; an unappetising pronunciation, but one phonetically identical to the Chinese characters meaning "to prosper". This weed is often stewed with dried oysters (*hou si*), which sounds like "good business". Not surprisingly, this dish is a standard inclusion on annual Chinese New Year menus, as are prawns (*ha*), which symbolise happiness.

Restaurant Chinese food in Malaysia is considerably more traditional and less novel. Dainty Cantonese *dim sum*, spicy Sechuan food, crispy Peking duck, shark's fin and other Chinese classics are available and cooked to high standards. Although many authentic mainland dishes still remain intact, some so-called Chinese food in Malaysia would baffle any mainland Chinese, just as "chop suey" and "egg rolls" confound many non-American Chinese.

LEFT: mee rebus, Malay-style noodles smothered in spicy gravy. RIGHT: for chicken rice, whole chickens are simmered in stock for extra flavour.

Go Indian

Although Indians make up only about 10 percent of the population, Indian stalls and restaurants proliferate. The majority of Indians are Tamils from the south Indian state of Tamil Nadu, whose food is hot and spicy and served with rice. But there are also northern Indian restaurants, dishing up milder fare with delicious breads like *naan* and *poori*. In addition, there are eateries run by Indian Muslims, who observe strict Muslim dietary laws.

Eating at one of the many south Indian "banana leaf curry" restaurants in Malaysia, you will experience one of the heartiest and

most colourful culinary spreads around. The banana leaf itself is not eaten, but acts as a natural, disposable green plate from which spicy dry *mysore* mutton, fried fish, chicken curry, red curried crabs, and a variety of spiced vegetables and pickles are eaten. The meal is often accompanied by fresh yoghurt to cool the palate, and cups of thin, spicy soup (*rasam*) to aid digestion. The meal is strongly seasoned with the dried spices used by Indians for thousands of years: chillies, cardamom, cloves, cumin, fenugreek, cinnamon, fennel and mustard seeds, to name just a few of the aromatics used. Fresh lime juice is almost always available to top it all off.

Malaysians would stand firm on the claim that India's greatest culinary contribution to Malaysia is the multi-layered, feather-light *roti canai* (flattened bread) – a flaky fried bread made of wheat flour, *ghee* (clarified butter) and a touch of milk for lightness. A stretchy dough is kneaded, rolled into balls, then dramatically tossed repeatedly into the air; the resulting dough is paper thin, and is folded and fried on a griddle to yield a crisp, flaky pancake. A popular breakfast item, *canai* can also be eaten at any time of

PRECISION CUISINE

Nothing in traditional Peranakan cooking is large or clumsy; every bite has to be equal in size, and measure approximately 2 centimetres (1 inch) in length.

the day. When visiting Indian hawker stalls, don't forget to try Indian *mee goreng* (fried yellow noodles), which are similar to the Malay version, but with slightly different spices, and Indian *rojak*, deep-fried fritters dipped in a sweet, hot sauce.

Peranakan cuisine

Peranakan food is a bi-cultural cuisine unique to Malaysia and its island neighbour, Singapore. It is a food of love, conceived by the interracial marriage of early Chinese immigrants and native Malays, resulting in the Peranakan, or Straits-born Chinese culture. These Nonya women combined the best of both cuisines, pro-

ducing delectable dishes for their Baba men.

Peranakan food subtly merges typical Chinese ingredients such as pork, soy sauce and preserved soya beans with Malay spices, *rempah* ingredients and the ever-present coconut milk and/or tamarind juice. Being non-Muslim, Peranakan pork dishes are everyday fare. Some favourites are *babi asam* (a tamarind-based pork curry), and pork satay, with pineapple-enhanced peanut sauce.

Duck, traditionally not consumed by Malays, is popular in Peranakan kitchens, where it is braised whole, or made into a curry or sour soup (*itek sio*). Chicken is also commonly used, transformed into varied dishes such as chicken *kapitan* (chicken in spicy coconut milk) and *encik kabin* (fried chicken with a tangy dip).

Much like Malay cuisine, Peranakan food evolved differently in different parts of the peninsula. *Laksa*, a classic Nonya dish, comes in two varieties: Melakan cooks favour *laksa lemak* (also called curry laksa) which consists of noodles, prawns and other toppings bathed in a *lemak* (rich) spicy coconut soup. Then there is *asam laksa*, a famous speciality of Penang Nonyas. This variety, with distinct Thai influences comprises noodles in a clear, fish-based soup, topped with raw cucumber and onion rings, pineapple chunks and mint sprigs.

Not only is Peranakan food delicious, it is also painstakingly prepared. Despite the many servants of old-style Peranakan homes, young Nonya women traditionally spent hours in the kitchen mastering the precise culinary skills that would please their would-be Baba husbands. Under the watchful eye of elder Nonya women, the girls would practice pounding *rempah*, and slicing and chopping everything in the correct manner.

Eurasian and colonial

Malaysia's other ethnically complex cuisine is Eurasian food. The mecca of this type of cooking is undoubtedly Melaka, which fell to Portuguese invaders in 1511. Although Portuguese rule ended in 1641, and Dutch sovereignty some 150 years later, three centuries of mixed marriages resulted in modern-day Catholic descendants of Portuguese, Dutch, Malay, Javanese and Indian ancestry.

Eurasian cuisine is typically multicultural: Malay herbs enliven Chinese cuts of pork, further enhanced by Indian mustard seeds and chillies. A famous dish is devil curry, a fire-and-brimstone name for a spicy dish based on a Goanese vindaloo, further pepped up with vinegar, mustard and chillies. Similarly, English dishes such as stews and roasts are transformed with the simple addition of soy or oyster sauce, green chillies, or sour tamarind juice.

Undoubtedly, though, the highlight of any Eurasian kitchen wafts through the air in the form of warm, buttery, baking aromas. Eurasian cakes are sinfully delectable – rich fruit cakes, and the infamous *sugee* cake: a rich yellow cake made with heaps of only the best churned butter (traditionally imported in a can), sugar, vanilla, and a mixture of wheat flour and gritty *sugee* (semolina). The result is a decadent tea treat favoured highly by most Eurasians.

Related to Eurasian cooking is colonial food – British dishes that were originally cooked by a hired help (almost always Hainanese Chinese). These cooks slipped Chinese seasonings such as soy sauce and oyster sauce into sedate English food, resulting in tastier roasts, and famous chicken and pork chops slathered with peas, onions and a gravy seasoned with garlic and soy sauce. The altered dishes met with little protest and have remained till today, in older hotels and locally-run Western restaurants across Malaysia.

Food from the jungle

Traditional Borneo food is hard to find outside the longhouses and remote villages. Rice is the staple, although some tribes still adhere to diets based on boiled sago palm and tapioca root. Raw meats and fish are preserved by smoking, or curing in salt. Jungle vegetables like bamboo shoots and fern tips are regular accompaniments, as are lashings of lime and chilli.

Nowadays, what is typical food in Sabah and Sarawak is in fact a Chinese- and Malay-influenced cuisine. From the Chinese immigrants this century, Borneo food has adopted ingredients like soy sauce, and stir-frying and other cooking methods; from the Malays, chillies, dried shrimp, and prawn paste (*belacan*). Using these ingredients, vegetables, jungle animals such as wild boar, and seafood from the coast and rivers are deliciously braised and stir-fried.

Stranger jungle fare can be found even on the peninsula. For those with adventurous spirits and strong stomachs, jungle-food restaurants can be found in many states. Johor, for example, boasts popular Chinese restaurants serving bullfrogs, wild-boar, snake, flying fox, civet cat and a host of seasonal "chef specials", which should be tasted first before being identified if they are to be enjoyed. Although the meats used may turn Western stomachs, the cooking is imaginative and the dishes usually tasty. ❑

LEFT: in "banana leaf restaurants", food is served on a natural, disposable green "plate". **RIGHT:** a sampling of spices and herbs used in Peranakan cooking.

LOCAL EATING HABITS

To be completely immersed in the whole Malay culinary experience, it is imperative to try at least once the traditional Malay way of eating, still practised in the average Malay home – with your fingers. It may look simple, but it is a skill to be mastered. Using only the tips of the fingers on the right hand (the left hand is considered unclean and never used), any Malay can pick, tear, and scoop with complete deftness.

Increasingly, however, outside the home many Malays use a spoon in the right hand, which is brought to the mouth, and a fork in the left, used mainly for manoeuvring food onto the spoon.

HAWKER FOOD AND OUTDOOR EATS

The best of Malaysia's food isn't served at fancy restaurants but at stalls set up by the roadside, in hawker centres, or in street-side coffee shops

Patronised by rich and poor alike, hawker stalls are found all over Malaysia, from urban sites beside busy highways, to idyllic seaside locations. Feeding and slaking the thirst of the nation is a round-the-clock affair: Malaysians, as a rule, live to eat and not the other way around. With such low prices who'd be bothered to cook, and as most hawkers specialise in only a few dishes, they have perfected their culinary skills to a degree where most people would prefer to eat out than in. Basic tables and stools are provided on-site. Hawkers will often ask if you want to *makan* – "eat there", or *bungkus* – "take-away".

WHERE TO EAT

Each state has its own famous outdoor eating centre. In Kuala Lumpur (KL), head for Chinatown's famed Petaling Street night market (*above*) for Chinese specialities. For Malay food don't miss the Saturday night market in Kampung Bahru. After dark in Penang, Gurney Drive offers an array of multi-ethnic treats by the sea. In Kota Bharu, have breakfast upstairs in the Central Market, and dinner at the car park, which turns into a night-time eating centre, offering mouth-watering Kelantanese delicacies. Melaka's best-known hawker scene is at the Glutton's Corner overlooking the Mahkota Parade shopping centre.

▽ **NASI LEMAK**
Malaysia's favourite breakfast consists of rice cooked in coconut milk, served with egg, cucumber, anchovies and a spicy *sambal* sauce.

▽ **SNACK TIME**
A variety of sweet and savoury snacks, go by the generic name of *kuih*. These stalls proliferate during the Muslim fasting month of *Ramadan*.

▽ **MORNING TEA**
On KL's Jalan Silang, office workers enjoy mid-morning snacks of banana-leaf-wrapped savouries, cakes, curry puffs and tarts.

△ **PENANG TREAT**
At Georgetown's Esplanade, hawkers prepare *rojak pasembur*, deep-fried seafood and tofu smothered in peanut sauce.

▷ **KL BREAKFAST**
KL's Masjid India area is popular for *roti canai* with *dhal* or lentil gravy, and accompanied by *teh tarik*, a sweet strong tea.

ROTI CANAI BREAKFAST

△ **CHINESE BREAD**
Deep-fried *yu char kway*, a Chinese snack, on sale near Georgetown's Campbell Street market, Penang.

△ **SATAY**
Marinated morsels of meat are grilled over a charcoal brazier for *satay*, a popular after-dark snack and the unofficial "national" dish.

▷ **INDIAN PANCAKE**
Roti canai is best eaten with your hands. Just tear off a flaky portion, and dip it into a saucer of *dhal* or lentil curry.

Walk through any Malaysian town mid-morning, and the most crowded eateries will usually be those serving *roti canai*. Its English description, an unleavened pancake served with dhal, just doesn't do it justice. It is deliciously light, flaky and crisp, the perfect vehicle to soak up spicy sauces and curries.

Most cooks show off their skills at the front of their shops; it takes years of practice to swing out the dough until it is paper thin. The theatrical flourishes when tossing the *roti* may appear excessive, but are needed to keep the pancake as light and flaky as possible.

A speciality of Indian-Muslim cooks, the origins of *roti canai* are obscure, and like many Malaysian favourites, it has evolved over generations into a strictly localised dish.

ARTS AND CRAFTS

Malaysia has always been proud of its rich craft tradition. Now a new breed of artists are pushing back the boundaries of contemporary Asian art

From prehistoric cave murals to cutting-edge contemporary oil painting, the story of Malaysian art spans over 2,000 years of creativity; traditional crafts, which still survive on the Malay peninsula's east coast and in the longhouses of Sarawak, could well have been around for even longer. Located at the heart of Southeast Asia, at the meeting of the ancient trade routes, Malaysian culture has always been heavily influenced by external influences; its arts and crafts a reflection of this cross-cultural interweaving.

Prehistoric art

Over two millennia ago, unknown artists painted abstract designs, human figures and animals on the walls of a cave near Ipoh, Perak. Meanwhile, across the South China Sea in Sarawak, artisans in the Niah Caves were also painting over 100 depictions of human figures and boats, in murals which stretch over 50 linear metres (165 linear ft). Cave paintings are rare in Malaysia and for many years scholars wondered who these artisans were, and what the drawings meant. Later discoveries of contemporary Orang Asli cave drawings in Perak, in Sarawak and in Sabah, suggest that the prehistoric artists were probably the ancestors of the more recent Orang Asli cave painters, and that the murals depicted the cultural and religious aspects of the original prehistoric painters' lives.

Malaysian crafts date back to the earliest human settlement. A Palaeolithic workshop for making crude stone chopping tools, excavated at Kota Tampan, Perak, dates to 38,000 years ago, while sophisticated flaked stone tools from Sabah's Tingkayu region can be traced back some 28,000 years.

Around 2,000 BC, during the Neolithic era, pottery and polished stone tools appeared. Wooden paddles and anvil stones were proba-bly used to produce some of the pottery, including sophisticated three-colour urns from the Niah Caves. This production method is still used today by Sarawak's Iban peoples.

In the remote highlands of Bario in Sarawak, and in the lowland wetlands near Santubong, there are some unusual rock carvings where

figures and spiral designs have been engraved into boulders. The only stone carvings in Peninsular Malaysia are a group of carved megalithic stones at Pengkalan Kempas in Negeri Sembilan. This group of three stones, of unknown origin and age, are one of Malaysia's greatest archaeological mysteries as they depict Hindu-type phallic symbols along with the Islamic script for Allah (God). Scholars are divided as to whether the carvings were done at the same time, or whether the Allah inscription was done later to sanctify a pagan site. Stone foundations of buildings and temples found in Kedah's Bujang Valley apparently supported a wooden infrastructure which has long since perished.

PRECEDING PAGES: an oversized Malaysian kite or *wau.* **LEFT:** fine art of handpainted batik. **RIGHT:** megaliths in Negeri Sembilan testify to early artistic leanings.

Wood-carving is a popular craft in Sarawak, where the Kajang people still carve wooden burial poles, or *klirieng*, to house jars containing ashes of deceased chiefs. The oldest surviving pole is 200 years old, but the tradition is believed to date back many centuries more. Other wood-carving traditions survive with the Mah Meri of Pulau Carey, Selangor, who carve legendary figures believed to be the spirits of their ancestors, and the Jah Hut of Pahang, who also sculpt their legends in wood. The Iban of Sarawak carve spectacular hornbill sculptures, while the upriver Kenyah carve mythical dog-god ancestors.

Examples of his work still exist and show how upper-class houses were constructed using no nails, with beautifully carved panels of floral patterns and verses from the Koran.

Metalwork and jewellery

From the first century AD, Indian and Chinese travellers told of legendary Malay kingdoms like Langkasuka and Chi Tu (Red Earth Land). They would describe ancient courts where rulers wore fabulous gold jewellery and dressed in "rose-coloured cloth" – possibly the first-known reference to Malay handwoven *songket*. It is hard to separate reality from fiction in these

Carving comeback

In the peninsula, wood-carving is undergoing something of a revival. There is a new interest in the old craft, and today Malay wood-carvings not only adorn the walls of museums, but decorate the foyers of banks, businesses and government offices, including that of the prime minister. Some of the finest antique wood-carvings can be seen on the panelling, pillars, windows and doors of the nation's oldest royal palaces, which were all built of wood. Encik Long of Besut, Terengganu, was a celebrated master carver, and during four decades of his century-long life he was the principal builder for the Raja of Besut.

fabled accounts, but by the time of the Melakan Sultanate in the 14th century, artisans and craftspeople were an integral part of the royal court. Many lived and worked in the villages beside the palace. Sultans, chiefs, nobles, and their wives and families were the moneyed class, and silversmiths and goldsmiths, silk-weavers, and wood carvers depended on royal patronage for their existence.

A royal wedding was the ultimate event and every artisan was involved in preparing the trousseau and the ceremonial items needed for such a prestigious affair. However, when the courts became more westernised, rulers started buying imported jewellery, clothing, and artefacts. The habit of betel-nut chewing went out of fashion, for instance, rendering obsolete the silver items used in its preparation, and forcing many artisans to hang up their tools. Similarly, many traditional arts and crafts are in danger of extinction.

Fortunately, however, in the predominantly Malay-populated regions of the peninsula's east coast, craftsmen and women have preserved their age-old practices. Today, silver-working, silk-weaving and wood-carving are all experiencing a huge revival. For example, silversmiths still thrive in Kota Bharu, despite having vanished elsewhere. These days, jewellery and functional pieces like fruit bowls, tea-sets and spoons are popular, and although past fashions called for different artefacts, the designs and techniques employed are the same. In Islam, it is taboo to use anthropomorphic figures, and many of the patterns are therefore inspired by flowers, branches and even clouds.

Early silverware is often of exceptional craftsmanship and some pieces, like the earliest surviving example – a royal Johorean betel-set from the early-18th century – employ a painstaking technique that is seldom seen these days. Probably the most fascinating of all the old pieces are leaf-shaped "fig leaves" which until the 19th century were the only clothing worn by little Malay girls.

In the 1800s, the Straits Chinese of Melaka and Penang, also known as Peranakan – whose ancestors were early Chinese traders who intermarried with local women – borrowed heavily from Malay silver and gold traditions to create their own craft, which is distinguishable from traditional Malay work by its designs which often feature birds and flowers.

Fabrics and weaving

Silk brocades, known as *kain songket*, have always been the favoured textiles for royal occasions, and these elegant woven cloths are still the preferred wear, not only for courtly occasions but for government functions. They are most often used as traditional bridal wear, when both the bride and groom are dressed in sumptuous brocade outfits. At a Kelantanese

> **MYSTIC CRAFT**
>
> Traditionally, a wood-carver would enter the forest to select his own timber and chant incantations to appease forest spirits.

weaver's showroom, a pale mauve colour is still sold only to royalty, and there are certain designs which are even now the prerogative of the traditional ruler.

Weavers are usually women who have learnt the craft from their mothers and grandmothers. The very best weavers worked for the palace, like the grandmother of one of Terengganu's top weavers, who was picked from two thousand local artisans of her day to become the sultan's head weaver. Like most other time-honoured crafts, *songket* weaving is practised in

Terengganu and Kelantan, and the techniques and looms used are the same as in the old days. Woven on a simple four-posted loom, the brocade consists of a coloured silk background with a floating weft of gold and silver threads. A distinctive part of every length is the *kepala*, a centre panel with a particularly elaborate pattern. The names of the designs echo the Malay fascination with nature and the countryside: one is known as "bamboo shoots", another "the tail feathers of a cock". Traditionally, nobles would design their own *songket* patterns. This legacy lives on today as a Terengganu prince, Tunku Ismail Tungku Su, continues to create new designs at his well-known workshop. Related to

FAR LEFT: Sarawakian burial pole. **LEFT:** traditional dress made of rich *songket*. **RIGHT:** a *songket* weaver.

the *kain songket* is *tekat*, an ancient craft of gold embroidery on rich, dark velvet. This luxurious material is popular among Malays for home furnishings, wall hangings, cushions and even bedroom slippers.

From Sarawak hails *ikat*, a unique woven fabric with a tie-dyed warp. Iban textiles serve many ritual purposes: newly-born babies are wrapped in them to ward off evil influences and in the past, trophy heads from headhunting expeditions were even draped with *ikat* cloths.

> ### CLASSY CLOTH
>
> Batik derives from the Malay word *tik*, meaning "to drip". It is thought that batik replaced tattooing as a mark of status in Malay culture.

ing block made from zinc strips bent into the desired shaped, and dipped in molten wax. However, the biggest success story is of hand-painted batiks, where the designs are drawn on the cloth using a *canting*, a "pen" filled with liquid wax, with the dyes then painted on with brushes. This latter method means that more colours can be used than with the vat-dyeing method, and the freehand designs are only limited by the artisan's imagination. Batik workshops are now opening up all over Malaysia, but the majority of craftspeople are based on the east coast of the peninsula.

Pottery and other crafts

Beside the Perak River, opposite the royal town of Kuala Kangsar, is the village of Sayong, renowned throughout Malaysia for the manufacture of *Labu Sayong*. Literally "Sayong Pumpkins", these gourd-shaped pottery water vessels keep liquids cool in even the hottest weather. The women of Sayong are the potters, and have been for more generations than they can remember. The pots are made in moulds from local clay, and then finished on the wheel where they are incised with freehand designs. After drying in the sun they are fired in small brick kilns. Both terracotta and black-coloured wares are made, with the latter obtaining their distinct colour from being buried in rice husks while they are still hot from the kiln.

In Sabah and Sarawak, the indigenous peoples are renowned for their skill in weaving baskets and hats. The nomadic Penan weave fine black and white baskets from split rattan. To find the best materials they often have to walk a day's journey deep into the forest, then they dry, split, and finally colour the rattan with dye made of forest leaves.

Batik

Batik cloth is often used to symbolise Malaysia. The national airline uses it for its uniforms, batik shirts are *de rigueur* as men's formal attire and are even compulsory dress at the nation's only casino. It is also worn as sarongs and used for the fashionable and traditional women's dress known as *baju kurung*. But batik-making is not a traditional Malay craft: it was introduced from Indonesia in the 1930s. However, although it is of recent origin, there is no denying that batik-making is now the nation's most popular craft.

Using a wax-resistant technique, the patterns are stamped onto lengths of cloth using a print-

Making mats from *nipah* palm or *pandanus* leaves is a more down-to-earth craft, though one that still requires great skill. Throughout the country, woven mats are an essential part of daily life, used on the floor in *kampung* houses, on beds, on the beach, in mosques, for drying food under the sun, and anywhere else that a convenient, light covering might be needed. Weaving begins at the centre of the mat and moves outwards, using dyes to produce simple criss-cross patterns. More professional weavers (mostly women) fashion hexagonal boxes of nipah palm leaves. In Sabah and Sarawak, floral and even pictorial stories are part of the woven mat's design.

Contemporary art

When the British colonial era introduced industrially-made goods, it was inevitable that traditional arts and crafts would go into decline. At this same time, however, new arts were being introduced like oil painting and watercolours. At first, Malaysian artists emulated Western styles, but after independence a new group of artists came into their own, creating their own brand of abstraction more in line with Islam. Hoy Cheong's epic series on immigration, Ahmad Zakii Anuar's smoke-blurred portraits and Lee Joo For's bonding of Eastern and Western visual language, to name but a few. Some of the new breed trained overseas, bringing a fresh angle to local traditions. During the 1960s and 1970s, artists were keen to distance themselves from local motifs in order to look "modern". However, after more than four decades of independence, Malaysian artists have come of age, and have rediscovered their roots while continuing the Malaysian tradition of blending both local and foreign influences. The result is a style uniquely their own. ❑

Three of the best known of this group are Latiff Mohidin, who uses indigenous motifs and the environment as inspiration; Syed Amad Jamal, who champions abstract expressionism; and, most famous of all, Ibrahim Hussein, whose linear abstracts can be seen at his gallery/workshop in Langkawi.

In the economic boom of the late 1980s and 1990s, a new breed of artists emerged whose works sold as fast as they were being produced: Rafiee Ghani's colourful "roomscapes", Wong

FAR LEFT: pumpkin-shaped pottery of Sayong, Perak.
ABOVE: an example of Rafiee Ghani's "roomscape".
RIGHT: contemporary Malaysian painter, Rafiee Ghani.

RAFIEE GHANI'S WORLD OF COLOUR

Kedah-born, and Kelantanese-raised Rafiee, one of Malaysia's hottest new artists, combines European styles with tropical Malaysian colours and patterns. His signature roomscapes are of everyday objects infused with extraordinary light and colour, bold and spontaneous in the tradition of Van Gogh and Matisse. His oil paintings celebrate his everyday life, but much of his inspiration is derived from his travels in Europe, Asia and Australia. Rafiee's big break came in 1993 with the success of his "Room of Flowers" exhibition, and he has exhibited widely ever since. His work can be seen at the Artist Colony in Kuala Lumpur's Lake Gardens.

ADVENTURE SPORTS

Forest-clad mountains, giant caves, roaring rivers and deep oceans make
Malaysia a challenging destination for the thrill seeker

Drenched in rain and sweat, too tired to pluck off yet another leech, you make the decision to slide the rest of the way down the almost vertical slope of soft clay. Through the drizzle, the welcome sight of smooth large boulders can be barely made out, beyond which is the source of the roar audible for the last hour: a 30-metre (100-ft) high waterfall, thundering down in fine spray.

This is adventure indeed, a 3-day trek in the rugged interior of a tropical rainforest. Malaysia's highland forests are also the source of swift, bubbling headwaters that run into massive river systems, offering superb rafting and kayaking. Some of these streams seep through the porous limestone massifs, forming huge cave systems waiting to be explored and mapped. Their tiny entrances are often masked by thick foliage – which is also why few cliff faces are available for rock-climbing. Those that are suitable, however, are excellent.

Outdoor pursuits

Malaysia's rainforests offer all manner of challenges to both body and mind; but this is largely ignored by its populace. Trekking is popular among boy-scouts and university students, but Malaysians are generally not fond of the outdoors. Blame it on the rain, blame it on the sun. Blame it on the mosquitos and the leeches, the sweat and the dirt. To the urban Malaysian, leisure means a family picnic in a carefully-landscaped park or at one of the easily-accessible beaches or waterfalls near town. Rural folk spend their free time on traditional art forms such as *wau*-flying (kite-flying) and top-spinning. And for the indigenous people, these challenges *are* part of daily life.

Yet adventure sport is slowly gaining ground among younger, more affluent Malaysians, whose exposure to western trends comes as a result of time spent abroad, at an overseas university or travelling. Sometimes, the interest is driven by Malaysia's expatriate community. The exception would be scuba diving, which, due to the heavy promotion of Malaysia's underwater attractions for tourism, is enjoying a massive growth in popularity.

For other adventure sports, however, the infrastructure is nascent, expertise is scarce, and sites undeveloped. Taking up these activities is also very expensive, as much of the equipment has to be imported – which is why they are largely limited to middle-income, city-dwelling 30-somethings. Nonetheless, there are clubs for kayaking, a mountaineering association (whose members were the force behind Malaysia's successful 1997 Mount Everest ascent), and a backpackers' association (which is trying to develop the Roof of Malaya Mountain Trail, a formidable trek covering seven of the peninsula's highest mountains). These are all, however, based in Kuala Lumpur.

PRECEDING PAGES: windsurfing on the wide open South China Sea, off the peninsula's east coast.
LEFT: whitewater action at one of several rivers in Sabah. **RIGHT:** the majestic Gunung Kinabalu.

Multi-sport expedition racing is gaining some interest. In the early 1990s, the punishing Raid Gauloises, the so-called Holy Grail of Expedition Racing, was held in the spectacular mountain, jungle and cave terrain of Mulu, Sarawak. Each team had to have one local participant, but these were mainly park guides and hardy natives. Then in 1998, a local team became the first Asian team to complete the other big international expedition race, the Discovery Channel Eco-Challenge.

Probably the greatest difficulty faced by rainforest-based adventure sports proponents in Malaysia is the humidity, which can reach close to 100 percent in the forest. Dehydration is another problem because of the heat. Luckily there is always an icy-cold river close at hand. In some areas, fortification is necessary against the threat of tropical diseases such as malaria.

The most challenging jungle-trekking is to be found in the country's mountainous interiors. In the peninsula, these concentrate in the backbone of Banjaran Titiwangsa (Main Range); in Sabah, the Crocker Range; and in Sarawak, the northern Mulu area. Countless routes can be taken, whether in the Livingstonian quest for

---

RAINY DAYS

Highland rivers can swell to Grade 5 rapids after a downpour. In some areas, "dry season" means that it only rains in the afternoon instead of all day.

---

waterfalls, or to scale a mountain, or simply to experience the many ecosystems that make up the rainforest. Hundreds of kilometres of trails wind through protected park areas, mainly serving conservation objectives. Other trails have been trammelled for generations by the indigenous people who still travel on foot to their remote villages. In wilder country, it is the animal trails along the steep ridges that form some kind of pathway through the thorny rattan- and liana-strewn undergrowth.

Many of the longer trails involve ascending to mountain tops, such as the 7-day hike to Gunung Tahan (2,200 metres/7,000 ft) in Taman Negara, and the 4-day ascent to Gunung Mulu (2,400 metres/7,900 ft). The popular overnight trail up the country's highest peak, Gunung Kinabalu (4,100 metres/13,400 ft) is relatively civilised, if stamina-sapping. Exciting country lies in the largely unvisited northern tracts of Banjaran Titiwangsa in the peninsula's Belum area, steep hilly terrain full of hidden waterfalls, and in Sabah's Maliau Basin, termed East Malaysia's last frontier.

Trekking is often a wet experience on muddy trails and across numerous rivers, sometimes by boulder-hopping. However, hot-footing it with a backpack is the best way to experience the amazing jungle, and have a chance to encounter the extremely elusive tropical wildlife. And because the Orang Asli and natives make the best jungle guides, it provides a chance to learn about remarkable and fast-disappearing ways of life.

Climbing the walls

Rock-climbing has long been popular among tiny pockets of enthusiasts. But the sport's best shot in the arm came in the early 1990s when, in line with world trends, Malaysia saw the advent of sport-climbing, which is more accessible than traditional climbing. The other factor was that climbing was part of the government's *Rakan Muda* youth programmes, prompting the growth of artificial climbing walls. In 1999, the first indoor climbing gym opened in Kuala Lumpur, the brainchild of Chan Yuen-Li, Malaysia's foremost climber. Chan is a pioneer who set up most of the sport routes in the natural rock around Kuala Lumpur.

All of Malaysia's rock-climbing surfaces is limestone, characterised by steep overhanging rock and often stalactites, which make routes tough (at least 6A French grade; climbing grades range from 3 to 9A). The cliffs are also high, usually 100 metres (300 ft), so paths have to be established from the ground up.

The most frequently visited rock-climbing spots around the capital are Batu Caves and Bukit Takun near Templer's Park. The former is easy to access and has sports routes. Takun is a more tradi-

TOUGH GOING

Malaysia makes for challenging climbs. Rock faces are always steep, cliffs are often high, and dense vegetation makes some faces almost impossible to scale.

water-level fluctuations, depending on rain; dry floors are often thick with guano. There are spectacular traverses, squeezes and stretches of tough ropework. There is plenty of clambering around massive stalagmites and crossing narrow bridges of fretted rock. No one knows how much more of Mulu remains to be discovered, and foreign caving groups come in on surveying expeditions virtually every year.

A brand new area north is also opening up for spelunking. This is Buda, described by

tional rock face, which involves a bit of a clamber through thick undergrowth to reach. However, both offer several interesting routes. The highest grade of climb locally is 7C.

Cave adventures

Superlatives abound when it comes to the caving haven of Mulu – largest, longest, most decorated. Mulu's giant caves offer superb adventure and technical caving opportunities. Most of the area's 200 km (124 miles) of surveyed passages are wet, with large and sudden

American caving expeditionists as "a literal garden of Eden complete with fruits, serpents and an eternity of virgin passage". Truly one of the most spectacular areas for caving in the world, among its wonders is the deepest vertical drop in Southeast Asia (140 metre/460 ft), accessible through challenging ropework amid thundering waterfalls. Another cave houses the region's greatest vertical relief at 465 metres (1,500 ft). Not surprisingly, Buda has been proposed as a state park or an extension of Mulu.

If pre-arranged, equipment and guides can be hired at the Mulu National Park headquarters. There are no caving clubs, but the Malaysian Nature Society has a caving group.

LEFT: rock-climbing near Batu Caves, Kuala Lumpur.
ABOVE: inside a cavern in Sarawak's Mulu Caves

On your bike

While old timber trails in the interior sometimes give hikers access to undisturbed forest, they are more popular with mountain bikers. There are no clubs as such, but various groups comprising mainly friends spend weekends exploring oil palm and rubber plantations, as well as secondary forest near towns. These provide everything from fairly simple trails to challenging hilly terrain, and the vegetation makes for much cooler riding than on the road.

CAPITAL WHEELS

Specialist mountain bike shops are centred in Kuala Lumpur, and sell a range of bikes and accessories. They are also a good place to find out about biking groups.

Wider and flatter jungle trails can actually also make pretty good, if tough, riding – with their root-covered paths, numerous river crossings, and breathtaking views. The Headhunters' Trail in Mulu, Sarawak is being developed for this, while another good trail is the dirt road on the border of Taman Negara which leads from Jerantut to the Kuala Tahan *kampung*, opposite the park headquarters.

Aerial sports

Parachuting and microlight flying are almost prohibitively expensive sports to take up in Malaysia, but instruction is available. A great place for both is Mersing, Pahang, the scenic springboard to the Johor isles. For microlights, the flight course takes in both the island-dotted sea and forested land, spectacular both in the early morning – when flying is best – and at sunset. A 20-hour training course leads to a Department of Civil Aviation, Malaysia, student pilot's licence. Mastering the open cockpit, two-stroke engined aircraft is an exhilarating – and more affordable – way to hone piloting skills for larger aircraft.

In Malaysia, microlights, also known as ultralights, are usually allowed to fly at a maximum height of 150 metres (500 ft), and a 5-km (3-mile) radius from the point of take-off, but the Mersing operation, a pioneer in setting local standards, has been given the green light for a 600-metre (2,000-ft) altitude and a 35-km (22-mile) radius ride along the coast. "Cowboy" operators abound, so check if the instructor is qualified and that a log book is maintained.

Like microlighting, skyjumping is offered by only a handful of operators. The Mersing operation is cleared for a height of 300 metres (1,000 ft). Another operator uses the Segamat Country Club, a golf course in Johor, for student jumps. The 2-day course includes ground training, and static jumps must be completed before freefalling is allowed. Equipment can be rented and jumps are charged according to height. Tandem skyjumping is also available.

Whitewater action

Malaysia's many rivers offer good whitewater experiences. One of the top sites is the spectacular Padas Gorge in Sabah. Tour operators usually offer rafting experiences on 8- to 10-seater inflatable rafts with river guides. Generally, whitewater tour operators are well-organised, experienced and provide safety equipment, a briefing, sometimes insurance, and lunch. In some places, competent paddlers can have a go at one- or two-person kayaks.

A centre of sorts for the sport has sprung up at Sungai Selangor in the peninsula, about 1½ hours from Kuala Lumpur. Attracting mainly daytrippers from the city, a run lasts between 3 and 4 hours. There are also all-day trips that go the entire length of the river. Sungai Selangor has about 15 rapids, most of them fairly simple, with a couple of technical stretches.

However, it is Cameron Highlands that is gaining fame for technical kayaking as the venue for a major international competition – The Camerons Descent. Multi-day destinations include Sungai Nenggiri in Kelantan, and Sungai Endau in the Endau-Rompin Park.

The big blue

Scuba-diving is the fastest-growing adventure sport in the country. Malaysia's precious coral islands offer a multitude of stunning possibilities, and with the gazetting of many sites as marine parks, tourists are flocking to them as snorkellers, and, increasingly, divers. Almost

dive destination, Sipadan. The island also has the country's only dedicated sports-diving hyperbaric chamber; others are in navy bases in Kuantan, Melaka and Lumut. Another up and coming dive destination is Layang Layang, on the other side of the coast.

Besides resort-based facilities which accept walk-in trade, fully-inclusive scheduled trips are offered by city-based operators, mainly from Kuala Lumpur, Kuala Terengganu and Kota Kinabalu.

Malaysia's reefs and marine life are among the world's richest and most diverse. Each dive destination, and sometimes dive spot, is char-

every diveable destination has operators offering tours, full equipment rental, and instruction in PADI, NAUI and/or SSI.

While there are internationally-rated dive centres, at the other end of the scale are operators who are not registered with dive agencies, or are lax about medical and safety equipment such as buoyancy compressors. The Malaysian Sports Diving Association is trying to set local standards and make insurance mandatory. The most developed facilities and services are in Sabah, off whose coast is the region's premier

acterised by endemics, from odd macro life in Mabul to pelagics in Tenggol, coral-wreathed wrecks in Labuan, to the huge diversity of marine life in Redang. Nitrox or technical diving is also becoming popular. Likewise photography, with some operators renting underwater cameras too.

Other seasports, while popular, do not enjoy such enthusiastic patronage. You'll find windsurfing at beach resorts, while sailing has a small, mainly-expatriate following among members of yacht clubs. Incredibly, there is a surfing group who head regularly to the east coast to take on what must be mere ripples compared to the surf in Bali and Hawaii. ❏

LEFT: paragliding panoramas
ABOVE: be prepared for encounters with sharks.

PLACES

*A detailed guide to the entire country, with principal sites
clearly cross-referenced by number to the maps*

The visitor's first impression of Malaysia when flying into Kuala Lumpur typifies the country. The view from the aircraft window is of a sweeping agrarian landscape, a deep green carpet of oil palm plantations; but then the plane touches down at an avant-garde international airport, one of the most advanced in the world.

Malaysia is a land of surprising contradictions: picturesque fishing villages and opulent hotels share the same sandy beach; cosy colonial resorts nestle on hillsides that host spirit-worshipping tribal ceremonies, while dense tropical forests are penetrated by the strains of karaoke. Throw in the cultural pastiche that is the Malaysian people, and the result is an irresistible combination of charm and adventure that is still just a glimpse of the "real" Malaysia.

Situated right in the middle of Southeast Asia, with a total land area of 342,000 sq. km (132,000 sq. miles), Malaysia is about the size of Japan, and has a population of 21 million. The country's infrastructure is well set-up for tourism and consequently, it is fairly easy and very safe to travel anywhere in the country.

Peninsular Malaysia juts out from the southern-most part of the Asian continent. The most developed part of the country is the west coast, dissected from the more traditional and rural east coast by a chain of mountains. Then, about 640 km (400 miles) of ocean – the South China Sea – separates the peninsula from the east Malaysian states of Sabah and Sarawak on the island of Borneo. With its own diverse ethnic tribes, lifestyles and the rich natural heritage, at times, this part of Malaysia seems almost a different country.

Geography has left an indelible stamp on today's Malaysia. The monsoons were what brought disparate cultures to her shores, bringing the religions that now hold sway, influencing architecture and even the model of government. The changing of the winds still affect the important fisheries industry, but for the tourist, it now signifies merely wet and less wet times to visit the country.

Since independence in 1957, Malaysia has faced a series of economic and political pitfalls. Each time it has emerged with the same clear-eyed determination to succeed. From an almost total dependence on raw commodities like rubber and tin, to a broad manufacturing base, Malaysia is now looking beyond that into 21st century global citizenship with hi-tech industries as its vanguard.

But Malaysia's soul is still very much in its *kampung* (villages) and its small town heartlands; in its rainforest and marine heritage; in its religious foundations; and in its cultural roots. And while the quest continues, all these have found some form in a unique Malaysian identity. ❏

PRECEDING PAGES: the majestic Batang Ai river in Sarawak; Pulau Manukan in Sabah's Tunku Abdul Rahman Park; Sultan Abu Bakar Mosque in Johor Bahru
LEFT: picture-perfect Pulau Tioman, where the musical *South Pacific* was filmed.

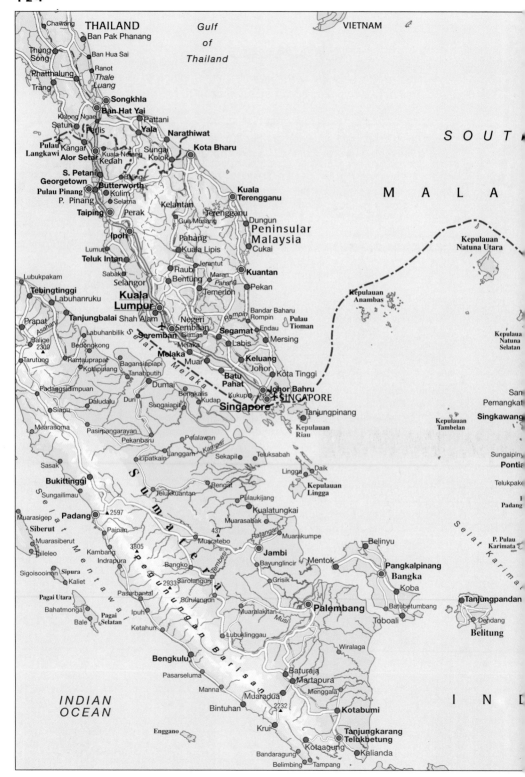

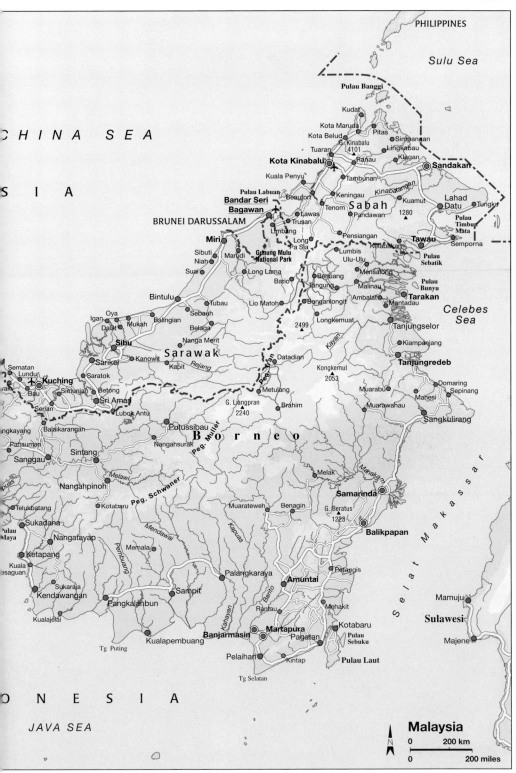

PHILIPPINES

Sulu Sea

CHINA SEA

SIA

Pulau Banggi

Kudat

Kota Maruda
Kota Belud   Pitas
                           Simpangan
Tuaran   G. Kinabalu   Lingkabau
         4101   Klagan
Kota Kinabalu   Ranau   ● **Sandakan**
                    Keningau
Kuala Penyu   Tambunan
Pulau Labuan   Beaufort   Kinabatangan   Kuamut   Lahad
Bandar Seri   Tenom   **Sabah**   Datu   Tungku
Bagawan   Lawas   Pandawan   1280   Pulau
BRUNEI DARUSSALAM   Trusan   Timbun
                   Limbang   Mata
Miri   Long   Pensiangan   Semporna
Sibuti   Marudi   Pa Sia   **Tawau**
Niah   Gunung Mulu   Lumbis
Suai   National Park Ulu-Ulu   Pulau
          Long Lama   Mensalong   Sebatik
               Bario   Benuang
Bintulu   Tangung   Malinau   Pulau
           Tubau   Bonganlongit   **Tarakan** Bunyu
Igan   Oya   Sebauh   Lio Matoh   Mantadau
Dalat   Mukah   Balingian   Longkemuat   Celebes
Sibu   Belaga   2499   Sea
Sarikei   Nanga Merit   Tanjungselor
       Kanowit   Datadian
Sarawak   Kapit   Rejang   Kiampanjang
Sematan   Kongkemul   **Tanjungredeb**
Lundu   Saratok   2053
● **Kuching**   Betong   Muarabu   Domaring
Bau   Simunjan   Metulang   Mahesi   Sepinang
Serian   **Sri Aman**   G. Liangpran   Brahim   Muarawahau
       Lubok Antu   2240   Sangkulirang
ngkayang   Balaikarangan
Pahauman   **Putussibau**
Sanggau   Nangahsurak   B o r n e o
Sintang   Melak
Melawi   **Samarinda**
Nangahpinoh   G. Beratus
Telukbatang   Kotabaru   Muarateweh   Benagin   1223
Sukadana   **Balikpapan**
Pulau   **Nangatayap**
Maya   Memala
Ketapang   Palangkaraya   Petangis
Kuala   **Amuntai**   Mehakit
esaguan   Sukaraja   Sampit   Mamuju
Kendawangan   **Pangkalanbun**   Rantau   Kotabaru
Kualajelai   Mehakit   Pulau   **Sulawesi**
Tg Puting   Kualapembuang   **Banjarmasin** ◎ **Martapura**   Sebuku
                   Pagatan   Majene
              Pelaihari   Kintap   **Pulau Laut**
         Tg Selatan

O N E S I A

JAVA SEA

Malaysia
0   200 km
N
0   200 miles

KUALA LUMPUR AND ENVIRONS

Young, vibrant and bursting with energy, Malaysia's capital is the epitome of a modern Asian city

First-timers expecting to see shanty towns, a populace in Oriental dress, and other "quaint" aspects of Asia, are in for a severe dose of disillusion when they actually reach Kuala Lumpur. What they get instead are skyscrapers of contemporary design, gleaming European and Japanese cars, sober-suited executives, and brand names from Marks & Spencer to Louis Vuitton.

The economic meltdown may have taken away some of its bite, but this Asian Tiger's capital is still a force to be reckoned with on the world stage. For Malaysians, Kuala Lumpur is the centre of everything: business, trade, finance, politics, arts, fashion, trends… in short, it all starts here. You feel it in the air, the mad pace of life, in the traffic-choked streets, the crowded malls, and the incessant beat of techno in the discos. And you feel it when at last you reach your hotel, peel off your dusty shoes and wash the grime from your face.

The capital sits in the Klang River Valley, referred to as the Klang Valley, an area of townships and large industrial estates linked by a network of highways. The Klang Valley is the hub of development, the economic magnet that draws in Malaysians hungry for money, experience, and a taste of big city life.

In the city, tourists like to head to the pockets of colonialism and old Asia, but cannot escape the thrust of modernity. They try to frame a picture of the old Moorish mosque with their camera, but it is impossible to exclude the metallic light rail tracks in the background. Even in a Chinatown wet market, a chicken-seller on a stool is consulting his stockbroker on his mobile phone.

The "real" thing does exist, in the *kampung* just outside the Klang Valley. For while "kampung" translates literally as "village", in city terms, it also carries connotations of being rural, rustic, almost backward. The Klang Valley is forward-looking, technologically-bonded, and even Western in outlook. But to many, it is also just a place to *cari makan*, to "earn a living". It is certainly not home, for home is still the *kampung* – where the heart is.

And so, during the major festive occasions of Hari Raya Puasa and Chinese New Year, hundreds of thousands *balik kampung*, return home to their villages or towns.

This annual exodus sees the highways deserted, hawker stalls closed, while the city's parks echo to the *caw caw* of crows. After the holidays, you can almost hear the machine grinding up again, and before long, it is throbbing once more with noise, chaos, and life. ❑

PRECEDING PAGES: the Kuala Lumpur city skyline at dusk.
LEFT: Jalan Petaling night market all lit up for the Chinese New Year.

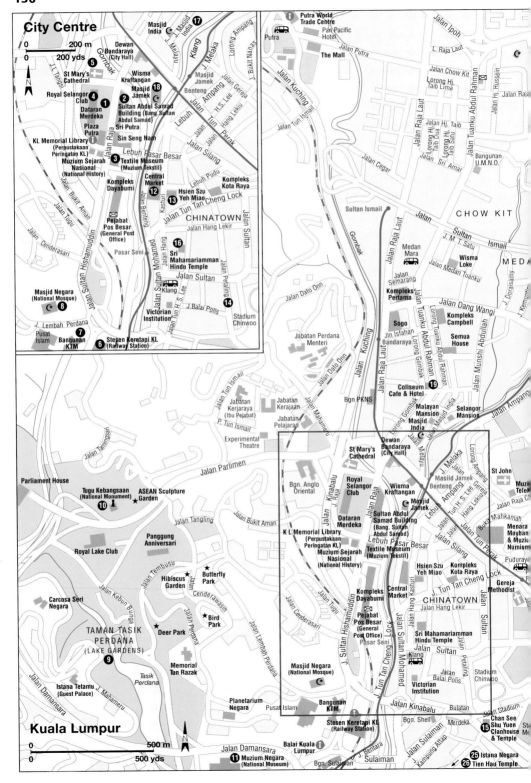

City Centre

0 — 200 m
0 — 200 yds

N

St Mary's Cathedral
Royal Selangor Club ④ ❶
Dataran Merdeka
Plaza Putra
KL Memorial Library (Perpustakaan Peringatan KL)
Muzium Sejarah Nasional (National History)
Kompleks Dayabumi
Pejabat Pos Besar (General Post Office)
Pasar Seni
Masjid Negara (National Mosque) ⑧
Pusat Islam
Bangunan KTM ❼
Stesen Keretapi KL (Railway Station) ⑥

Dewan Bandaraya (City Hall)
Wisma Kraftangan
Masjid India ⑰
J. Masjid India
J. Melayu
Klang
Gombak
J. Tangsi
JLN. Raja
Masjid Jamek ⑱
Sultan Abdul Samad Building (Bang. Sultan Abdul Samad)
Sri Putra
Sin Seng Nam
Lebuh Pasar Besar
Textile Museum (Muzium Tekstil) ③
Central Market ⑫
Hsien Szu Yeh Miao ⑬
Kompleks Kota Raya
Lebuh Pudu
Jalan Silang
Jalan Tun Perak
Lebuh Ampang
H.S. Lee
Hang Lekiu
Masjid Jamek
Benteng
Jalan Gereja
Lorong Ampang
Bukit Nanas
Jalan Raja Chulan

Jalan Sultan Mohamed
Kasturi
Jalan Tun Tan Cheng Lock
CHINATOWN
Jalan Hang Lekir
Sri Mahamariamman Hindu Temple ⑯
Jalan Sultan ⑭
Klang
J. Balai Polis
Victorian Institution
Stadium Chinwoo
Jalan Petaling
Jalan Sultan
H.S. Lee

Masjid Negara (National Mosque)
JLN. Sultan Hishamuddin
JLN. Bukit Aman
Jalan Tugu
Jalan Cenderasari
J. Lembah Perdana
② ⑤ ④

Kuala Lumpur

0 — 500 m
0 — 500 yds

N

Parliament House
Tugu Kebangsaan (National Monument) ⑩
ASEAN Sculpture Garden
Jalan Tangling
Jalan Parlimen
Jalan Bukit Aman
Panggung Anniversari
Royal Lake Club
Jalan Tembusu
Hibiscus Garden
Butterfly Park
Bird Park
Deer Park
Carcosa Seri Negara
Jalan Kebun Bunga
Cenderawasih
TAMAN TASIK PERDANA (LAKE GARDENS)
Jalan Perdana
Memorial Tun Razak
Tasik Perdana
Istana Tetamu (Guest Palace)
J. Mahameru
Jalan Damansara
Jalan Lembah Perdana
Planetarium Negara
Pusat Islam
Bangunan KTM
Stesen Keretapi KL (Railway Station)
Balai Kuala Lumpur
Jalan Damansara
Muzium Negara (National Museum) ⑪
Bgn. Sulaiman
J. Bentara
Jalan Sulaiman ⑨

Putra World Trade Centre
Putra
Pan Pacific Hotel
The Mall
Jalan Putra
Jalan Kuching
Jalan Ipoh
L. Raja Laut
Jalan Chow Kit
Lorong Hj.
Jalan Tuanku Abdul Rahman
Jalan Hj. Hussein
Jalan Raja
Jalan Raja Laut
Lorong Hj. Taib Lima
Taib Lima
Jalan Hj. Taib
Lorong Hj. Dua
Lorong Hj. Satu
Bangunan U.M.N.O.
Jalan Sri. Amar
Jalan Cegar
Sultan Ismail
CHOW KIT
Jalan
Sultan
J. M. T. Satu
Ismail
Medan Mara
Wisma Loke
MEDA
Jalan Semarang
Jalan Medan Tuanku
Kompleks Pertama
Jalan Tuanku Abdul Rahman
J. Doraisamy
Jalan Dang Wangi
Jalan Munshi Abdullah
Sogo
Jln Isfahan
Lorong Tuanku Abdul Rahman
Lorong Gombak
Kompleks Campbell
Semua House
Coliseum Cafe & Hotel ⑲
Malayan Mansion
Selangor Mansion
Masjid India
Jalan Ampang
Lorong Gombak
J. Masjid India
Lorong Hj.
Jalan Raja Laut
Gombak
Jabatan Perdana Menteri
Jabatan Kerjaraya (Ibu Pejabat)
P. Tun Ismail
Jabatan Kerajaan
Jabatan Pelajaran
Experimental Theatre
Jalan Tun Ismail
Jalan Mahameru
Bgn PKNS
Jalan Dato Onn
Jalan Kuching
Dewan Bandaraya (City Hall)
St Mary's Cathedral
Royal Selangor Club
Wisma Kraftangan
Bgn. Anglo Oriental
JLN. Raja
Jln. Kinabalu
Dataran Merdeka
Masjid Jamek
Sultan Abdul Samad Building (Bang. Sultan Abdul Samad)
K L Memorial Library (Perpustakaan Peringatan KL)
Muzium Sejarah Nasional (National History)
Textile Museum (Muzium Tekstil)
Jalan Tugu
Kompleks Dayabumi
Pejabat Pos Besar (General Post Office)
Pasar Seni
Masjid Negara (National Mosque)
Jalan Cenderasari
JLN. Sultan Hishamuddin
Lebuh Pasar Besar
Hsien Szu Yeh Miao
Kompleks Kota Raya
J. Tun Tan Cheng Lock
Central Market
Jalan Hang Kasturi
CHINATOWN
Jalan Hang Lekir
Sri Mahamariamman Hindu Temple
Jalan Sultan Mohamed
Klang
Jalan Sultan
Jalan Balai Polis
Victorian Institution
Jalan Petaling
Stadium Chinwoo
Jalan Kinabalu
Bulatan
Masjid Jamek
Benteng
Jalan Tun H. S. Lee
Jalan Gereja
Lebuh Ampang
Jalan Silang
Jalan Tun Perak
St John
Bukit Mahkamah
Muzi Telek
Jalan Raja Ch
Menara Mayban & Muzi Numism
Puduraya
Gereja Methodist
J. Tun Tan Cheng Lock
Jalan Stadium
Merdeka
Bgn. Shell
Jalan Sulaiman
Chan See Shu Yuen Clanhouse & Temple ⑮
J. Kampung Attap
Istana Negara ㉕
Tien Hau Temple ㉖

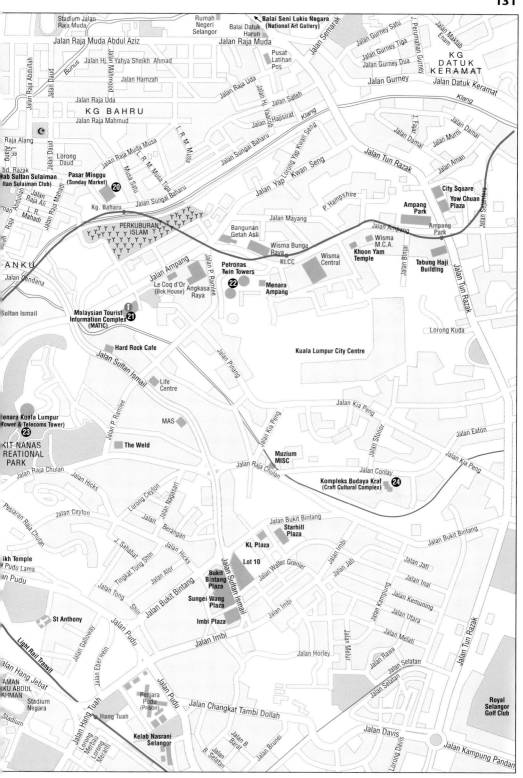

KUALA LUMPUR

From colonial mansions and the bustle of Chinatown to the modern magnificence of the Twin Towers, Kuala Lumpur represents the true essence of today's Malaysia

Map on pages 130–31

A mining outpost 100 years ago, a dynamic Asian city today, Kuala Lumpur is the capital of Malaysia and home to 1.6 million people. With its constant facelifts and ever-rising skyline, Kuala Lumpur – or KL, as it is popularly known – embodies the aspirations of a nation working hard to carve its niche in an era of globalisation.

It is therefore in KL that the East-West and old-new juxtapositions are most apparent. Stately old mansions of eclectic style, traditional mosques and Hindu temples are squeezed between concrete high-rises and steel and chrome office blocks. Trendy 30-somethings trade pleasantries with traditionally-garbed shopkeepers. *Feng shui* and Islamic values blend in global deal-making, while even in the face of leading-edge technological innovation, a fortune teller is consulted. With its variety of sights, food and shops, cosmopolitan Kuala Lumpur offers something for every visitor.

Bare beginnings

The most popular tale of how KL got its name is the simplest: the miners and traders who first came in search of tin poled up the river to where the Klang and Gombak rivers converge. The Gombak estuary was the highest point upstream that the miners could land their supplies for prospecting tin in Ampang, a few kilometres further inland. They named the settlement Kuala Lumpur, which means Muddy Estuary in Malay. By the 1860s, the landing place had become a flourishing village.

However, these were turbulent times, and fierce rivalries over mining claims and water rights led to gang clashes and bitter feuds. Finally, the predominantly Chinese settlement was put under the leadership of Yap Ah Loy, the *Kapitan China* or Chinese headman. The *Kapitan* warred against crime, built a prison and quelled revolts. Under his supervision, KL obtained some semblance of a township.

Then Frank Swettenham, the British resident of Selangor, moved his administration to KL. Brick buildings were introduced and street by street, the wooden shanties were pulled down. In 1886, the country's first railway line connected KL to the coastal town of Klang.

As the state capital of Selangor, KL grew to become the centre of administration, business and trade. In 1946, it was established as the headquarters of the Federation of Malaya, with its development intensifying after independence from the British in 1957. But KL truly came of age in 1974, when it became a unit of its own called Wilayah Persekutuan (Federal Territory). Today, it is the seat of government for the whole of Malaysia.

LEFT: coloured umbrellas in front of the Dayabumi Complex.
BELOW: Malay cultural show.

Fountain detail from the Dataran Merdeka.

BELOW: the Royal Selangor Club faces the green expanse of the *padang*.

Colonial core

KL's central attractions are close enough together to cover on foot. To reach the sights that are a little further away, hop into a taxi, commuter train or monorail (LRT) – but walking is definitely quicker during the traffic-choked peak hours. Alternatively, there are plenty of city tours that cover the main sights in KL as well as its surroundings. You can book with local tour companies, and major hotels. Or make up your own tour by hiring a taxi for the day (negotiate the price before you set off).

A good starting point for your walking tour is in the city's historic centre at **Dataran Merdeka (Independence Square)** ❶. Flanked by graceful cupolas and Moorish minarets, the square first saw life as a *padang* or green. This was the playing field of a club at which the colonial community congregated. Apparently, it was also in the *padang* that the British flag was lowered for the last time on 31 August 1957.

Today, Dataran Merdeka is the venue for national events such as the colourful parades held in conjunction with Hari Kebangsaan (National Day) and Malaysia Fest in October. Casting a 100-metre (328-ft) high nationalistic shadow on the green is the world's tallest flagpole, which rises from an underground entertainment complex and car park.

The most photographed of Moorish buildings facing the green is the imposing **Sultan Abdul Samad Building (Bangunan Sultan Abdul Samad)** ❷. The former colonial administrative centre, it now houses the High Court and Supreme Court. Constructed between 1894–7, it was the first of the Moorish-style buildings introduced to the country by two Public Works Department architects, A.C. Norman and A.B. Hubbock. Both men had spent some time in

India, and deemed that an architectural style featuring Moorish, Indian and Arabic motifs would best suit a predominantly Muslim country, apparently ignoring the fact that the Malays already had a highly developed style of their own.

Sir Charles Mitchell, the governor of the Straits Settlements at the time, thought the building a ridiculous extravagance, and was heard to say: "The tin won't last forever, you know." One wonders what he would have had to say about the multi-million ringgit Petronas Twin Towers.

At one end of the Sultan Abdul Samad Building sit the **Sessions and Magistrates Courts**, with their twin tower-flanked entrances. On the other end, also built in the distinct Moorish style, is what is now the **Textile Museum (Muzium Tekstil)** ❸ (open daily 9am–6pm). The museum's four galleries gracefully showcase the country's rich weaving heritage, from the gold-threaded *songket* to the Sarawakian *pua kumba*.

Opposite, the **Muzium Sejarah Nasional** (National History Museum) continues the Moorish tradition, while next door, the **KL Memorial Library** (Perpustakaan Peringatan KL) is striking in being the only neo-Rennaisance style building in the lot. Both are open to the public.

Facing the Sultan Abdul Samad Building across Dataran Merdeka is the **Royal Selangor Club** ❹, built in 1884 in mock-Tudor style. The club was sometimes known as the Spotted Dog, a derisive allusion to the club's emblem of a running leopard. Today, senior government administrators and prosperous businessmen prop up the long bar where the British once sat over their *stengah* (literally half, meaning half a peck of liquor).

Completing the square is the neo-Gothic **St Mary's Cathedral** ❺, which was built in 1894. It is one of the oldest Anglican churches in this region.

Map on pages 130–31

TIP

The Plaza Putra complex underneath Dataran Merdeka houses one of the busiest theatres in KL, the Actors' Studio, which is also the name of the theatre group – pick up a brochure from them or call: 03-2945400.

BELOW: the Moorish-inspired Sultan Abdul Samad Building.

Victorian station

The southern end of the Moorish design stretch is capped by the Kuala Lumpur Railway Station and Bangunan KTM. En route to these from Dataran Merdeka on Jalan Sultan Hishamuddin, is the **Kompleks Dayabumi** (Dayabumi Complex) with its filigree-like Islamic-design arches. It is most impressive at night when it is floodlit. At its base is the **Pejabat Pos Besar** (General Post Office).

Beyond this sits the **Stesen Keretapi Kuala Lumpur (Kuala Lumpur Railway Station)** ❻. To arrive by rail in KL is a fantastic experience as turrets, spires, minarets and arches greet the eye in every direction. The station was constructed to the standards applied to Victorian public buildings all over the empire. So much so, in fact, that construction was once held up because the roof did not meet the specifications stipulating that it support one metre of snow! The station was completed in 1911 and its platforms have been crowded ever since. The intra-city KTM Komuter trains and the luxury Singapore-Bangkok bound Eastern & Oriental Express also stop here.

Within the railway station there is a post office, eateries, a tour information counter and budget-priced rooms for backpackers. The station's wonderfully colonial **Heritage Station Hotel** retains an air of faded grandeur which renovations have fortunately managed to preserve. The original lift is still in operation for a leisurely ride upwards, while the lobby and restaurant downstairs have lofty ceilings with spinning fans.

Opposite the station is the **Bangunan KTM** ❼, headquarters of Malaysian Railways. This was the last of the Moorish buildings to be erected. Down the road from this pair of buildings is the **Balai Kuala Lumpur** information centre (open Monday–Friday 8.30am– 4.45pm; Saturday 8.30am–1pm). It has few brochures but the staff are helpful and will be able to give you directions.

Heading back to Dataran Merdeka, you will see the **Masjid Negara (National Mosque)** ❽, the main Muslim prayer centre in KL. Its Grand Hall, busiest on Fridays, can accommodate 8,000 worshippers. Completed in 1965, this was one of the country's first post-independence constructions. The jagged 18 points of the star-shaped roof represent the 13 states of Malaysia and the five pillars of Islam. Its five-hectare (13-acre) garden encompasses the tombs of Malaysia's most celebrated dignitaries including the country's pioneers of independence.

A garden retreat

Downtown KL is so crowded with buildings that the visitor may begin to wonder if there are any green spaces in the city apart from Dataran Merdeka. However, right in the middle of the city is its largest park, **Taman Tasik Perdana (Lake Gardens)** ❾.

The Lake Gardens (open Monday–Saturday 10am–6pm; Sunday and public holidays 8am–6pm) and their surrounding attractions are actually perched on a number of adjacent hills. The gardens themselves comprise 92 hectares (240 acres) of undulating green with magnificent trees and flowering plants. Popular with locals and visitors alike, they are especially crowded at weekends. Early morning and evening,

BELOW: a lasting British legacy – the Victorian KL Railway Station.

in particular, you'll see joggers puff their way past picnickers, hand-holding lovers and old Chinese folk going through their *tai chi* routines. It is a great place to watch the KL family at play.

For a taste of wildlife, the **Bird Park** and **Butterfly Park** (open 9am–5pm; entrance fee) house local and foreign species in pretty, forested enclosures. The **Planetarium**, which has been recently renovated, sits in a carefully thought-out garden. It has a 36-cm (14-inch) telescope, a theatre, and the Arianne IV space engine used to launch Malaysia's first satellite, the Measat I. Other attractions in the gardens include an orchid garden and deer park.

On the fringes of the gardens is the members-only Royal Lake Club, founded by breakaways from the Selangor Club in the early 1900s. Of much greater interest is a pair of colonial mansions that overlook the gardens. The **Carcosa Seri Negara**, built in 1896, was once the official residence of the British governor of Malaya and is now an exclusive luxury hotel. The neighbouring **Istana Tetamu** (Guest Palace) is a reserved for visiting foreign dignitaries. The latter was built in 1913 for the British King, who never visited the country.

Fallen heroes

On another hill opposite the gardens stands the solemn **Tugu Kebangsaan (National Monument)** , commemorating those who died in the struggle against the communist insurgency in the 1950s. Modelled on Washington DC's famous Iwo Jima Monument, the galleries at its base record the names of the units who fought, including British, Australian, Fijian, Maori and Malay troops.

Nearby is the **Cenotaph**, erected by the British to commemorate the soldiers who died in world wars I and II. At the base of the hill is the ASEAN **Sculpture**

Opposite Lake Gardens is the Tugu Kebangsaan, a tribute to those who died in the communist insurgency of the 1950s.

BELOW: Lake Garden's oar-boats.

TIP

The Museum Garden Shop in the National Museum's grounds sells Kelantanese coconut craft and ceramics from Kedah. It also has a range of Asian knick-knacks.

Garden, a symbol of the solidarity among the 10-member regional group.

A little down the road is the **Parliament House**, which appears on the back of all Malaysian coins. The 1960s building is usually not open to visitors.

Nearby, history is on display in the Minangkabau-roofed **Muzium Negara (National Museum)** ❶ (open 9am–6pm; entrance fee) on Jalan Damansara facing Jalan Travers. Its galleries showcase local culture (including the reconstruction of a Malay *kampung* (village), natural history (including an extensive mounted insect collection), and arts and craft. Particularly well-known are its thematic exhibitions; about eight are staged each year. The museum's extensive reference library, with its original manuscripts and charts, is accessible to the public with permission from the curator.

Head back towards Dayabumi Complex and cross the river to get to **Central Market** ❷. A former fruit-and-vegetable market, this Art Deco showpiece was saved from demolition by conservation-minded architects, who eventually won an award for their restoration and renovation efforts. It is currently a favourite hangout for KL's youth.

Central Market has it all, from key-chains and batik scarves, to traditional basketry and woodware from all over the country, as well as preserved foodstuffs. Artists will paint your portrait for you or inscribe a dedication on a pencil-holder. There is often an event or exhibition happening – if you're lucky you could catch a *wayang kulit* (shadow puppet) performance or *bangsawan* (traditional Malay theatre) production in full swing. Outside the building, buskers and medicine men give their own impromptu shows.

From Central Market, head down Jalan Hang Kasturi to the oldest temple in Kuala Lumpur, the **Hsien Szu Yeh Miao (Temple of Szu Yeh)** ❸. Make sure you duck your head to avoid the low-hanging awning poles, and walk past the alley's food stalls to arrive at the temple gate.

Built in 1884 by Yap Ah Loy, the first headman of old KL, the temple is rather small and dark, its ceiling blackened by non-stop smoke curling up from the joss-sticks below. Fine examples of wood carvings illustrate scenes from the various Buddhist canons. A framed photograph of Yap Ah Loy sits on a side altar, looking more like a kindly and gracious saint than the tough and exacting leader he was in reality.

Chinatown

Arriving at this point, you're in the vicinity of Chinatown, whose main streets are Jalan Sultan, Jalan Tun H.S. Lee and Jalan Petaling. For the inveterate shopper and connoisseur of exotic oddities, Chinatown is a paradise. Chinese apothecaries display their herbs and medicines in porcelain pots or beneath glass counters amid more familiar international brands. There are jewellers and goldsmiths, casket and basket makers, dry goods stores, pet shops, herbalists, frame makers and haberdashers. Modernisation wields its hand in air-conditioning and contemporary decor, but there is still plenty to experience.

The tourist trade has long realised the area's magnetic draw. Here are any number of backpackers, and at night you'd be hard-pressed to find local patrons at

BELOW: Central Market shopper.

the Jalan Hang Lekir open-air eateries. Still, local bypassers stare as hard at the visitors as the latter do at them.

The term Chinatown is often used interchangeably with **Jalan Petaling ⓮**, site of the famous night market. Better known as Petaling Street, this section of town is as different at night and in the day as, well, night and day. The action begins at dawn, to the delicious aroma of traditional dumplings and breads filled with red-bean paste and chicken curry. The wet market is the place to find Chinese housewives haggling for fresh chicken slaughtered on the spot, greens of all kinds, and chrysanthemums for their altars. Be warned, though – the smells are something else. As the city wakes up, stalls begin to line both sides of the road and pedestrians zig-zag from coffeeshop to fruit stall and back, impervious to the heavy traffic. A respite from the crowd and heat can be found in the interior of the **Chan See Shu Yuen Clanhouse and Temple ⓯**, near Bulatan Merdeka. Built in 1906, it is decorated with elaborate ceramic glazed tiles and ornamentation, and intricate wall paintings.

Street eats

At midday, office executives begin to fill the eateries. Chinatown is reputedly where the best Chinese street food can be found, from all sorts of noodles to pork ribs soup (*bakut teh*) and roasted meat snacks. There is "home-made" *dim sum* (little Chinese dumplings and pastries) from 6am, mooncakes for the autumnal Moon Festival, and bittersweet herbal brews to cure all sorts of ailments at the roadside medicinal drinks stalls.

Petaling Street assumes its festive air from 5pm. A section of the street closes to traffic for the *pasar malam* (night market), where the stalls, restrained all

Map on pages 130–31

Chinese dim sum dumplings are heavenly when freshly steamed. Look out for them in Chinatown.

BELOW: Jalan Petaling by day.

Hindu devotees who make the annual pilgrimage from KL's Sri Mahamariamman Temple to Batu Caves, skewer their bodies with metal rods and carry great steel structures as penance for favours asked from the gods.

BELOW: Sri Mahamariamman Temple

day at the kerbs, take over the road, joined soon by twice as many again, are erected at lightning speed. Here you can find all the "genuine" copies of brand name watches and tee-shirts, as well as videos of movies that haven't even made it to the local cinemas yet. The line of canopies traps air, humans and smells as you jostle single-file through a medley of stalls hawking precious stones, antiques and household goods. First rule of thumb when buying: shop around. Second rule of thumb: bargain.

However, this being Malaysia, Chinatown is not all Chinese. At the end of Jalan Tun H.S. Lee sits the old **Victorian Institution**, built in 1893 in an incongruous English cottage style. This was the city's first boy's school. It has now been turned into a drama hall.

Then, parallel to Petaling Street on Jalan Bandar is one of KL's most famous Hindu temples, the **Sri Mahamariamman Hindu Temple ⑯**. Its towering gate is decorated with an explosion of colourful gods entangled in an arresting design of South Indian origin. Built in 1873, it occupies an important place in Hindu religious life. This is the starting point each January for the annual Thaipusam pilgrimage of penance to the Batu Caves temple, just outside KL. On other days, women and children sell strings of fragrant jasmine in the, as pavements here are called, "five-foot-way" and a man in a traditional *dhoti* sarong keeps watch by a shoe rack for those wishing to enter the temple courtyard. Devotees emerge from prayer, their foreheads smeared with sacred white ash.

Off Petaling Street behind the Traffic Police Headquarters is a little street called **Jalan Balai Polis**, where a new Chinatown is being born. Here, a charming row of pre-war shophouses has found a new lease of life as the centre for the young Mandarin-speaking Chinese of KL. Among the shops is the *Happy Days*-style Halo Café, a smoke-free café fashioned after the folk song cafés of Taiwan, where wannabe singers hope to be spotted by a talent scout. Its sister establishment at the corner, Halo Rock Café, is more pub-like, and dishes up hard rock. In between the two is the Old China Café and Gallery, a Nonya restaurant-cum antique shop, where food is served on antique furniture, and virtually everything in the restaurant is for sale. There are also several tea houses along the street and in Jalan Panggung. For the uninitiated, these offer a chance to learn about the ancient Chinese art of serving and drinking tea.

Indian and Muslim flavours

On the other side of Dataran Merdeka lies an entirely different experience. This is **Jalan Masjid India ⑰**, where Indian silks, flowery saris and glittering hand-made jewellery are the order of the day. After six every evening, portable kitchens with tables and chairs take over the street, offering food which is as spicy as you can stand it.

Eating al fresco is definitely more enjoyable than dining in a large restaurant, where the atmosphere can be contrived, and enthusiastic air conditioning can make you long for winter clothing. Food stalls set up under the stars are common all over the city; those along the riverbank attest to their popularity.

A prominent landmark on Jalan Masjid India is a

mosque erected at the site of one of the town's first mosques. Follow the river-bank towards Jalan Tun Perak and you will reach **Masjid Jamek (Jamek Mosque)** ⓲, standing proudly still at the historic meeting place of the Gombak and Klang rivers. This elegant structure, adapted from a Moghul mosque in North India, is an oasis of serenity once you enter the palm-tree filled grounds through the *sahn* or walled courtyard. At sunset, a mirrored glass skyscraper nearby gives a mystical reflection of the mosque.

From Dataran Merdeka, go along **Jalan Tuanku Abdul Rahman** and explore its interesting shops. Named after the country's first Prime Minister, the area's most written-about restaurant is the **Coliseum Café and Hotel** ⓳. Serving customers for more than 60 years, its bar was once the favourite watering hole for planters, miners, government officials and soldiers. The decor has changed little since those days, and the service by grumpy Chinese waiters certainly harks back to a bygone era. Today, its steaks continue to attract attention for their quality and price. Next door to this establishment is one of the country's first cinemas, the **Coliseum Cinema**, built in the 1920s.

For six days a week, Jalan Tuanku Abdul Rahman is crowded with traffic, but every Saturday night it becomes a pedestrian mall, with stalls offering goods to be had from the bigger shops by day for half-price (or even less).

There are more street markets at **Chow Kit**, where Jalan Tuanku Abdul Rahman crosses Jalan Sultan Ismail. Despite efforts to clean it up, the area retains its shady character, with stalls selling cheap items and Malay eats, while above the roar of the traffic, the air is rent with raucous pop music. Look out for a small crowd gathered in one spot and you may find a snake charmer, or a medicine man proclaiming the miracle attributes of his wares.

Map on pages 130–31

BELOW: a rare sight in the city – a carefully-groomed Triumph.

TIP

Tourism Malaysia has a good collection of travel industry material in its library on the 24th floor of the Putra World Trade Centre. Use of the library is free (open Monday–Friday 7.30am–4.30pm, Saturday 7.30am–1pm, closed lunchtime).

BELOW: Malaysian pottery.
RIGHT: a downtown flowershop.

On the right, off Jalan Tuanku Abdul Rahman on the way to Chow Kit, **Wisma Loke** poses as another reminder of KL's past. This charming Chinese townhouse was built by Chinese mine owner Cheow Ah Yeok, a contemporary of Yap Ah Loy. Sporting classical Greco-Roman arches and pillars, it also has balustrades of glazed jade-coloured porcelain from China, Melakan tiles and a "moongate" within. Bought later by another self-made millionaire, Loke Yew, this was the first house in KL to be lit by electricity.

At the other end of Chow Kit stands a structure very much of this century: the 40 storey-high **Putra World Trade Centre (PWTC)**, which was built at infamous cost, and houses government offices as well as the head office for Tourism Malaysia, the massive Putra Concert Hall and a conference complex.

Next door is the Pan Pacific Hotel with elevators riding on the outside of the building, affording an interesting view of the area. Across the road is a modern shopping centre, **The Mall**.

Saturday's Sunday Market

For yet more *pasar malam* (street market) head for **Kampung Bahru** off Jalan Raja Abdullah near Jalan Ampang. Literally meaning "new village", Kampung Bahru came into being in 1889, and has stubbornly remained a Malay *kampung* while Malaysia's most progressive city grew around it. Even though brick has replaced many of the original wooden houses, to enter the "village" is to leave behind the sounds and smells of a city.

Sheltered by the blocks of flats here, the **Pasar Minggu (Sunday Market)** **20** springs to life, not on Sunday, but on Saturday night – although it does last into the early hours of Sunday morning. The *pasar* is well worth a visit for its exclu-

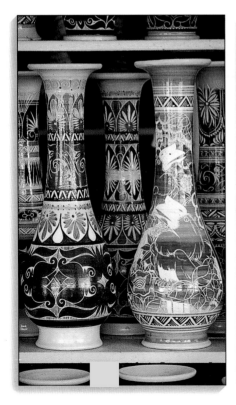

sively Malay offerings. *Songkok* (fez), prayer books, Islamic calligraphy, batik *sarungs*, and all kinds of handicrafts are on sale at the stalls, including vases, traditional earthenware pots (*labu*), Kelantan silverware and the richly embroidered *songket* from Terengganu. Besides the ubiquitous *satay*, here is where you find a large choice of Malay cooking, from *nasi lemak* (coconut rice with various condiments) to *bubur* (rice porridge) and spicy regional delights.

Map on pages 130–31

Golden Triangle

Further up from Kampung Bahru, historic **Jalan Ampang** presents a very different aspect of urban architecture. Forming a boundary of KL's Golden Triangle business district, its row of old tin miner's mansions is gradually being dwarfed by steel and concrete giants of contemporary design. However, many are being conserved, particularly at the upper end of Jalan Ampang past Jalan Tun Razak, which now houses embassies and consulates.

One of the best preserved of these mansions is the **Malaysian Tourist Information Complex** (MATIC) ㉑, a tourism and theatre complex at the Jalan Sultan Ismail junction. Built in 1935 by a wealthy Chinese tin mogul and rubber planter, Eu Tong Sen, the chateau served as the war office for the British Army, and later, the Japanese Army. When Malaysia gained its independence from British rule in 1957, it saw the first sitting of the new nation's Parliament. It was also the scene for installation ceremonies for Malaysia's kings, and over the years it continued to play various prominent roles in the nation's history. In the late 1980s, it was refurbished and commissioned for its present use. A one-stop visitor centre with booking desks and information counters, MATIC is also a centre for Malaysian culture.

Look out for bargain-priced batik at the Central Market.

BELOW: MATIC is housed in what was once a tin millionaire's mansion.

Ride a trishaw for a novel way of seeing the city. Be sure to settle on the fare first before taking off.

The stipulations of a 100-year-old will are preserving the grandeur of another 19th-century Jalan Ampang mansion. **Bok House**, which is now a restaurant called Le Coq d'Or, has retained much of its original flavour because its owner decreed that it never be sold, nor its design or decor changed. Behind its porticoed verandahs, Italian marble floors and 18th-century paintings, is a charming tale of love and revenge. Bok House was built by a poor young man, Chua Cheng Bok, who fell desperately in love with the daughter of a wealthy mine owner whose house stood on Jalan Ampang. However, the old man forbade the couple to marry. Bitterly disappointed, the young suitor put all his energies into his work, determined to prove that he could make it in the world. Eventually, he was able to build his own mansion – right next door to his enemy's, overshadowing it in size and magnificence. Bok's house still stands, while the arrogant miner's house has long since disappeared.

Tall Towers

The city's newest landmark is on Jalan Ampang and currently holds the record for the world's tallest building, or, rather, pair of buildings: the **Petronas Twin Towers ㉒**. Soaring some 451.9 metres (c.1,500 ft) above the traffic-congested streets, its identical towers – linked midway up by a skybridge on the 42nd floor – reach an auspicious 88 storeys. Designed by Cesar Pelli, these glass and stainless steel buildings combine Islamic patterns with state-of-the-art engineering techniques (see *page 89*).

The Twin Towers are actually office blocks, and make up a section of a larger development called the **Kuala Lumpur City Centre** (**KLCC**). Sitting on what used to be KL's racecourse, the development includes a cinema com-

plex, the largest shopping centre in KL (the ultra-modern Suria KLCC) and an oil and gas museum. There is also an art gallery and a small but magnificent concert hall, the first dedicated classical music venue in Malaysia. The development also has a pretty landscaped park.

Unfortunately, visitors have no access to the view offered by its great height. Instead, head down the road to **Menara Kuala Lumpur** ❷ (open 10am–10pm; entrance fee). Also known as the KL Tower, this 421-metre (1,380-ft) structure is, nevertheless, of impressive height. The public observation platform reveals in one glance KL, its surrounding hills, and as far away as the casino playground of Genting Highlands in the peninsula's mountainous backbone, the Main Range. The Islamic-influenced tower also has a souvenir shop, revolving restaurant and the world's highest MacDonald's.

High life

The fulcrum of modern consumerism in Malaysia is the intersection of Jalan Sultan Ismail and Jalan Bukit Bintang, an area of expensive shops, high-class restaurants, international hotels and party-till-you-drop nightlife. You will find a number of large shopping malls in this area: Sungei Wang Plaza and the adjacent Bukit Bintang Plaza offer more than 500 shops, including the best bookstores in KL; Imbi Plaza concentrates on computers and software; the upmarket Starhill Plaza is the place for branded designer wear and fashionable eateries; and flashy Lot 10 has its European designer boutiques.

In a quiet KL enclave off Jalan Raja Chulan is the arts and craft centre of **Kompleks Budaya Kraf (Craft Cultural Complex)** ❷ (open 10am–6pm) in Jalan Conlay. A larger, quieter and more upmarket version of Central Market,

Along Jalan Ampang is the Khoon Yam Buddhist Temple. This oldest Chinese temple in Kuala Lumpur has been extensively renovated.

BELOW: the soaring Menara Kuala Lumpur at dusk.

MULTIMEDIA SUPERCORRIDOR

Cult techno-mag *Wired* once called it "the planet's most seductive technopark", a quote later seized upon by the *International Herald Tribune*. They were referring to Malaysia's MSC, the Multimedia Supercorridor, which is anchored in KL by the Petronas Twin Towers. At the other end of the 50 by 15 kilometre (31 by 9 mile) corridor is the Kuala Lumpur International Airport (KLIA) in Selangor.

Though effectively still an experiment, the MSC is meant to leapfrog the country into the knowledge-based world economy of the new millennium. The idea is to invite international participation to explore new ways of doing things in tomorrow's information-driven environment. The Malaysia node would physically be on the corridor of an "intelligent" state-of-the-art infrastructure, linked to an international collaboration of companies, regions and communities via a high-bandwidth fibre-optic backbone. Among its components is Putrajaya, the "cyber" seat of government which will eventually take over Kuala Lumpur's administrative role.

Advising the government on the ambitious project is an international panel, comprising the likes of Microsoft's Bill Gates, Netscape Communication's James Barksdale, and NTT's Jun-Ichiro Miyazu.

Map
on pages
130–31

TIP

The Golden Triangle is also where you'll find KL's great night life. The hot spots are along Jalan Sultan Ismail near Concorde Hotel and behind it in the bungalows along Jalan Kia Peng.

BELOW: pottery in the Artists' Colony, Komplexs Budaya Kraf.
RIGHT: the glittering Petronas Twin Towers.

it comprises a collection of shops offering traditional and contemporary designs for anything a souvenir-hunter could want, including handwoven textiles, woodwork, batik, basketwork, silver and pewter, native products and pottery. There are also demonstrations of *songket* cloth weaving, batik printing and silver and copper tooling. The building at the back houses a small museum (entrance fee).

Arts and crafts

In one corner of the sprawling complex is the Artists' Colony, a conglomerate of nine open-air wooden work spaces in the shape of *wakaf* (traditional Malay gazebo). Here, 18 resident artists ply their trade to the sound of Malay rock songs on their radios. The colony presents an excellent opportunity to talk to newly-established and up-and-coming artists, watch them at work, and even buy paintings directly from them.

Indeed, for art lovers, KL has many galleries, some of which are works of art in themselves, such as the minimalist Petronas Art Galley (KLCC) and the charming Gallery Taksu off Jalan Dato' Keramat. A sampling of the broad spectrum of local art can be found in the **Balai Seni Lukis Negara** (National Art Gallery) (open 10am–6pm) in Jalan Temerloh. The modern building has three galleries showcasing experimental, permanent, and temporary works.

Down the road from the Golden Triangle is the **Istana Negara (National Palace) ㉕**, the official residence of the *Yang Di-Pertuan Agung* (king). The country has a new *agung* every five years as the position is rotated among its sultans. The palace began life as the town house of a wealthy Chinese businessman and was sold and converted into a palace in 1926. Typical of colonial mansions, it has large balconies and gardens; not so typical is its golden domes. Yellow is the colour for royalty, and only kings may walk on the welcoming yellow carpet while politicians and visiting dignitaries use red. Royal garden parties, investitures and receptions are held here, but the *agung* normally lives in his own palace, every sultan having his own "mini" palace in the capital.

Beyond the National Palace and further south along Jalan Syed Putra is a small road which climbs a steep hill (Jalan Kerayong). Follow it and you will find yourself at another commanding view of the city. On this hill stands the massive **Tien Hau Temple ㉖**. Built in 1985 with the contributions of several Chinese multimillionaires, each purportedly donated large sums of money to build one pillar of the temple – just count the pillars! Although it is known that the cost of building the temple was phenomenal, the exact figure remains a firm secret.

The temple's ornate features make it a popular backdrop for local television productions. A much-utilised community centre, the complex has a large conference hall for meetings, performances and weddings; a restaurant; and youth and women's clubs and offices.

The temple itself, with its many large and small roofs, sits right at the top of the hill. There is even a small garden inside, which can be viewed perfectly from any angle. The building itself is an incongruous mixture, gaudy yet impressive, mystical yet decidedly worldly. ❑

SELANGOR

Map on page 150

The area of Selangor around Kuala Lumpur is the developed hub of Malaysia's industrial economy. But beyond the hinterland, the landscape yields to limestone cliffs, caverns and jungle trails

Heading west from **Kuala Lumpur ❶** on the Federal Highway, massive Moorish arches announce that you are departing the Federal Territory and entering the state of Selangor. According to the Tourism Malaysia brochure, this marble *pintu gerbang*, flanked by ancient Selangor canons, was erected in 1974 "to mark the sacrifice" made by the Sultan of Selangor in ceding Kuala Lumpur to the Federal Government as the national capital.

More than two decades later, more land has been ceded for the new national capital, Putrajaya, the intended heart of the ambitious information technology-driven Multimedia Supercorridor (MSC), which runs through Selangor. At the southern end is the 100-sq. km (36-sq. mile) **Kuala Lumpur International Airport (KLIA)**, one of Asia's largest airports: so large, in fact, that it has a Formula One racing circuit running within its perimeter. Near Putrajaya is Cyberjaya, the MSC's dedicated "intelligent" city for multimedia companies. Currently, the view of this area that greets you as you fly into the KLIA, is still a muzzy pattern of oil palms.

Mining roots

Like Kuala Lumpur and Perak, Selangor grew rich on tin, prompting power struggles and civil wars in the 19th century. Selangor's original Minangkabau settlers were displaced by the Bugis, who established the present sultanate at Kuala Selangor. In 1894, Selangor was among the first four states in the British Federated Malay States (FMS) which later became Malaya and then Malaysia.

Before reaching the state capital, **Shah Alam ❷**, the busy Federal Highway goes through the huge residential satellite town of Petaling Jaya (PJ), whose population commutes daily into KL. Shah Alam was built in 1963 and is more of a quiet suburb than administrative centre, with large houses, tree-lined boulevards, and numerous roundabouts. It is also a centre for heavy industry, including Proton, the national car project developed with Mitsubishi of Japan. You'll see a lot of Protons on Malaysia's roads; the company commands about two-thirds of the local car market, due mainly to high duties imposed on foreign models.

The Sultan of Selangor resides on a hilltop in the lavish Istana Bukit Kayangan. But the jewel in the city's crown is the state mosque, the **Masjid Sultan Salahuddin Abdul Aziz Shah**. Known also as the Blue Mosque, it features some of the Islamic world's tallest minarets and largest domes, decorated with Islamic calligraphy. Its worship hall is bigger than London's St Paul's Cathedral, and can accommodate 16,000 worshippers.

LEFT: limestone interior of Batu Caves.
BELOW: the Blue Mosque.

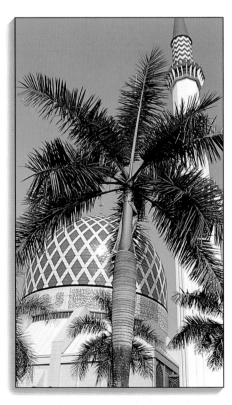

Seafood capital

At the western end of the Federal Highway, **Klang ❸**, the former state capital, conceals a colourful and violent past. Given its commanding position near the mouth of the Klang River, it was obvious that whoever possessed the town controlled the lucrative tin trade. Klang became a centre of fighting during the Selangor Civil War of the 1870s. Raja Mahdi, one of the chief protagonists, built his fort on the hill where the neo-classical municipal offices now stand.

Across the bridge in the old town is a former warehouse called the **Gedong Raja Abdullah**, built in 1857 by Raja Abdullah, one of Mahdi's principal opponents in the civil war. The warehouse exemplifies traditional Malay workmanship and has been converted into a tin museum, bringing Klang's exciting past to life. Klang is linked to KL by the KTM Komuter train system, which ends in Port Klang.

Port Klang (Pelabuhan Klang) ❹, 8 km (5 miles) by road from Klang, is best known for its wonderful seafood restaurants at Pandamaran. The major seaport for Kuala Lumpur and the Klang Valley, it is one of the fastest growing container ports in Southeast Asia. This is also the base for local cruise ship companies, as well as port-of-call for ships from Singapore and other foreign lines. Packages from a 3 day/2 night duration cover destinations such as Singapore, Melaka, Penang and Langkawi, as well as Phuket, which is known for its beaches, and southern ports in Thailand.

For shorter trips, boats and ferries from the port go out to the various islands in the Klang River delta, a favourite spot with weekend anglers. Two hours away through monotonous mangrove scenery is **Pulau Ketam** (Crab Island), probably the last Chinese fishing village on stilts in the state. Unfortunately,

BELOW:
Pulau Ketam's seafood bonanza.

cleanliness is not its strong point, although it offers cheap and excellent seafood.

Head south for about 17 km (11 miles) to get to **Pulau Carey** ➎, home to the most famous of indigenous craftsmen, the Mah Meri Orang Asli traditional wood-carvers. The Sungai Bumbun Mah Meri tribe is best-known for its dream-inspired spirit masks and unique *Moyang Tenong Jerat Harimau* tiger sculpture. Turn right at Teluk Panglima Garang, then right again to enter the Golden Hope estate road, and finally left at the fork. There is a tiny shop opposite the house of the leading woodcarver, Pion Anak Bumbon, which also happens to be the woodcarving centre. Unfortunately, demand for the work isn't high enough to make it worthwhile for many to be full-time artists. Fortunately, the designs are documented in a voluminous research text which doubles as both a "bible" of authenticity and a sort of sales catalogue for potential buyers of the unique craft. Visits to the settlement must be arranged with the Department of Orang Asli Affairs (tel: 03-5590375).

Historic Selangor

The road south from Pulau Carey leads via Jenjarom to yet another old Selangor capital, **Jugra** ➏, which, unlike Klang, is completely out of the development limelight. On the hill overlooking the village and estuary are the graves of Selangor royalty and noblemen. The ruins of some old government buildings can be seen below. Standing amid the paddy fields are the abandoned palace, built in the 1800s, and the equally elaborate mosque where the sultan used to pray. Both are fine examples of late 19th/early 20th-century architecture.

The nearby **Morib** is not one of Malaysia's most beautiful beaches, but is nevertheless a popular weekend getaway for Klang Valley residents. It is also

Map on page 150

TIP

If not venturing to Pulau Carey, you may like to know that Mah Meri craft can also be bought in Cameron Highlands (*see Hill Stations, page 160*).

BELOW: Mah Meri woodcarving, Pulau Carey.

historically significant for being the landing place of the Allied forces in 1945, ending the Japanese occupation of the peninsula.

Bird sanctuary

About 45 km (28 miles) north of Klang is the pretty, peaceful town of **Kuala Selangor** ❼ on the Sungai Selangor estuary. This was the 18th-century base of the state's Bugis rulers whose mausoleums are now a tourist attraction. The fort was built by the Dutch in the futile attempt to control the tin trade, and it still stands at **Bukit Melawati**, complete with cannons that point out to sea. Today, however, they are merely iron sentinels to the **Kuala Selangor Nature Park** ❽ (entrance fee; tel: 03-8892294), which they overlook.

Protecting the area's coastal mangroves, and therefore its fisheries industry, the park is a joint project between the Malaysian Nature Society (MNS) and the state government. Over 160 species of birds have been recorded here, and an estimated 100,000 birds pass through during their annual migrations south. Artificial ponds that blend in beautifully with the surroundings attract the birds, surrounded by nature trails and observation hides – don't forget your binoculars. A pioneering attempt to breed endangered milky storks is also being undertaken here in a large aviary. The park has accommodation as well.

There are several interesting Chinese fishing villages around Kuala Selangor, where salted fish and fishballs are prepared, and some great seafood restaurants. Further along the riverbank at **Kampung Kuantan**, hundreds of *kelip-kelip* (fireflies) alight on the branches of the overhanging trees; for a truly other-worldly experience, book yourself on a river trip at the jetty (tel: 03-8892403), which starts at nightfall in good weather.

BELOW: Hindu devotees at Batu Caves during the Thaipusam festival.

A limestone shrine

One of the most amazing sights in Malaysia is Thaipusam, the Hindu festival of penance, which occurs at the end of January. As a sign of repentance for past sins and to demonstrate their vows of reformation, devotees often carry *kavadi* (offerings) to a temple, from a simple milk jug on the head to wooden frames decorated with flowers and fruit and supported by long thin spikes pinned into the body.

The most sacred temple for this festival is the cave shrine at **Batu Caves** ❾. A bold limestone outcrop about 13 km (8 miles) north of Kuala Lumpur, this is the final destination for the rippling sea of devotees who follow the procession from the Sri Mahamariamman temple in Kuala Lumpur and painstakingly climb the 272 concrete steps that lead up to the cave. The pigeons and monkeys that generally rule the area disappear in the face of this massive human onslaught.

On normal days, the temple is peaceful. The massif's main cavern, known as the Cathedral Cave, is a huge vault pierced by stalactites that point downwards for 6 metres (20 ft). Eerie shafts of light streak down from gaps in the ceiling high above. Another cave at its base is decorated with colourful and intricate drawings depicting Hindu legends. A row of Indian vegetarian shops at the base of the temple serves cool, refreshing coconut juice.

Batu Caves is also popular with adventure sports exponents. There are about another 20 caves within the massif, and the **Dark Caves**, open only to MNS tours (tel: 03-2879422) has narrow passages where you could encounter bats and creepy-crawlies. The other side of the cliff is popular with rock-climbers, as is **Bukit Takun** located further north along the old trunk road (Route 1).

Map on page 150

Tamed jungles

The Takun area is also home to several parks, offering easy tracks, and pools and waterfalls for swimming. Among them is the popular Templer Park (Taman Templer), and scenic Hutan Lipur Kancing (Kancing Forest Reserve). But better trails wind through the 600 hectares (1,500 acres) of the **Forest Research Institute and Museum (FRIM)** ❿ at Kepong, a few kilometres west of Batu Caves. The country's top forest research facility, FRIM has experimental plantations, arboreta, and a traditional medicinal plant plot, as well as an excellent forestry museum and library. The MNS runs nature education courses here.

Malaysia's wildlife is on show at the **Zoo Negara dan Akuarium** (National Zoo and Aquarium), 13 km (8 miles) from central KL by way of Jalan Genting Klang. Its collection includes a nice display of birds, reptiles such as pythons, *seladang* (the world's largest wild buffalo), tapir, crocodiles, tigers, and of course, the orang-utan.

Royal Selangor pewterware, a uniquely Malaysian craft.

Off Jalan Genting Klang, in a suburb called Setapak, is the headquarters of the famous **Royal Selangor**, the prime mover of the home-grown pewter industry, whose designs are sold the world over. Pewter is made from a combination of antimony, copper and refined tin. The factory holds tours and has a host of quality souvenir items for sale. ❑

BELOW: a canopy of Kapur trees at FRIM.

THE NORTHWESTERN PENINSULA

This is an area of immense variety, spliced in the middle by a mountainous jungled backbone, Banjaran Titiwangsa

Heading north out of Kuala Lumpur is like heading through the country's so-called first wave of development – this is the land of tin and rubber, and, nearer the Thai border, rice. Global demand and phenomenally high prices for the first two natural resources were behind the peninsula's rapid growth from the late 19th century till the middle of the 20th century.

Perak's Kinta River Valley was once the tin capital of the world. Now, a daisy-chain of huge mining ponds sit in silence amid deserts of stark, bleached sand and the odd tin dredge made of wood; but life is returning to this seeming desolation. The lakes are slowly evolving into a wetland habitat, attracting many species of both native and migrant bird, some never seen here before. Elsewhere, the concrete and metal of industrial parks are testament to the new manufacturing industries, so vital to the state's continued economic progress.

Some former mining towns remain frozen in time – Papan, Batu Gajah, Pusing. Others retain their charming old-world core but have continued to build on that early prosperity, and are thriving – Ipoh, Kuala Kangsar, Taiping.

However, while many rubber plantations have been supplanted by the more lucrative oil palm, visitors will still pass through acres of this early fortune-maker, thanks to a new rubberwood furniture industry utilising fast-growing, high-yield strains. In the irrigated plains of Kedah and Perlis, paddy covers much of the land in this, the country's largest rice-growing area.

Limestone is another feature of the north. Large outcrops dripping with vegetation dot Perak and Perlis, and make up the entire islands of the Langkawi archipelago. Swathed in mist at dawn, the limestone hills are inspiration for any number of Chinese brush paintings, while the earliest evidence of prehistoric human civilisation in the country can be found among the caves.

On the isles, it is always holiday time. Penang continues to bewitch with its plethora of Buddhist temples, cluttered lively city streets, and golden beaches. More long sandy beaches beckon at Langkawi, still sleepily enwrapped in legend; likewise Pangkor, still following the rhythms of the sea, as it has throughout the ages. ❑

PRECEDING PAGES: rows of terraced vegetable plots in the highland resort of Cameron Highlands.
LEFT: palms reign supreme on Langkawi's beaches.

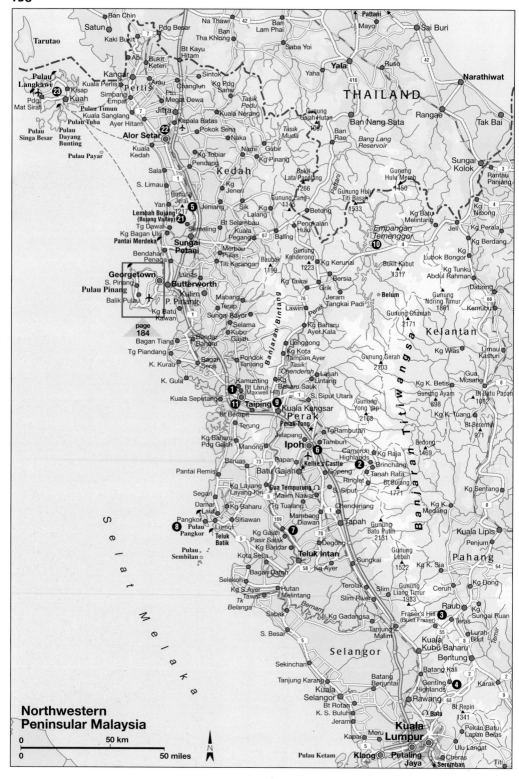

Northwestern
Peninsular Malaysia

0   50 km

0   50 miles

N

HILL STATIONS

With their temperate climates and tranquil gardens, the high hill stations of central Malaysia are as popular with tourists today as they were with the European settlers before them

The insufferable heat drove them to the hills. Once there, they pushed back the jungle and created little pockets of England with rose gardens and mock Tudor bungalows; from that point on, life in the colonies assumed a more bearable aspect for the British. Today for much the same reason – cooler climes, those little snapshots of Englishness – tourists flock to the former hill stations of Maxwell Hill, Cameron Highlands and Fraser's Hill. Some of the buildings have been taken over by multinationals as hillside retreats, others are now hotels, while yet more new high-rise developments attempt to emulate their colonial predecessors – with varying degrees of success.

Restful retreat

The oldest hill station, and the one least touched by time, is **Bukit Larut (Maxwell Hill) ❶** in Perak. Rising above the serene Lake Gardens of Taiping, it is largely responsible for Taiping being the wettest place in the peninsula. Bukit Larut has no golf courses, fancy restaurants or swimming pools, only a few jungle walks and a badminton court. However, the attraction for visitors is the cool air and the vistas: thick mist-laden jungles below and clouds that wash off the Straits of Melaka (Selat Melaka) from Penang to Pangkor.

Large bungalows, complete with fireplaces, sit at different elevations of this 1,000-metre (3,300-ft) high hill. The road that climbs up it was constructed after World War II with the "help" of Japanese prisoners-of-war, but before that, anyone who wished to reach the top but did not fancy hiking had the choice of going by pony or sedan chair. At one time, the trail was used by porters carrying heavy loads of fragrant tea downhill. Now the tea plantations are no more, leaving only the **Tea Garden House**, midway up, with its view of Taiping and the Lake Gardens. A handful of labourers keep the jungle at bay and the gardens neatly manicured.

Access to the hill is denied to private vehicles. Instead, government-owned Land Rovers serve as mountain taxis departing every hour between 8am–6pm. They take eight seated, and two standing at the back, hanging grimly on to the top bar. The one-lane road is steep and narrow; at sharp bends the jungle suddenly parts to reveal the green land below divided into a pattern of roads and fields.

The air becomes brisk, and the sun is lost in mist and clouds. The 12-km (7½-mile) journey takes 40 minutes, and you are deposited at the front step of your bungalow. At the foot of the hill sits a war cemetery of Commonwealth soldiers who died in the Japanese invasion. Nearby is a large freshwater swimming pool fed by a waterfall.

BELOW: mist-shrouded Cameron Highlands.

BELOW:

harvesting tea in Cameron Highlands.

The tea highlands

Crewcut tea bush rows lend the rolling hills of **Cameron Highlands** ➋ a soft green glow in the dewy early light. Suddenly the eye catches sight of a tiny figure in a bright scarf, basket on back, moving meticulously among the rows – it's a tea-picker! You raise your zoom lens, and suddenly realise that "she" has a moustache. The tea industry, like all other labour-intensive industries in Malaysia, now employ Bangladeshi workers – male ones at that.

The vast tea plantations are the distinguishing characteristic of this most developed of Malaysia's hill stations, which peaks at 1,800 metres (5,900 ft) above sea level. Some of them offer tours, except on Mondays, and no tea is plucked on Sunday.

The prettiest estate is at Sungai Palas in the highest town of Brinchang; the oldest tea-processing factory is the one built in 1929 in the Farlie estate near Habu, in which original processing technology is still used; and the most accessible plantation to photograph is the Bharat Tea Estate near Tanah Rata, which has a teahouse but no tours. The first two estates belong to local giant Boh Tea, who also have a chain of "tea cafés" in big cities.

Incidentally, the South Indians brought in by the British to work in the plantations are into their second generation. Well-educated youngsters now run the factory tours or work in shops in town and behind hotel reception desks.

Although Camerons, as it is called, is actually part of Pahang, it can only be reached through Tapah in Perak. Buses run every hour and taxis can be chartered from here. Tapah is also on the train route, and there are express buses from Kuala Lumpur and Penang that go all the way to Brinchang.

For those with their own transport, there is a turning off the old trunk road just

north of Tapah that leads via Chenderiang to the gorgeous **Lata Kinjang**, a towering multi-step waterfall visible from the North-South Highway. Concrete steps lead up to a spray-misted suspension bridge. Orang Asli guides who live at the foot of the falls can guide you to other cascades and to their *durian* fruit orchards in the forest for a fee, but you need to get permission from the Forestry Department in Tapah to enter the area, which is a forest reserve.

From Tapah, the Camerons road twists its way uphill for 90 km (60 miles) through a dense forest of coniferous trees, thick ferns, and clusters of bamboo that add the touch of a Chinese scroll painting. Camerons is particularly well-known for its tree ferns and wild orchids. While you're travelling up, you will pass Orang Asli on motorbikes, or on foot carrying butterfly nets, on their way to their villages which dot the hills.

Ringlet is the first and rather ugly little settlement at the 45 km (30 miles) marker. Push on, and 4 km (2½ miles) later you will reach the **Sultan Abu Bakar Lake** (Tasik Sultan Abu Bakar), an artificial body of water formed by the damming of Sungai Bertam for Camerons' hydroelectric scheme, which is one of the country's oldest. Perched on a bluff above the lake is the first Tudor-style hotel, which has sweeping views of the valley.

Map on page 158

Cameron Highlands is home to many rare species of butterfly.

Vegetables and inns

Farmlands begin after passing the lake, the cultivated terraces that have earned Camerons the nickname of vegetable capital of the peninsula. Here also, the Chinese farmers have employed Bangladeshi workers. An interesting trend among these growers is the move towards organic farming, thanks to pressure against pesticide use. About 15 km (9 miles) further on lies **Tanah Rata**, the principal township, a bustling tourist centre with hotels, shops, and restaurants.

This development must be a far cry from the sight that caused such excitement to William Cameron, a government surveyor on a mapping expedition in 1885, who reported "a fine plateau with gentle slopes shut in by the mountains". This area was unknown even to the locals in the lowlands. Shortly afterwards, tea planters, then farmers, claimed the plateau, and built a road to carry their produce to market.

Today, Tanah Rata is popular with Malaysian families, college students and diplomats alike Boy scouts with knapsacks on their backs thumb rides up the winding hills, while Singaporean tourists from the south lounge on colonial-style verandahs, munching fresh strawberries and cream. To some, arriving from the tropical lowlands, it seems somewhat incongruous to arrive at Tanah Rata and find logfires lit every night, and Devonshire tea and English breakfast on menus. But the local steamboat soup dish is also popular, and among the Chinese hotels are several very good Indian restaurants, serving simple snacks and meals that agree well with the climate here.

Check out the excellent Yung Seng souvenir shop at No. 23 on the main road, which has beautiful native craft, including the wonderful Mah Meri masks of Selangor, and Temiar fishing traps, as well as craft from other Southeast Asian countries.

BELOW: a temperate haven in the tropics.

Cameron's Trails and Tours

One day in 1967, while on holiday in the region, the American Thai-silk entrepreneur Jim Thompson went out for an evening stroll along one of the highlands' many trails. He was never seen again.

Even today, spirit-world, wild-animal and conspiracy theories surround the disappearance of the highlands' most famous missing person. Somehow this has added weight to the otherwise standard precautions requiring visitors to tell someone which trail they are taking and to stick to the paths.

All Cameron's maps include walking trails – the Fotofocus Discovery Map is detailed and descriptive. The roads themselves make good walks, and there is a paved walkway all the way from Tanah Rata to Brinchang. A fairly easy and popular trek at Tanah Rata is the 1-hour **Robinson Descent** (Path 9) which starts at the falls and goes downhill to the power

station – the last stretch is fairly steep though. The longer and flatter **Boh Road** trail (Path 9A) branches off to the left at the top of Path 9 and leads to the Farlie Boh Tea Estate road near Habu. Another easy route is **Parit Falls** (Path 4), a flat 20-minute stroll from the Garden Inn hotel to Taman Sedia.

All these trails join up with the circular **Gunung Bereman** track (Path 8 from Robinson Falls and Path 3 from Parit Falls). The trek is steep and you need to cross some streams. It takes about 3 hours to reach the 1,800-metre (5,900-ft) peak, but the sunsets and sunrises are great – bring a tent and warm clothes if you intend to camp out. Path 3 actually ends in Brinchang at the golf course, or joins Path 2, to go past the hilltop Sam Po Buddhist temple into town. The Bereman track splinters at various parts, so ensure you take the path you really want to take, or you could end up somewhere else.

There is actually a trail that leads from Brinchang just north of the town, up to **Gunung Brinchang** (Path 1). It is a long 4-hour trek, though a fairly easy one, but can be wet and slippery after rain. Keep your eyes open for pitcher plants in this damp and fern-rich mossy forest.

There are several interesting tours out of Brinchang and Tanah Rata that go off the beaten track but require minimum numbers. Wilderness Journeys (tel: 05-4912073) based in the Equatorial Hotel specialise in nature interpretation. Their programmes include treks to the highland cloud or mossy forests at Gunung Brinchang (half-day) and Gunung Irau (2 day/1 night), tours to Semai Orang Asli villages, and the jewel in the crown, a Rafflesia Tour, which is run only when guides encounter a patch where this rare parasite, the world's largest flower is, or is close to, blooming. Trekking packages start at RM40 for a half-day tour.

Other tour companies offer a half-day jungle trekking tour that takes in a waterfall, and an all-day tour that covers a tea plantation, a visit to a Semai Orang Asli village, and picturesque cave waterfalls. Contact Jade Holidays at Brinchang (tel: 05-4912318). Tours start at RM25 and they do pick-ups from your hotel. ❏

LEFT: the carnivorous pitcher plant.

En route to Brinchang is an authentic replica of an English Inn, **The Smoke-house Hotel**, with a well-kept garden and ivy-covered walls of stone. Inside the cosy living rooms are stuffed chintz settees and old photographs, clocks, kettles, and other characterful remnants of the British colonial era. The bedrooms are gorgeous but expensive. Behind the inn is one of the country's oldest golf courses, which survived tigers, vegetable-farmers, and World War II to become the 18-hole course it is today, overlooked by a cosy pavilion equipped with a bar and a restaurant.

There is lots of accommodation available along this stretch of road, before you hit **Brinchang** and the Kea Farm area, the heartland of the farms and nurseries growing Camerons' other big product: flowers. This once pretty area has become a mess of exposed and eroded hillslopes and unsightly high-rise development, a scene compounded further by tacky attractions such as Cactus Valley, the Rose Centre and Butterfly Farm. The peak is also at the tail-end of the new Lojing road that links to Ipoh. According to environmental reports liberally quoted in newspapers, the development has raised temperatures around the main towns by a couple of degrees; wearing a sweater during the day is now a thing of the past.

The only worthwhile sight here is the **Sungai Palas Tea Estate**, whose steep road winds 6 km (4 miles) up to Camerons' highest peak at 2,031 metres (6,663 ft), Gunung Brinchang and panoramic views of the forested valley. This also makes quite a nice – if long – early morning walk that takes in the colourful periwinkles growing freely among the tea bushes, a couple of vegetable farms, and bird-filled forest near the top.

You'll find maps, tourist information and tours in Tanah Rata and Brinchang.

Map on page 158

TIP

Bicycles are available for hire at the goldsmiths, Kedai Emas Loon Hing, on the main road.

BELOW: the mock-Tudor Smokehouse Hotel in the Cameron hills.

Tea in the garden

Much quieter is **Fraser's Hill (Bukit Fraser)** ❸ in Selangor, although its past is rather more colourful. The hill resort is named after Louis James Fraser, an elusive English adventurer, who had long disappeared when the hill station was built in 1910. He apparently ran a notorious gambling and opium den here for local miners and planters, as well as a mule train, and later, a transport service in the lowlands.

The 1,500-metre (5,000-ft) high resort is scattered over seven hills on which sit a series of English greystone bungalows, surrounded by neat English gardens blooming with roses and hollyhocks. The tiny town centre around the clock tower has some rather disastrous newer additions, and there are also high-rise hotels which fail to blend with the landscape.

A better bet is to go with the economical if run-down bungalows, now state-run. The prettiest and most expensive accommodation is **The Smokehouse Hotel**, a replica of the Camerons outlet, where you can also enjoy Devonshire tea or apple pie in the lovely garden. The road to the inn leads on to Jeriau Waterfall, once a pretty picnic spot, but now permanently silted, the result of resort development years ago.

Because of its proximity to Kuala Lumpur, Fraser's is crowded at weekends, but there are enough walks and trails to take you away from the madding crowd. The ring road around the 9-hole golf course makes a pleasant two-hour walk, and brings you past the old bungalows and newer resorts. Like the one in Camerons, the picturesque golf course is very old. It was carved out of an old tin mine, and is one of the few public courses in the country.

There are also eight jungle trails of varying lengths, all named after pioneers who built up the resort. The trails are well-marked and easy to follow. The newest is the steep 6-km (4-mile) **Pine Hill Trail** which leads to breathtaking views. The trails run through hilly dipterocarp forests which boasts some of the richest birdlife in the peninsula, hence the high chance of bumping into groups standing rock-still and peering intently through binoculars. There are an estimated 270 local and migratory species in the forest.

If you have your own transport, there are good drives around the area, such as the second loop that goes past the holiday bungalows of multinational corporations. In fact, having your own transport is really the only way to get to the resort. Otherwise, it is a one-hour bus journey from Kuala Lumpur (100 km/60 miles) to Kuala Kubu Baharu, from where you have to board a second bus which takes another one and a half hours to get to the top. The last 8 km (5 miles) is a narrow winding road, on which a one-way traffic system is in place between 7am–7pm; odd hours for going up, even for coming down. It was along the winding road from Kuala Kubu Bahru that British High Commissioner Sir Henry Gurney was ambushed and killed by communist guerilhas in 1951.

If you arrive at the gate too early, you could have tea at the Gap Resthouse, or else drive down to a small but scenic waterfall along the main road that leads to the town of Raub.

BELOW: tee off in Fraser's Hill, Selangor.

Gamblers' paradise

Newer hill resorts are popular, but lack the charm of the three "oldies". A definite study in contrast is **Genting Highlands** ❹, 2,000 metres (6,600 ft) above sea level. Just one convenient hour from Kuala Lumpur, it is actually visible from the capital, a mystical palace of pleasure shrouded in mist, on top of Banjaran Titiwangsa (Main Range), the mountain range that runs down the centre of the peninsula.

However, at close quarters, nothing could be more prosaic. For Gentings as the locals call it, is the Las Vegas of Malaysia, a rambling complex of hotels, theme parks and a casino, the country's sole gambling den. And it is something people either love or loathe. Ignoring the originally lush surroundings through which it took such effort and cost to cut, the complex is entirely artificial, giant boulders included, and it is possible to not surface for sunshine the whole time you are there. Gentings just never goes to sleep.

The whole development comes under Genting Highlands Resorts, owned by businessman Lim Goh Tong, who mooted the idea for the resort, spending seven years alone to build the steep road. Gentings has just kept growing in every way, although there is talk that its large revenues are being dented by the increasingly popular cruise liners which operate casinos in international waters.

Gentings' casino is one of the largest in the world and offers the gamut of games, both Western and traditional Chinese like *tai sai*. There are also rows of slot machines and computerised racing. Suits are compulsory for men, or you can opt for a batik shirt, Malaysian formal wear, which can be rented at the door. In accordance with Islamic law, a sign over the casino entrance warns that Muslims are forbidden to try their luck here.

Map on page 158

Batik shirts are considered formal wear and will allow men entry into the Gentings' casino.

BELOW:
Genting Highlands theme park.

Map on page 158

Accommodation is plentiful and cheap, because the real money is raked in at the casino. A range of food is available, yet sharing tables is not unusual at weekends and public holidays. The outdoor theme park, set around an artificial lake, has rollercoasters, boat rides, and a monorail. The indoor theme park houses the largest video/virtual reality arcade in Malaysia. There are also two theatres which feature international magic acts or cabaret dinner shows, and famous singers are occasionally flown in from Hong Kong. Tip: Save your jungle shoes for the other hill stations.

Things are a little less manic 10 km (6 miles) down the hill at the Awana Golf and Country Club, which has an 18-hole golf course and panoramic views. However, driving up the winding road to the casino at night through thick mist can be harrowing.

Express buses from Kuala Lumpur's Puduraya Bus Station run daily to the cable car complex at the foot of the hill. The ticket cost covers the cable car ride. Buses are not allowed up the steep road. There is a special taxi stand at Puduraya servicing Gentings. If you drive, make sure you don't lose your way in the huge maze of featureless carparks.

Aboriginal treasures

Gentings can be accessed from the capital via the Karak Highway or the considerably more pleasant old Pahang Road through Gombak. At Gombak, you might want to pop into **Pak Ali's House** (Rumah Pak Ali) for a quick look at the interior of a traditional Sumatran-style house, which is open to visitors.

About 15 km (9 miles) down the old Pahang road is an excellent **Orang Asli Museum** (Muzium Orang Asli, open 9am–5.30pm). Sitting on a hill at an Orang Asli settlement, it provides a fascinating insight on the Malaysian peninsula's aboriginal peoples. A good range of exhibits such as old photographs, artefacts, handicraft, and tools and implements used in daily life, make this museum well worth a visit.

A new highlands road has been in the pipeline for over 10 years to link Gentings to Frasers and Camerons. However, it continues to receive public opposition because of fears it will affect the water catchment and biodiversity of the highlands.

Another (relatively) new resort is **Gunung Jerai ❺**, Kedah's highest peak. The 1,217-metre (3,993-ft) high limestone massif has commanding views of the surrounding rice plains and the Main Range. On the other side, you can see across the Straits of Melaka into Penang, and even as far as Langkawi island. Part of the **Sungai Teroi Forest Recreation Park** (Hutan Rekreasi Sungai Teroi), which has some forest trails, the hill is also home to a forestry museum. At its peak sits a pretty resort. A Hindu shrine was discovered in this area in the late 1880s, but no further excavations have been done.

Jerai is accessed from Sungai Petani or Gurun from the North-South Highway. Turn off Guar Chempedak. If you don't have your own transport, jeeps can ferry you up the 13-km (8-mile) winding road between 9am–5pm. Alternatively, if you are energetic enough, a mountain track goes right up to the peak. ❏

BELOW: Orang Asli child.
RIGHT: jungles of Sungai Teroi.

PERAK

It was once the wealthy tin-mining centre of Malaysia. Now the home of the country's longest-surviving sultanate, Perak woos the tourist dollar to its beaches

Map on page 158

I t started with tin in the 19th century. But like the claws of an excavator, mining has held Perak in its grip ever since. But while tin built Perak all those years ago, it is the state's limestone hills that have today become the building blocks of the nation.

In Bahasa Malaysia, *perak* actually means "silver". But it was the "silver" of the tin revolution that lined Perak's coffers, making it one of the wealthiest states in the land. The accompanying feuds and power struggles prompted greater British intervention in the whole country, eventually shifting the centre of power from the old capitals along the Perak River to the tin-rich areas of Larut and Kinta.

When the bottom fell out of the industry in the 1980s, entire towns shut down. However, thanks to industrialisation and the rapid pace of development in the country, the state's limestone hills are now feeding huge cement factories.

LEFT: the stately Ubadiah Mosque.
BELOW: one of many temples embedded in the rockface around Ipoh.

The town that tin built

The Kinta Valley remains Perak's leading district, and its main city, **Ipoh** ❻, the most prosperous of its settlements. Like Kuala Lumpur, Ipoh started as a landing stage at the point at which the river became unnavigable, springing up as a messy shanty-town almost overnight on the ancestral land of Dato' Panglima Kinta, the local Malay territorial chief. However, when Ipoh took over as state capital from Taiping in 1937, it was the best-planned town in the peninsula, with broad, regularly laid-out streets. It is now Malaysia's second-largest city, with a population of half a million.

Nestled in the craggy bosom of limestone outcrops and the more distant hills of the Main Range, Ipoh boasts excellent amenities and quality accommodation. **Old Town** on the west side is where you'll find the *Padang* (Town Green), the epitome of every Malaysian town with a colonial past. Surrounded by the Royal Ipoh Club, court houses, municipal library and the stately **St Michael's Institution**, today, it is the scene of important matches, school athletic meets, and parades. Also in Old Town, near the **Masjid Negeri (State Mosque)** and the Clock Tower, is the Moorish **Stesen Keretapi Ipoh** (Ipoh Railway Station), whose silver dome, graceful arches, and interminable colonnades, bear a striking resemblance to the Kuala Lumpur Railway Station.

East of the river lies the **D.R. Seenivasagam Park** (Taman D.R. Seenivasagam) which, typical of most public parks in Ipoh, hosts large dawn gatherings of *tai chi* practitioners. Here, groups faithfully go through all forms of the martial art, some using swords and fans too.

Succulent pomelo, very similar in taste and texture to the grapefruit, is found everywhere in Ipoh.

BELOW: colourful paintings from the cave walls of Perak Tong temple.

Down the road on Jalan Panglima Bukit Gantang is the **Muzium Darul Ridzuan** (Darul Ridzuan Museum, open Sunday–Thursday 9am–5pm; half day Saturday). The century-old mansion used to be the residence of Malay chieftains and British officials, but now showcases the state's history, including of course, the story of tin.

Grand mansions in huge grounds still sit along the prestigious **Jalan Sultan Azlan Shah**, commonly referred to by its old name, Tiger Lane. Along this road is also the **Geology Museum** (Muzium Geologi, open Monday–Friday 8am–4.15pm; Saturday 8am–12.45pm). It has over 600 examples of minerals, an exhibition on tin ore, including one of the best examples of cassiterite in the world, and a fine collection of precious stones.

About 15 minutes' drive east of town is **Tambun**. Among its attractions are the Tambun Hot Springs, rather ugly public baths, the National Stud Farm, where thoroughbred race horses are raised, and the Tanjung Rambutan Waterfall. Tambun is also home to an Ipoh speciality, the *pomelo,* a luscious grapefruit.

Temples in the rock

However, Ipoh's undisputed top attractions are its cave temples. The naturally hollowed insides of the Kinta Valley's limestone formations, so reminiscent of southern China, have served as homes for ancient peoples as well as hideouts for bandits.

They are also spiritually significant for both Buddhists and Hindus. Devotees have built entrances to these temples that range from the simple to the ostentatious; sometimes entire buildings complete with red-tiled pagoda roofs "grow" out from the rock. Walking into the dimly-lit interiors, with their altars, the

smell of incense and the occasional echoes of bats and swallows, can make for a heady experience for the uninitiated.

The largest of the rock temples is south of Ipoh on the old trunk road, near a line of stalls selling pomelos and local biscuits. The ornate **Sam Poh Tong** dates back to the 1890s when a passing monk found the cave and made it his home and meditation base for 20 years until his death. Today, a group of monks and nuns follows in his footsteps.

Statues of Buddha are dotted everywhere, even among the stalagmites and stalactites. A stiff climb up 264 steps leads to a panorama of Ipoh and its surroundings. Of renown is the temple's pond of small turtles; visitors can buy spinach to feed them. Turtles are Chinese symbols of longevity.

Close by is the **Gua Kek Lok Tong**, known also as the Brass Temple after its gleaming statues. You can walk through the cave to the back where its dog's teeth of limestone formations frame a peaceful green valley of ponds and hills.

Another famous cave shrine is the **Perak Tong**, 6 km (4 miles) north of town on Jalan Kuala Kangsar, the old trunk road. Traditional Chinese paintings adorn the walls and relate traditional folk tales and legends. Built in 1926 by a Buddhist priest from China, the temple has more than 40 statues of Buddha, the central figure rising 13 metres (40 ft) high.

Caves and castles

The prettiest view of Ipoh's limestone hills is just past the city as you head south on the North-South Highway. Unfortunately, this gives way briefly to blasted rock, precious material for the country's development, before coming to the imposing Gunung Tempurung limestone massif. One of the show caves,

Map on page 158

On the same limestone massif as Sam Poh Tong is a giant Mercedes Benz logo, presented to the city by the German manufacturer in thanks for the huge purchases by rich miners.

BELOW: Buddhist statues (left) crowd a shrine in Sam Poh Tong, and (right) the temple exterior.

Look hard enough in the countryside of Perak and you may spot abandoned wooden tin dredges, a sight from yesteryear when tin was king in Perak.

BELOW:
Kellie's Castle has a fairy-tale air.

Gua Tempurung (open 9am–5pm, tel: 05-011-540775) can be accessed from the Gopeng interchange and 2 km (1 mile) down the old trunk road south. The turnoff is at the pretty Kampung Gunung Mesah.

Used variously by tin miners and communists on the run, the 1.9-km (1-mile) long river passageway is now accessible via an illuminated walkway. The concrete pathway climbs up to the 180 metre by 120 metre (540 ft by 360 ft) Alam Cavern, the biggest of the five chambers, and also passes through interesting formations such as gigantic stalagmites and flowstones.

Tours run from a 40-minute basic trip to the 4-hour grand tour, which involves a river stint. There are morning and afternoon sessions for the longer tours, and guides will bring in a minimum of two. Weekends and public holidays can be crowded with tour buses, after which graffiti appears on the walls, to be painstakingly cleaned off by management. Camping is allowed on site.

The old trunk road in Perak goes through mainly flat and open land, offering vistas of deserted mining pools over the bleached scars of tin tailings and glimpses of the wooden *palong* (tin dredges).

An incongruity among these ruins is that of a Scottish Castle, about 5 km (3 miles) from Batu Gajah, half an hour from Ipoh. **Kellie's Castle** (open 7am–6.30pm; entrance fee) was built by a William Kellie-Smith, a rubber plantation owner who made his fortune in Malaya. Smith brought in Tamil workers from southern India to build the house, which was meant to be a reminder of home, but, sadly, it was never finished; Smith died while on a trip to Portugal. During the war, the castle was used by the Japanese as an execution area, hence its reputation for being haunted. Overlooking a river, the mansion is almost overgrown with wild fig and banyan trees, and still has a fairy-tale air about it.

Historic river valley

For centuries before the tin boom, Sungai Perak provided the only access to the state's interior. The river valley stretches from the royal town of Kuala Kangsar, to the coastal village of Beting Beras Basah, near the town of Bagan Datoh. The main area of Malay settlement, this was also the scene of some of the most dramatic events in Perak's history. Now good roads run along either side of the banana tree-lined banks, through villages which were once the homes of the state's greatest heroes.

Throughout the valley, there are about 20 tombs of Perak's sultans, all carefully marked and cared for by the villagers. Some of the graves have become *keramat* (shrines) visited by humble folk in search of blessings or favours. It is also a tradition that a newly-installed Sultan of Perak must pay his respects at every shrine, travelling by boat, before he can truly be accepted as ruler.

Perak is the only state whose royal house can claim direct descent from the sultans of Melaka. The sultanate is also one of the world's longest surviving monarchies, going back to the 7th century.

Some of these graves can be found in one of the country's most important sites, which saw the first local uprising against British colonialists. Now a well-organised tourism complex, **Pasir Salak ❼** was where the state's first British resident, James Birch, was assassinated in 1875 while bathing in the river. The local ringleaders, Dato' Sagor and Dato' Maharaja Lela were executed. Today, there are memorials at the complex to both the British and local heroes.

The complex (open Monday–Friday 10am–5pm; weekends 10am–6pm) is a beautiful collection of original and reconstructed buildings of historic value blended into a peaceful kampung. Of particular note is the architecture, which has elements of Perak's *rumah kutai* (old houses) – two originals sit in the compound. The historical tunnel (entrance fee), which is also the information centre, features a diorama giving a good overview of the country's history. A new resort in the complex offers a Malay kampung homestay experience, with riverview chalets and, for large groups, a traditional welcoming ceremony performed by the kampung folk.

To get to Pasir Salak, which is 70 km (40 miles) from Ipoh, head south from the city on the old trunk road towards Kampung Gajah through Bota or Batu Gajah. The journey there passes Bota Kanan which has a hatchery for river terrapins, the *labu* (traditional pottery) area of Pulau Tiga, and fruit orchards, particularly of the pungent *durian*.

Island in the sun

If you can't make it to the beaches of the peninsula's east coast, **Pulau Pangkor ❽**, off the coast of Perak, is pleasant. The well-signposted road there from Ipoh goes through Sitiawan to Lumut, the principal base for the Royal Malaysian Navy.

Pangkor is a smaller, less developed version of Langkawi, and is popular with locals, Taiwanese and Germans. Public holidays find it packed, and prices double, but off-peak, the taxi drivers play draughts, and the isle is enveloped in a lovely lazy atmosphere.

There are many versions to the origin of the island's

Map on page 158

A Hindu shrine near Kellie's Castle, erected for the plantation workers has, among the figures of animals and gods, a man in a green suit and topee hat – could this be an image of the castle's architect, Kellie Smith?

BELOW: rock inscribed with the coat-of-arms of the Dutch East India Company in Pangkor.

TIP

Teluk Intan, the chief town of Lower Perak, has an unusual claim to fame. The century-old clock tower has its own Tower of Pisa-style tilt.

name; one is that Pangkor derived from the Thai "pang koh", meaning "beautiful island". Like so much of Malaysia, the isle's place names are legend-inspired. For instance, the northern Pantai Puteri Dewi (The Beach of the Fairy Princess) is named after a princess who flung herself off a cliff when she learned of the death of her suitor during battle. However, for the Malaysian school-child, Pangkor is better known for the historic treaty signed there in 1874, granting the British entry into the Malay states for the first time. From Lumut, ferries run to the Pangkor jetty every 15 minutes from 6.30am–7pm. The fast ferry takes about 20 minutes, while the slower ones take twice as long.

The beach resort stretch is on the western side of the island, and has great sunset views. The only means there from the jetty is by taxi-vans at government-fixed rates. However, the closest beach, **Pasir Bogak**, is only 20 minutes' walk away. The most established of the beaches, Pasir Bogak is by no means the prettiest, but it does make a good base from which to explore the island by rented bicycle or motorcycle. Cyclists should note, though, that the island is pretty hilly. Pasir Bogak has plenty of accommodation and places to eat.

North of Pasir Bogak is the prettier **Teluk Nipah**, packed with virtually identical backpacker accommodation. There are a couple of souvenir shops and a good Chinese seafood restaurant here. Don't be surprised to see a horn-bill or two sitting on an electricity pole outside your resort. In the adjacent beach, **Coral Bay**, is a hawker centre. As with Teluk Nipah, the waters here are lovely, and great for snorkelling. Just before Teluk Nipah is **Teluk Ketapang**, where turtles sometimes come ashore to lay eggs.

Heading north again through rainforest, the road cuts inland at a narrow point of the island. The left branch goes to the upmarket Pan Pacific Resort on the lovely Beach of the Beautiful Princess, more popularly called Golden Sands. There is a nine-hole golf course in the hotel's grounds. The beach and hotel facilities are open to day visitors for a fee.

BELOW: salted fish being sun-dried in Pangkor.

Head out through more rainforest, and the lovely kampung-style Teluk Dalam Resort spreads out before you. Just before the road reaches the fishing villages on the east coast, there is a jungle trek to Pasir Bogak that climbs **Bukit Pangkor**, offering good views.

Tourists and traditions

Little has changed in the eastern villages of **Kampung Sungai Pinang Kecil** (better known as SPK, also a ferry stop) and **Kampung Telok Kechil**, with their quaint tiny wooden houses on stilts over the water. Despite tourism being well-established, the island's economy is dependent mainly on the sea. The villages are therefore alive with activity when the bright yellow boats leave and return from their night stints. To reach any of the jetties, just head right through the courtyard and what looks like someone's living room – ingeniously-converted warehouses! At SPK, drop in at the famous **Hai Sap Hei satay fish factory**, where sea produce is dried, packed and sold.

South of the island in the middle of a *kampung* sit the remains of a **Dutch fort** built over 300 years ago in an attempt to control Perak's tin trade and to fight the tyranny of piracy in the Straits of Melaka. Recon-

Map on page 158

structed by the National Museum in 1973, features of the original building still survive such as the Dutch East India coat-of-arms chiselled on a boulder close to the fort. Later adventurers have added their own "messages". A fisherman who is immune to snake bites used to demonstrate his affinity with the creatures close by, but has since retired. On a large rock opposite the fort is the remains of a drawing of a tiger mauling a boy. The drawing has been crudely etched in and the child is believed to be the son of a Dutch dignitary who disappeared mysteriously in the forest.

Smart resorts

Off the coast of Pasir Bogak is the exclusive patrons-only **Pangkor Laut Resort** on a small island of the same name. The resort was one of the first in Malaysia to build chalets on stilts that extend into the sea. The island's most famous feature is Emerald Bay, a gorgeous beach with powdery, white sand and clear, blue waters. The resort has its own ferry from Lumut.

Lumut is a well-developed jump-off point for Pangkor, with tourist information, money-changers, car-parks, and food. It is busiest during Pesta Laut (Sea Festival) in August, a popular local attraction. Pangkor can also be crowded at this time and during the Malaysian school and public holidays. Because Lumut sits on the Dinding River, it has no beach, but it does have some good accommodation, and is a quiet, pleasant getaway.

Often, locals don't even cross to Pangkor, but head for **Teluk Batik**, a public beach 5 km (3 miles) from Lumut which is packed with food stalls, seafront A-frame accommodation for backpackers, and classier hotels on the headland and inland.

BELOW: gorgeous Emerald Bay, Pangkor Laut

Golden dome, royal town

Perak's royal capital, **Kuala Kangsar** , is a lovely garden town about 35 km (20 miles) north of Ipoh across the Perak River. Within walking distance of the town's attractions is the quiet Government Rest House on Jalan Istana, which overlooks the river. It also has a charming little museum.

Follow Jalan Istana past the Old Residency to reach Bukit Chandan, where the huge golden dome of the century-old **Masjid Ubadiah** (Ubadiah Mosque) gleams. Its striking and symmetrical domes and minarets make it one of the most photographed Muslim buildings in the country; if it is reminiscent of Kuala Lumpur's Moorish architecture, it is because it had the same architect.

Beyond the mosque, the road circles the Sultan of Perak's palace, the modern **Istana Iskandariah**, with its rather watered-down Moorish architectural elements. Next to it is the smaller but more dignified and charming **Istana Kenangan** (open daily 9.30am–5pm). Its name translates as the Palace of Memories and it served as a temporary residence while the Istana Iskandariah was being built. The original construction was in accordance with Malay tradition, without a single nail or architectural plans. Subsequent preservation attempts have not remained faithful to this requirement, however, but the building is still a beautiful example of Perak architecture. It is now a royal museum and contains an interesting collection of mementos and photographs of the Perak royal family. All displays are in Bahasa Malaysia, however, although a guide is sometimes available to bring tourists around.

Kuala Kangsar is also home to one of the pioneer batch of rubber trees that arrived here in the 1870s as seeds from Brazil and eventually took over the country. One of these first trees is found near the agricultural office in town.

BELOW:
Istana Kenangan
in Kuala Kangsar.

Though some plantation owners have switched to oil palm because of higher revenues, others are cashing in on rubberwood, an important new commodity for Malaysia's booming furniture industry.

Close by is the Malay College Kuala Kangsar (MCKK). Founded in 1904 as a residential school for the sons of the Malay aristocracy, it is now the seedbed for a good cross-section of Malaysia's political establishment.

On the outskirts of Kuala Kangsar, about 20 km (30 miles) along the Ipoh–Enggor road, is the pottery district of Sayong, also once the home of sultans. Turn off at the bridge and turn left again to get to Kampung Kepala Bendang, the original potter's village, and you will be greeted by scores of vases, ashtrays and ornaments drying in the sun all along this dirt road. The most famous of the traditional designs is the black *labu*, gourd-shaped water pitchers with broad bases and tall narrow spouts that keep cold water really cold.

Map on page 158

Sayong is well known as a centre for these characteristic gourd-shaped pottery.

Waterfall haven

From the highlands of the Main Range spring the waters of Sungai Perak, the second-largest river in the peninsula. The river's flow is controlled by Malaysia's largest dam, 150 km (95 miles) upstream from Kuala Kangsar on the Temenggor River tributary. Once a "black area", where armed forces fought the communists, the region is still largely covered by thick mountainous jungle, and forms the northernmost part of the wildlife corridor stretching through Taman Negara and Endau-Rompin. It has one of the best remaining populations of large mammals in the country, including endangered species such as the tiger, Sumatran rhino and Malayan bear.

Cutting through the area is the spectacular East-West Highway to Kota Bharu. This is probably the only public place you'd see a road sign warning of elephants crossing. The road bypasses the picturesque **Temenggor Empangan (Temenggor Dam)** ⑩, where there is a resort and floating chalets for fishermen.

BELOW: Temenggor is dotted with pretty waterfalls like this.

The jungles of Temenggor south of the highway are slowly opening up to nature enthusiasts due to the attention brought to it by the Malaysian Nature Society. MNS is trying to push for it to be gazetted as the **Greater Belum** state park, encompassing the Belum area north of the highway up to the Thai border. Belum proper is still restricted, but tour agencies market Temenggor as Belum, after the MNS scientific expeditions.

Temenggor is dotted with numerous beautiful towering waterfalls accessible through steep, rugged terrain across swift rivers, on ridges used by the Orang Asli to collect rattan, that follow trails left by animals such as deer or elephants. Among the area's popular sites are the seven-step thundering **Kertch Waterfall**, where the lucky could catch sight of the giant Rafflesia bloom, and the eight-step **Kelaweh Waterfall**, with a lovely campsite at its spray-misted base.

Animals are difficult to spot, but there are plenty of fresh hoof-prints and droppings on the ground and claw-marks on trees. Trails are flanked by tall hill dipterocarp trees, medicinal plants and shrubs underfoot, and of course, the thorny rattan that grabs at sleeves and flesh. The leech-phobic would do well to

stay away. The dryer months are traditionally in the first half of the year, but "dry" is a relative term here.

Tour guides arrange entry permits but the District Office might sometimes require a meeting with foreigners. All groups are guided by the Orang Asli, who comprise the peaceable and friendly Temiar and Jahai peoples, and a tour usually includes a night at their thatched hut villages and a little *berse-wang* (traditional dance) performance.

The jump-off point to Temenggor is **Grik**, one and a half hour's drive from Kuala Kangsar on a scenic and winding road. Serenely shrouded in mist in the early morning, the town has basic accommodation, including a government resthouse, and lots of eateries, though serving local food only. During the communist warfare years, Grik was the compulsory check-in point for the daytime-use only East-West Highway.

Town of everlasting peace

South of Grik is **Taiping** , the former state capital. The town with the heaviest rainfall in the peninsula has one of its loveliest names: "everlasting peace" in Chinese. The name derives from the ending of the bloody struggles between rival Chinese mining factions in Larut after the Treaty of Pangkor was signed.

The town's atmosphere is epitomised by the beautiful **Lake Gardens** (Taman Tasik), whose serene lakes and ancient raintrees were established at an abandoned tin mine on the edge of the town in the 1890s, long before the word ecology was in use. In the grounds is a nine-hole golf course and the rustic 50-hectare (120-acre) **Taiping Zoo**. A road leads to Bukit Larut (Maxwell Hill), Malaysia's oldest hill station (*see Hill Stations, page 159*).

There is so much rain in Taiping that its residents place bets on what time it will fall. The bookie's office is a downtown hawker centre with a zinc roof and a digital clock put in by the punters.

BELOW: the Lake Gardens of Taiping.

The entrance to the gardens is marked by a number of architectural gems including the colonial town hall and the government offices. The **Perak Museum** (Muzium Perak), housed in a venerable Victorian building, is the oldest in the country. Its collections include some excellent natural history and ethnology displays. The **Ling Nam Temple** is the oldest Chinese temple in Perak, and within it there is a model of a boat dedicated to the Chinese emperor who built the first canal in China.

Mangrove magic

Taiping was also the terminus for the country's first railway line, – now disused – which ended in Kuala Sepetang (Port Weld) on the coast. The road there passes the old fort of **Kota Ngah Ibrahim**, named after the Malay territorial chief of Larut who grew rich through the tin trade, but was unable to control the turbulent Chinese factions producing the wealth.

The road also leads to the **Matang Mangrove Forest** (Hutan Baleau Matang), which has a park with boardwalk going through a sustainably-managed mangrove forest, which has been harvested for charcoal for nearly 100 years. The traditional charcoal kilns make an interesting visit as do the fishing villages, but you might need to find a guide for this. Enquire at Taiping.

A portion of the mangrove swamp further north near Bagan Serai is the **Kuala Gula Bird Sanctuary**. Hundred of birds, including rare species, feed and nest here. Between August and December, thousands of migrant birds make this their pit-stop en route south to Australia. The sanctuary is also home to otters, monkeys, and the ridge-back dolphin. There is limited and basic accommodation here. For information and bookings, contact the Wildlife Department. ❑

Map on page 158

Despite its name, Kuala Gula Bird Sanctuary is also home to monkeys and other small animals.

BELOW: gnarled buttress roots of the fig tree.

THE PERAK MAN

He was about 40–45 years old, they believe. And he was given a proper burial, complete with stone tools, and meat offerings from five different animals as well as shellfish from the river; the shells covered the floor. When they found him 11,000 years later, he was remarkably well-preserved, and still in his original foetal position.

The "Perak Man" is the peninsula's oldest skeleton. He was discovered in a cave in the Lenggong vicinity near Grik by prominent archaeologist Dr Zuraina Majid, who had also uncovered the country's oldest stone tools nearby, potentially dating back 100,000 years. The "Perak Man" is thought to be an ancestor of the Negrito Orang Asli people, a small hunter-gatherer tribe regarded as the oldest inhabitants in the peninsula.

The Lenggong stone tools in Kota Tampan were also discovered intact. Anvils, stone hammers and tools in various stages of being made – complete with flakes and chips – suggest that the site was a tool factory. It was abandoned all those years ago when a volcanic eruption spewed clouds of ash that buried everything – the same eruption that created Lake Toba in Sumatra. Stone tool factories have also been excavated in Tingkayu, Sabah, and Kubang Pasu, Kedah.

CHICK BLINDS: OLD FASHIONED URBAN ART

Malaysian streets are always vivid and colourful, but when shopkeepers lower their chick blinds, the street fronts take on a whole new look

Made of split bamboo or thin wooden rods laced with twine, these sun blinds, known as *bidai* in Malay, serve a dual purpose.

Not only do they shade the colonnaded verandah in front of the shop, known as the "five-foot-way"; they also provide the shopkeeper with the perfect canvas to advertise his goods and services, giving every street a distinct and vibrant character.

With the advent of modern, Western-style shopping malls, some pundits have predicted the demise of the shophouse, and with it the chick blind. This may be true in some Malaysian cities, but in most smaller towns, rows of traditional shophouses prevail and their useful and colourful awnings are still prolific, and as popular as ever.

SIX CENTURIES OF HISTORY

Chick blinds have a long and colourful history. When the notorious Mongol leader Tamerlane and his "Golden Horde" sacked the Indian city of Delhi in 1398, it was noted that the tent openings of the much-feared conquerors were covered with blinds made of thin wands lined with rose-coloured silk. Indeed, the name is thought to derive from the Mongol word *tchik*.

Malaysia's chick blinds first appeared on the front of colonial bungalows in the 19th century, and were most probably introduced as a tropical architectural element from British India. Traditionally, the blinds were painted in black and white stripes, and lined with navy-blue muslin, which is the preferred backing fabric on urban chick blinds even today.

▷ **SARONGS FOR SALE**
In Kuala Terengganu, a Malay woman and child leave a shop through the "door" of its chick blind, which advertises "Rajah Brand" men's sarongs.

△ **FUNKY ROLEX**
The world's best-known watches honour a jewellery shop's blind in Taiping, Perak, a town where streets of traditional shophouses still survive.

△ **NOON GLARE**
Hawkers sell tropical *duku* fruit in front of a wall of chick blinds in the main street of Bagan Serai, Perak.

◁ **SPIDER SARONGS**
Men's *pelikat* sarongs come in a variety of brands, including *Chop Laba Laba*, or "Spider Brand".

"FIVE-FOOT-WAY" SHOPS

The long colonnaded space, known as the "five-foot-way", or *kaki lima* in Malay, which fronts all traditional rows of shophouses is said to have originated in a directive by Sir Stamford Raffles, founder of Singapore.

Raffles decreed that all urban buildings should have "a verandah of a certain depth, open to all sides as a continuous and open passage on each side of the street", so people could walk comfortably along, sheltered from the fierce heat of an equatorial sun or a monsoon downpour. However, it wasn't long before hawkers began exploiting these shaded spaces and the "five-foot-way" shop came into being.

Some are merely extensions of the shops behind, or additional display spaces for already crammed premises, but others are individual, cupboard-sized establishments often known as Mamak shops, because they are run by Indian-Muslim Malaysians, colloquially known as Mamak. These miniature shops still survive in many of Malaysia's rural towns.

▷ **STOMACH PILLS**
"Chi-Kit" pills, a Chinese remedy for stomach ailments, are advertised on this chick blind at a Taiping Chinese pharmacy.

▽ **ANONYMOUS ART**
In Taiping, songbirds in bamboo cages share hanging space with a chick blind advertising a popular brand of milk powder.

▷ **BRIDAL TAILOR**
In Kuala Kangsar, Perak, a tailor advertises his speciality – Western-style wedding attire. Some artworks, like this one here, are painted to the client's specification; others, like those advertising brand-name goods, recur in many towns.

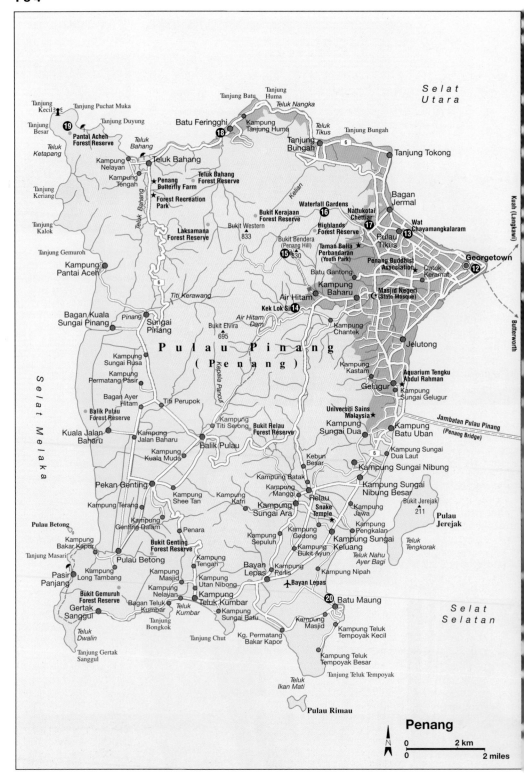

Penang

Selat Utara

Selat Selatan

Selat Melaka

**P u l a u   P i n a n g
(P e n a n g)**

Georgetown ⑫

Tanjung Kecil
Tanjung Besar
Tanjung Puchat Muka
Tanjung Duyung
Teluk Ketapang
⑲ Pantai Acheh Forest Reserve
Teluk Bahang
Kampung Nelayan
Kampung Tengah
Tanjung Keriang
Tanjung Kalok
Tanjung Gemuroh
Kampung Pantai Acen
Bagan Kuala Sungai Pinang
Sungai Pinang
Pinang
Kuala Jalan Baharu
Balik Pulau Forest Reserve
Kampung Sungai Rusa
Kampung Permatang Pasir
Bagan Ayer Hitam
Titi Perupok
Kampung Jalan Baharu
Kampung Kuala Muda
Pekan Genting
Kampung Terang
Kampung Genting Dalam
Penara
Pulau Betong
Kampung Bakar Kapor
Tanjung Masari
Pasir Panjang
Kampung Long Tambang
Pulau Betong
Bukit Genting Forest Reserve
Bukit Gemuruh Forest Reserve
Gertak Sanggul
Teluk Dwalin
Tanjung Gertak Sanggul
Bagan Teluk Kumbar
Kampung Nelayan
Kampung Masjid
Kampung Utan Nibong
Kampung Teluk Kumbar
Teluk Kumbar
Tanjung Bongkok
Tanjung Chut
Kg. Permatang Bakar Kapor
Kampung Sungai Batu
Kampung Tengah
Bayan Lepas
Kampung Perlis
Kampung Sepuluh
Kampung Gedong
Kampung Bukit Ayun
Kampung Kafri
Kampung Shee Tan
Kampung Sungai Ara
Kampung Manggi
Kampung Batak
Relau
Snake Temple ★
Kampung Jawa
Kampung Pengkalan
Kampung Sungai Keluang
Teluk Nahu Ayer Bagi
Kampung Nipah
✈ Bayan Lepas
⑳ Batu Maung
Kampung Masjid
Kampung Teluk Tempoyak Kecil
Kampung Teluk Tempoyak Besar
Tanjung Teluk Tempoyak
Teluk Ikan Mati
Pulau Rimau
Bukit Jerejak 211 ▲
Pulau Jerejak
Teluk Tengkorak
Kampung Sungai Nibung
Kampung Sungai Nibung Besar
Kampung Sungai Dua Laut
Kampung Sungai Dua
Universiti Sains Malaysia ★
Kampung Batu Uban
Jambatan Pulau Pinang (Penang Bridge)
Kebun Besar
Kampung Kastam
Gelugur
Aquarium Tengku Abdul Rahman ★
Kampung Sungai Gelugur
Jelutong
Kampung Chantek
Butterworth
Kuah (Langkawi)
Tanjung Tokong
Bagan Jermal
Wat Chayamangkalaram ★ ⑬
Pulau Tikus
Penang Buddhist Association ★
Datuk Keramat
Masjid Negeri (State Mosque) ★
Kampung Baharu
Batu Gantong
⑮ Bukit Bendera (Penang Hill) 830 ▲
Taman Belia Perbandaran (Youth Park) ★
⑰ Nattukotai Chettiar ★
Highlands Forest Reserve
⑯ Bukit Kerajaan Forest Reserve
Waterfall Gardens ★
Kelian
Air Hitam
Kek Lok Si ⑭ ★
Air Hitam Dam
Bukit Elvira 695 ▲
Kepala Pancur
Bukit Western 833 ▲
Laksamana Forest Reserve
★ Forest Recreation Park
★ Penang Butterfly Farm
Teluk Bahang Forest Reserve
Teluk Bahang
Teluk Bahang
Kampung Tanjung Huma
⑱ Batu Feringghi
Teluk Tikus
Tanjung Bungah
Tanjung Bungah
Teluk Nangka
Tanjung Batu
Tanjung Huma
Bukit Relau Forest Reserve
Kampung Titi Serong
Balik Pulau
Titi Kerawang
Kampung Pantai Aceh
6
6
6
6

Penang

N

0   2 km
0   2 miles

PENANG

A rich heritage and a mystic, spiritual core – as well as fine beaches and wonderful food – make the island state of Penang a perennial favourite among visitors to Malaysia

Map on page 184

Temples shrouded in incense smoke and palm-fringed beaches have been attracting curious visitors to **Penang** for several hundred years. One of the most famous islands in Asia, Penang is also perhaps the best-known tourist destination in Malaysia.

Throughout history, Penang has changed names like the seasons. Early Malays called it Pulau Ka Satu, or Single Island. Later it appeared on sailing charts as Pulau Pinang, or Island of the Betel Nut Tree. The British renamed it Prince of Wales' Island, and finally, with Malaysia's independence, it became Pulau Pinang once again. But romance, sustained by tourist brochure copywriters, is hard to dispel: Penang is also the Pearl of the Orient, Gateway to the East, and the Isle of Temples.

The trade

From the mainland, the 7-km (4-mile) **Penang Bridge** (Jambatan Pulau Pinang) offers exhilarating views of the harbour and the jagged skyline of condominiums and office blocks set against the hilly centre.

A very different aspect would have greeted English trader and adventurer Sir Francis Light in the 18th century, but he saw the advantages of having the island – then under Kedah – as a station for Britain's East India Company. Light saw Penang as a base to replenish company ships on their long haul to China in the flourishing tea and opium trade, and serve as a headquarters to further British interests in Southeast Asia.

Light, fluent in Thai and Malay, and a familiar figure in the Kedah court, persuaded the sultan to trade Penang for British protection against threatening Thai and Bugis enemies. But the British did not honour the agreement, and going to war only saw Kedah lose more land to the Empire – this time on the mainland, named Seberang Prai by the Malays.

To encourage trade and commerce, the British made the island state a free port; no taxes were levied on either imports or exports. This strategy worked and in eight years, the population increased to 8,000, comprising many immigrant races – Chinese, Indians and Bugis, among others.

Today, the state of Pulau Pinang or Penang as everyone calls it, comprises Seberang Prai (or Butterworth as it was formerly known) on the mainland and Penang island, linked by both the bridge and 20 minute-interval ferry services that run 24 hours a day. The ferries carry both passengers and vehicles; ferrying your car over costs the same as the bridge toll and you pay at the Seberang Prai side. The ferry terminus at the Seberang Prai is linked to bus, taxi and railway stations – the transport goes all the way to Thailand.

BELOW: travelling salesman in Georgetown.

The clock tower opposite Fort Conwallis in Georgetown was a gift from a Chinese millionaire to celebrate Queen Victoria's Diamond Jubilee in 1897.

Different faces

Like most cities of Asia that juxtapose the glass and concrete of the new with the tile and teak of the old, Penang has several dimensions. A newcomer can arrive by ferry, be transported by trishaw to a Chinese hotel on Lebuh Chulia in the heart of Chinatown, eat at the outdoor food stalls, visit the waterfront villages, and after two weeks, leave Penang having never stepped into anything built after World War II. On the other hand, another visitor may have cocktails at the poolside overlooking the sea while getting a golden tan, dine in a gourmet restaurant, and never brush shoulders with a Chowrasta Market butcher in town.

But vibrant **Georgetown ⑫** is the heart of Penang. Named by the British after King George III, it is unmistakably Chinese, its narrow streets congested with pedestrians, vehicles, signboards and temples. The best way to experience it is on foot, or you could hire a trishaw for the day – but bargain first. By trishaw, the city passes by in a kaleidoscope of changing colours, and even in the rain, the driver zips you into a plastic covering, and pedals slowly through the wet streets. At night, there is a special romance about riding in the glow of neon signs and blinking lights.

An excellent route that takes in the main sights is the signposted Heritage Trail – ask for a map from Tourism Malaysia (tel: 04-2619067; open 9am–5pm) near the **Clock Tower Ⓐ**. The trail starts at **Fort Cornwallis (Kota Cornwallis) Ⓑ**, the place from which probably the most costly cannon ball in history was shot. When Francis Light was clearing land for his settlement, the thick undergrowth proved arduous work for the sepoys, Indians employed as soldiers by the British and other European powers. The disgruntled sepoys had no compunction in complaining, so Light loaded a cannon with silver dollars and fired it into the

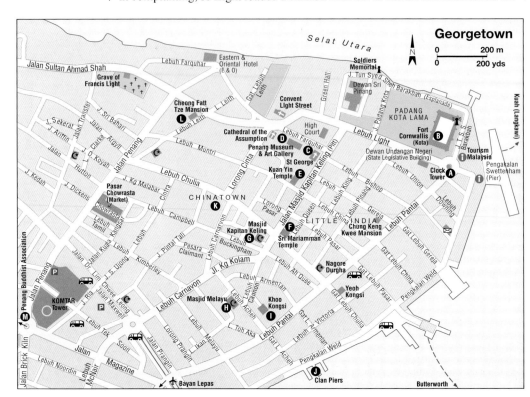

jungle. This was enough to get them all to work to retrieve the coins; and before long the land was cleared and the first camp established.

Maps:
Area 184
City 186

Magical cannon

Originally a wooden structure, Fort Cornwallis was rebuilt with convict labour in the early 1800s. Today, the old fort's precincts have been converted into a public park and playground. Its ramparts are still guarded by old cannon, the most venerable and famous of which is Seri Rambai, presented by the Dutch to the Sultan of Johor in 1606. Seven years later, it was captured by the Achehnese and taken to Acheh, where it remained for almost 200 years. The cannon was then sent to Kuala Selangor in the quest of a Bugis alliance. After the British bombarded Kuala Selangor in 1871, the cannon was brought to Penang. Like most ancient cannon, Seri Rambai is attributed with magical powers; it is believed that women desiring children will have their wish fulfilled if they place flowers in the cannon's barrel and offer prayers.

TIP

Public buses cover the whole the island but follow no timetable. Bus terminals are at Lebuh Victoria and Jalan Dr Lim Chwee Leong. Fares are low and you can go around the island in one day with an early start.

Next to Fort Cornwallis lies the *padang* (town green) and the Esplanade (Jalan Tun Syed Sheh Barakbah). The handsome 19th-century colonial **State Legislative Building** (Dewan Undangan Negeri) stands at one end of the Padang; at the other, near the entrance to Fort Cornwallis, traffic circles the Clock Tower, which was presented to Penang by a rich Chinese *towkay* (businessman), Cheah Chin Gok, in commemoration of Queen Victoria's Diamond Jubilee.

The dignified and well-designed **St George's Church Ⓖ**, built in 1818 on nearby Lebuh Farquhar, is the oldest Anglican church in Southeast Asia. Sir Francis Light lies buried in the frangipani-shaded cemetery down the road, along with a host of other notables of old Penang, many of whom succumbed

BELOW: colonial State Legislative Building.

Dragon figurine at Penang's Kuan Yin Temple, dedicated to the Buddhist Goddess of Mercy.

BELOW: giant joss stick at the Kuan Yin Temple.

early in life to the rigours of the climate and dangers of life in the tropics.

In the **Penang Museum** ⊙, on the same side of the street as St George's Church, visitors can peer into a Chinese bridal chamber created in the lavish style of the 19th century, or see a bejewelled *keris*, the dagger Malays used for protection and for prestige. The **Penang Art Gallery** upstairs displays work by local artists, including batik, oils, graphics and Chinese ink drawings.

Also along Lebuh Farquhar is the site of Georgetown's oldest hotel, the E&O Hotel, an institution which once played host to guests such as Rita Hayworth and Somerset Maugham. You, however, will not be able to stay the night; it has been undergoing renovation for some years, with no definite re-opening date.

Houses of worship

Three of the state's oldest worship houses are in the Jalan Masjid Kapitan Keling area. Along that road is Penang's oldest Buddhist temple, the **Kuan Yin Temple** ⊖, which is also the most humble and crowded. The temple belongs to the people in the street – the noodle hawkers, trishaw riders, and the workers building cupboards, repairing bicycles or selling sundry goods. A Buddhist deity who refused to enter Nirvana so long as there was injustice on earth, Kuan Yin typically personifies mercy. She is ever-present on Chinese altars, whether Taoist, Buddhist or Confucian, and is perhaps the most beloved divinity.

Jalan Masjid Kapitan Keling leads into the tiny "**Little India**" where saris, garlands, and jewellery deck the stores, and the spicy scent of curry wafts through the air. Indian merchants arrived in Penang with the British, as did the sepoys and Indian convicts, who built the first roads and filled in the swamps on which the town now stands. Assimilated into local society, it is not surprising to find their descendants fluent in Tamil as well as in Bahasa Malaysia, English and some Hokkien.

In Lebuh Queen sits the state's oldest place of worship for Hindus, the **Sri Mariamman Temple** ⊕, which was built in the 1830s, and boasts an ornate South Indian gateway. However, many Indians who came to Penang were Muslim, and the state has a large Indian-Muslim population, whose delicious *nasi kandar* rice and scorching-hot curry dishes are relished by all Malaysians. Their oldest place of worship, and the state's oldest mosque is on Jalan Masjid Kapitan Keling. The Moorish **Masjid Kapitan Keling (Kapitan Keling Mosque)** ⊕, erected in 1800, is named after the Indian-Muslim merchant headman, or *Kapitan Keling*, Caudeer Mohudeen, who was responsible for its construction. Head into Lebuh Armenian, which is flanked by early 19th-century shophouses originally belonging to Malays and Sumatrans. An octagonal minaret at the end of the road marks the entrance to the **Masjid Melayu (Acheen Street Mosque)** ⊕, which is a mixture of Egyptian and Javanese styles.

Narrow alleyways off the bustling roads lead to quiet rows of Chinese homes, with carved lintels and elaborate doorways. The small family temple erected on Gat Lebuh Gereja (Church Street) by millionaire Chung Keng Kwee is a good example. Inside the temple, a lifelike bronze statue of Chung in the robes of a Chinese mandarin stands resplendent. Chung made his fortune from the tin mines in Larut, Perak, and was one of the leaders of the Chinese factions in the Larut Wars of the 1860s.

As you walk around Georgetown, you will keep coming across clan houses, Chinese guild halls that honour both ancestors and outstanding members. Sitting in compounds surrounded by houses, they are reached through narrow entrances. Among these are the Yap Kongsi on Lebuh Armenian and the Cheah Kongsi on Gat Lebuh Armenian.

Map on page 186

King of the clanhouses

The most elaborate of these, however, is the **Khoo Kongsi ❶** at the junction of Jalan Masjid Kapitan Keling and Lebuh Acheh. Designed to capture the splendour of an imperial palace, it has a seven-tiered pavilion, "dragon" pillars and hand-painted walls engraved with the Khoo rose emblem. The original design was so ambitious that conservative Khoo clansmen cautioned against it, lest the emperor of China be offended. After eight years, the building was completed in 1902; but on the first night after it was finished, the roof mysteriously caught fire. Clan members interpreted this as a sign that even the deities considered the Khoo Kongsi too palatial for a clan house. The Khoos rebuilt it on a more modest scale. A recent 15-month renovation process costing RM3 million and painstakingly put together by 16 Chinese artisans using traditional Chinese materials has restored the house to its former splendour.

At Georgetown's waterfront near the ferry terminus, entire villages belong to clans. These are the **Clan Piers ❷**, comprising wooden houses perched on stilts over the sea, which in the pre-condominium era, were the most outstanding feature to greet visitors who travelled to the island by ferry. Each of the six

BELOW: the ornate entrance of a Georgetown clanhouse.

THE CHINESE CLANHOUSES

Chinese immigrants arriving in Malaysia in the 19th century fell under the protection and control of clan associations, whose functions were not unlike those of medieval European guilds: to promote the interests of their members and provide help to those in distress. You'll find the ancestral halls or *kongsi* of associations such as the Khoo, Ong, Tan and Chung clans scattered all over Georgetown.

Many of these clan houses are beautiful pieces of traditional Chinese architecture and house important antiques and artwork. But there is concern about their future, as well as the surrounding shophouses, due to the abolition of the Rent Control Act in 2000. The Act limits the rent that owners could charge tenants, but it is feared that its abolition will see owners looking to maximise profits by re-developing the land, or selling it off for money-raking high-rises. Current tenants, some of whom have lived in the same house for generations, might also be evicted. The Penang Heritage Council is lobbying hard to save these important buildings. The Khoos, for instance, are also planning to turn the buildings around their *kongsi* into a cultural and heritage village, with souvenir and other shops and budget accommodation.

Wooden clogs like these are more charming as wall hangings than foot wear. Find them in Penang's Chinatown.

villages has its own temple, and houses just one clan, except for one "mixed" village. Therefore, on Lim's Pier, you'll find only members of the Lim family, while Tan's Pier is the sole property of the Tan clan. Nearly all but the Chews have abandoned the fishing trade, but all the houses are occupied, and no one minds if a visitor strolls along the plankwalks.

Backpacker alley

Life in the hotch-potch of streets and alleys of **Chinatown** looks like it has been lived the same way since the immigrants got off the boat. At dawn, goods are unloaded at century-old shophouses, the lorries blocking half the already-narrow road. In the coffeeshops, old men exchange daily news over cracked cups of coffee with bread and *kaya* (coconut jam). For shopaholics, there are antiques and curios galore, as well as more contemporary items such as leather goods and batik. Second-hand bookstores are treasure-troves of old tomes, as well as the latest John Grisham left behind by backpackers in Lebuh Chulia.

The desire to soak-up this atmosphere has ensured that Lebuh Chulia's tiny old Chinese hotels have held out against time (and in some cases, badly-needed renovation). From a cracked window here, you can catch sight of a funeral procession through the streets, complete with drums and gongs and mourners. In the afternoon, a lion dance might be staged to bring luck to a new sundry goods shop – a noisy affair with more drums and gongs. Come evening and it could be a Chinese opera that draws an audience on plastic stools to watch heavily painted faces pantomime classical tales of old. In Chinatown, you can never tell where and when you might find a bargain or a baritone.

The hotels are "supported" by cafés offering "Western food", tours, bicycles

BELOW: rooftop patterns of Chinatown.
RIGHT: Chinese opera in action.

Map on page 186

for hire and money-changers. The backpacker row extends to Lebuh Leith, on which enterprising entrepreneurs have turned a row of heritage buildings into trendy restaurants and pubs. Here also is the carefully-restored late 19th-century **Cheong Fatt Tze Mansion** ❶, which has a unique blend of Eastern and Western architectural styles (guided tours 11am Monday, Wednesday, Friday, Saturday; entrance fee).

Georgetown has lots of small and friendly pubs, some of which keep a "family album" of snapshots showing just about every traveller who has ever walked in and bought a drink. They provide jukeboxes for dancing, games machines for entertainment and barmaids for conversation.

Jalan Penang (better known as Penang Road) is the main shopping bazaar, and it ends in the towering air-conditioned KOMTAR shopping complex at the top of a bus station, which also houses a tourist information centre and a Malaysia Airlines office. Take a ride up its probing circular tower for a bird's eye view of the city (entrance fee).

Take a walk through **Pasar Chowrasta** (Chowrasta Market), between Lebuh Campbell and Jalan Chowrasta. A wet market with the customary wet market pong, it has a section facing Penang Road that offers the Penang specialities of local biscuits and preserved nutmeg and mango prepared in a wide variety of styles. On Jalan Chowrasta is the row of *nasi kandar* (mixed curry rice) stalls whose food is reputed to be the best in the country.

Food is Penang's favourite export to the rest of the country. Here, hawker centres commandeer every corner, the most famous of which (and you pay the price for it) is on the seaside **Gurney Drive** stretch, open in the evenings. However, wander into the **Pulau Tikus** area behind Jalan Burma, and you pay far less

BELOW: *kachang puteh* or nuts vendor in Pulau Tikus market.

for food that is perhaps twice as good. Pulau Tikus is also the heartland of the *Baba-Nonya*, descendants of Chinese immigrants who married into and absorbed Malay culture, including wearing batik *sarungs* and the adoption of local spices and coconut milk in their unique style of cooking. Also known as *Peranakan* (locally-born) and Straits Chinese, these communities are predominant in the British Straits Settlements states of Penang, Melaka and Singapore.

Temples of incense

Be prepared to get soaking wet if you visit Wat Chayamangkalalam in June, during the Thai Songkran festival. Mischief-makers hurl water-filled plastic bags on passers-by on the pretext of "purifying" them.

The eve of Chinese New Year at the **Penang Buddhist Association** on Jalan Anson is a more formal affair compared to the mad rush of devotees at other temples. Association members busily arrange bright flowers, fruits and coloured cakes on a large, shiny table of blackwood imported from Canton. Enthroned on the high altars are six white marble statues of Lord Buddha and his disciples. Crystal chandeliers from Czechoslovakia hang overhead, and the walls are decorated with paintings depicting Buddha's path to enlightenment. A teenage girl patiently leads her dignified grandfather across the wide marble floor, where a seated congregation chants praises to Lord Buddha.

As temple bells tinkle, the chanting rises to usher in the new year. Outside the front door, beggars sit quietly chatting amongst themselves. They know benevolence is a precept of the Chinese New Year and they receive it passively.

Ordinarily, the large, luminous hallway that dominates the Chinese Buddhist Association is the most serene sanctuary in Penang. The building, completed in 1929, reflects the desire of a Buddhist priest who wanted to indoctrinate his followers with orthodox rites and ceremonies. Joss-stick hawkers or paper-money burners are not found here. Prayers are considered

BELOW: The Thai inspired Wat Chayamangkalaram.

the essence of Buddhist worship, and the association cherishes the simplicity inherent in its Buddhist faith.

The variety of Buddhist worship in Penang is so striking it makes every temple a new experience. One can enter the gigantic meditation hall at **Wat Chayamangkalaram**  and find a workman polishing the left cheek of 32-metre (100-ft) long Reclining Buddha. The *wat*, on Jalan Burma, is a Thai Buddhist monastery. Gigantic *naga* serpents, mystical creatures that link earth to heaven, form the balustrades at the entrance, while fierce-visaged giants tower over the doorways in the role of otherworldly bodyguards.

Another form of Buddhist worship can be seen in the **Burmese Temple** on the other side of the road. A Buddha with a haughty, yet serene expression is worshipped here. Another shrine is surrounded with a moat over which "heavenly" bridges fly. On either side are Buddha images. Little shops in the shaded walkways sell little pink and green lotus flower-shaped candles to worshippers, who leave the lighted candles reverentially in front of the shrines.

Maps:
Area 184
City 186

Naga, or serpent guardian at Wat Chayamangkalaram.

Inspired by a vision

Penang's loftiest temple sits on a hilltop at Air Hitam, 6 km (4 miles) from the Buddhist Association. **Kek Lok Si** , the largest Buddhist temple in Malaysia and one of the largest in the region, owes its existence to Beow Lean, a Chinese Buddhist priest from Fujian province in China who arrived in Penang in 1887. As the resident priest of the Kuan Yin Temple in Lebuh Pitt, so impressed was he by the religious fervour of Penang's Buddhists, that he decided to found a monastery. This hilly site at Air Hitam is supposedly reminiscent of Fujian.

The main buildings were completed in 1904, and the great Pagoda of a

BELOW: joss stick offerings at Kek Lok Si temple.

Million Buddhas, erected in 1930, is dedicated to all manifestations of the Buddha, hence its name. It is renowned for the three architectural styles it contains: a Chinese base, a Thai middle section and a Burmese top.

When completed, in addition to being a centre for Buddhist devotion, Kek Lok Si became an instant tourist attraction. The stone walkway from the base to the top is flanked by arcades of souvenir stalls, and you pay "voluntary" contributions for the privilege of ascending the pagoda.

Kek Lok Si is split into three tiers spread over a rocky incline. The three "Halls of the Great" honour Kuan Yin, goddess of mercy; Bee Lay Hood, the Laughing Buddha; and Gautama Buddha, founder of the faith. It is here that the monks pass their hour in prayer. The Tower of Sacred Books on the topmost tier houses a library of Buddhist scriptures and Sutra, many of which were presented by Emperor Kuang Hsu of China. An edict from the same emperor, cemented into a wall of this block, grants imperial approval to the establishment of the temple.

A 3-km (2-mile) road from Kek Lok Si winds its way up to the **Air Hitam Dam**, with an 18-hectare (45-acre) lake reflecting the lush green foliage of the surrounding jungle. The cool air and steep road is popular with walkers and joggers in the early morning and late evening.

Hill with a view

Jalan Air Hitam also leads to **Bukit Bendera (Penang Hill)** ⓯, established as a quiet getaway in 1897, and saved about 80 years later from large-scale commercialisation by public petition, a rare people-power victory. However, there is little of interest at the top. The best part of the experience is the ride in the

BELOW: the funicular railway at Penang Hill.
RIGHT: the Kek Lok Si Temple.

Swiss-modelled funicular railway (6.30am–9pm; fee). As it climbs, a panorama of the sea, islands, hills and valleys slowly unfolds.

You can also hike up Penang Hill on a trail that starts from the **Waterfall Gardens** ⓰, also known as the Penang Botanic Gardens; if you aren't so keen on the idea of a hot, sweaty trek, you'll enjoy strolling through the gardens. This mature and beautifully-cultivated showcase of tropical plants is about 2 km (1 mile) from Pulau Tikus, with waterfalls that start over a hundred metres above the gardens and cascade through the greenery. On holidays, families round up relatives for a picnic lunch by the stream, while barefoot children romp on the rocks or play follow-the-tourist. Benches are scattered throughout the gardens and provide pleasant resting spots in the shade.

Atop a hill and reached only by a long flight of steps is the Hindu shrine of **Nattukotai Chettiar** ⓱. Every January, this becomes the centre for the Hindu festival of penance, Thaipusam. After a period of fasting, devotees carry devotional *kavadi* structures made of steel, and pierce their flesh with skewers. Many consider the processions here more dramatic and interesting than the one in Kuala Lumpur's Batu Caves. Certainly, more coconuts are smashed in Georgetown's streets, including by non-Hindus, who see no harm in amassing some good luck too.

Feringghi beach

But for many visitors, it is the beach that beckons. Penang's holiday beaches are in the north, from Tanjung Bungah to Batu Feringghi and Teluk Bahang. The road up from Jalan Tanjung Tokong follows the curve of the land, twisting up and around a hill, or skirting the fringe of the sea. Rocky headlands divide the shoreline into small bays and coves, each with a different character and charm. Although the waters are not as clear as on the east coast, the beaches are still popular for swimming and sunbathing.

The northern beaches are self-contained, with no need for visitors to venture down to town. There is the full range of accommodation, from apartments for longer-stay guests, to beachside places for backpackers, and a bus station, post office, clinic, grocery shops and a host of souvenir outlets. At night, the naked bulbs and blaring music of a *pasar malam* (night market) add to the bustle. Car and bicycle hire is available, and most hotels have a free shuttle service to Georgetown; there are plenty of taxis too.

Activities are centred around **Batu Feringghi** ⓲, one of the most popular beach resorts in Southeast Asia. This is where the famous luxury hotels are clustered, including the Minangkabau-roofed Rasa Sayang at the start of the stretch. However, small inns and motels are plentiful too, as well as accommodation offered by villagers. Likewise, the whole range of eateries can be found here, from air-conditioned steak and seafood restaurants to hawker stalls under winking fairy lights.

Yahong Art Gallery opposite the clinic is a storehouse of some of the finest arts, crafts and antiques of Malaysia and China. It is also the home of Chuah Thean Teng, the internationally-acclaimed Father of

Map on page 184

Watch out for pesky monkeys in Penang's Waterfall Gardens, some of which can be aggressive. Feeding them is discouraged but the notice is often disregarded.

BELOW: Batu Feringghi beach.

Cocoa pods are cultivated in Penang. Look out for the bright orange papaya-like fruits.

BELOW:
Giant moth, Penang
Butterfly Farm.

Malaysian batik art. His sons are all talented artists too, and their work is on display and for sale in the gallery.

If Batu Feringghi is too busy for you, 6 km (4 miles) further down the coast is the fine Teluk Bahang beach, dominated by the luxury Mutiara Hotel. En route you'll find the **Pinang Cultural Centre**, where arts and craft demonstrations are given. There is also a dinner-show.

Teluk Bahang has little save a batik factory and other souvenir shops. Further down the road is the **Penang Butterfly Farm** (open 9am–5pm), where large varieties of butterflies and unusual insects are bred. A couple of minutes down the road is a **Forest Recreation Park**, good for a picnic. For more trekking and resort-free beaches, head towards the **Pantai Aceh Forest Reserve** ⑲ where there are trails to Muka Head, a favourite boy-scout camping-spot. At the fishing village at the entrance of the forest reserve, you can arrange for a boat to pick you up. The sea can be choppy though.

The road to Batu Maung goes down the west coast and around the island. Here, a different Penang begins: an agrarian world, quiet, peaceful and thinly populated.

Round the island

As much as the port is Chinese, so is the countryside Malay. The winding and sometimes mountainous round-island road runs for 74 km (46 miles), a journey you can cover in air-conditioned buses with guides, (book through hotels and tour agencies) or rented chauffeured cars with or without guides.

The road through the rolling hills offers striking views of the island dropping to the sea far below. Dense, damp jungles are interspersed with the plan-

tations of pepper, clove and nutmeg that lured Arab, Spanish, Portuguese and other Western traders to this part of the world long ago. When in season, nets are spread out below the *durian* trees in the orchards, to prevent damage to the fruit, which drops when ripe. Visitors throng the temporary roadside stalls, savouring the pungent flesh or haggling over prices.

At Titi Kerawang, there are waterfalls and a serene view of the Indian Ocean. The natural freshwater pool is filled from the waterfalls, and is suitable for bathing, although a big water pipeline mars the scenery.

Kampungs and footprints

As you head south, the scenery gives way to paddy fields. Several small roads branch off to the coast, usually the commercial link between a fishing village and the trunk road. It was in small villages such as these that the few Malays lived when Francis Light established the first settlement.

Although updated with brick, the *kampung* houses look much the same today as they did 100 years ago. If you have your own transport, it is worthwhile turning off into the coconut tree-lined paths to explore a village. Malays are proud of their homes, and many have pretty courtyards planted with flowers and fruit trees. The smiles are inevitably warm, with locals always ready to make your acquaintance.

As you head to the east coast, bustling urbanity starts to rear its head. Turn off to **Batu Maung** ⑳, about 3 km (2 miles) from the Bayan Lepas Airport, and you will reach a shrine built around a footprint in stone, believed to be that of Admiral Cheng Ho, the Chinese Columbus. The well-kept shrine sits in a beautiful Chinese garden that overlooks the jetty and fishing boats of the village.

Map on page 184

BELOW: Malay *kampung* house.

At the Snake Temple, pit vipers are venerated by the Chinese because of their kinship to the mythical dragons of Chinese folklore.

BELOW: Cheng Ho's footprint, Batu Maung.
RIGHT: sunset at Batu Ferringhi.

Villagers believe that Cheng Ho called at this spot on one of his seven voyages to Southeast Asia. On Pulau Langkawi, 96 km (60 miles) further north, is a similar footprint. The two are believed to be a pair, and anyone who lights incense sticks and places them in the urns at the shrine will enjoy good luck and great fortune.

There are a couple of large restaurants here which are famous for their seafood. Walk down from the shrine past the eatery next door, and you'll come to a garden of incongruous statues, ranging from mythical Indian and Chinese gods, to Snow White and the Seven Dwarfs, and the Statue of Liberty. The garden is neglected, which is sad, for the choice and juxtapositioning of these figures is an ironically accurate summary of Malaysian life.

Silicon and sleepy snakes

If you take the right fork from Batu Maung to go north, you will pass behind the airport and cut through the **Bayan Lepas Free Trade Zone**, the Silicon Valley of Malaysia. The huge area of sanitised, unimaginative blocks is the home of high-technology industries, ranging from microchip-manufacturing multinationals such as Intel, to success-hungry export-orientated local giants.

These factories have now completely hemmed in the Temple of Azure Cloud, more popularly known as the **Snake Temple**. Here, venomous pit vipers, doped perhaps by the incense, lie coiled around everything: altars, shrines, incense burners, candlesticks, vases, tables, underfoot and overhead. However, the air of mystery surrounding the temple, and the reason why the reptiles would congregate here has vanished, together with the lush jungle behind it; today the temple is now just another commercial attraction.

A highway runs the length of the east coast from here to Georgetown. This is built on reclaimed land, and Penangites joke about how this has changed the shape of the island; before it resembled a tortoise, whereas now it looks more like a rather pregnant one.

More microchips

The mainland section of Penang state is nearly twice as large as the island, a thriving industrial area built around Seberang Prai (Butterworth) that has become one of the world's leading producers of microchips, disk drives and other computer parts. Both sides of the North-South Highway and the approach to the Penang Bridge are covered with sprawling high-tech factories. Amid the factories, in Seberang Jaya, east of Seberang Prai, is the **Penang Bird Park** (open 9am–7pm), a lush garden with over 200 species of tropical birds from around the world. The birds are all housed in specially designed homes, including a huge walk-in aviary and geodesic domes.

Another patch of green is the 37-hectare (92-acre) **Bukit Mertajam Recreational Park**, about 18 km (11 miles) from the Penang Bridge. It has numerous walking trails for trekkers and rest huts when you tire. Near its entrance is the stark white **St Anne's Church**, a well-preserved 19th-century colonial relic. It is the site of a candlelight procession each year on the Feast of St Anne's. ❑

Map on page 184

KEDAH AND PERLIS

Map on page 158

The most traditionally Malay of the northern states, Kedah and Perlis offer the modern traveller ancient Hindu settlements, lush mountain parks and the carefree resort isle of Langkawi

I t beckoned, a bluish-grey mass which towered in the distance, and so civilisation took root in the land. At 1,200 metres (3,900 ft), Gunung Jerai in the state of Kedah served as a lodestar to early merchant voyagers; it was at its foot that the peninsula's first centre of civilisation established itself.

But Kedah's position at the crossroads of Southeast Asian trade also exposed it to constant danger. Initially controlled by the great trading empires of Funan in Vietnam, and then Sri Vijaya in Sumatra, Kedah later became part of the Melaka sultanate. Until the beginning of the 19th century, Kedah's rulers were remarkably successful in preserving their independence. However, despite having put their faith in British power (and losing Penang in the process), Kedah fell to the Thais, and Perlis had to be given up as well. Both states were transferred to British suzerainty in 1909, but the mainly Malay population somehow managed to maintain their way of life, unlike other peninsula states.

Ancient temples

Unlike the sailors of old from across the Bay of Bengal, modern-day travellers approach **Gunung Jerai** on the North-South Highway through **Sungai Petani**, Kedah's second-largest town and the country's fastest-growing. Close by, at a slower but no less intense pace, one of the largest archaeological sites in the country, dating back to the 5th century, is being uncovered.

After over a century of digging, archaeological finds from the edges of villages, riverbanks and the foot of jungled hills point to many more treasures in the whole area between the **Lembah Bujang (Bujang Valley) ㉑** and **Sungai Muda**. This is the site not only of one of the earliest Hindu settlements in Southeast Asia, but also an earlier Buddhist phase, and there is even the possibility of a prehistoric Malay settlement before that. About 10 ancient *candi* (temples) have been excavated and restored, the largest and best-preserved being the Candi Bukit Batu Pahat (Temple of the Hill of Chiselled Stone). Inscriptions in Sanskrit, porcelain pieces from China, Indian beads, and glassware from the Middle East point to the site's importance as an international entrepot.

The area now comes under the administration of the **Muzium dan Taman Arkeologi Lembah Bujang** (Lembah Bujang Archaeological Park and Museum), whose museum (open 8am–4.30pm) showcases important finds, and has a display of photographs and models. Pretty landscaped paths lead to the four closest restored temples. Guided tours of the site must be pre-arranged (tel: 04-4572005). To get there, exit the North-South Highway at Sungai Petani and head towards Bedong, turning left to Merbok and the

LEFT: Langkawi fishermen heading home.
BELOW: neolithic stone tool from Bujang.

In the predominantly Malay-Muslim states of Kedah and Perlis, men wearing the songkok (fez) on Friday prayer days are a common sight.

museum. Taxis can be chartered from Sungai Petani, but there are no buses.

Beyond Merbok, the road winds prettily on and eventually turns south to **Tanjung Dawai**, a postcard-perfect fishing village on the Muda Estuary. A ferry (but not for cars) crosses the estuary to Pantai Merdeka, a popular beach which can also be reached from Penang by road.

Sungai Petani is also the jump-off point on the spectacular East-West Highway to the peninsula's east coast. The road goes via Baling, overlooked by a spectacular limestone massif, and Grik in Perak, an important post during the communist threat of the 1960s.

The rice capital

To get to the state capital of Alor Setar, head north from Sungai Petani on the highway. Here the country flattens out, and depending on the season, oceans of rippling green or gold or brown fallow ground merge with the distant cloud-flecked hills of the Main Range. This is the country's Rice Bowl, producing half the locally-grown rice. There are biannual harvests, thanks to the massive Muda Irrigation Project, which covers 127,000 hectares (300,000 acres). This is one of the few schemes financed by the World Bank which has fulfilled the aims of its sponsors and provided adequate returns. A much older irrigation canal actually runs alongside the old main road from Gunung Jerai to Alor Setar. Built in the 19th century by Wan Mat Saman, the then *menteri besar* (chief minister), the canal is perfectly straight throughout its long length, a feat achieved by aligning kerosene-fuelled flares.

Alor Setar ㉒ generally serves as a springboard to the holiday isle of Langkawi, but it does have some fine architecture along the main road, Jalan

BELOW: sun-ripened rice paddy fields in Kedah state.

Pekan. The large **Zahir Mosque** (Masjid Zahir), built in 1912, has the graceful colonnades and domes of Moorish tradition. Opposite it is the **Muzium Di-Raja** (Royal Museum), a former palace interesting for its layout as well as its royal family displays, including Sultan Abdul Halim's African animal trophies.

Map on page 158

Sacred orchestra

Next to the museum is the charming Thai-style **Balai Besar** (Great Hall), built in 1898. Used as an audience hall by Kedah's sultans of old to receive public petitions and hear grievances, today it is the site of ceremonial and state functions. The **Balai Nobat** down the road plays a unique function: it houses the instruments (*nobat*) of Kedah's royal orchestra. Comprising a horn, three drums and a gong, only four such orchestras exist in Malaysia today, the others being in Terengganu, Selangor and Johor.

Kedah's is reputedly the oldest, a gift from Melaka's last sultan. The *nobat* is considered sacred and an important part of the regalia of state: no Kedah sultan is considered a legitimate ruler if he has not been installed to the accompaniment of the nobat. The Kedah *nobat* is also played on other state occasions when the sultan is present, and may be heard daily during the Muslim fasting month, when it is played for five minutes before the end of the day's fast from the tower-like Balai Nobat. Permission to see the *nobat* may be obtained through the state secretariat opposite.

Further down Lebuhraya Darul Aman, near the stadium, is the **Muzium Negeri** (State Museum) (open 10am–6pm). This is another Thai-style building, with collections that include Chinese ceramics as well as exhibits from the Bujang Valley.

BELOW: Crown of Kedah monument in the capital, Alor Setar.

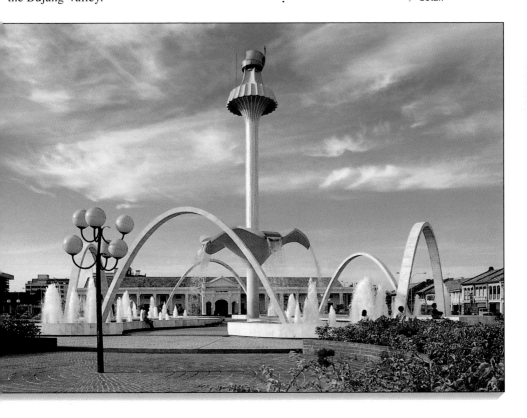

Outside the capital

The highway north of Alor Setar ends in **Bukit Kayu Hitam**, the exit point to Thailand. There is an uninteresting duty-free emporium there, and a market that is popular with locals. About one-and-a-half hours' drive east of the capital is **Pedu Lake** (Tasik Pedu), a dammed lake retreat in peaceful surroundings that attracts anglers and golfers. The road there goes through tiny wooden settlements among rolling oil palm and rubber plantations.

Ikan bawal or pomfret from Kedah's coastal waters

Seafood *a la* spicy Malay style is best at the small fishing village of **Kuala Kedah**, 12 km (7 miles) west of Alor Setar. The local *ikan panggang* (barbecued fish) and chilli crab are favourites, as is the Thai-influenced noodle dish, *laksa*.

On the other side of the river is the well-preserved fort, **Kota Kuala Kedah**, the state's last defence against the invading Thais in 1821. Although Kedah's aristocracy was either killed or taken prisoner within the hour, the fort held out for another six days before it, too, fell. This disaster marked the beginning of 20 years of subjugation to Siamese rule. In the midst of Kuala Kedah's wooden warehouses and fish market is a modern jetty, serving Langkawi's holiday-makers. The Perlis jump-off point to the island, Kuala Perlis, is a busy but not particularly attractive fishing village; it does, however, have some excellent seafood restaurants.

Kuala Perlis is about an hours' drive from **Kangar**, the capital of Malaysia's smallest state. **Perlis** is really an extension of the Kedah plain, but the scenery is even more rustic, the peaceful atmosphere more lulling. Unlike Kedah, stark, limestone outcrops stand like sentinels over the flat rice fields. Spectacular and mysterious, many contain subterranean caves, with flora and fauna unique to limestone habitats. The vegetation here is also more similar to Thailand's, with the canopy turning a golden autumnal brown during the marked dry season.

BELOW: Kuala Perlis is the jumping-off point for Langkawi.

While the North-South Highway ignores Perlis completely, the railway line goes through **Arau**, the royal town. The Malaysian railway system meets its Thai counterpart 50 km (30 miles) north at **Padang Besar**, which has a market that comes alive at weekends. You can also cross into Thailand by road via Padang Besar, but a more spectacular drive is west through the hills to **Kaki Bukit** (literally "the foot of the hill"), a former tin-mining outpost comprising a charming wooden Chinese village. **Gua Kelam**, a tunnel used for mining, is now the area's main attraction although some caves near the Wang Kelian border are being developed for tourism. The road from here goes to Satun in Thailand.

Legendary isle

Once upon a time, **Pulau Langkawi** ㉓ was a sleepy island believed to be under a spell cast by a legendary princess, Mahsuri, who lived in the 14th century and was unfairly executed for adultery. It is largely through the efforts of Kedah-born Prime Minister Mahathir that it has been elevated to the status of international tour destination, complete with direct air links to Germany. Malaysia's Father of Independence, Tunku Abdul Rahman, was also Kedahan, and a large number of political leaders are northerners.

A beautiful limestone cliff and forest archipelago of over 100 islands, some of which are mere rocks that vanish at high tide, Langkawi is being marketed as a modern-day legend. Ferries service the main island between 8am–6pm from Kuala Perlis at hourly intervals (40-minute journey), Kuala Kedah every 90 minutes (1-hour journey), and once a day from Penang (2½-hour journey). Boats also go to Satun in Thailand four times a day. During the monsoon months of July to September, seas can be choppy, and services may be cancelled. Malaysia Airlines operates daily flights from Alor Setar, Penang, Kuala Lumpur and Singapore Airlines from Singapore (the Munich connection is via LTU International Airways).

Maps:
Area 158
Island 206

Perlis is the only Malaysian state whose royal leader is known as Rajah rather than Sultan.

Tax-free shopping

Langkawi's duty-free status has succeeded in injecting life into the island. From the jetty to the main town, **Kuah Ⓐ**, nearly every shop is crammed with chocolates, electronic items and household goods. Not all items are a bargain, but alcohol and cigarettes are exempt from Malaysia's heavy "sin" taxes on Langkawi; however, visitors are only allowed to bring out 1 litre of alcohol and a carton of cigarettes after a minimum stay of 72 hours. The old market is a good place to buy Indonesian batik and Chinese-made towels. Trendy craft shops are moving in with hand-painted fabrics and Asian curios.

Yet more shops sit on the reclaimed land which starts right next to the jetty. Here you'll see an enormous statue of an eagle; among the many interpretations of its name, Langkawi is thought to derive from the word *helang*, Bahasa Malaysia for "eagle". The statue of the majestic creature about to soar is a powerful allegory, one might say, for the tremendous success of the island resort.

LEFT: a Langkawi resort at sunset.
BELOW: a fisherman waits for a bite.

There is a range of hotels and good seafood restaurants at Kuah, but the more enjoyable option is to find accommodation at one of the island's many beaches, and head into town for a spot of shopping.

Coves, coral and caves

Langkawi has good roads that go round the island. Cars and motorbikes can be hired at the jetty, in town or Pantai Cenang, the most popular beach. Alternatively, book yourself into a half-day guided tour with any tour agency at Kuah. Most visitors head for **Pantai Cenang B** in the southwest, an hour from Kuah by bus and less by taxi. The beach here is lined with places to stay, while opposite are restaurants, souvenir shops, and yet more accommodation. There is something for every budget, from the luxury Pelangi Beach Resort, to rooms in well-tended gardens and A-frame huts.

The road leads south to **Pantai Tengah C**, which is quieter and more upmarket, but doesn't have such a nice beach. The road ends at a new marina resort

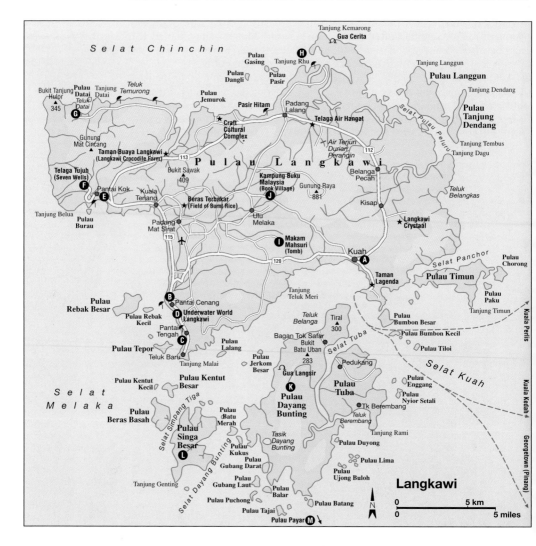

and an awful bowling and cinema complex at **Teluk Baru** (literally New Bay), built on, yes, reclaimed land. En route to Pantai Tengah is **Underwater World Langkawi ⓓ** (open 10am–8pm) which showcases over 5,000 sea and fresh-water species. One highlight is a 15-metre (50-ft) glass tunnel within a giant salt-water tank with larger species such as sharks, stingrays and turtles.

At the upper end of Cenang is the **Muzium Padi** (Rice Museum), which cel-ebrates the staple of the Langkawi folk. Further past the airport, the road winds through lush forest and you are suddenly met by a gorgeous view of the beach – breathtaking, especially at sunset. This is **Pantai Kok ⓔ**, a quiet stretch set dramatically against black jagged peaks cut out against the sky. The backpack-ers have been moved on, leaving only moderately-priced hotels.

Head towards the peaks, which are part of the Gunung Mat Cincang moun-tain range. The road ends in a trail to **Telaga Tujuh ⓕ** (Seven Wells). Legend has it that the mountain fairies come to this series of pools to bathe and wash their long hair with tree roots and sweet plants. However, they vanish at the sight of a human, leaving behind a fragrant and lingering perfume, which you may or may not catch a whiff of when you're bathing in its cool waters. Note, however, that the pools evaporate in the dry season.

Rock of ages

The Mat Cincang formation is the oldest rock in the peninsula, and a good look at the sedimentary structure can be had at the end of the road at **Teluk Datai ⓖ** in the north. Datai is the location of the exclusive resort called The Datai, an award-winning Balinese-influenced resort with a golf course and private beach. Another exclusive resort is at the mangrove stretch of **Tanjung Rhu ⓗ**, further

Map on page 206

Langkawi villager weaving nipah palms for roof thatching.

BELOW: Pantai Kok, Langkawi.

east, which has scenic views. Gua Cerita across the straits is rather overrated as a cave attraction; try the rest of the 24 caves that dot the islands, including **Gua Kelawar** (Bat Cave) in the southeast, set among mangroves and **Gua Tanjung Dendang** on Pulau Dayang Bunting.

Outside the glitzy tourist beaches, Langkawi's predominantly Malay population of 43,000 maintain their peaceful agrarian lifestyle in much the same way they did before their home was catapulted into the limelight. The older *kampung* folk do not participate in the tourism industry – hotel staff are overwhelmingly from the mainland – and visitors are generally ignored, particularly in December during the Lima maritime and aerial exhibition when there is not a single free room to be found on the island.

From Tanjung Rhu, continue along the road to Kuah for about 5 km (3 miles) to reach **Durian Perangin Waterfalls** (Air Terjun Durian Perangin), which, unlike Telaga Tujuh, never runs dry. Back on the main road, another turning to the left goes to Barn Thai, a unique Thai restaurant in the middle of a mangrove swamp that features live acts.

Bookworms' paradise

From Kuah, head west to go inland for 12 km (7 miles) to reach the tomb of **Makam Mahsuri (Mahsuri's Tomb)** ❶ (open 8am–6pm, entrance fee), which honours this local heroine; her tomb has in fact become a shrine, and locals believe that anyone visiting Langkawi must pay their respects here when they visit the island. On a parallel road sits the **Kampung Buku Malaysia (Book Village)** ❷ (open 9.30am–6pm), a collection of eight bookshops beautifully set among trees and a babbling brook. The bookshops are in traditional Malay

TIP

Tanjung Rhu is probably the last place you can get *mee gulung*, a Langkawi speciality dish on the verge of extinction due to the high cost of *udang galah* (tiger prawns).

BELOW: Durian Perangin waterfalls.

LEGENDARY PLACE NAMES

Langkawi's legends are legion and often more interesting than the places they celebrate. The "main" tale concerns Mahsuri, accused of adultery by the jealous chief's wife. At her execution, white blood spurted out, confirming her innocence. Before she died, Mahsuri laid a curse upon the island's next seven generations.

Immediately after, the Thais attacked Langkawi, and the villagers at **Padang Mat Sirat** burned their rice fields rather than let it fall into Siamese hands – few grains remain at **Beras Terbakar** (Field of Burnt Rice).

A Romeo and Juliet-type legend is behind several other place names. A union between a couple was refused by the girl's parents, and in a family feud, pots and pans were thrown at **Belanga Pecah** (broken pots). The gravy jug landed at **Kuah** (gravy), while jugs of boiling water formed the **Telaga Air Hangat** hot springs. The fighting ended when the two fathers were transformed into mountains – **Gunung Raya** and **Gunung Mat Cincang**.

Tasik Dayang Bunting got its name after a Kedah princess, forbidden to marry her lover, fell pregnant after drinking from the lake. The angry king banished her to the island where she drowned herself in the lake and became a rock.

buildings, and specialise in antique and second-hand books, particularly Asian and Islamic texts. You can also access the Internet from these stores. When you return to Cenang, take the southern coastal road, Jalan Bukit Malut, to enjoy some spectacular views.

Langkawi's maze of islands is full of secret channels, narrows, inlets and bays. Shadowed cliffs, topped by dense virgin jungle, reach up to 600 metres (2,000 ft) and drop abruptly into the sea. Three are inhabited by fishermen, the sea gypsies, and it is also obvious why pirates who preyed upon the trading ships in the Straits of Melaka sought refuge here.

Pulau Dayang Bunting Ⓚ, the second-largest island of the group, has a unique deep fresh- and salt-water lake, whose ice-cold waters are believed to aid conception. (Its name translates as Island of the Pregnant Maiden). Next to it is a bird and animal sanctuary, **Pulau Singa Besar** Ⓛ, an interesting hilly island with a boardwalk that meanders through mangrove, sandy and rocky coastline. Sun-soakers can enjoy the gorgeous beaches on some of the other islands, including **Pulau Bras Basah**. Boats from Tanjung Rhu, Pantai Cenang and Kuah tour these islands in about 4 hours, but you have to book the whole eight-seater speedboat. The Langkawi Yacht Club at Kuah also does sunset tours.

Marine life is richest at **Pulau Payar** Ⓜ, a marine park, one bumpy hour by boat from the main island. While underwater visibility is rarely more than 3 metres (10 ft), it has lots of life, including sharks that come right up to shore, encouraged by hand-feeding visitors, and colourful soft coral blooms on wrecks in deeper waters. Book with dive operators on the mainland, or if you're interested in snorkelling and a picnic, any boat operator. There are also dive sites at the neighbouring islets of Segantang, Kaca and Lembu. ❑

Map on page 206

In Mawat village is the tomb of Princess Mahsuri, who, falsely accused of adultery, took her own life.

BELOW: legendary lake in Pulau Dayang Bunting.

THE SOUTHERN PENINSULA

Village and city, ancient and modern – the contradictions are more obvious in the south than elsewhere

Standing as it does today at the silted rivermouth, it is barely conceivable that tiny Melaka (Malacca) once ruled world trade, and was responsible for the spread of Islam throughout the Malay peninsula. Although the world still congregates at Melaka, these days it is to gawp at its ruins and relics, and to ride in its riverboats, while the main trade with local merchants is in cheap souvenirs and T-shirts.

Melaka is the undisputed top tourist draw of the southern stretch of the peninsula's west coast. To keep the tourists coming, and coming back, the state takes great pains to keep its artefacts dusted, and monuments spruced up. The authorities have also "developed" newer attractions in other parts of the states, particularly in Ayer Keroh.

It was under the benign rule of Melaka that the people of the neighbouring Negeri Sembilan were able to remain true to the traditions and customs of their native Sumatra; this is most visible today in their architecture, notably the large sweeping roofs reminiscent of buffalo horns. Like Melaka and Johor, the rural parts of the state comprise clusters of charming *kampung* with neat front yards, orchards bursting with local fruit, and a lovely lazy air.

But Negeri Sembilan is no backwater. The state is setting itself up to tap the land and labour needs of the fast-developing Klang Valley. The imminent arrival of the new national nucleus of government and IT industries, and the new aviation hub of Sepang, right on the Selangor-Negeri Sembilan border, offers further opportunities for the state.

Johor has reaped the economic benefits of its prime location next to Singapore. Besides road, rail and shipping links, a pipeline carries precious water to the island nation, a point of contention which crops up whenever there are differences between the two countries. Vast tracts of Johor are made over to rubber, oil palm and pineapple plantations; the state is a prime producer of these goods.

Johor's towns are relatively uninteresting, except perhaps for Muar, which bears a striking resemblance to Melaka – it was to this rivermouth port that the last Sultan of Melaka fled from the Portuguese. Inland, however, is the Endau-Rompin National Park (Johor), a magnificent swathe of primeval rainforest set aside for conservation and nature-based tourism. ❏

PRECEDING PAGES: Melaka village tykes.
LEFT: harvesting oil palm at one of numerous plantations that dot Johor state.

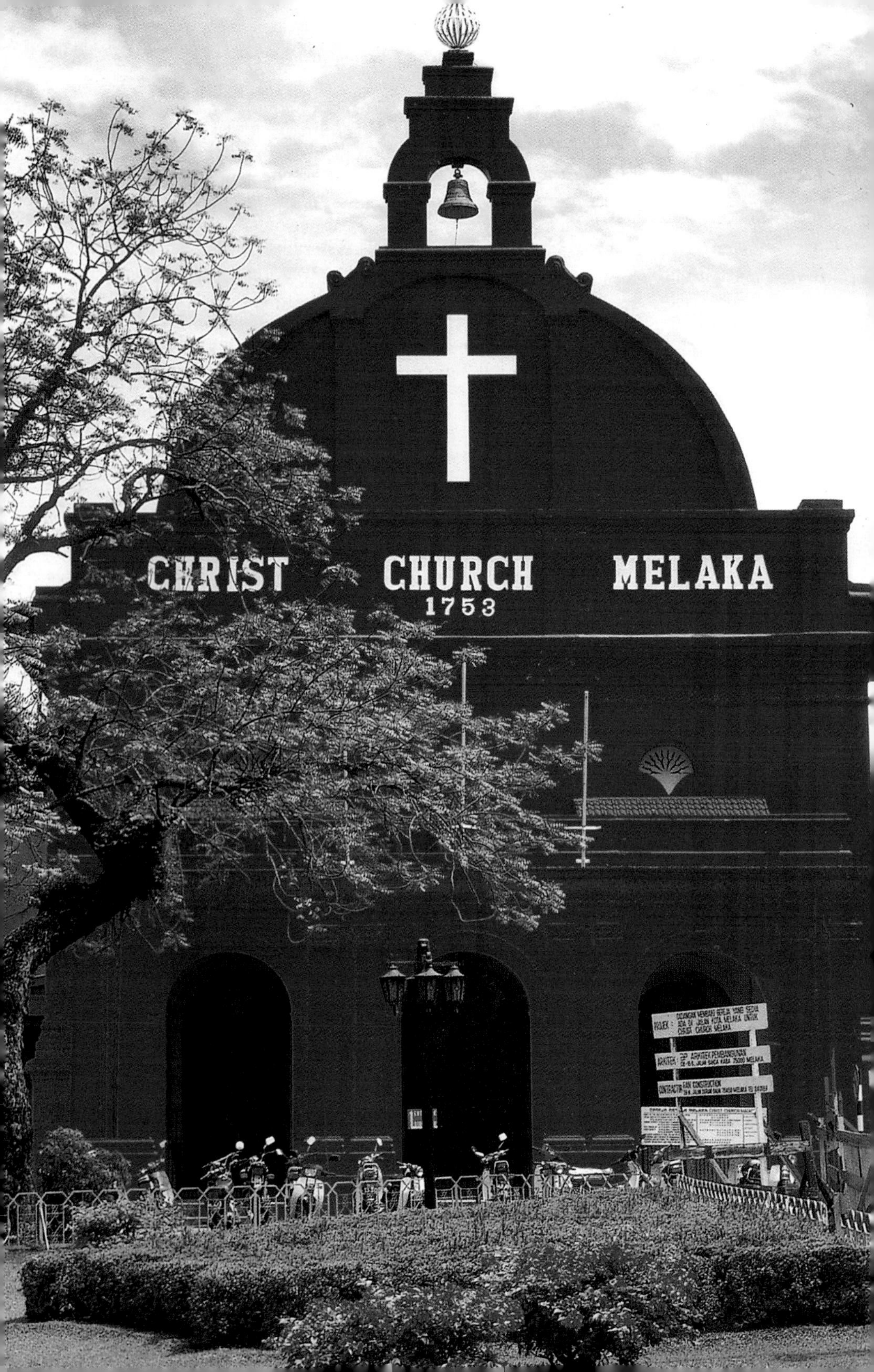
CHRIST CHURCH MELAKA
1753

MELAKA

Map on page 216

The site of both the first settlement on the peninsula in the 1400s, and of the declaration of Independence in 1957, Melaka can truly be called the birthplace of Malaysia

History is everywhere in **Melaka (Malacca)** ; peeping out from odd corners, hinting truths from epitaphs, outlined in the weathered face of a fisherman. Melaka is a town with a glorious past; about four centuries ago, a Portuguese chronicler and frequent visitor said, "Whosoever holds Malacca has Venice by the throat". However, that golden grip lasted a mere 100 years. Today Melaka is in a grip of another kind. Every weekend, you'd be hard pressed to find local car licence plates among the Singaporean vehicles that jam the narrow streets. And often, among the ruins of ancient buildings, are radiant white-gowned brides posing alongside patient grooms – photos for perpetuity where the now has been eternal for centuries.

Glory days

In the 1400s, Melaka was a small settlement of sea gypsies, scraping a living as fishermen and farmers. Then Parameswara arrived, a Malay prince fleeing from his own invaded domain of Tumasek, Sumatra. While out hunting in the area, he encountered a tiny *kancil* (mousedeer) which managed to intimidate his dogs; he took this as a sign that this should be the site of his new capital.

By the end of the 15th century, Melaka had become the centre of a great trading empire and held an undisputed claim over the southern Malay peninsula, as well as East Sumatra opposite. From every seafaring nation they came – Persians, Arabs, Tamils, and Bengalis from the west; Javanese, Sundanese and Sulus from the archipelago; Chinese, Thais, Burmese, and Khmers – in search of profit through trade, piracy or plunder. Each in turn left something of their culture behind.

The small colony of Chinese merchants, in particular, stayed behind to found the Peranakan community, which has become one of the most striking and colourful Chinese fraternities in Malaysia today. The Baba men and Nonya women (or Straits-born Chinese) are descendants of the Chinese pioneers who accepted the practical realities of living in a Malay community, but upheld the social and religious norms of their forefathers in Fujian.

It was also through Melaka that the Islamic faith came to Malaysia. Malays have been Muslims since the second half of the 15th century, when rich Moorish merchants from Pasai in Sumatra settled in Melaka. From here Islam spread throughout the peninsula, and eventually to its neighbouring islands.

Geography was responsible for Melaka's multicultural history. Located at the mouth of the Melaka River, astride the maritime route linking the Indian Ocean with the South China Sea, it was at Melaka that the monsoon winds met. Sturdy junks from China

LEFT: Melaka's crimson Christ Church.
BELOW: a Melakan Baba merchant.

TIP

Trishaw drivers
actually make fine
guides, as they know
the sights and speak
English. Not only
might you learn that
the Portuguese came
"a much much long
time ago" but also that
along the seafront
there is a great stall
that sells some of the
best fried *mee hoon*
(vermicelli) in
Malaysia.

and Japan, loaded with silk, porcelain and silver, were driven up the Straits of Melaka by the northeast monsoon. Likewise, the traders from the Indonesian archipelago, with their crafts, spices and sandalwood. At the port, their cargo was exchanged for Indian and Middle Eastern cloth, carpets, glassware, iron and jewellery. When the winds changed, the southwest monsoon assisted the same vessels to return to their homes.

Taking note of this, the West decided that they should assume control of the hub of this lucrative trading operation, and Melaka's golden age came to an end when it fell in 1511 to the Portuguese. The port was theirs for more than 100 years, before they were ousted by the Dutch. After 150 years of occupation, the Dutch in turn ceded the land to the British.

Reflections of a river

Melaka's past is contained within its 1-km (½ mile) historic centre, easily covered on foot or by a leisurely trishaw ride through the narrow streets. The best place to begin your tour is right in the town centre, near the bridge built on the site the Portuguese made their final successful assault on the town. There you will find the helpful Tourist Information Centre (open 9am–4.30pm, tel: 06-2836538), where you can grab maps, brochures and also book the excellent 45-minute river cruise up **Sungai Melaka** – at high tide, the boats depart hourly from 10am from the jetty behind the centre or the Heeren Street jetty on the opposite bank.

At the jetty are battered junks whose high bows and raised poop decks stir thoughts of their distant cousins who once brought Admiral Cheng Ho's dragon court entourage from China to Melaka all those centuries ago. These days, the

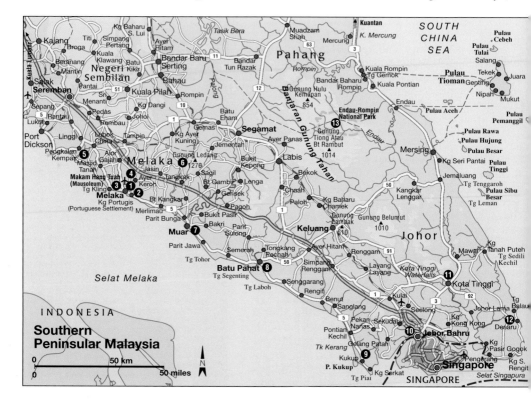

labourers crossing the narrow gangplanks carry no exotic spices or silks, but instead lug the bulky sacks of charcoal that fire the aroma-filled kitchens of Melaka. The river cruise goes past century-old townhouses and warehouses, and ends in a traditional Malay village.

Dutch shapes

If you're hot-footing it, try and get hold of a map of the Heritage Trail, which takes you through the main sights. On the east riverbank is a neat little square with a clock tower, surrounded by terracotta-red buildings and a church. They are distinctly Dutch; you almost expect to see tulips rather than tropical blooms in the flower pots.

Facing what is sometimes known as the Red Square, is the **Stadthuys (Town Hall)** Ⓐ (open 9am–6pm; entrance fee). This building, constructed of incredibly thick walls and massive hardwood doors supported by studded, wrought-iron hinges, served as government offices for more than 300 years. Today, it houses the **History Museum**, which tells the story of the city from the time it was an ancient Malay kingdom to the present. The museum's collections include old coins and stamps, Portuguese costumes from the 16th century, and old sepia photographs of Melaka life. The Stadthuys itself is an antiquity. Erected in 1650, it is the oldest known Dutch building still standing in Asia. The handsome **General Post Office** on Jalan Laksamana is also of Dutch origin, and is now the **Youth Museum**.

On the embankment near the entrance to the Stadthuys is an ancient memorial whose significance has been lost in time. The stone fish with an elephant's head is believed to be a Hindu legacy predating even the Melakan sultanate.

Maps:
Area 216
City 218

Dutch-built Stadthuys or Town Hall dates back to 1660.

LEFT:
European-inspired architecture.
BELOW: Melaka River.

Perpendicular to the Stadthuys is the fabled **Christig Church ❸** whose bricks were shipped all the way from Holland. Melaka's masons then faced them with local red laterite. The church is full of old, engraved tombstones, many telling a grim tale about the hardships the early European settlers faced. The immense rafters within the nave were each carved from a single tree and above the altar a wooden crucifix hangs from the iron hoops fastened to the wall. When the church was first in use, it had no pulpit. The pastor would sit in a chair that had ropes running to the hoops. When the time came for him to deliver his sermon, his sextons would winch him halfway up the wall.

Outside the church is the century-old **Tan Beng Swee Clock Tower**, presented to the town by the wealthy Tan family. The small water fountain nearby was built to commemorate the Diamond Jubilee of Queen Victoria. Four white *kancil* (mousedeer) surround the fountain – a reminder of Melaka's origins.

Formidable fortress

The only remnants of original Portuguese architecture are on the slopes of St Paul's Hill, behind the square. When the Portuguese conquered Melaka, they were determined to make it one of the mightiest strongholds in the Orient. Hundreds of slaves and captives hauled stones from demolished mosques and elaborate tombs to build the **A Famosa** fortress.

The fortress eventually enclosed the entire hill, and withstood attacks for 150 years, until it was finally breached in 1641 by the Dutch after an 8-month siege. However, the Dutch did not find a rich and prosperous port of the fabulous East, as they had expected. The city they had struggled so hard to conquer lay in near-total ruins. The Dutch lost no time putting things in order, rebuilding the

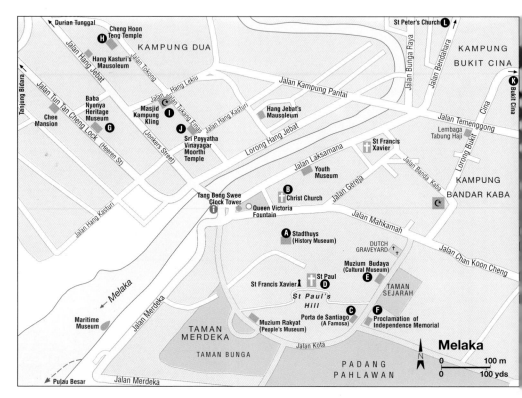

Map on page 218

city with a Dutch flavour, and repairing the fortress and renaming the bastions. Melaka was soon a well-defended port once again.

Unfortunately, when the British occupied Melaka at the beginning of the 19th century, they decided to blow up the fortifications to prevent the Dutch from reclaiming it. The walls and gates were badly damaged and all that was left is what stands today: the **Porta de Santiago C** – a gate without a wall.

At the top of St Paul's Hill are more ruins. In 1521, a chapel, later renamed **St Paul's Church D**, was built by a Portuguese *fidalgo* to fulfil a vow he made on escaping death in the South China Sea. It was later taken over by the Jesuits, who completed the building and painted it white, so that it could serve as a guidepost for ships out on the Straits. The famous Jesuit missionary St Francis Xavier conducted mass in the church during his several visits to Melaka. After his death near Canton, his body was interred there for some months before being taken to Goa in India.

The Dutch discontinued services in St Paul's Church when their own Christ Church was built. However, the engraved tombstones that line the inside walls are testament to its continued use as a place of burial thereafter.

Mahmud's palace

At the bottom of the hill is an elaborate reconstruction of Sultan Mahmud's 15th-century wooden palace as described in the *Sejarah Melayu* (*Malay Annals*). This is the **Muzium Budaya (Melaka Cultural Museum) E**, which displays aspects of Melaka's royal culture, including clothing, weapons and furniture, as well as a diorama of the court (open 9am–6pm; entrance fee). More museums lie around the west side of St Paul's Hill.

The remains of Jesuit missionary St Francis Xavier were temporarily interred in Melaka's St Paul's Church after his death in 1552.

BELOW: what is left of the Portuguese A Famosa fort.

A Peranakan Townhouse

The front of the house is so decorative, it is like a heady visual perfume: brightly-coloured tiles, wooden shutters, large gold Chinese characters on the black signboard, and those elaborate doors. It is distinctly Oriental, but the floral plaster motifs look Western. And yet the whole is unified. This is the Peranakan townhouse.

Described as Chinese Palladian, the architectural style of these buildings of the Malaysian Straits Chinese is a unique meld of Victorian, Chinese and Malay. Lining the streets of Melaka's old town, they are also found in Penang's back streets and in selected nooks of Singapore. But the Melaka buildings are among the oldest townhouses in the country, dating back to the 17th century. Those along Jalan Tan Cheng Lock are particularly elaborate because they were status symbols for their affluent owners.

The houses have two sets of doors. The main wooden doors, with their intricately carved panels, are left open during the day to let air in. The second outer set, are swinging half-doors based on the Malay *pintu pagar* (literally, fence door). On either side are large square windows with vertical bars and sometimes shutters. Above the windows are air vents, which are sometimes decorated.

A Peranakan townhouse is much longer than its entrance suggests. In fact, it can be seven times longer than it is wide. The centrepiece of the main or reception hall is usually an altar, large and beautifully carved. More likely than not, the deity among the candles and burning joss-sticks would be the white-robed Kwan Yin, goddess of mercy, flanked by tall vases of fresh chrysanthemums which are replenished daily.

Twin arched entrances lead to the sitting room. The main furniture would usually be imported blackwood furniture inlaid with mother-of-pearl and marble. These are usually set against the walls, from where portraits of ancestors in gilded frames peer down.

Behind the sitting room is the dining room and, right at the back, the huge kitchen. In between would be one or more courtyards or air wells to let light into the otherwise dark house. The courtyards serve as indoor gardens with potted plants, a fountain, and a well or large ornate jar filled with water.

The bedrooms sit upstairs at the top of a wooden staircase with balusters. The rooms and bathrooms are capacious and carry through the elements of carved lacquered wood, embroidery, and porcelain. Sometimes, the bedrooms have windows that open into the landing, complete with shutters.

Many of these beautiful houses are being restored and renovated for commercial purposes. The best preserved, complete with furniture and ornaments, is probably the Baba-Nonya Heritage Museum on Jalan Tun Tan Cheng Lock. Others have been converted into hotels or restaurants, dishing up spicy Nonya food with varying degrees of success. For the times the food does not live up to its fame, the old-world ambience usually manages to make up for it. ❑

LEFT: the ancestral altar is often the focal point of a traditional Peranakan home.

The **Proclamation of Independence Memorial**  (open 9am–6pm; closed Monday) is housed in the former Malacca Club House, a 1911 Dutch building which was the centre of British colonial social life. Its displays chart Malaysia's campaign for independence, including historic documents, films and artefacts. An obelisk outside commemorates British soldiers killed in the Naning War, a farcical affair in the early 1830s, which took two military expeditions over two years to subdue Penghulu Dol Said, the defiant chief of the principality of Naning. The local hero is commemorated at his birthplace (*see page 226*).

The museums face the **Padang** (town green) where Tunku Abdul Rahman first announced Malaya's independence from British rule. Today, it is the scene of a nightly sound-and-light show that recounts the history of Melaka. It also serves as the "walking track" for traditional Melaka bullock carts (RM1 per person). Beside the *padang*, a lane flanked by handicraft stalls leads to a row of food-stalls across from the huge Mahkota Parade shopping mall. Between the park and the river is the disappointing **Melaka Maritime Museum** (open 9am–9pm). Its contents are mainly artefacts gleaned from shipwrecks in the Melaka Straits.

Map on page 218

Detail from an ornate wall tile of a typical Peranakan house. Antique tiles such as these are on sale at Melaka's Jonkers Street.

Antique streets

Head back to the bridge near the Red Square, and cross over to a completely different experience. The west bank has always been the main centre of Melaka's shopping and business activities; a maze of ancient and narrow streets. **Jalan Tun Tan Cheng Lock** – called Heeren Street by the Dutch – is named after a leading Baba politician and architect. His family house and the palatial town-houses of several other prominent Chinese families line the street, flaunting Peranakan tiles and carved wooden doors.

BELOW: Melaka's Baba Museum.

At No. 48–50 is the fascinating **Baba Nyonya Heritage Museum**  (open 10am–4.30pm Saturday–Wednesday; 9am–12pm Thursday), where you can explore the unique interior of a typical Peranakan house. The family which owns the house gives guided tours and can tell fascinating stories about some of the architecture and curios, including blackwood tables and chairs from China and the sumptuous traditional wedding costumes.

Parallel to this road is Jalan Hang Jebat, better-known as **Jonkers Street**, Melaka's main tourist drag. The street contains every imaginable trade, and a few others besides: spirits importers, hairdressers, wooden shoe stores, coffin makers, apothecaries with Chinese herbs on display, signwriters, an acupuncture clinic, furniture makers, and increasingly, souvenir shops and restaurants.

Above all, however, Jonkers Street is antique haven. There are heavy brass irons with receptacles for hot coals, wooden bullock carts, ornate oil lamps, Peranakan-style furniture inlaid with mother of pearl, opium beds and altar stands, Victorian clocks and early gramophones, brass urns and marble statues, silver trinkets and Chinese wedding beds, as well as rare stamps and coins, and Malay *keris* (daggers).

On yet another parallel road, **Jalan Tokong**, are three of the oldest places of worship in Malaysia. The **Cheng Hoon Teng Temple** , or Temple of Bright

Kuih lapis, a multi-coloured Peranakan dessert made of rice flour, coconut cream and sugar.

Clouds was founded in 1645 and is the oldest Chinese temple in Malaysia. It was originally built by a fugitive from the Manchu conquest, and was later restored and embellished by local Chinese leaders. The temple is dedicated to three deities: the main altar to Kuan Yin, the goddess of mercy, and the others to Kwan Ti (also known as Kwan Kung), the god of war who "triples" up as the patron saint of wealth and tradesmen; and Ma Choe Poh, the Queen of Heaven. Look up and you will see that the carved roof, ridges and eaves are elegantly decorated with exquisite Chinese mythical figures, animals, birds and flowers, of coloured glass and porcelain. Step through the massive hardwood gates, and you feel you are stepping back several centuries. Among the wood carvings and lacquerwork within is a stone inscription commemorating Admiral Cheng Ho's visit to Melaka in 1406.

Mosques and temples

Along the same road, now called Jalan Tukang Emas, is the **Masjid Kampung Kling (Kampung Kling Mosque) ❶**, the town's oldest mosque, built in 1748. It sports a typical Sumatran design, with a three-tiered roof and rather Chinese-like minaret. This style is characteristic of Melakan mosques. (Another good example is the mosque in Tranquerah, 2 km (1 mile) away.) The cemetery encloses the tomb of Sultan Husain of Johor, who ceded Singapore to Sir Stamford Raffles in 1819.

Nearby is the **Sri Poyyatha Vinayagar Moorthi Temple ❷**, built in the 1780s by the Hindu community of Melaka. The country's oldest Hindu temple, it is dedicated to Vinayagar or Ganesh, the Elephant God, one of the most popular deities among Malaysian devotees.

BELOW: Antique Peranakan silver belt.

A princess's legacy

There is another historical hill, a little away from the historic centre – which houses 12,000 graves. Hills are auspicious burial grounds, according to the principles of *feng shui* (Chinese geomancy), for they block evil winds and offer the spirits of the ancestors a good view over their descendants. But while most names and dates on the tombstones on **Bukit Cina (China Hill)**  have been eroded, what remains eternal is the legacy of a Ming princess.

Map on page 218

When Sultan Mansur Shah was in power, he carried on a diplomatic war of wits with the Emperor of China, which grew to be legendary. Around 1460, a Chinese ship sailed into Melaka's port. The entire interior of the vessel was delicately pinned with gold needles, and the message to the sultan read: "For every gold needle, I have a subject; if you could count their number, then you would know my power."

The sultan was impressed. He sent back a ship stuffed with bags of sago and the message: "If you can count the grains of sago on this ship you will have guessed the number of my subjects correctly, and you will know my power." This so moved the Chinese emperor that he sent his daughter Hang Li Poh, to marry the sultan. She arrived with no less than 500 ladies-in-waiting. The sultan gave them "the hill without the town" as a private residence and promised that the land they occupied would never be taken away from them. To this day, Bukit Cina belongs to Melaka's Chinese community. Several of the graves on Bukit Cina date back to the Ming dynasty and are among the oldest Chinese relics in Malaysia.

The princess's followers built a well at the foot of the hill, whose waters soon became as legendary as her marriage contract. After Admiral Cheng Ho drank from the well, its water attained an extraordinary purity. It never dried up, even during the most severe drought, and many believed that if a visitor drank from it he would return to Melaka before he died. Now the **Perigi Rajah** (Sultan's Well) is protected by wire mesh. It has still not dried up and is as pure as ever. Many young Chinese still come to see the landmark and snap some pictures.

Head northwest from here to get to Jalan Bendahara and **St Peter's Church** ❶. The church was built in 1710 by the descendants of Portuguese soldiers given amnesty by the Dutch when the Portuguese garrison was forced into submission.

Today, except for the occasional wedding or funeral, not much goes on at the church. However, on Easter weekends, Melaka-born Catholics try to return to their hometown to attend the mass at St Peter's. On Good Friday itself, thousands of people – Chinese, Eurasian and Indian – take part in a candlelit procession. A life-sized statue of Christ, crowned with thorns and draped in deep purple robes with gold embroidery, is solemnly borne above the devout Catholic congregation. The churchyard becomes a sea of flames from the lighted candles, accompanied by the mournful sound of hymns. After the solemnity of the mass, the crowds gather outside the church to catch up with friends, and children in their Sunday best romp around the lawns.

BELOW: painted temple door, Melaka.

The Portuguese today

The legacy the Portuguese left behind is of far greater significance than mere ruins like the A Famosa fort. "I gave to each man his horse, a house, and land," wrote Alfonso d'Albuquerque in 1604, when he reported with pride to Portugal that 200 mixed marriages had taken place.

On direct orders from the king, d'Albuquerque encouraged the garrison's men to marry local women. Such intermarriages flourished and soon women were even sent out from Portugal to marry local men. The Portuguese were instructed to treat local people as equals; d'Albuquerque himself would courteously escort local women to their seats in church, as though they were members of the nobility.

Therefore, the descendants of Sequiera, Aranjo, Dias, d'Silva and d'Souza remained loyal to Portugal through blood ties and religion. After 400 years, a number of Portuguese Eurasians in Melaka still continue to speak Cristao, a medieval southeastern Portuguese dialect spoken nowhere else now.

At the **Portuguese Settlement (Kampung Portugis)** ❷, 3 km (2 miles) from Melaka's centre, near the beach, there's a community of about 500 Eurasians, mostly fishermen. Their unpretentious dwellings resemble Malay kampung houses with wooden walls and tin roofs, in soft hues of blue and green.

There is little of commercial tourist value here, except for restaurants that serve Portuguese food and cultural performances on Saturdays. But linger and you just might meet young boys who sing beautiful ballads in Portuguese; their sisters could well show you a dance which their grandmother was taught by her grandmother; and an old man at a fruit stall might tell tales about a secluded tunnel from St John's Fort to St Paul's Hill, in which the Portuguese hid all their treasures before the Dutch overran Melaka.

BELOW: Portuguese relic from Melaka's early days.

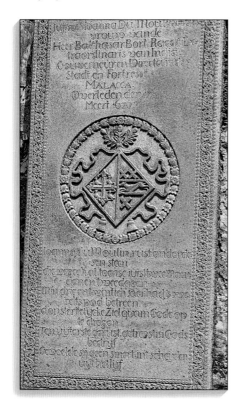

Some of the best places to meet local people are in the open-air cafés around **Portuguese Square** (Medan Portugis), which serve spicy seafood dishes and ice-cold beer.

Local customs

Each year in June, at the Festa de San Pedro, the fishermen decorate their boats with bunting and sacred texts. An open-air mass is conducted and after the boats have been blessed, the evening is spent in merrymaking. Another unusual custom called Intrudu (Introductions) is celebrated on the Sunday preceding Ash Wednesday, when the residents wear fancy costumes and throw water over one another. Even those at home are not spared. The merrymakers make a point of visiting their friends at home, and drenching them with water as soon as they open their doors. To show there are no hard feelings, they are then invited in for refreshments. Later in the day, men dress up as ladies and the ladies dress as men, and go around selling cakes and fruits.

Beyond Melaka town, paddy fields stretch into the low hills and numerous side roads cut through groves of rubber and fruit trees, and past peaceful villages and compact market towns. Traditional Malay houses, with curving gables, carved eaves, wide-fronted verandahs and tiled entrance steps are commonplace all the way from Tanjung Kling in the north to Merlimau in the south. The house of the Penghulu (chief) of **Kampung Merlimau** is a particularly fine specimen of this architecture, boasting delicate wood carvings and art nouveau tiles. It is sometimes open to visitors if the owners are in the mood.

Tanjung Kling, about 10 km (6 miles) from Melaka, has a resort but beach-lovers are not advised to flock to it. You'll find some luxury, resort-style condominiums here, but the sea is not very clean and is sometimes infested with jellyfish. The northern beach of Tanjung Bidara suffers similar problems. However, the seafood is generally good, particularly at Klebang Besar and further north at Pantai Kundor.

Between Tanjung Kling and Pantai Kundor is **Hang Tuah's Mausoleum (Makam Hang Tuah)** ❸. Hang Tuah was a local Malay hero of legendary stature who, even till today, epitomises a subject's absolute loyalty to the ruler. He led a band of brave and noble warriors – who were also childhood friends – in the court of Sultan Mansur Shah. However, Tuah was unfairly disgraced over the sultan's consort by a jealous rival and banished from the court. His most loyal friend, Hang Jebat, went amok at this injustice and created havoc through-out the sultanate. Tuah returned, and, though torn apart by the dilemma, killed Jebat on the sultan's command. Jebat's mausoleum lies in Jalan Tukang Kuli.

This classic tale, known to every child, is at the heart of the Malay psy-che. The warriors have also been immortalised in books, drama, and in 1998, Malaysia's first home-grown animated movie. Tuah's soul – some say in the form of a crocodile – is believed to reside in a well in Kampung Duyong. The waters of the well are reputed to have medicinal value, and bring good luck to those who drink at it.

Map on page 216

A Eurasian couple decked out in Portuguese costume for a cultural event.

BELOW: Portuguese descentants still speak Cristao, an antiquated dialect.

Map
on page
216

Zoos and clubs

Visitors entering Melaka town from the North-South Highway may choose to come in through **Ayer Keroh** ❹, about 12 km (8 miles) from the city. At the Air Keroh Recreational Forest, 70 hectares (170 acres) of jungle have been tamed to provide walks, deer reserves, picnicking spots and camping sites.

Numerous "tourist attractions" are spread along the road, some typical, others not so typical: a butterfly park, a crocodile farm, a fish world, a tennis centre, a *feng shui* (geomancy) garden, and a huge water theme park with rides. There is also a **Taman Mini Malaysia** (Mini-Malaysia Complex), which features model houses representing the traditional architecture of the various states, along with cultural and entertainment programmes. Next door is a mini-ASEAN, a similar park showcasing the architecture of the countries in this 10-nation Association of Southeast Asia Nations grouping. Nearby is the Melaka Zoo, with boating and refreshment facilities. Several good golf courses dot the area, a result of the huge growth in interest in the sport in recent years.

The old road to Seremban and Kuala Lumpur goes through the district of Alor Gajah and passes **Naning**, the principality whose chieftain defied the British in the 19th century. Dato' Dol Said now rests in his tomb by the roadside. Near his grave and around this area are some 90 mysterious stone megaliths called *batu hidup*, translated as "living stones" because of the belief that they grow. In fact, stones like these can be found scattered throughout the neighbouring state of Negeri Sembilan as well, with a famous cluster at **Pengkalan Kempas** ❺ just across the Sungai Linggi border. Some carry Islamic inscriptions, while others act as gravestones, yet others simply offer no explanation as to their origin or purpose. ❑

BELOW: a Melakan bullock cart with a creative touch.

Minangkabaus of Negeri Sembilan

The sweeping, peaked-roofed "buffalo horn" architecture is the most distinguishing feature of the Minangkabau culture of **Negeri Sembilan**, Melaka's northern neighbour. It appears everywhere; in the National Museum in Kuala Lumpur, at luxury hotels fringed by swaying palms, even at a petrol station at a highway lay-by. The roofs have come to signify not just Minangkabau, but Malay and Malaysian.

It is indeed a proud tribute to the heritage of a group of Malay settlers from west Sumatra who first made their new home in the fertile valleys and hills behind Melaka, attracted, as was the world, by the port's remarkable success. They brought with them their style of architecture and, protected by the Malay sultans, continued adhering to the *adat pepatih* customs which govern laws, political organisation, traditions, and social systems.

The small principalities founded by the original settlers formed the nine *luak* or states that became the federation of Negeri Sembilan. Today, although the modern state is divided into districts, the *luak* remain. However, the violent clashes over tin that resulted in British intervention in the 1800s reduced the number of *luak* to five.

Negeri Sembilan's ruler is not a sultan but a Yam Tuan Besar or Yang Di Pertuan Besar (translated as "He Who is Greatest"), who resides in Sri Menanti, 30 km (18 miles) from the administrative capital, Seremban.

Minangkabau culture and history is housed at the **Teratak Perpatih** (State Museum) within the grounds of the **Taman Seni Budaya** (Cultural Handicraft Complex) at the Seremban/Labu exit off the Kuala Lumpur-Seremban Highway. The museum's main building is a 19th-century palace from Kampung Ampang Tinggi that has been carefully reconstructed here. The museum showcases a fine display of ceremonial *keris* (daggers), Bugis and Minangkabau swords, and royal ornaments. Next door is the **Rumah Minang-**

kabau, another fine piece of Minangkabau architecture. Unlike the palace's attap roof, the Rumah Minangkabau has a cover of wooden shingles. The main building has handicraft displays and weekly cultural performances such as the *tarian piring* (plate dance) and *dikir rebana* (drumming).

Green hills and landscaped gardens provide the setting for the beautiful **Museum Diraja Sri Menanti** (Royal Museum of Sri Menanti) in the royal capital. A former palace, it was built in 1903 without a single nail. The timber structure sits on 99 pillars, representing the warriors of the various *luak*. It ceased to be a royal residence in 1931, when a new palace was completed in the shape of the blue-tiled **Istana Besar** nearby.

The great, sweeping roofs of the Istana prove to be the crowning glory of the otherwise featureless state capital of Seremban. A fine contemporary use of that traditional style, the **State Legislative Assembly Building** houses various government departments. Opposite it is a gem of neo-classical architecture, the **State Library**. ❑

RIGHT: great sweeping roofs typify traditional Minangkabau architecture.

JOHOR

Its proximity to Singapore makes the state's capital and resorts a favourite with visitors from the island nation; but leave the bustle behind, and you'll find some of the most beautiful habitats on earth

Map on page 216

Beware the Causeway clog that daily heads south from Johor Bahru, the capital of Malaysia's southernmost state, into Singapore. On weekdays, the 1-km (½-mile) road and rail link between the two countries is filled with thousands of Johoreans commuting to their jobs in the Lion City by bus, car, motorbike and on foot. The bottleneck is reversed on weekends, when Singaporeans flock to Johor to take advantage of the lower ringgit to shop, party, and relax in its waterfall, beach and island resorts.

It is a symbiotic relationship extended to investments as well, fuelling Johor's development and making prices in its capital and in the Singaporeans' favourite haunts among the highest in the peninsula. Still, Johor has not lost its agricultural roots, with its hinterland almost completely covered with oil palm, rubber and pineapple plantations amid virgin rainforest .

Johor evolved its own identity after the fall of the Melaka sultanate to the Portuguese in the 16th century. The last ruler, Sultan Mahmud, fled to Johor and turned it into a powerful trading empire. Its old capitals along the protected reaches of the Johor River were moved to the Riau archipelago, making them more accessible to trade – and attacks. Johor not only had to fend off the Portuguese, and the Dutch, but also the Acehnese in Sumatra, and later, the Bugis, losing Singapore to the British in 1819.

LEFT: Johor Bahru skyline across the causeway from Singapore.
BELOW: waiting for the school bus.

A turning point

At the end of the 1800s, Johor was the fiefdom of a *temenggung*, an official of the sultan. Abu Bakar, who became *temenggung* in 1862, elevated himself to maharaja, and in 1885 was acknowledged by Britain as Sultan of Johor.

Sultan Abu Bakar was educated in Singapore by English clergy. He spoke fluent English and cultivated ties with influential Europeans in the business world. Under his rule, the foundations of modern Johor were laid. In 1866, he moved his capital to Johor Bahru, transforming it into a thriving new town.

The sultan used western methods of policy-making and administration, introduced a modern bureaucracy and gave Johor the first constitution written for a Malay state. Thus he was able to defer the appointment of a British "advisor" to help him rule his state. He maintained good relations with Englishmen in Singapore and London, and was the first Malay ruler to visit England, becoming a personal friend of Queen Victoria. Johor was therefore the last Malay state in the peninsula to come under direct British control.

Many of Johor's Malays are of Javanese descent, and known for *kuda kepang*, a trance dance set to hypnotic gamelan music, in which the dancer is said to possess magical and visionary powers.

Waterfalls and tombs

The North-South Highway stretch from Kuala Lumpur to Singapore is a boring, flat, ruler-straight road which encourages the tendency to speed or doze. Entering the state from Melaka on the highway, a turnoff at Tangkak towards Segamat leads to **Gunung Ledang (Mount Ophir)** ❻. While popular with hikers, they unfortunately often leave the mountain litter-strewn. Here, Sagil Falls tumbles off the 1,276-metre (4,186-ft) peak into clear pools below. Ledang has a legend attached to it of a magical princess who finally thwarted the attention of a persistent Sultan Mansur by demanding a cup of his son's blood.

The right turnoff from Tangkak goes to the **Muar** ❼, considered a cultural centre for *ghazal* music and *kuda kepang* dances. Sited at a river mouth, Muar is a pretty town with neo-classical government buildings, traditional Malay houses and a pleasant tree-lined walk along the river at Tanjung.

Back on the North-South Highway, a left turnoff further south leads to **Pagoh**, home to the tombs of two Melaka sultans, and **Kampung Parit Pecah** in which stand the 99 graves of an entire village, wiped out – according to legend – by a single spear about 500 years ago. The spear was supposedly tossed by a jealous lover into the chest of a bridegroom at his wedding, removed and tossed again, eventually killing everyone, including the bride.

The highway leads on to **Ayer Hitam**, a popular stopover with coffee shops and rows of street stalls heavily laden with souvenirs, *durian* cakes, peanut nougat and other local produce as well as fresh and preserved fruits.

Half hidden by the stalls is the Claycraft Coffee House, where patrons sit on stoneware stools and drink out of dainty ceramic tea cups; the other half of the tables is crowded with arty relics. There is more pottery south in a village called Machap, including the famous **Aw Potteries** behind whose Minangkabau-style showroom is the studio where you can watch craftsmen at work.

From Ayer Hitam the road to the coast ends at **Batu Pahat** ❽. This is Johor's other Malay cultural heartland, not that this is reflected in its faceless urbanity. However, Batu Pahat is home to one of the last few genuine *kuda kepang* troupes. The town is more notorious for its floods at high tide, but is also known for its cheap and good Chinese food.

A more scenic way to get to Batu Pahat is via the coastal road from Muar. The road goes through little *kampung* and orchards whose goodies are heaped upon roadside stalls during the fruiting season. This road meanders past vast pineapple plantations, and finally ends in a Chinese village raised on stilts above the water. This is **Kukup** ❾, which prides itself as being the southernmost town of the Malay peninsula, and indeed the Asian continent. Late afternoon is the ideal time to arrive in Kukup, when the sun is low over the sea and the evening breezes begin. However, it is not to watch the sunset that the hordes descend on Kukup, especially from Singapore. It is to eat chilli crabs, for which Kukup is justifiably famous. The restaurants do not have fancy decor – and some do not even have walls – but they do have atmosphere and great food, if you care to look past the unsanitary toilets. There is a golf resort here and hotels in town.

BELOW:
colourful Aw pottery in Ayer Hitam.

Abu Bakar's legacy

The best-known place in **Johor Bahru** ❿ is probably its immigration point leading to Singapore. Johor also has a less crowded 2-km (1-mile) second link to the island nation at Tanjung Kupang and ferry connections at Tanjung Belungkor and Kukup.

Downtown JB (as the city is known) seems unaffected by the economic downturn, with new air-conditioned shopping malls and high-rise buildings taking shape by the day. Remnants of old Johor can be found behind **Jalan Ibrahim** in old shophouses where Chinese and Indian traders sell everything from spices and joss sticks to tailored suits and the latest colour TVs. Scattered among the shops are cheap Chinese restaurants and Indian cafés specialising in the popular South Indian banana leaf rice and *roti canai* (Indian bread).

Nearby, along Jalan Terus, are the elaborate Rajamariamman Kovil Hindu temple and a Chinese Taoist shrine. At the crest of the nearby hill is the gleaming white spire of St Joseph's Catholic Church. The old colonial train station is in this neighbourhood too.

The State Secretariat Building, **Bangunan Sultan Ibrahim** crowns the top of Bukit Timbalan. A huge Saracen-style building with arches, columns and enclosed stone balconies, it bears a gold seal of the State of Johor on its massive front doors.

The impressive **Royal Abu Bakar Museum** (open 9am–6pm; entrance fee) is a bit further down the waterfront, overlooking the Johor Straits. The stark, white structure with sweeping lawns was commissioned by Sultan Abu Bakar in 1864 as the primary royal residence. Over the last century, the **Istana Besar (Grand Palace)** has hosted royalty such as the Duke of Edinburgh (Queen Vic-

Map on page 216

Ice-cold lime juice is the perfect accompaniment to spicy South Indian fare served on banana leaves.

BELOW: a spice merchant in Johor Bahru.

TIP

If travelling to Kukup
from Singapore, avoid
the traffic jam on the
causeway by taking
the ferry from Tuas to
the Kukup pier.

toria's son), Archduke Franz Ferdinand of Austria (whose assassination sparked World War I) and the future King Edward VIII of England (who abdicated to marry Wallis Simpson).

Although it remains in royal hands, the palace was opened to the public in 1991 as a museum dedicated to the golden age of Johor. Rather reminiscent of visiting the aristocratic homes of rural England, there is no other museum in Southeast Asia quite like it.

The *dewan* (audience hall) is now a gallery detailing the history of the Johor sultanate, while the Grand Palace itself is crammed with antiques and strange knickknacks. The four-poster teak beds in the state bedrooms have British-made Corinthian-style columns dating to the 1860s. The bedrooms are still used for the lying-in-state of deceased members of the royal family. Down the hall is the opulent Reception Room, with a Baccarat crystal table and chairs. The Throne Room, with its matching gilt thrones, is used each year for investiture ceremonies on the sultan's birthday. The opulence of the Banqueting Room has to be seen to be believed.

The surrounding **Istana Gardens** has rolling parkland, immaculate lawns and several flower gardens, while just uphill from the Dewan is a Japanese garden and tea house presented by Crown Prince Hirohito on his state visit to Malaysia in 1936. Within the grounds' handicraft centre sits Mawar House, a carefully restored traditional Johor Malay house.

The next landmark along the waterfront is the **Masjid Sultan Abu Bakar** (Sultan Abu Bakar Mosque), completed in 1900. A bizarre blend of Italian rococo, classical Greek and traditional Muslim styles, the interior is decorated with Corinthian columns, crystal chandeliers and Oriental carpets. At the front

BELOW:
modern mosque
architecture, Johor.

of the main hall are a fabulously ornate gilt *minbar* (pulpit) and an ancient grandfather clock. Hawkers frequent the mosque grounds selling prayer rugs, velour wall hangings and other souvenirs.

Much further along the waterfront is **Istana Bukit Serene**, home of the present ruler. The huge Art Deco-style complex is off limits to the public, but you can get a good view of the palace from Jalan Sekudai along the waterfront or Jalan Straits View. Its expansive grounds contain a private air strip, a huge satellite dish, an orchid garden and a menagerie.

Nightlife draws many customers from Singapore, attracted by cheaper drinks and a relatively more "liberal" atmosphere, although the JB town council attempts to crack down on less salubrious spots from time to time. Still, the city has numerous nightclubs, discos, hostess clubs and karaoke lounges.

Golf and thundering falls

Back in the early 1990s, at the start of the golf boom, Johor took to developing resorts by the dozen. It therefore boasts the largest number of courses in the country. The best known include the 18-hole Royal Johor Country Club, Desaru Country Club and Palm Resort Country Club, not far from Senai Airport.

Many of these golf and country resorts are in the **Kota Tinggi** ⓫ area. Kota Tinggi is a small, quiet town with a loud splash. About 15 km (9 miles) northeast of the town are its famous waterfalls (entrance fee), the bottom-most section of which thunders down 36 metres (118 ft) to the polished rocks below. The entire area is cemented and steps lead up to the third and highest tier. Weekends find the large natural pools and surrounding tree-rooted slopes commandeered by the locals. Chalet-type accommodation and Malay hawker food is available.

From Kota, a trunk road goes south through fruit stalls and golf resorts to the golden beaches of **Desaru** ⓬, which is practically a Singapore resort. Many Singaporean visitors travel via the ferry between Tanjung Belungkor, 60 km (37 miles) from Desaru, and Changi Point in Singapore. There is a service four times a day between 9am–6pm, and the ferries carry vehicles too. The big hotels at Desaru provide transfers to the ferry terminal for a fee.

Thanks to free-spending Singaporeans, accommodation in Desaru is expensive – even the no-frills chalets. However, there is a good variety, from a theme park-type 700-roomer to a golf resort and camping grounds, all sandwiched between the beach and forest. Because there is little more than a go-kart circuit at Desaru – not least the absence of the normally ubiquitous *warung* (food stalls) – resorts provide the gamut of activities from watersports to mountain bikes and racquet games.

However, there are interesting side trips from Desaru. About half-an-hour away on the Kota Tinggi road is a turnoff that goes through an oil palm plantation to **Johor Lama** (old Johor) on Sungai Johor. This was once a great trading centre and royal capital, boasting one of the most powerful forts in the area, and probably the peninsula's largest. Today, however, Johor Lama is a sleepy village, and only grassed-over massive ramparts remain of the old fort.

Map on page 216

BELOW: golf is a favourite activity in Desaru.

Tanjung Balau, 5 km (3 miles) from Desaru, has an excellent fishing museum (open 9am–5pm; entrance fee) which charts the industry's history, traditions and methods, and includes displays of traditional boats. The museum fronts a firm, white sandy beach, and the *kampung* has new chalet-type accommodation. Seafood buffs should not miss out on the excellent Chinese-style delicacies at **Sungai Rengit**, 25 km (16 miles) south.

Endau-Rompin National Park in Johor is home to 71 palm species, which comprises 18 percent of Malaysia's palms – all indigenous – and more than 50 percent of its rattan varieties.

Land of palms

The road from Ayer Hitam to Mersing cuts across the state's rainforest heart, 20,000 hectares (49,000 acres) of which are the Johor section of the **Endau-Rompin National Park** . Named after the Endau and Rompin rivers, the park forms the southern end of the peninsula's wildlife corridor that stretches through Taman Negara up to Belum on the Thai border.

A fine example of ancient virgin lowland forest, the park's gems are its extensive palm forests, pebbly beaches and large rivers of amazing clarity whose headwaters plunge into cascades and waterfalls. A conservation area, it is being developed by the Johor Park Corporation (tel: 07-2237471) in consultation with the Malaysian Nature Society (MNS). There are chalets and dormitories at the Staging Point (open 8am–5pm), and four campsites within the park.

The Tourist Information Centre at Mersing (tel: 07-7995212) has comprehensive information on the park, and travel agencies run tours from there, Kuantan, Kuala Lumpur and Johor Bahru. Johor Parks can arrange boat transfers from the Felda Nita jetty, 25 km (16 miles) from Mersing, as well as accommodation at the Staging Point and Orang Asli guides into the park. They also rent out camping equipment, but food has to be bought outside.

BELOW: gigantic umbrella palm at Endau Rompin.

The boat ride from Felda Nita takes about 2 hours; at the Staging Point, you need to register, get your entry permit and pay park fees (including camera fees and insurance). The largest base camp is **Kuala Jasin**, 7 km (4 miles) away, accessible on foot or by boat. Sited at the Jasin-Endau river confluence, it has great swimming areas, including a 8,000-sq. metre (78,000-sq. ft) pool. There are hornbills at dawn, and you can observe deer and monkeys from a hide.

The **Janing Ridge** trek can be accessed from here: a steep climb to an amazing palm forest. The trail from Kuala Jasin goes all the way to the park's star attraction, the Buaya Sangkut waterfalls, and is a 6-hour, 8 km (5 mile) trek. The first bit is fairly flat, going through riparian (river) vegetation, with some waist-deep rope-aided river-crossings, but the later stages involve some steep stretches. Most people camp at the end of the flat section at Batu Hampar, tackling Buaya Sangkut the next morning.

En route to Batu Hampar are two base camps. **Kuala Marong** overlooks the still, clear Sungai Marong, whose waters were at one time the purest of any river studied in Malaysia. A side trail goes to **Tasik Air Biru**, better known as Blue Lagoon, a deep shady pool that makes for a refreshing swim.

The falls at the **Upeh Guling** base camp has remarkable "bath-tub" formations at the top of rocks, probably formed when pebbles lodged in crevices were spun round by flowing water. There is also a tiny island here, Pulau Jasin, which enjoys a remarkable diversity of plants, including wild orchids and four species of the carnivorous pitcher plant.

Batu Hampar also has playful cascades and huge sun-baked boulders. From here, a steep ascent kicks off the section to Buaya Sangkut, and the undulating trail goes through changing vegetation, including the peaty *kerangas* forest, usually found only in lowlands. The umbrella palms, whose leaves reach 4 metres (12 ft) in length, just get bigger and bigger. The leaves function as roofs for the huts at Batu Hampar, fashioned using Orang Asli techniques. Incidentally, the umbrella palm leaf really does work as an umbrella in a downpour!

There is an alternative trail that climbs the final hill – this is actually part of Janing Ridge, and therefore covered by thick palm forest, mainly the indigenous *Livistona endauensis* fan palms.

Map on page 216

White crocodile

At the 40-metre (130-ft) **Buaya Sangkut Falls**, seemingly static pools of water tumble down into rugged boulders, the most spectacular being the lowest of the three-step falls. The falls, first sighted on a helicopter reconnaissance of the park, has a charming Orang Asli legend to it, as do many of the sights. Translating as "stuck crocodile", the reptile in question was a mythical albino that had died in battle with a snake, and whose carcass got caught in the falls. The battle was over the hand of a lass of immense beauty, whose father made a drum of the croc's skin. Unfortunately, he hung it over his daughter's bed, and one night, it fell and killed her. Some say the rocks at a certain point at the waterfall's top-most level bear a striking resemblance to a crocodile. ❑

Come nighfall, look out for fluorescent forest mushrooms in Endau Rompin National Park.

BELOW: Wagler's pit viper, Endau Rompin reserve.

THE PENINSULA'S EAST COAST

A world away from its brash western brother, the rural east coast is picture-postcard Malaysia: traditional and unhurried

If ever a mountain divided a land, the peninsula's Banjaran Titiwangsa (Main Range) has, isolating the peninsula's east coast from the progressive west coast. As such, it has retained its rich cultural identity through the ages, despite the ravages of satellite TV. And while it remains economically less advanced, it is also relatively buffered from west coast financial and environmental woes.

Embracing the states of Kelantan, Terengganu and Pahang and the eastern half of Johor, the east coast is as indisputably Malay as it is proudly rural – particularly in the staunchly Muslim north. Local dress dominates, especially among the women who are like colourful butterflies in their batik *tudung* (head-scarfs) and *baju kurung* (Malay dress). Local dialects reign, so that even west coast speakers of Bahasa Malaysia find it difficult to follow a conversation.

The economy remains rooted in fishing and rice cultivation, as it has been for generations. Traditional implements have been replaced by newer, larger, faster models, but the boats of Kelantan, for one, are still splendidly decorated. The fishing industry is celebrated in various museums, themselves fine examples of Malay architecture.

The coastline is a continuous broad beach that invites you to jump into the sea at virtually any point. Here sit peaceful, timeless villages, palms bending out over a bright blue sea, while islands beckon from the hazy horizon. The most pristine beaches of tropical paradise ilk are found on the islands. Here, the shallow waters are the clearest in the peninsula, lapping gently on white sand or crashing against giant boulders.

Underwater, the colourful landscapes are fascinating, and the diversity of life staggering. The east coast islands make up the majority of Malaysia's 38 marine parks, which protect fragile and important habitats.

As noisy as any big city is the cacophony of insect noises, bird calls and animal cries in the rainforest interiors of the east coast. Among the world's oldest ecosystems, the million-year-old forests make up conservation and tourism sites such as Taman Negara, the oldest national park in the peninsula, and the freshwater wetland of Bera, where the indigenous Orang Asli maintain their lifestyles, so closely intertwined with the ways of the land. ❑

PRECEDING PAGES: river tributary just metres away from the sun-drenched shores of Malaysia's east coast.
LEFT: teeing off at Tioman island.

Eastern Peninsular Malaysia

0 — 50 km
0 — 50 miles

SOUTH CHINA

SEA

Peninsular
Malaysia

MERSING AND ISLES

With long sandy beaches, unpretentious resorts, crystal-clear waters and beautiful coral reefs, these South China Sea islands achieve the difficult feat of being both popular and unspoilt

Map on page 240

Whoever planned **Mersing**  knew how to make the most of her views. Seen from the coast-hugging roads of this bustling fishing and jump-off port, its postcard vistas of the offshore island silhouettes have brought it considerable fame. Despite lost-looking beach-seekers at the jetty, Mersing itself retains its peaceful small-town character.

You need a car to enjoy the winding evening drives to **Kampung Sri Lalang** en route to Endau north of town (turn right just after the bridge), and through **Teluk Iskandar** on the Sekakap road (turn right at Jalan Nong Yahya opposite the hospital). There are no beaches for swimming, but lookout points and hotel rooms overlooking the sea almost make up for it.

For a bird's-eye view of the sand, surf and greenery, try out the microlight aircraft instructional flights at the **Flyright Air-Sport** facility 6 km (3½ miles) down the Sekakap road (open daily 7am–7pm). Aim for either the misty early mornings or glowing sunset evenings – strictly no photography though.

On public holidays, Mersing's mini stadium sometimes plays host to the *kuda kepang* performance, a Javanese trance dance seldom seen outside Johor. Enquire at the friendly Mersing Tourist Information Centre (METIC) near the jetty (open Monday–Friday 9am–4pm; half-day Saturday; tel: 07-7995212).

BELOW: winging it on a microlight off Mersing.

Because of its proximity to the area, Mersing is becoming a reference point for tours to the Endau-Rompin National Park (*see Johor chapter, page 229*). More accessible, and popular with locals are the recreational forests of **Gunung Belumut** and **Gunung Lambak**, inland from Mersing along Route 50.

However, the South China Sea islands are the prime objective of the madding crowd. Over 60 volcanic isles in crystal-clear waters make up the Johor group, six of which have tourist facilities. The Mersing jetty is also an established springboard to the popular Pahang island of Tioman. These islands are protected by their marine park status and are home to prolific and diverse marine life, much of which is endemic to the area. Some of these islands are closed during the monsoon months of November–Feburary.

Mythical Tioman

The largest of these islands, **Pulau Tioman** , is popularly believed to be named after the *burung tiong* or mynah bird, said at one time to proliferate the isle. In legend, it is said that the island was created when a dragon, which emerged from Lake Cini inland, froze into rock while waiting interminably for its mate.

There is a mention of Tioman before AD 1,000, in what was perhaps the first guide to Malaysia. Arab traders of the time noted in their "sailing directions" that Tioman offered good anchorage and freshwater springs. Much later, the island's twin southern peaks at Mukut (called "Ass's Ears"), were a guide to Chinese traders between the 12th and 17th century, as evidenced by shards of Ming and other pottery found on the beaches and in nearby caves. Some of the pottery now sits in a lovely little museum at Tioman's Tekek beach. Despite the treasures so far unearthed, it is widely believed that the waters around this crucial trading pitstop harbour many more sunken treasures in the forgotten holds of unknown wrecks. To add to the island's mystique, Tioman has also found celluloid immortality in the guise of the mythical Bali Hai island in Hollywood's *South Pacific.*

Beach life

Today, Tioman's beaches continue to attract tropical isle fans, and divers and snorkellers who have come to revel in the marine park's underwater life. The main beaches fringe the west coast, and all are lined with small chalet-type accommodation run by local Malay families. A sea-bus (speedboat) services the beaches between 8am–6pm.

The tiny town "centre" is at **Tekek**, where you'll also find the jetty, airstrip and shops. The long beach, shaded by casuarina and coconut trees, is fronted with chalets and restaurants. Further inland on the other side of the road are *kampung*-style chalets. Despite the development, during the low season Tekek feels pretty much like the *kampung* it always was. The island's only road goes south from here to the island's one large resort, the Berjaya Tioman Island Resort, which also has a golf course. North of Tekek are the smaller beaches of **Air Batang** (better known as ABC after the original chalet operation there) and **Salang**, which also have some interesting mangrove areas.

BELOW: white-sand beaches are plentiful on Tioman.

South of Tekek are **Nipah**, a quiet chalet-only stretch, and **Mukut**, way down south at the base of the Twin Peaks, whose view of the wide expanse of blue ocean is obscured by neither islands nor passing ships. Mukut also has lots of fresh springs and a couple of waterfalls, the precious water for which the ancient mariners must have been thankful. Two other stretches on the west coast are not so pretty: Genting which sits on rocks and Paya, which has no beach to speak of, although both have plenty of accommodation.

Juara is the sole beach on the east coast, a long white stretch with relatively little tree cover, great for sun-seekers but it has no coral reefs at all. This is more of a backpackers' stretch, and can be reached from the west coast by sea-bus (2-hour journey) or by a jungle trail which starts at the jetty.

The 2- to 3-hour jungle trek across the island emerges next to the airport at Tekek, from which point you can take a sea bus back. The trail is paved in some stretches, steep in others, and climbs into thick lush forest. Another trail goes from Tekek to Batang Air and Salang.

Giant reefs

Tioman has large coral reefs on the west coast, most of which are close to shore. A feature of its marine life is its giant seafans, particularly at the top dive spot of **Pulau Tulai** or Coral Island, whose shallow waters are also popular with snorkellers. Cebeh provides for some fine swim-throughs, and there are pretty, submerged coral gardens at Golden Reef. Rengis, opposite the resort, is an accessible site with an occasional slight drift. Jahat is a good site south of Mukut. It is common to spot hawksbill turtles in the waters too, as well as groups of spiny lionfish. Walk-ins and packages are available at the seven dive

Map on page 240

TIP

Be careful of sandflies on Pulau Besar's beaches; the bugs are particularly nasty in the cool evenings.

BELOW: all set to dive on Tulai.

TRICKY ISLAND LOGISTICS

Getting to the isles from Mersing can be a bit messy. First of all, there are three types of boats – the speedboat is twice as fast as the slow boat, while the fast boats refer to the ferries. Secondly there are no schedules, except for Tioman (at least three times a day from 7.30am) and Rawa (once a day at noon). Generally, what boat you take and when you leave depends on the size of the group, and your choice of resort and island. Try to book both accommodation and boat ticket beforehand, especially if your dates coincide with Malaysian and Singaporean public and school holidays. If you can rustle up enough passengers, you can charter the entire boat.

Nine big boat operators servicing all islands belong to the Persatuan Bot-bot Sewa Pelancong Daerah Mersing (Tourist Boat Rental Association of Mersing; open 8am–4.30pm; tel: 07-7991222), who are at the Plaza R&R near the jetty. Like tour agencies, they can also arrange accommodation at all the islands. Seagull is the other big operator with three ferries that depart in the morning, but only to Tioman. Then there are various small operators, some connected to the resorts, and all congregated at the Plaza and jetty area. You can also check out pictures of their boats before you get on.

The blue parrot fish makes an audible crunching sound when it feeds on coral polyps.

shops on the west coast beaches, as is full equipment rental. Instruction is offered too, and technical diving is gaining impetus here.

The 55 km (35 miles) to Tioman can be covered in an hour by scheduled ferry from Mersing (try to get there in the morning), or Tanjung Gemok near Kuala Rompin in Pahang. Boats service Genting, Tekek, ABC and Salang. All boats back to the mainland depart Tioman at 7.30am. A high-speed ferry also services Singapore.

An even quicker way to get to Tioman – with some spectacular scenery thrown in – is on board the Malaysia Airlines or Pelangi Air Twin Otter from Kuala Lumpur, Kuantan and Singapore.

Island cluster

Johor's islands south of Tioman are also covered in jungle and have some good reefs; the islands are particularly popular with Singaporeans. All tour agencies offer the same 3-day/2-night package regardless of destination island: this comprises transfers, accommodation, tours (including snorkelling), and all meals including a barbeque. An all-day island-hopping trip in a 10–12 seater boat can also be arranged. This covers a few of the nearest islands and hire of snorkelling gear, but you usually have to bring your own lunch.

The closest isle to the mainland, and the largest, is **Pulau Besar ❸**, one hour away. Pulau Besar is one of a trio of islands, including Pulau Tengah (which was once used as a refugee camp for Vietnamese boat people) and Pulau Hujung, which are popular with day-trippers. However, Pulau Besar is the only one with accommodation, which comprises mainly basic chalet operations, and one two-star hotel. There is also a dive facility here. Trails from the sandy beaches lead to small plantations and wooden *kampung*.

BELOW: snorkelling off Pulau Rawa.

About the same distance from Mersing is the tiny **Pulau Rawa ❹**. The island was once one of the top destinations, but it has declined in popularity somewhat in recent years. Rawa has only one resort, in which Johor royalty have a share, and it has dive facilities but no divemaster. The marine life is nothing to shout about, but most visitors don't mind. They go there simply to enjoy its lovely beach – also on the island-hopping tour list – and do nothing. For the energetic, there is windsurfing, snorkelling, canoeing and fishing available.

Pulau Tinggi ❺, a 40-minute trip from the mainland, has a towering jungled peak, hence its name (*tinggi* means "high"). Like Tioman's mountains, this 650-metre (2,100-ft) giant was used as a navigational marker by Chinese mariners, and is mentioned in their literature as the "general's hat island". There is lots of accommodation here, mainly budget chalets. Two islets nearby have some marine reefs.

Much further away are **Pulau Aur ❻** (3–4 hours) and **Pulau Pemanggil ❼** (4–5 hours). Transport here is by chartered boat only, and is arranged through the respective resorts. Despite the distance, the islands are very popular, particularly for fishing and diving. Accommodation is plentiful but basic, and takes the form of longhouses and dormitories with common bathrooms. The best beach at Aur is actually on a

Map
on page
240

neighbouring islet, Pulau Dayang, which has a dramatic granite rock face looming over its sole resort. Sea fans characterise its reefs, and experienced divers can explore a World War II Japanese wreck another 1½ hours east. The main island is hilly and good for trekking. Secluded Pemanggil has turquoise lagoons and offshore pools, and great shallow waters for snorkelling.

Deep south

Johor's southern-most pair of holiday islands is accessible from Tanjung Leman, a staging point on reclaimed land about 2 hours south of Mersing. The ferry takes half-an-hour to reach Pulau Sibu Besar and Pulau Sibu Tengah; speedboats do the journey in 20 minutes, but it's a bumpier trip.

Pulau Sibu Besar ❽ has a longer history of tourism, and therefore has more accommodation, although the bulk of it is basic. A large island, it also offers some good walks that weave through its small, forested hills. In the *kampung*, modern solar panels stand out among the traditional wooden houses – they are part of a government-subsidised power programme.

The smaller **Pulau Sibu Tengah** ❾ is being promoted as a one-island, one-resort destination, the same tagline as Rawa. A huge three-star resort sprawls over 8 hectares (20 acres) of beachfront, offering a gamut of activities including snorkelling and DIY batik.

One option is to do an all-day island-hopping tour covering these islands from Tanjung Leman. Perched near the islands are also some *kelong*, traditional fishing huts on stilts sunk deep into the ocean floor, which are open to visitors. Popular among anglers, you'd need to bring sleeping bags; food can be arranged. Enquire at the Tanjung Leman staging point. ❏

BELOW: Pulau Tinggi's peaks are among the highest in the island group.

PAHANG, TERENGGANU AND KELANTAN

On the beaches of the peninsula's beautiful east coast, sun-soakers and coral-lovers mingle happily with the local folk whose families have fished its waters for generations

Map on page 240

Kuala Lumpur

The Malays say the *pokok rhu* or casuarina only grows near the sound of surf. So it is these trees that flourish along the peninsula's east coast, virtually one long surf-lapping beach running through four states. Between November and February however, the *rhu* are lashed about mercilessly by angry winds which also whip up the seas – this is the monsoon season, where entire villages and even towns are inundated with water.

But this is the reality of life for generations of fishing folk who live on these beaches, their difficult but quiet existence untouched by MTV and stock market fluctuations. Even the towns seem laid back, and hold fast to age-old traditions both culturally – mainly Malay – and religiously – predominantly Islamic.

Old settlements

There is a long history of human settlement in the east coast region. Neolithic finds have been made in Sungai Pahang, while Kelantan's prehistoric finds were in interior caves. Pahang was also mentioned in Chinese texts as being a vassal of the 13th-century trading empire of Sri Vijaya, and Kelantan is thought to have been under its wing too.

Terengganu, meanwhile, was established as a cornerstone of Malay settlement when a 14th-century Islamic inscription was discovered there. The find established Terengganu as the first place in the peninsula to embrace Islam, before even Melaka, whose colonisation of the east coast states only happened in the 15th century. Islam has retained its strongest hold here. The Thais, who ruled Kelantan and Terengganu before British intervention, have also left their mark in the local architecture, dialect and art forms.

The east coast is linked to the west by several main routes through the spectacular Main Range: the Karak Highway (Kuala Lumpur–Kuantan), the Gua Musang road (Kuala Lumpur–Kota Bharu), and the East–West Highway (Penang–Kota Bharu). Along the coast, Route 3 hugs the shore from Mersing all the way to Kota Bharu. It is a lovely drive, interrupted occasionally by livestock – and their droppings – and grinning children on bicycles. Go off the beaten track to a small fishing village, and a friendly gesture will be returned with a smile, or perhaps an invitation to tour the village where the soothing rhythms of Malay life have endured for centuries.

Kuala Rompin, near the Pahang-Johor state border, is a new tour destination, mainly as a jump-off point to the relatively undeveloped Pahang section of the Endau-Rompin Park (enquire at the Forestry Depart-

LEFT: colourful motif of a Kelantan fishing boat.
BELOW: kite maker in Kota Bharu.

TIP

If pressed for time, the inland Route 14 is the quicker link between Kuantan in Pahang state and Kuala Terengganu further north – but be forewarned that the drive is much less picturesque.

ment), and to Pulau Tioman from the Tanjung Gemok jetty down south. It is also being promoted as the *udang galah* (tiger prawn) city, in particular the Leban Condong area near the Lanjut Golden Beach Resort. Some travel agencies offer a four-wheel-drive tour to Jakun (Orang Asli) settlements inland at Iban (10 km/6 miles) and Kampung Aur (25 km/15 miles).

Islam, royalty and polo

At the mouth of the massive Sungai Pahang is the Pahang royal town of **Pekan** ❿, the former state capital. The sultan's palace, the **Istana Abu Bakar**, has an enormous polo ground which doubles as what must be the flattest golf course in the world. On 24 October each year, the town is injected with festivities for the sultan's birthday celebrations.

The **Muzium Sultan Abu Bakar** (Sultan Abu Bakar Museum) has excellent displays on old Pahang, royal family memorabilia, and ancient Chinese glassware and ceramics. Nearby are a mausoleum and two handsome, white-marble mosques with a riot of golden domes. About 5 km (3 miles) from town is a silk-weaving centre at Kampung Pulau Keladi.

Kuantan, the Pahang state capital, 44 km (27 miles) north of Pekan, is pretty uninteresting but has an excellent Tourist Information Centre opposite the Kompleks Teruntum on Jalan Mahkota (open Monday–Friday 9am–4.30pm; Saturday, half-day; tel: 09-5161007).

The town serves more as a springboard to inland attractions such as **Gua Charah** (30 km/19 miles away), **Sungai Lembing** (45 km/28 miles away), and the seven-step **Berkelah Waterfall** (70 km/44 miles away). Most visitors prefer to stay at the pleasant **Teluk Chempedak Beach**, 1 km (½ mile) out of town,

BELOW: Muslim schoolgirls in *tudung* (headscarf).

featuring the usual eateries, pubs and both upmarket (the Hyatt Kuantan) and budget accommodation. An alternative is to opt for one of the many resorts just north of Kuantan in **Beserah**. Known for its dried salted fish, a handful of Beserah's denizens still employ tough lumbering water buffaloes to transport fish from their boats on the beach to the processing areas.

Fun in the sun

From here, it's one long beach resort stretch all the way up to Kota Bharu. About 35 km (22 miles) from Beserah at the Terengganu border is the resort area of **Cherating ⓫**, a *kampung* squeezed out of its gorgeous crescent-shaped golden beach by tourism.

Originally a backpackers' haunt, the accommodation has moved upmarket and there is now a range, including a Club Med resort – Asia's first – on a private beach north. There are restaurants galore, souvenir shops (including DIY batik) and pubs; weekends can be one long party starting from Thursday, with the arrival of big city folk. Somehow, though, the area has avoided the claustrophobic feel of some other resort beaches, and maintains its friendly, relaxed air. A huge map at one of the two turnoffs to Cherating from the main road gives more information.

Local buses linking Kuantan and Kuala Terengganu stop on the main road from where you can walk in. Some resorts organise river trips and tours, and there are also two travel agencies (respectively at tel/fax: 09-5819957, with Internet facilities, and 012-9285404), who can also arrange transport to nearby islands as well as onward legs of your journey. Popular tours are to Gua Charah in Sungai Lembing (5-hour trip with a stopover in Kuantan) and

Salted fish being sun dried is a common sight along the east coast.

BELOW: the upscale Hyatt Kuantan.

TIP

Cukai town in Terengannu boasts some of the best baked stuffed crab in the east coast – the restaurants are clustered on the main road facing the river.

Tasik Cini (7-hour trip, including a boat ride and visit to the Orang Asli village). However, minimum numbers are required, so you could end up losing out playing the waiting game.

Near Club Med at Pantai Chendor, sea turtles lay their eggs at night from May through to September. The Fisheries Department is experimenting on-site hatching here and the tiny **Sea Turtle Information Centre** next to the club is well worth a visit, particularly to see its two live turtles in a pool.

Terengganu treasures

Cross into Terengganu and you hit oil country. When black gold was struck in Terengganu in the 1970s, the first buildings to come up in Cukai were the banks, so the story goes. The multi-million ringgit oil and natural gas industry has changed the face of Terengganu's oil stretch beyond recognition. Villages now wear whitewashed brick faces, former fishermen and farmers sport imported overalls and hard hats, and grocery shops stock German beer, Edam cheese, and Japanese seaweed for the cosmopolitan mix who now call Terengganu home. Terengganu contributes about 60 percent of Malaysia's total oil production, but 95 percent of revenues go to federal coffers. As such, fisheries remain the state's main income-earner.

The huge drilling rigs are 200 km (125 miles) offshore in the South China Sea, but giant steel structures, snaking pipelines and bullying tankers dominate the scene from Kemaman to Paka. Before and after office hours, the traffic slows to a crawl in this stretch.

Yet there are some pretty beaches, notably at Kijal. However, it is only at Dungun that the messy industrial scenery falls away and dignified fishing villages and paddy fields reclaim the landscape. Dungun, a dreamy little seaside town and port is a jump-off point to **Pulau Tenggol ⑫**, 13 km (8 miles) offshore. Actually a group of islands, it is a diving destination that features underwater cliffs and boulders. Its deep dive profile attracts a good selection of pelagic (deep water) marine life.

Inland from Kampung Pasir Raja is the majestic **Cemeruh Waterfalls**, 300 metres (1,000 ft) of white water thundering down a sheer rock face. To get there, you need three days through pitcher plant and palm country, across cascades and rapids. Guided tours can be arranged at Kuala Terengganu.

Ancient mariners

North of Dungun, a desperate battle is being waged on a 13-km (8-mile) stretch of golden beach. This is the **Rantau Abang Turtle Sanctuary ⑬**, and the fight is against extinction for Malaysia's oldest marine creature – the sea turtle. This is an important nesting ground for four species of turtle, including the 500-kg (1,000-lb) leatherback, which lays eggs at only six beaches in the world.

Between May and September, females struggle up the beach to lay their eggs at night, shedding "tears" in the process. What is rarer is the sight of the tiny hatchlings running to sea before dawn. Turtle-watching has long been popular entertainment

BELOW: mending fish nets for the next workday.

on the east coast, but is itself under threat due to diminishing populations. With the leatherback almost extinct, tour operators now market sightings of the smaller green and hawksbill turtles, but these are also at risk. A wealth of information on turtles, including some depressing statistics, is displayed at the Fisheries Department's small information centre at Rantau Abang (open May–August, 9am–11pm; September–April, Saturday–Wednesday 8am–4pm, Thursday 8am–12.45pm).

Do take note of the do's and don'ts of watching turtles. Lights and noise can scare off the females. Picking up hatchlings could tamper with the imprinting process which registers the nesting location; imprinting takes effect when they run from the beach to the sea. Shining lights at the hatchlings also distracts them – they are guided by the white breakers in the ocean. Distracting them also causes them to use up energy from the tiny yolk sack that they survive on for the 3 or 4 days it takes them to get to driftlines, out of reach of predators. The Fisheries Department employs boys to scour the beaches nightly for landings, and eggs are relocated to hatcheries, away from predators, both four- and two-legged. Sightings are shared with chalet operators around the centre, so they can wake up guests for a sleepy, but worthwhile trek. Flash photography is a strict no-no; souvenir shops have plenty of postcards.

Kampung living

Just south of Kuala Terengganu is the district of Marang, dotted with picturesque villages. **Marang ⓮** beach is an old favourite of backpackers, although fancier establishments are muscling in. The inland villages, however, are just waking up to tourism. *Gula melaka*, screwpine palm sugar, is still baked in bamboo

---

Map on page 240

Extensive research to help turn the tide against sea turtle extinction is being conducted at the Sea Turtle Research Unit at University Pertanian Malaysia. Pledge your support in cash and kind. Visit their website at http://www.upmt.edu.my/seatru

BELOW: leatherback turtle heading back to sea.

TURTLE WATCH

Nobody knows what happens between the time sea turtle hatchlings swim out into the moonlit sea and are spotted years later as juveniles, perhaps hundreds of kilometres away. Indeed, question marks surround this marine reptile: why does it swim so far away? Why does it return to the same beach to lay eggs? Why do more come up to nest some years than others?

Malaysia's Fisheries Department has been collecting data on the giant leatherback since the 1960s, artificially hatching eggs, and carrying out awareness programmes. Yet, the largest of the four species is almost extinct: there were 1,800 landings in 1956, and just 210 in 1994. The tiny olive ridley is endangered, while the green and hawksbills have also dwindled in numbers. Why?

The most obvious human threat to turtles is the eating of eggs. Fisheries officers are trying to combat this by paying collectors for eggs which they then hatch artificially, but they are constrained by budgets. Turtle mortality due to fishing nets and propellers is also high. Uncontrolled tourist activities can be another killer. But the pollution that affects their habitat is the hardest to monitor – plastic bags that strangle them, or pollution that kills the coral reefs and marine life on which they feed.

Chillies are central to Malay cuisine. Ask before you dig into a dish. If the food proves too fiery, downing a glass of milk instead of water will usually do the trick.

BELOW: basket and mat weaver in Terengannu.

over traditional stoves, while old ladies sit in the shade of *nipah* huts, stitching away at a new "roof" for a beach resort. Tree-climbing monkeys deftly pluck young coconuts whose sweet cool juice makes a refreshing drink. A cruise up the Marang River offers views of mangrove forest from whose banks peep monkeys, iguana and sometimes, otter.

Marang is also only half-an-hour by boat from **Pulau Kapas** ⑮ and **Pulau Gemia**, which are good for snorkelling and easy diving. Just before hitting Kuala Terengganu, you will pass the **Masjid Tengku Tengah Zaharah**, also known as the floating mosque. Combining the modern and traditional, its serene white reflection gives an illusion of being afloat in the water.

Setting its own pace

Despite its affluence born of the state's plentiful sources of oil, enough of **Kuala Terengganu's** ⑯ old charms remain to save it from facelessness. Possibly the east coast's oldest port, the pulse of the state capital is felt most keenly in the waterfront **Pasar Besar** (Central Market) in the early morning. This is when fresh produce pours in: glistening fish by the lorry-load (the main fishing port is now in Chendering), while coconuts and *pandan* (screwpine) leaves arrive by boat from Pulau Duyung. Though less publicised than the much-photographed Central Market in Kota Bharu, this wet market is just as lively and colourful. Housed also in a concrete building, produce is sold downstairs and in the court-yard while the handicraft shops fill the first floor.

This bustle spills out into Jalan Bandar, a narrow and congested crescent-shaped street lined with Chinese shophouses. This is **Chinatown**, Kuala Terengganu's original thoroughfare, where the architecture dates back to

when Terengganu was an independent sultanate. Stroll down this street, or take a trishaw, still the most popular means of transport in downtown Kuala Terengganu. Peek into the narrow doorways – the houses seem to stretch back forever – and you might see an old lady sipping tea. The young and the trendy are moving in, though, mainly to open art and handicraft shops; this is also where many of **Pulau Redang's** resort operators are located.

Just beyond the market in the direction of the river mouth is a broad esplanade which faces the **Istana Maziah**, the official residence of the sultan, who actually lives in another palace a few kilometres away. The Istana resembles a French country house and was built at the beginning of the century to replace an older palace destroyed by fire.

Across from the Central Market is an island, **Pulau Duyung**, whose master craftsmen were, once upon a time, responsible for the unique fishing boats with decorated fore- and main-masts, and bowsprits called *bedor*. Today, the island has lost its allure, as only a couple of shipyards survive by building yachts for Australian, American and other foreign boating enthusiasts.

Terengganu's heritage

Little remains of Terengganu's beautiful traditional Malay architecture, but the best is preserved in the grounds of the **Terengganu State Museum Complex** (open 9am–5pm; closed on Tuesday; entrance fee).

Malaysia's largest museum sits on the site of the town's first settlement, but its main buildings are obscenely outsized replicas of the real thing, four well-preserved wooden houses with Islamic motifs and shades of Chinese and European architectural influence.

Map on page 240

BELOW: kite-flying is popular in the east coast.

Terengganu batik is generally more expensive than that of the northern-most state of Kelantan. The designs in the former state are finer, and involve more skilled workmanship.

The excellent fisheries and seafaring open-air galleries showcase the gamut of boats, including two original hand-built wooden galleys used for trade in the 19th century. The museum is in Losong, which has charming kampung houses and is home to the famous Terengganu *keropok lekor*, a fishy cracker found only here and Kelantan.

Like Kuantan, Kuala Terengganu has its own beach. **Pantai Batu Buruk** is a coconut tree-fringed sandy stretch with lots of eateries – try out the local *nasi dagang* breakfast if you can stomach rice and fish curry in the morning. There is also a three-star hotel and budget accommodation here.

Arts and crafts

Though village life in Terengganu has been urbanised, many of the traditional arts it fostered are as alive as ever. Seasonal fishing and farming brought village folk leisure, and from leisure came time to devote to their arts. Folk dances, shadow plays and traditional games such as kite-flying and top-spinning were celebrated during festivals after a harvest. Many processions and rituals were related to the spirit of the rice paddy, a carry-over from ancient animistic beliefs. Today, village festivals are rarer since farmers are busy planting rice twice a year instead of once, and the Islamic doctrine discourages customs connected with spirit worship.

Chendering, 8 km (5 miles) south of town, houses some commercial handicraft centres, including the government-sponsored **Pusat Pengeluaran Kraf Terengganu** (Craft Product Centre), which has an apprentice programme for weaving, stitching and brassware. Their showroom also shows off products from the surrounding villages, but you would need a guide to locate

BELOW: batik being sun dried in Terengannu.

them. Here also is the headquarters of the **Noor Arfa Batek House**, the country's largest hand-drawn batik producer, where you can watch batik being made and try your hand at it too.

Jewels in the sea

Like jade in an ocean of clear blue, Terengganu's islands are the most beautiful in the peninsula, and worshipped by sun-soakers and coral-lovers.

Merang, 28 km (17 miles) north of Kuala Terengganu, is the jump-off point to **Pulau Redang** ⑰ and the smaller **Pulau Lang Tengah**. A range of accommodation is available, virtually every one with dive facilities. However, there are no scheduled boats, so visitors have to book beforehand for packages with travel agents in any of the east coast capitals or Kuala Lumpur.

Lang Tengah is less crowded and is good for easy diving but has limited accommodation and access to water. Redang, 2 hours from shore, is famous for its great visibility and diverse sites. Comprising nine islands, it is also probably the peninsula's most researched island. A pleasant cross-island track through rainforest connects the pristine wide beaches of fine white sand at Pasir Panjang and Teluk Dalam. There is also a small traditional Malay fishing village on stilts where you can stop for *teh tarik* (tea) and local *kuih* (cakes).

However, diving is what has carved the island's fame. The Marine Park jetty alone has prolific marine life, including a resident Moray eel. Night dives at the submerged reefs are particularly fascinating. There is also a high chance of bumping into a member or two of the large green turtle population. In situ hatching is being carried out here, as well as a research programme involving volunteers (*see Margin Note on the Sea Turtle Research Unit on page 251*).

Map on page 240

Crown of thorns starfish are extremely destructive to reefs as they feed off the coral beds.

BELOW: Redang's talcum powder beaches are divine.

TIP

It doesn't matter what you wear (or don't) on the islands, but spare a thought for a vastly different culture by making sure you are decently clad when you visit a *kampung*.

In the first quarter of every year, a crown-of-thorns clean-up is done by divers and resorts. The starfish gobbles up coral beds, and just like in the movie *Aliens*, cutting them up only creates more of them; instead, they have to be individually picked off the coral and buried on land.

Legend has it that two birds turned to stone and became the gorgeous **Pulau Perhentian Kecil** ⑱ and **Pulau Perhentian Besar** isles, 27 km (17 miles) from shore. *Kecil* and *besar* mean "small" and "large" respectively. The jetty is at Kuala Besut, an unspoilt fishing village where fishing boats make a dramatic show at dawn and dusk. Slow boats reach the isles in 1½ hours and operate between 9am–2pm. Speedboats take 30 minutes, but it's a bumpy ride.

Accommodation at Kuala Besut is limited, but the jetty is well serviced by buses and taxis from any major town. Boats and accommodation can be booked at the jetty complex. Try the Persatuan Pengusaha Pelancongan Pulau Perhentian (Association of Perhentian Island Tour Operators). Walk-ins are common, but book beforehand during public holidays.

Perhentian Besar has a wider range of accommodation spread along the bay facing the smaller island, including the three-star Perhentian Island Resort. Rock-bottom accommodation can still be found at Pasir Panjang on Perhentian Kechil, site of the first backpacker invasion. It has become really crowded here; the island's body-lined beach attests to its popularity. However, water remains a problem in the dry July/August period.

The traditional fishing village on Perhentian Kecil is interesting, particularly at the day's end when the villagers converge on the waterfront for a gossip, surrounded by squealing children at play. The village also sells groceries and other necessities.

BELOW: two for the pot – a grinning lobster fisherman.

The diving here is more leisurely compared to Redang, and the shallower waters are good for snorkelling. There are nine dive facilities in all, each offering instruction. Gardens of soft coral – which grow to huge sizes – lots of shells, and large boulders make for an attractive underwater playground.

Malay enclave

A few kilometres from the Thai border lies **Kota Bharu** , the cradle of Malay culture. Although it is ruled by the opposition fundamentalist Muslim Parti Islam or PAS, Kelantan's capital is not corseted by the party's stringent policies but is, instead, vibrant with life and colour.

Kota Bharu has one of the best-known wet markets in Malaysia. The **Pasar Besar** (Central Market) on Jalan Tengku Chik is where traders – traditionally women – sit in their colourful headscarfs and traditional *baju kurung* on raised dais among vegetables and *keropok lekor*. Upstairs is a shopping haven for east coast crafts, particularly batik and silverwork.

Just beyond the market is a cluster of museums around the old palace, **Istana Balai Besar**, which was built in 1884. Next to it is the pretty **Istana Jahar**, another palace that is now the museum of royal traditions and customs. Its displays are a good introduction to traditional Kelantan life and culture; it also has an excellent weapons section. The **Pusat Kraftangan** (Handicraft Village) is notable more for its traditional architecture than its contents. Nearby are the **Muzium Islam** (Islamic Museum), another attractive traditional wooden building, and the more modern **Istana Batu** (Royal Museum) which houses memorabilia of the current sultan.

Kota Bharu's cultural pastimes are showcased at **Gelanggang Seni** (Court of

Map on page 240

TIP

All museums in Kota Bharu are open 10.30am–5.45pm, but are closed on Friday as it's a Muslim prayer day; all charge an entrance fee.

BELOW: the Central Market at Kota Bahru.

Map on page 240

All in a day's work – monkeys trained to pluck coconuts.

BELOW: reclining Buddha of Wat Photivihan.

Arts) on Jalan Mahmood. Check the latest schedules at Tourism Malaysia at Jalan Sultan Ibrahim (tel: 09-7485534; open 9am–4.30pm). Unless you are lucky enough to chance upon festivals in Kota Bharu or its surrounding villages, this is the best place to view these artforms. In a small *wakaf* (rest hut) outside the main hall, old men tune their instruments, and exponents of traditional Malay self defence, *silat*, take to the stage. On the green, the *gasing* (top) spinners are ready to spin down their prized tops onto a concrete square. From here, the tops are removed with a wooden pallet onto dowels. The trick is to keep your top spinning longer than anyone else's. The drummers then beat out rhythms on the rows of colourful *rebana*, huge drums fashioned out of logs.

Wayang kulit (shadow puppet plays) and the Thai-influenced dance-theatre *mak yong*, two of the loveliest Malay artforms, are banned from performance in the state, because they are considered anti-Islam. Luckily, the *wayang kulit* troupes in Terengganu, Kedah and Perlis are alive and thriving. *Mak yong* and its sister artform *manohra*, however, look set for a steady decline into obscurity.

Surprising surroundings

Kota Bharu is surrounded by a patchwork of villages among rice paddy fields and orchards. What might seem surprising in a predominantly Muslim state is the number of Thai *wat* (temples) between Tumpat and Pasir Mas. Among them is the **Wat Photivihan**, which houses the country's largest statue of the reclining Buddha. Some villages even celebrate Thai festivals, like the Songkran water festival.

Tumpat is the terminus for the eastern railway line from Segamat. Across the border in Thailand, the line whisks travellers all the way to Bangkok. Head out

of Kota Bharu on Route 3 to reach what is reputed to be the oldest surviving mosque in Malaysia (although the Melakans might dispute that). The 18th-century **Masjid Kampung Laut** (Kampung Laut Mosque) was originally on the banks of Sungai Kelantan but was moved out of flood's harm to Kampung Nilam Puri 10 km (6 miles) south of Kota Bharu. Built of stout chengal wood and without nails, it has a pyramidal two-tiered roof, typical of a Javanese mosque.

A great place to watch Kelantan's colourful fishing boats is at the picturesque estuary at **Pantai Dasar Sabak** ⓴, 13 km (8 miles) north of the town. The boats leave at dawn and return at about 3pm, when it is all bustle with the unloading of the catch and the washing of boats. The beach also has a 20th-century claim to fame: it was here, on 8 December 1941, that the Japanese began their brutal march south to Singapore. (The attack on Pearl Harbor was not to take place until 95 minutes later – 7 December on the other side of the dateline.)

Weekenders head for the city's most famous beach, PCB or **Pantai Cahaya Bulan** (Moonlight Beach); the acronym actually used to stand for Pantai Cinta Berahi – The Beach of Passionate Love – in pre-PAS days. Still, PCB remains a handicraft haven. The gold-threaded *songket*, *wau* (kites) large and small, and rows of batik hanging in the sun beckon souvenir-hunters on the 5-km (3-mile) road to the beach. ❑

Kampung Games

Every Malaysian is a *kampung* kid at heart; so says Lat, Malaysia's favourite cartoonist who has a series of books contrasting the easy, down-to-earth *kampung* lifestyle with the mobile-phone and pager-punctuated life of the modern yuppie.

Despite the city-dweller's groomed image and array of gadgets, every holiday in Malaysia results in airports and highways jammed with city residents returning to their villages – *balek kampung*. Their *kampung* are their roots, and bound up in this are the traditional pastimes enjoyed there.

Throughout most of the country, **top-spinning** is a teenage game, but in the Malay *kampung* of the northeast coast, a champion spinner is the village hero. Requiring great strength to spin, tops vary from a simple wooden cylinder to fantastic streamlined discs with spindles trimmed with inlaid gold; large ones can be as big as dinner plates. With the harvest completed and all the rice stored, farmers traditionally settled down to watch and bet on the top local team. Contests feature either the endurance spinners – record times for spinning are about two hours – or the strikers who spin down 7 kg (15 lb) fighting tops faster than a speeding bullet.

Another traditional entertainment most popular in Malaysia's northeastern states, **kite-flying** was enjoyed in the 15th century. Today, great pride is still taken in the design and the hand-crafting of each aerodynamic piece of art. The paper *wau* (kite) comes in unique shapes, and bamboo pieces are often attached underneath a kite to produce a melodic humming sound (*degung*). Contests are still held for serious kite-flyers, and today, international kite festivals are held in Malaysia, drawing participants from both European and Asian countries.

Sepak takraw, a traditional *kampung* game, uses a ball about the size of a large grapefruit, made of woven rattan strips, and weighing 170 grammes (less than ½ pound). The aim of the game is to keep the ball in the air as long as possible by passing it from one player to another, using all parts of the body except for the forearms and the hands. The game requires acrobatic flexibility and practised skills, and is exhilarating to watch.

Congkak is a game requiring more wits than physical skill. Comparable to backgammon, *congak* features a wooden boat-shaped "board" and marbles or seeds. The *congak* board has two rows of holes in which the marbles are placed, and the object of the game is to have the most marbles to finish.

The best childhood memories come from games provided by nature. The pea-sized, red saga seeds from the large saga tree, for example, are used in a game of accuracy much like marbles. The game of pick-up-sticks is played with coconut twigs or satay skewers; chicken feathers are stuck into a flat rubber disc, and this *catek*, resembling a shuttlecock, is kept in the air while being nimbly kicked using only the instep of one's foot. Even conker-like rubber seeds are the centre of numerous, imaginative kampung games, all still fresh in the minds of almost every Malaysian. Just go ahead and ask. ❑

RIGHT: top-spinning is taken very seriously in the northeastern states of Malaysia.

THE BANGAU MARITIME FIGUREHEADS

Carved spar holders, or bangau, adorn these colourful fishing boats, and are found only on the Malaysian peninsula's east coast

When engines began replacing sails from the 1950s onwards, it was thought that the *bangau* would become extinct. But, defying all predictions, these colourful objects have been retained, because the spars are still used as gaffs for landing fish and for poling into shore.

In ancient times they were more than utilitarian objects – the *bangau* also served as a repository for the spirit of the boat, and its presence was believed to help keep the boat safe from storms and sea demons.

Bangau are found from the northern shores of Kelantan – notably adorning the boats known as *perahu bauatan barat* at Pantai Dasar Sabak – to Terengganu in the south, where they act as figureheads on the curved bows of *kolek* boats.

FIGUREHEAD FASHIONS

Bangau take on various forms. Some are shaped like birds, others of the *naga*, a legendary sea serpent, while a few are even fashioned after figures in traditional shadow-puppet plays. Some prows are even shaped and painted to resemble the *garuda,* a demonic birdman from Kelantanese mythology. Were they originally made to ward off the *naga umbang*, a marine dragon that according to legend lurked in the depths of the sea? Another legendary tale has the *garuda* residing in the top of a huge coconut palm – a symbolic represention of heaven – which rises out of the centre of the ocean.

Although the spiritual significance of the *bangau* has been long forgotten, the tradition of keeping them and the boats they adorn still decorated, survives.

△ **PAINTED PROWS**
A naga "dragon" adorns a prow at Pantai Dasar Sabak, Kelantan.

◁ **THE "ONGKAK"**
Sitting opposite the bangau, the *ongkak* often resembles figures from the shadow-puppet plays.

BIRD-LIKE BOAT SPIRITS

Bangau means "cattle egret" in Malay. It is thought that originally the boat fittings resembled these birds, who, while rarely seen flying over the sea, were perhaps chosen for their symbolic value due to their well-known liking for fish.

Most *bangau*, however, bear no resemblance to this bird, although bird shapes are sometimes used. Their fanciful designs probably have something to do with the strict Islamic edicts banning the portrayal of anthropomorphic figures.

At Kelantan's Pantai Baru near Bachok, a *bangau* takes on a parrot-like look (*above*), but the colours are highly imaginative.

Further south, at Penarik, Terengganu (*below*), a *bangau* keeps the long neck of its namesake but its garish blue colouring is merely for ornamentation.

△ BEACHED BANGAUS
One of the east coast's most picturesque vistas is this rainbow-coloured fleet lined up under the coconut palms at Pantai Dasar Sabak, Kelantan.

◁ BOAT FIXER
When rough monsoon seas keep boats in port, fishermen repair their craft for the next season.

△ DEMON DESIGN
Trident-wielding demons were perhaps originally painted on boat hulls to scare off "sea devils".

◁ BOAT BEACHING
Each day at Pantai Dasar Sabak, Kelantan, the fishing fleet is physically hauled up onto the beach.

▷ BLUE BANGAU
The tuft of feathers on the head of this *bangau* could have originally mimicked the bright orange feathers which the male egret sprouts during mating season.

Map on page 240

EASTERN INTERIOR

Inland from the east coast lies the dark green heart of Malaysia, a land of lakes and forest, of wild animals, ancient myths and the sublime beauty of Taman Negara

In the still of morning, before the first breath of wind, surreal sculptures of dead wood stand perfectly reflected in the mirror of **Tasik Kenyir ㉑**, Southeast Asia's largest artificial lake. Nineteen hills were inundated to feed the 37,000 hectares (90,000 acres) of water needed to run the hydroelectric power station that supplies about 8 percent of the nation's electricity.

However, the statuesque tree trunks that used to be the lake's outstanding characteristic have been removed, except in its northern fingers. Nonetheless, Kenyir's numerous tributaries continue to be an anglers' favourite, with numerous freshwater species including the *kelah* and carnivorous *toman* (snakehead).

About 14 waterfalls dot the area's 340 thickly-forested islands. The multi-tier 152-metre (500-ft) **Lasir Waterfall** is 45 minutes south of the jetty by boat; and **Tembat Waterfall**, a series of five furious rapids and gorgeous giant sun-baked boulders, is an hour north. You'll find campsites on the pebble-beached **Petuang** and **Saok** rivers, popular fishing spots. Otters, eagles and amphibians are common; if you are lucky, you might spot elephants or the elusive black panther.

LEFT: Orang Asli tribesman and his blowpipe.
BELOW: thundering Sekayu waterfall during the rainy season.

The road to Kenyir

The main gateway to Kenyir is the **Pengkalan Gawi** jetty, an hour from Kuala Terengganu. Buses from the latter go to Kuala Berang, 15 km (9 miles) from Kenyir; take a taxi for the rest of the journey. There are also overnight buses that go direct from Kuala Lumpur (Hentian Putra) to Pengkalan Gawi.

The visitor's centre has a pleasant view, but little else beyond that. Day-trippers can hire boats at the landing near the dam. There are two groups of operators (tel: 010-9340101), who offer various tours in eight- to 10-person fibreglass boats. They also have dubious-looking double-decker houseboats that cruise the lake and can sleep 15 people on mattresses. The operators can arrange stays at the resorts too, but contact numbers of the resorts are also published in the Tourism Malaysia Tasik Kenyir brochures and tours can also be arranged from Kuala Terengganu. All resorts offer the same deal: accommodation, all meals, boat transfers, jungle-trekking, a visit to a waterfall and unlimited use of facilities.

En route to Kenyir is the picturesque seven-step **Sekayu Waterfall** (entrance fee) near Kuala Berang. A 25-minute walk up a flight of steps takes you to the top, the least slippery spot for a swim. Kuala Berang was the site of the first Malay settlement in Terengganu, but nothing remains of the original dwellings. Also discovered here was Malaysia's oldest Koranic inscription. The 14th-century *Batu Bersurat* is now in the state museum.

En route to Pahang's hinterlands from Kuantan, the turnoff to **Sungai Lembing** ㉒ leads to a towering limestone cliff, **Gua Charah**, whose inner cave houses a 9-metre (30-ft) long limestone statue of a reclining Buddha built by a Thai Buddhist monk. The taxing climb up to the ledge is rewarded by a great view. The cathedral-sized outer cave has thin shafts of light filtering down through cracks hundreds of metres above. There are other caves to explore but a guide is needed. On the same road is the world's second-largest and deepest tin mine, open to tours if prior arrangements are made with Pahang Consolidated Ltd. For details, enquire at Sungai Lembing.

About 16 km (10 miles) inland from Sungai Lembing is **Gunung Tapis**, a mountainous nature park with rapids, fishing and trekking. It takes a 1½-day climb to reach the peak. Enquire at the dormitories-only Sungai Lembing Tapis Resort, who arrange guides and transport (tel: 09-5411339/5412154).

Mountain skyscapes

Fantastic skyscapes over islands of *pandanus* (screwpines) at sunset; boat-wide "paths" through long submerged grass; and from June to September, fragile pink waterlilies and white lotuses on immense velvet leaf carpets. This is **Tasik Cini (Lake Cini)** ㉓, a rare river-floodplain of 12 interlocking lakes about 100 km (62 miles) inland from Kuantan.

Cini is fascinating for its two main forest types – the riverine forest of massive trees and lianas overhanging the narrow Sungai Cini; and the swamp vegetation, the most prominent of which are the *pandanus*. This is also home to monkeys and birds, including large flocks of hornbills, and kingfishers and broadbills that flash a brilliant blue across the water.

BELOW:
Tasik Cini, Pahang.

Myths and monsters

A lost city, probably Khmer, is believed to lie 12 metres (40 ft) below the lake's surface but Cini is probably best known for its mythical *naga*, a Loch Ness-type monster whose origins are a spiritual dragon-creature of local Orang Asli folklore. Another version tells of how two of these mythical creatures evolved to become the islands of Tioman and Daik.

The Jakun maintain some elements of their traditional lifestyle, planting rice paddy and fishing; they also make fine handicrafts, now predominantly targeting tourists. Try your hand at the blowpipe at Tanjung Puput and Kampung Gumum. There is also basic accommodation and tours at the latter.

By road, Cini is off the Kuantan-Segamat Highway (Route 12), then 32 km (20 miles) from the Pahang bridge turnoff. This goes to Kampung Gumum and the government-owned Rimba Resort Tasik Cini. The latter has a range of accommodation, a restaurant, and public toilets. A jetty here with an association of 19 boatmen (tel: 09-4567160 for Tok Ki), offers the lake tour at a more reasonable rate than the association of 15 boaters at the Tourism Complex at the Kuala Sungai Cini rivermouth (tel: 09-4201196) which lies further down that road. Use the latter's services if you plan to access Cini by boat from Kampung Belimbing off the Karak Highway on the other side of the massive Sungai Pahang; the rate is RM70 per four-passenger boat. If you want to be dropped off at your accommodation, the fare is double. All boatmen can ferry you to the campsites that dot the place.

A worthwhile day trip would cover the dank, winding Sungai Cini, half the lakes, and a short jungle trek from the resort to Kampung Gumum, one of three trails in the area. A longer day trip brings you to the **Mentenang Waterfall**,

Map on page 240

TIP

The best storehouse of tales from the rich Jakun oral tradition, is probably Tok Batin, the headman at Kampung Gumum – although the local boatmen are good sources too. You would need a translator though.

LEFT: waterlily at Cini. **BELOW:** Orang Asli blowpipes.

TIP

Club Med Cherating
usually sends
busloads of tourists to
Lake Cini on Mondays,
and weekends are
usually busy for boat
operators.

while an overnight option is **Gunung Cini**. Tours can be arranged from Kuantan and Cherating. Public transport runs from Kuantan and Pekan to Cini town; call the resort and they will pick you up. An express bus also goes to Cini from Kuala Lumpur's Mara Bus Station.

Unfortunately, all is not well at Cini. The leafless trees at the waters' edge are the result of a bungle by authorities on a dam built in the early 1990s to regulate water fluctuations; it let in too much, and was knocked down too late, killing off large numbers of the huge *tembusu* trees. The current, British-designed dyke is the third attempt to get it right. Behind the beauty of the increasingly abundant water lilies is also the ominous sign that the lake is getting shallower; the ecosystem has not found its balance yet.

Ancient lifestyles

A similar lake experience is to be had at **Tasik Bera (Lake Bera)** ❷, 1½ hours from Cini. Though the largest freshwater lake in Southeast Asia, its waters are contained in narrower "fingers" rather than the open lakes of Cini, thanks to the greater abundance of screwpine.

Bera's 26,000 hectares (64,000 acres) of wetland and swamp ecosystems are protected under the Ramsar Convention as a wetland of international importance. Like Cini, the water rises up to 3 metres (9 ft) in the wet months of September to January, blessing the rivers with fish, and making the post-monsoon months the best angling period. As the boat snakes through the narrow channels, a splash of colour in the orchids amid ferns and epiphytes catches the eye. Less obvious are the pitcher plants among the tall reed fields. Above, a hawk wings its solitary way, keeping a keen eye out for supper.

BELOW:
view from the
East-West highway.

The Ramsar Convention also protects traditional human use of the area, allowing the Orang Asli of the Semelai tribe to maintain their lifestyles, living in bamboo and bark huts, using traditional implements to trap fish for the lucrative aquarium fish industry, and fashioning handicrafts from forest products. An interesting tradition is the collection of *minyak keruing* resin from the *keruing* tree, used for making torches, boats and perfume.

Tourism however, is new to this remote area. Bera's resort has rooms, dorms, campsites and covered platforms overlooking the serene waters. Packages include a 3-day/2-night lake tour, trekking and Semelai experience, birdwatching tours, and a homestay programme with the Semelai. Three trails run around the area and there are also canoes and mountain bikes. Further north at Sudin jetty, a boat operator offers fishing and lake tours.

Bera is difficult to access, but the resort does pick-ups for a fee from Temerloh and the Triang train station.

Map on page 240

Rainforest thrills

There is shuffling and grunting, but the torchlight picks out only a pair of eyes. Is it the black-and-white king of camouflage, a tapir? Or, against all odds, one of the park's remaining 40-plus Sumatran Rhino? The experience afforded by the five animal hides in **Taman Negara** ㉕ is among the attractions that have made it arguably the best-known of Malaysia's protected areas. This granddaddy, which simply translates to "National Park", sprawls over 430,000 hectares (100,000 acres) across three states, with the bulk being in Pahang. Looming over all this is the central massif of Gunung Tahan, the peninsula's highest peak.

BELOW: Taman Negara at dawn.

Jungle bananas are these in Taman Negara look inviting but are unsafe to eat.

Taman Negara offers everything from a leisurely 2 days' fishing to a 2-week jungle safari, a muddy crawl through bat-infested caves to a splashy ride through Sungai Tembeling's rapids. The park's hundreds of kilometres of trails are kept cleared and well-marked, and meander through fascinating lowland dipterocarp and riverine forests, climbing to stunted montane vegetation.

Bird-watching is a delight. Kingfishers, bee-eaters, fishing eagles and osprey abound, and even if you don't see them, you'd certainly hear them, in particular the hornbills' unmistakable squawk. Besides monitor lizards, the larger denizens such as elephants, black panther, *seladang* wild ox and tigers are virtually impossible to spot, so learn to identify their tracks. Nonetheless, sit quietly in the jungle, and you might be rewarded with the sight of a troupe of long-tailed macaques in the treetops.

The aboriginal Batek communities are no longer a common sight around the headquarters, preferring a nomadic lifestyle deep in the forest. You might occasionally bump into them on a trail or see their temporary huts. The Batek have a natural dignity; don't be too quick to turn them into a tourist spectacle with the click of a camera. But don't be surprised if they demand RM5 if you do insist on clicking. The Senoi and Semak Abri tribes outside the park area, however, live more contemporary lifestyles and are more open to visitors.

Riding the Tembeling

BELOW: jungle canopy walk at Taman Negara.

Permits are required to enter the park and there is a fee for cameras – arrange at the Parks and Wildlife Department or your travel agent. Entrance to the park is usually by river from the Kuala Tembeling jetty, although a rough road also goes to the Kuala Tahan *kampung*. However, the covered 14-seater longboat ride is a great way to cover the 35-km (20-mile) journey on Sungai Tembeling. The 2-hour trip can take twice as long if the river level is low; sometimes, passengers have to disembark and wade while the boatmen negotiate the shallow waters.

Kuala Tembeling is accessed from Jerantut, where express buses and the Gemas-Tumpat trains stop. From Jerantut, take a 30-minute taxi to the jetty. Tours to the park that operate from major cities and Jerantut include transfers to and from the park.

Accommodation in the park ranges from campsites to luxurious chalets under the Taman Negara Resort. Budget accommodation is available outside the park in the *kampung* and at Nusa Camp. There is a 50-sen river shuttle between the park and the *kampung*, and a riverbus run by Nusa Camp services the main jetties on Sungai Tembeling. Boats within the park must be arranged through the Wildlife Department.

At Kuala Tahan, visitors can book accommodation, arrange trips and get information and maps at either the Wildlife Department or the Taman Negara Resort. The resort and Nusa Camp have good maps and guides to the park, and provide information to non-guests as well. They also rent out camping and fishing gear if you make prior arrangements.

The park's excellent interpretation centre, squashed into the resort grounds, provides a great introduction to the park, including information on trails and rainforests in general. Videos are screened at 2pm and 8.45pm. Short trails can be done yourself, or you can hire nature interpretation guides. Guides are compulsory on the major trails, and guided tours are included in packages.

Walks in the wild

The most popular walk is the half-hour trek to the **canopy walkway** (open 11am–3pm; entrance fee), a rope-and-ladder bridge among the tops of trees, up to 27 metres (80 ft) up. The 400-metre (1,300-ft) long walkway gives visitors a rare chance to experience the shoots, fruits and pollinating insects of the canopy at close quarters. This trail is part of the longer loop which goes to **Tabing Hide** and **Teresek Hill** with its views of Gunung Tahan.

Another popular trek is to **Gua Telinga**, a wet, ear-shaped cave (hence its name *telinga*) where you crawl through guano beneath bats clustered on the low ceilings. The lucky could spot a cave racer, a long white snake that feeds on the bats. Fist-sized toads and insects like spiders and cockroaches are plentiful too. Although they may be unnerving to many people, all the fauna in the cave are harmless to humans.

A leisurely alternative is to glide under arches of trees up the small pretty **Sungai Tahan**, and soak in **Lata Berkoh**, a natural jungle jacuzzi formed by a bank of cascades. Lata Berkoh is popular with anglers, as is **Sungai Keniam**, which can be reached on foot or by boat. The trail to the latter, Rentis Keniam, takes in the large caves of Gua Luas, Gua Daun Menari, Gua Kepayang Kecil and Gua Kepayang Besar, which also boast prolific cave fauna. It's a good 2-day trek, camping out at the caves or the popular **Kumbang Hide**.

For long-haulers, two options are the **Air Terjun Empat Tingkat** (Four-Step

Map on page 240

TIP

Taman Negara Resort and Nusa Camp run buses (RM25 one way) daily between Kuala Lumpur (departing 8am) to Kuala Tembeling (departing 1.30pm), which are open to non-guests, but book beforehand.

BELOW: sun-baked boulders at Sungai Tahan.

Map on page 240

TIP

The best time to fish in Taman Negara is during the drier months from February to March, and June to August; equipment can be hired. For bait, local fishermen use riverside fruits.

BELOW: Malayan Tapir.
RIGHT: face to face with pandanus plants, Lake Cini.

Waterfall) and the ultimate, **Gunung Tahan**. Each involves a 7-day trip where you need to carry your own camping gear and food. Both follow the same route along Sungai Tahan until the Teku tributary fork. There are numerous river crossings and a stretch where you have to climb 27 hills – all in 1 day.

The waterfall is a major tributary of Sungai Tahan that plunges down the eastern flanks of Gunung Tahan and Gunung Gedong. The undulating trek up to the Tahan peak, at 2,187 metres (7,175 ft), involves an exhilarating climb through montane oak and cloud forests. There is an alternative route to the peak, which takes 3 days, but it starts at Merapoh town north of Jerantut.

Other trails snake around the 36 hectares (90 acres) of forest bordering the park that belong to Nusa Camp. There are a couple of waterfalls, and the steep Bukit Warisan trek has great sunrise and sunset views of the rainforest canopy with its amazing diversity of trees.

The jungle by night

A night in an animal hide is your best chance to observe wildlife, much of which is nocturnal. These huts-on-stilts are near salt-licks, where animals come to drink. Arrive at the hides early, say around 5pm. Cooking is not allowed, so bring a packed supper, a powerful flashlight, and insect repellent, and settle down to wait. Binoculars are handy. Take turns to "watch", shining the torch every 10 minutes or so. Nosy jungle rats will help keep you awake.

As night falls, the forest comes alive with sounds and ghostly "spirits" flitting between the trees – fireflies and beetles with fluorescent wings and tails. Deer and tapir are the most common sightings, and you'll see lots of spiders and snakes moving about in the undergrowth. An alternative would be to go on a night walk, where you can pick out luminous mushrooms or a slow loris, flying squirrel or civet cat.

Southwest of Taman Negara is the lesser known but no less interesting **Kenong Rimba Park** ㉖, whose specialities are birds and insects. From dawn, the 128-sq. km (49-sq. mile) park is alive with the sounds of birds, including the unique call of the white-rump shamma and the thwack of the Malayan whistle thrush smashing its breakfast of snails on a rock. You might even spot the *belalang dewa* in action, grasshoppers which display locust-like behaviour in travelling in groups, decimating vegetation in one go.

A 2- to 3-hour trail loops around the park, taking in Kenong Rimba's many limestone caves and types of vegetation. There's **Gua Batu Tangga**, a huge cave believed to provide shelter for elephants. **Gua Hijau** is named after its mossy green walls, while **Batu Kajang** has folkloric connections: according to legend, it is a boat carrying a king's messenger that had been turned to stone. A more challenging route is the undulating 5-day trek to **Gua Batu Putih**, which has a delightful crystal-clear stream.

Kenong can be accessed from **Kuala Lipis**, the old Pahang capital. Kuala Lipis is also on the Segamat-Tumpat train route (get off at Batu Sembilan). A 20-minute longboat ride down Sungai Jelai goes to the park at Tanjung Kiara where there are chalets and a campsite. Tours can be arranged at Kuala Lipis. ❏

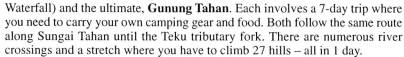

SARAWAK

Once, the much-feared tribes of Sarawak were after enemy heads. Nowadays, they're chasing tourist dollars

Even today, the name Borneo evokes a sense of the exotic – of adventure and a journey into the unknown. Visions of impenetrable jungle, of headhunters and jungle-dwelling tribes, of white *rajahs* (kings) and great riches refuse to fade. And yet today's Sarawak, in the heart of Borneo, is a fast-changing reality.

As loggers move ever further into the wild, deep and dark jungles become accessible, their secrets lost forever. Express boats bring once remote settlements and longhouses within reach, and trips that used to take weeks of battling fast-flowing rivers have been reduced to as many hours as powerful engines churn upriver.

While the white *rajahs* and headhunters are long gone, Sarawak's tradition of open hospitality continues, making Kuching Southeast Asia's friendliest city. You'll always be made welcome, whether by Chinese women offering free samples in the market, or in an Iban longhouse, where you might sit chatting with the chief over a glass of heady *tuak*, Sarawak's ubiquitous home-brewed rice wine.

While Sabah and Sarawak share a common heritage, each with a history that involved the British, their developments took different paths. Sarawak's white *rajahs* had great respect for their Dayak subjects and their rule took their predilections into account. Sabah grew as a trading post, with a more pragmatic and certainly less romantic attitude towards its native inhabitants. As a result, modern Sarawak retains its cultural integrity and pride in traditions.

This sprawling state makes a great introduction to Borneo. Even those with little time to spare can gain a rudimentary understanding of the country and the cultures of its people by visiting the award-winning Sarawak Cultural Centre just outside Kuching. But those with more time can look forward to some rich experiences: the enigmatic caves of Niah, deep in the interior, with their relics of cave dwellers from 40,000 years ago; the national heritage site of Mulu with caves so large that their statistics astound the senses; further afield, the cool Bario Highlands, which bring contact with the warm hospitality of the Kelabits and the chance to trek through pristine jungle.

After a longboat trip upriver, visiting a longhouse, and perhaps even witnessing a longhouse celebration or *gawai,* the taste of Borneo is firmly instilled. If you are lucky enough to hear the haunting music of the *sape* and witness the dance of the hornbills, memories of Sarawak will live in the heart forever. ❑

PRECEDING PAGES: "The Pinnacles" – razor-sharp granitic formations at Sarawak's Mulu National Park.
LEFT: Iban warriors in battle gear strike a pose. Thankfully, headhunting is not practised any more.

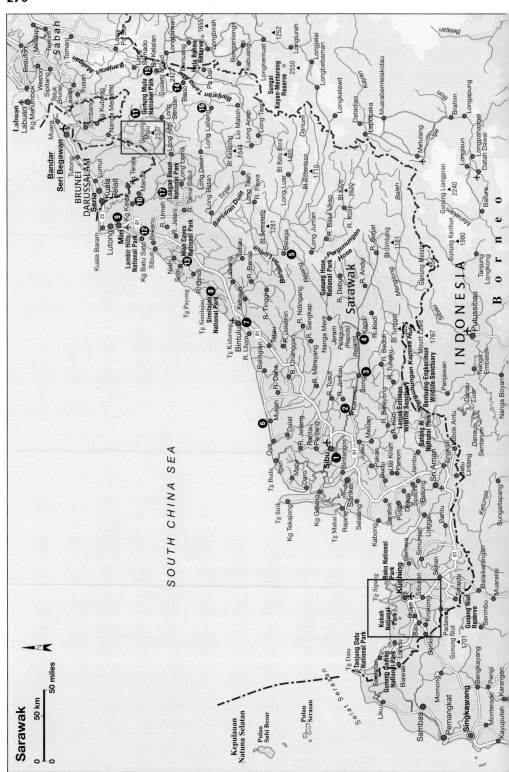

Sarawak

SOUTH CHINA SEA

Banjaran Maligan

Sabah

BRUNEI DARUSSALAM

Bandar Seri Begawan

Gunung Mulu National Park

Hulu Bahau Reserve

Sungai Kayan-Mentarang Reserve

Loagan Bunut National Park

Niah Caves National Park

Lambir Hills National Park

Banjaran Dulit

Pergunungan Hose

Gunung Hose National Park

Sarawak

Similajau National Park

Bintulu

Gunung Gading National Park

Lanjak Entiman Wildlife Sanctuary

Batang Ai National Park

Pergunungan Kapuas Hulu

Batang Entiman Wildlife Sanctuary

Bentuang-Engkarimun Wildlife Sanctuary

INDONESIA

Borneo

Bako National Park

Kuching

Kubah National Park

Gunung Niut Reserve

Tanjung Datu National Park

Kepulauan Natuna Selatan

Pulau Subi Besar

Pulau Serasan

Selat Serasan

Singkawang

N

50 miles

50 km

KUCHING AND THE SOUTHWEST

Kuching has held on to much of its original character while new development spreads further away from the old town centre. The result is one of the most charming towns in Southeast Asia

Maps:
Area 285
City 278

hen British adventurer James Brooke made his way up the winding Sarawak River in his ship, the *Royalist*, he had little idea what was in store for him, or that in a few short years he would be ruling a whole country. It was 1839 and an uncle of the Sultan of Brunei asked Brooke to help settle disputes amongst the country's fighting factions. To the amazement of all, he managed to talk both sides into a harmonious truce. Even more incredible to the Brunei overlords was his insistence that the lives of the rebels be spared and that they be allowed to return to their villages. Thus, Brooke gained the friendship of the Dayaks, the Malays and the Chinese. In return, the Sultan agreed to Brooke's demand that he be given the title of Governor and Rajah of the Sarawak region, thus initiating the "rule of the White Rajahs" – a rule that lasted three generations and over 100 years. Brooke's admiration for the character of the Dayaks led to a long and fruitful relationship, and the novelty of the Brookes' rule became its essence: justice without favouritism.

Exploring Kuching

Winding through lowland *nipah* swamps, the Sarawak River has always been the focal point for Sarawak's capital city, **Kuching** . This delightful old trading town is suffused with old memories, enhanced by the many colonial buildings that have withstood the march of 20th-century progress. People are friendly and hospitable with time to stop for a chat. Amid the noisy traffic, the shophouses squeezed between the bustling markets of the main bazaar and the stately old buildings give the capital an elegant and dignified air. History has always seemed close to the present in Kuching and until the early 1990s, the town centre had changed little from a century ago, when pressures to modernise led to new roads and improvements to the riverfront.

No visit to Borneo is complete without at least a day or two spent in the Sarawak capital. Scattered around Kuching's colonial heart stand the buildings that played such an important part during the Brookes' rule. A Heritage Walk has been devised that covers many of these buildings. The best time to make an on-foot exploration is early morning, or break it up and continue after 4pm, when the heat of the day has begun to pall.

Take one of the gaily painted *tambang* – the small ferry boats leave as soon as they have sufficient passengers – from the various jetties or *pangkalan* along the Kuching Waterfront. First stop is the **Astana** Ⓐ. Built in 1870 for the newly married second Rajah, Charles Brooke, it is now the official residence of Sarawak's head of state. Several renovations later, it

BELOW:
Dayak woman.

Cat sculpture outside the Hilton hotel in Kuching. Incidentally, the city's name translates into "cat" in Malay. According to one theory, Kuching was named after the fruit 'buah mata kuching'(cat's eyes), which grows locally.

consists of three bungalows, supported by square brick pillars, with the low, spreading roof giving shade to the interior. You cannot enter the building, but you may walk in the grounds.

Fortified town

A little further downriver is **Fort Margherita ❸** (open 10am–6pm; closed Fridays) which holds a commanding position overlooking the town. The first of a series of forts that lined Sarawak's main rivers, Fort Margherita was built in 1879, at a calm and peaceful time. The fort was never used for its intended purpose during the Brooke era; the only time it came under attack was during a Japanese air raid in World War II. No severe damage was caused, however, and since the war, the quaint fort has been used mainly as a barracks by the police force. It also houses the surprisingly interesting **Police Museum**. The best time to visit is in the morning; for security reasons, you must produce a passport or ID to enter.

Back across the river is Kuching's **Square Tower ❻**, (no formal opening times, tel: 426-093 for an appointment) an imaginative building built in the same year as Fort Margherita. Its architecture harks back to the Victorian era's fascination with medieval culture. Although equipped with a real dungeon for prisoners, the tower later came to be used as a popular dancing hall.

Next door, also at the beginning of the Kuching Waterfront park, is the renovated **Sarawak Steamship Building**, which houses a fast food restaurant and next to that is the Sarawak Tourist Information Centre, which offers brochures, advice and information in a cool air-conditioned haven.

Once a collection of godowns and trading stores, the old waterfront was

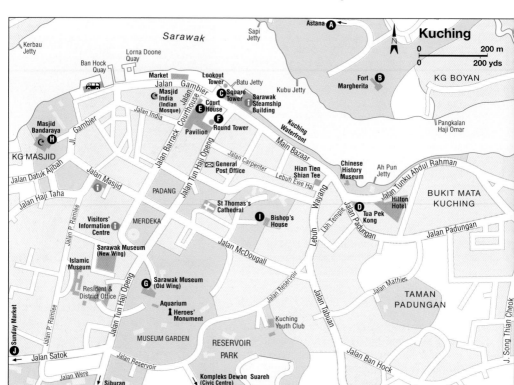

greatly transformed in 1993 to become the **Kuching Waterfront**, a kilometre-long stretch of recreational areas, gardens, walkways, stalls and restaurants, dominated by the impressive white edifice of the **Hilton Hotel** right at the end of the walk – the beginning of the main upmarket hotel area. The park is extremely popular with locals, who can be seen enjoying themselves here at all hours of the day and night. At the down-river end of the Waterfront Park, the one-time Chinese Chamber of Commerce building has been transformed into an interesting **Chinese History Museum** (open 9am–6pm; closed Fridays).

Crossing the road from the Waterfront one reaches Sarawak's oldest, and possibly prettiest, Chinese temple. Devoted to **Tua Pek Kong ❶**, its construction in the late 18th century marks the strong Chinese presence in Sarawak. The Chinese community trades not only in the main towns and cities, but also up-river, with trade boats stocked like floating supermarkets, or others attached to remote longhouses, supplying down-river goods and building up a network of trade and news wherever they go.

The street facing the Waterfront is known as **Main Bazaar**, whose shops now form the main tourist area – a shopping mecca not just for touristy souvenirs but with pieces to interest serious collectors. Many of the old shophouses are taken over by travel companies, handicraft and antique stores specialising in primitive arts.

Continue along the Main Bazaar until you reach the **Court House ❺** – a quietly impressive colonial building, standing stolidly beneath shading trees. Each morning Rajah Charles Brooke would ceremoniously wander in from his home across the river, fresh flower in his buttonhole, to meet with Dayak chiefs and hear their grievances before doling out justice befitting the situation. Built

Map on page 278

BELOW:
Fort Margherita was named after Charles Brooke's wife.

in 1874, the clock tower was added in 1883. The **Charles Brooke Memorial** stands facing the courthouse, erected in 1924. On closer scrutiny, this unimposing obelisk reveals four superbly crafted copper plaques depicting in turn, an Iban warrior, a Chinese courtier, a British soldier and a Malay warrior.

Turning left up Jalan Tuan Abang Haji Openg, it is a short walk to the odd-looking **Round Tower ⑤**, built in 1886 to house the town dispensary. Brooke seems to have had a predilection for fortifications; the Round Tower was meant to double up as a fort in times of attack. Adjacent is the **Pavilion**, with its elaborate frontage – very different from Kuching's other colonial buildings. Built as Kuching's medical headquarters, it is undergoing redevelopment into a costume and textiles museum, along with the the Round Tower.

Victorian treasure trove

Across the road is the impressively-columned **General Post Office** (open 9am–5pm), built in 1931 by Vyner Brooke, the last rajah. The road continues up, past the grassy square of the Central Padang to the **Sarawak Museum ⑥** between Jalan McDougall and Jalan Tun Haji Openg (open daily 9am–6pm; free admission).

This is perhaps the most important place of interest for the visitor. Naturalist and co-founder of the theory of evolution along with Charles Darwin, Alfred Russell Wallace spent many months in Borneo, exploring and collecting specimens. He became a particular friend of Rajah Charles Brooke, who with Wallace's encouragement, built the museum to house a permanent exhibition of native arts and crafts, and specimens from Wallace's own extensive collection. The Brookes were steadfast in their sense of justice. They suppressed

Naturalist Eric Mjoberg who was the first to climb Sarawak's highest mountain, Gunung Murud in 1922, was one of the more famous curators of the Sarawak Museum.

BELOW: the Sarawak Museum is dedicated to the soul of Borneo.

crime and established peace in the state, but wisely refrained from imposing any "civilised" versus "primitive" comparisons upon the native cultures. The Rajahs insisted upon capable curators, whose Western expertise was to serve only to illuminate the ethnological richness of Borneo and the vivid expressions of the societies it nourished. The facade of the museum, however, betrays another influence. Its architecture was influenced by Charles Brooke's French valet, after a house in Normandy.

Spirit of Borneo

While its sense of mystery disappeared along with the marvellous old teak floors during its modernisation, the museum still invites hours of exploration. It is divided into two buildings, separated by busy Jalan Tun Haji Openg. But the museum's exhibits take you far beyond the paved streets of Kuching and into the heart and soul of Borneo.

In the days of head-hunting, human skulls were hung from the rafters of Iban longhouses; the skulls were said to contain a powerful magic.

One display case in the museum is devoted to the Kenyah people, who have names for 60 varieties of ancient glass beads, each one with a special value. Another houses figurines carved 2,000 years ago by the now-extinct Sru Dayaks. An entire corner of the museum has been transformed into a walk-in replica of an Iban longhouse, with simulated fires, human skulls hanging from the rafters, as well as a warrior's elaborate headdress and weaponry resting at his bedside; you almost expect him to walk in and sound the battle cry.

The Sarawak tribespeople's great love of adornment is reflected in the high walls of the interior, painted with flowing designs. A museum employee found one end of a Kenyah longhouse at Long Nawang completely covered with a majestic mural celebrating "The Tree of Life" and he returned to Kuching and commissioned painters to reproduce it.

BELOW: art on display at the museum.

The old wing of the museum has an eclectic character that recalls a succession of spirited curators, as well as the great diversity of Sarawak. The enthusiastic influence of scholar Tom Harrisson, who first came to explore Sarawak in the 1920s as an Oxford undergraduate (and later returned to make his home here) can be seen in many of the collections. There is a human dental plate on display that was found in the stomach of a 6-metre (20-ft) crocodile. A rhinoceros horn cup that can detect poison is another item. If the drink was contaminated, the liquid bubbled to the top: since princes were always trying to poison one another, rhino horn was in high demand during the days of the dynasties.

The old museum is joined by a footbridge over the road to the new **Museum Annex** completed in 1983. Here galleries display more of this cultural treasure trove; the lifestyles and customs of the nation's various tribes are well documented, and there is a reconstruction of the Niah caves where people lived 40,000 years ago. Videos and slide-shows cover such Sarawakian topics as the Great Golden Hornbill (Sarawak is often referred to as the "Land of Hornbills"), life in the jungle, and popular tribal dances.

Over the road bridge is the **Visitors' Information Centre**, where permits for National Park visits can be obtained from the helpful staff. Continue down

Jalan Barracks, past the Padang and the Central Police Station and turn left into **Jalan India**, a colourful jumble of shops and small businesses, little changed from 50 years ago.

Veer left into Lebuh Market, the old market street that leads to the golden domes of decorative **Masjid Bandaraya (Kuching Mosque)** , which overlooks the river. Built in 1968, it replaced the much older wooden structure built in 1852 that burned down. Retrace your steps along Lebuh Market to Jalan Gambier, where opposite the market, a spicy aroma emanates from the open sacks of spices on display. This collection of colourful shops marks what was once the main trading area. Indian Muslim traders, following the Chinese example in the 18th century, headed for Sarawak to set up textile shops and moneylending stalls; the area still exudes a faint aura of the exotic east. Across the street are a few examples of the old buildings that once lined this end of the Main Bazaar.

The **Masjid India** (Indian Mosque), in between Lebuh India and Jalan Gambier, was built by Indian Muslim traders in 1876. The streets around the mosque are a labyrinth of small Indian shops and spicy curry-scented restaurants. Continue the walk through this colourful area back to the Courthouse.

Chinese influence

Like many Malaysian towns, Kuching has its share of ornate Chinese temples. Apart from the Tua Pek Kong temple mentioned earlier, there is the **Kuek Seng Ong Temple** on Lebuh Wayang. Built in 1895, the temple is the traditional place of worship for Henghua fishermen, praying for good catches and a safe return from the sea. The temple is dedicated to the god Kuek Seng Ong, whose

BELOW: Kuching Mosque overlooking Sarawak River.

figure is placed on a sedan chair on the 22nd day of the second moon, and carried through the town's main thoroughfare.

Worthy of note is one of the oldest buildings in Kuching, the sprawling **Bishop's House ❶**, located behind the temples and shophouses of Chinatown, It was built in 1849 by James Brooke for the Rev. Thomas Francis McDougall and his wife. With his typical astuteness, Brooke selected McDougall as the first Anglican Bishop of Kuching because he had previously been a surgeon. Nearby is **St Thomas's Cathedral**.

The popular **Sunday Market ❼**, which attracts Dayak tradesmen from the surrounding countryside, is situated on the outskirts of town at Jalan Satok. The stallholders arrive and set up market on Saturday afternoon and continue until midday Sunday. All manner of strange foodstuffs – jungle produce, wild boar, bats, lizards, monkeys and turtles – are on sale here, alongside fruit, vegetables and fish.

A more recent addition to the Kuching cityscape is the blue- and gold-domed **Masjid Negara** (National Mosque), which stands across the river in a newer part of town, an example of modern Islamic architecture.

Sarawak's western beaches

Sun worshippers, beach lovers and golfers head for **Damai Beach ❷** near Santubong, just 30 minutes by road from downtown Kuching. The pioneer resort here, Holiday Inn Damai Beach, has been joined by the Holiday Inn Damai Lagoon and the Santubong Resort. As well as the various watersports offered by the resorts, an 18-hole golf course and jungle walks on Mount Santubong increase the recreational options.

Maps:
Area 285
City 278

Temple detail from Kuching's Kuek Seng Ong temple, dedicated to protecting fishermen.

BELOW: fruit stall, Kuching.

TIP

There are traditional
dance performances
at the Sarawak
Cultural Village
at 11.30am and
4.30pm each day.
Call 846-411 for
more information.

For a fine introduction to Sarawak's varied cultures, visit the state's award-winning **Sarawak Cultural Village ❸**, (open 9am–5.30pm; entrance fee) adjacent to Damai Beach. Spread across 6 hectares (15 acres) of jungle at the foot of Santubong Mountain, the park has authentic dwellings of the six main cultural groups, staffed by friendly helpers wearing the appropriate dress. The village offers demonstrations of traditional arts and crafts, as well as daily cultural shows which incorporate Iban, Kayan, Kenyah, Melanau and Malay, Chinese and Bidayah dances.

The fishing village of **Santubong ❹** is also worth a visit. The village dates back to the Tang and Sung dynasties, between the 9th and 13th century, when it was an important trading centre. Ancient rock carvings of Hindu and Buddhist influence have been discovered around the river delta.

Other beach resorts further along the coast include the **Santin Resort ❺**, hidden among mangroves 30 km (20 miles) west of Kuching. Tour buses leave the capital and take you to the jetty, where a boat zips you to the resort, which is inaccessible by land. There are boats to take you snorkelling and a fine beach lined with casaurina trees. With prior permission, you may be allowed to visit the turtle sanctuary of **Pulau Satang Besar ❻** where precious turtle eggs are closely guarded.

Longhouse tours from Kuching

While you are in Sarawak, one thing you must do is to visit a longhouse (*see page 294–5*), and enjoy the chance to see an integrated community living under one roof. It is also great fun and the friendly and hospitable Iban people generally enjoy a bit of outside company.

BELOW:
Sarawak Cultural
Village hostess.

The Iban and most of the Orang Ulu build their dwellings near rivers, which once offered their only means of access. Now many are accessible by road. Many interesting longhouses are accessible from Kuching, mostly around the **Batang Ai Dam**, situated about 275 km (170 miles) north of Kuching, near the headwaters of the **Batang Lupar**. The dam is fed by several tributaries where many longhouses are found.

Visitors were previously encouraged to head out on their own, but now, unless you are invited by a longhouse inhabitant, it is advised to use a tour operator. Many have built their own tourist accommodation nearby, ensuring more privacy for both the longhouse dwellers and the visitors, and ensuring that the inhabitants benefit from the visits.

The best known river is the **Skrang**, the first river to open to tourism, but the river inhabitants along here have been subjected to visitors for many years and their enthusiasm has worn off. Ask your tour company about the **Lemanak River**, the **Engkari** or **Ulu Ai** which is surrounded by virgin rainforest and is a boat ride from **Batang Ai National Park**.

One of the best longhouse experiences is offered by Borneo Adventure (*see Travel Tips*) tour company at the eco-award-winning **Nanga Sumpa** longhouse on Ulu Ai. The longhouse inhabitants have benefited from their visitors who enable them to earn a little more cash without needing to compromise their lifestyle.

Sarawak's other longhouse experience is the **Hilton's Batang Ai Longhouse Resort**. Opened in 1994, overlooking the dammed lake, the upmarket resort features "longhouse living with all the modern conveniences" but lacking the community atmosphere. Make your choice. Facilities include air-conditioning, hot water and a modern restaurant. Since the primary reason for coming here is the jungle, the resort offers nature walks, jungle treks and boat trips, as well as excursions to nearby Iban longhouses and the open-air market at **Sri Aman**.

Sarawak's national parks

An abundance of nature can be enjoyed at the many national parks accessible from Kuching. Some parks can be enjoyed as day trips, although all deserve a longer visit.

Gazetted in 1957, **Bako National Park (Taman Negara Bako)** ❼ was Sarawak's first, and it offers some of the best chances to see native animals in the wild. Situated on a peninsula at the mouth of the Sarawak River, Bako's relatively small area of 30 sq km (10 sq miles) is uniquely rich in both flora and fauna, offering examples of almost every vegetation group to be found in the state. Primary rainforest covers one side of the peninsula, while the other side offers a picturesque coastline of steep cliffs and sandy bays with beaches for swimming. Mud flats and sand bars support a great diversity of sea birds, as well as peculiar red crabs and mud skippers.

While it is possible to visit Bako on a day trip, the rewards are greater if you stay for one night at least – a visit of two or three nights is recommended. Some people stay for a month, relaxing in the natural environment and exploring all the park has to offer. Catch the sun setting over the coloured limestone

Map on page 285

BELOW: Iban dancer.

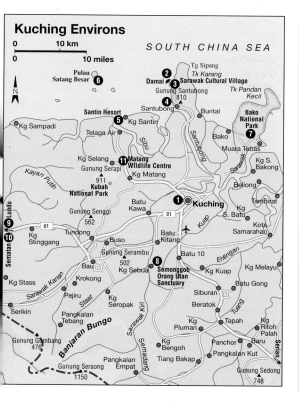

Feeding times at the
Semonggoh Orang
Utan Sanctuary are
from 8.30–9am and
2.30–3.30pm so time
your visit carefully.

karsts of the main beach, and enjoy the unearthly experience of walking in the luminous forest at night.

The dry plateau is home to the bizarrely beautiful insect-eating flowers known as *nepenthe*s or pitcher plants; eight species exist within the park's confines. The coastal swamp forest is a favoured retreat of the proboscis, or long-nosed, monkey, the long-tailed macaque, bearded pig and sambar deer, some of which find their way down to the beaches.

Within the park is a good system of well-marked paths, and on arrival at the Park Ranger's Office you will be given a guide map. So, set down your things in your accommodation, and get ready to explore the wonders.

A magnificent plankwalk leads through a tidal mangrove forest that changes character throughout the day with the rise and fall of the sun, and the ebb and flow of the tide. Here in the early morning, when the water is low, lucky visitors may encounter the shy proboscis monkey or the silver leaf monkey, feasting on the young leaves. Tread quietly and keep your eyes wide open. The popular **Lintang Trail** leads through nearly all the vegetation types and up to the arid plateau where pitcher plants can be found among the scrub.

Within the park, accommodation is available at the resthouse, dormitories and chalets at the headquarters at **Teluk Assam**. A small shop supplies basic provisions which you can cook yourself, or the canteen offers a perfectly acceptable menu. Beware the cheeky long-tailed macaques who will try their best to find their way into your chalet kitchen or even steal food right off the table in the main dining area. They are a basketful of trouble, providing high entertainment for onlookers. Book accommodation with the helpful staff in Kuching at the Visitors' Information Centre, close to Sarawak Museum.

BELOW: sunset in Bako National Park.

At **Semonggoh** ❽ you'll find Sarawak's first orangutan sanctuary, 22 km (14 miles) southwest of Kuching. This is another must-visit excursion and a great chance for an encounter with these delightful creatures. Rehabilitation for orphaned babies and creatures who have been kept as domestic pets is an ongoing process as they are taught to climb trees, find food, make nests and otherwise survive in the wild. It is also the home for hornbills, monkeys and honey-bears.

Remote islands

The little-explored western part of the state has more surprises for those who want to visit. The now reasonable road west leads to **Lundu** ❾ and **Sematan** ❿ where remote beaches – try Pandan Beach near Lundu – are only one of the attractions. Out from Sematan, a relaxed little fishing village, are several deserted islands, one of which, **Talang Talang** is a turtle sanctuary. Permission to visit the far west of the state can be obtained from the local district officer; accommodation in self-contained chalets is available.

More national parks have recently opened up in the northwest. The town of Lundu is the access point to **Gunung Gading National Park**. Gazetted in 1983, the mountainous park covers an area of over 41,000 hectares (101,100 acres), on both sides of the Lundu River. Within the park are waterfalls and a trail to the summit of Gunung Perigi, a trek that takes about 8 hours. Giant Rafflesia blooms can be found in the park, and chalets are available.

In Sarawak's southeast corner you'll find **Kubah National Park**, a small park of 2,230 hectares (5,500 acres), which is only 21 km (13 miles) from Kuching along good roads, making it easily accessible. Within its confines are streams, waterfalls and bathing pools. A 5–6 hour return trail leads to the park's highest peak, **Gunung Serapi,** while the most popular, the waterfall trail, leads through dipterocarps with plankwalk sections in front of the waterfall. Kubah makes a good day trip from the capital; chalets are available for longer stays.

The **Matang Wildlife Centre ⑪** is some 14 km (9 miles) further along, although you can also get to this reserve via the 3–4 hour Ulu Rayu trail from the Park Headquarters. Endangered species are contained in large enclosures within the rainforest allowing perusal by visitors.

Gazetted in 1994, **Tanjung Datu National Park** is one of Sarawak's newest and smallest parks, covering an area of just 1,379 hectares (3,400 acres). Right at the westernmost tip of the state, the park has clear rivers and fine corraline beaches with unspoiled reefs. It is accessible by boat from Sematan and the whole journey takes around 3½ hours – but there is no accommodation available.

Batang Ai National Park and **Lanjak Entiman Wildlife Sanctuary** are favoured haunts of orang-utan, gibbons, barking deer, leaf monkeys and wild boar as well as several hundred species of birds. Both areas are located in the Sri Aman Division, north of the Batang Ai hydro-electric dam. Once past the Batang Ai dam – a 4-hour trip from Kuching – the journey to the park takes about 2 hours upriver by longboat. There are no facilities in these two reserves as yet, but Borneo Adventure has accommodation at **Wong Tibul**, on the boundary of Batang Ai National Park; excursions into the park can be arranged from there. ❏

Map on page 285

BELOW: Orang-utan at Semonggoh.

SIBU AND CENTRAL SARAWAK

Sibu is the bustling gateway to the Rejang, Malaysia's mightiest river. A trip upriver will reward you with a glimpse of the lives of the Orang Ulu and Iban peoples of the region

Map on page 276

Beyond Kuching, cosmopolitan city life fades away and the innumerable rivers that mark Sarawak's green interior become the highways to remote inland settlements. **Sibu ❶**, capital of Sarawak's third and largest district, is an easy-going and predominantly Chinese town, where trishaws are still in service and where the fish markets overflow with gigantic freshwater species such as carp and the much-prized *kolong,* which finds its way to the elegant dining tables of Hong Kong. Timber money has made Sibu rich and the sprawling town, abounding with glitzy hotels and karaoke bars, is home to some of Sarawak's wealthiest families. Visitors tend not to linger in Sibu – often just staying overnight after arriving from Kuching by boat, before leaving to travel upriver the next morning.

The expressboat port and surrounding market area is the town's busiest spot, presided over by the imposing seven-tier pagoda that is part of the **Tua Pek Kong Temple**. From the top of the pagoda is a magnificent view of dozens of expressboats lined up along the wharf, with boards in front denoting their destinations and a clock showing their departure times. The busy atmosphere lends a hint of adventure and of journeys into the unknown.

Although it is possible to take a bus from Kuching to Sibu, your bones will be considerably rattled by the time you arrive. It is far more pleasant to take the expressboat which heads down the Sarawak River, out to the South China Sea then up the **Rejang River** via **Sarikei**. Alternatively, there is a 40-minute flight, giving a wonderful view of the never-ending jungle with its milk-coffee rivers snaking their way through the low-lying *nipah* palm swamps. Flights to further up the Rejang River, to Kapit and Belaga, are also available.

LEFT: tributary of Sarawak's mighty Rejang River.
BELOW: nomadic Punans help to transport goods.

Heading upriver

From Sibu, expressboats, long and narrow, rather like wingless 747s, depart regularly. They head downstream to Sarikei and Kuching, and upriver *(ulu)* to Kapit, and also past the treacherous Pelagus Rapids to Belaga. Tourists mingle with an assortment of other passengers: Chinese merchants taking their wares to distant longhouses; river and inland officials (usually Iban) going about their business; the odd longhouse dweller returning home after a visit to the big city, or schoolchildren who attend school in Sibu but return to their family longhouses for the holidays.

Because of extensive logging, expressboats now run to several of the major tributaries of the Rejang – a marvellous network that enables visitors to get around at little expense and with great ease – a situation much changed from the heady and hilarious days of Redmond O'Hanlon's explorations in *Into The*

Heart Of Borneo. Other, much earlier travellers had to do it all the hard way, by hiring boats themselves. Although expressboat prices are fixed, hire of longboats is expensive (even for locals) and heavily dependent on the water level, weather, time of day, river currents and how willing the boatman is to hurry his journey to fit your schedule. For foreigners, prices will naturally be much higher and a spot of astute but friendly bargaining is in order. Unless you take a direct express to Kapit, the expressboat stops along the way at the smaller settlements of **Kanowit** ❷ and **Song** ❸, from where local expressboats can be taken to visit longhouses up these rivers.

On the river, boats and longboats, and timber tugs work their way up or glide down-river on the Rejang. Sarawak's longest river is also the natural highway for the timber industry, and you are likely to see huge rafts stacked with logs floating downstream. Should one of these hazards become waterlogged, they present considerable danger to outboard motors; with that very danger in mind, the express boats have their undercarriage lined with steel and there is always a spare propellor shaft lashed to the roof.

Kapit – the upriver capital

The day starts early in **Kapit** ❹ as the siren call of the first expressboats sound through the misty dawn. As the boats fire up their throbbing and powerful engines, passengers down their last cups of morning coffee, ready to start their journeys on the river.

BELOW:
the Rejang River in
the glow of dusk.

To those who live far up the Rejang River, the bustling market town is the big city. Kapit has electricity 24 hours a day, shops (selling goods at considerably higher prices than back in Sibu), hotels equipped with luxuries like TV and air

conditioning and fast food outlets selling fried chicken, pizza, ice cream and other doubtful big city delights. As a marked contrast, the daily morning market is filled with tribal women coming to town to sell their produce, before heading off to the local provision shops to buy longhouse necessities.

Only 2½ hours upriver from Sibu, and in spite of all these modern improvements, the sprawling centre still retains the atmosphere of a frontier town, bearing marks of it's origins when the Brookes established it as a trading post and fort town. **Fort Sylvia**, built in 1875 by Charles Brooke, was placed strategically to prevent the movement of the Orang Ulu downstream and the Ibans moving further *ulu* or upstream, to avert more full-scale wars. Constructed solidly of *belian* or ironwood, the fort has withstood generations of floods, which in some years reached halfway up the walls. Today the fort houses the **Kapit Museum**, with excellent ethnographic displays on the main peoples of the area.

Kapit lies in the heart of Iban country, Sarawak's largest indigenous population. Ibans were once the headhunters who gave Borneo its romantic and primitive reputation. Some understanding of their culture will help the visitor to see that they were not merely bloodthirsty in an anarchic way.

To bring good fortune to the longhouse, and fame and a bride for themselves, young Iban warriors would (and some still do) set out from home to travel "the world". Status would be acquired in the form of tattoos telling of their bravery, and the heads of a few enemies brought home to imbue the longhouse with protective spirits. Only warriors of equal strength were killed, and never children, women or the old and sick. Sadly, these traditions were much misunderstood by the 19th-century writers who revelled in writing lurid stories about the headhunters of the Iban tribes.

Map on page 276

An Iban woman weaving the pua kumbu, a traditional fabric used for ceremonial purposes.

BELOW:
Iban tattoos are heavily symbolic.

TIP

The Sarawak Tourism Board has organised a homestay programme which allows visitors to stay with selected families to sample a slice of traditional Malaysian life. Contact the board at tel: 082-240 620

Beyond Kapit is **Belaga ❺** – the last urban centre on the Rejang, after which it is longhouse communities all the way. Reaching Belaga means coursing through the **Pelagus Rapids**, marking the natural boundary between the Iban territory below and the Orang Ulu beyond. These rapids are the most treacherous navigable waterway in the state, and possibly in the whole of Borneo. The 2½ km (1½ miles) stretch is a series of whirlpools and waves as the river rapidly loses altitude. Many lives and boats have been lost in this maelstrom; riding the rapids atop an expressboat (ready to jump off in case of trouble) provides high excitement. When the water is low – from May to August – only small longboats can struggle through, although some do try to negotiate the perils in a speedboat.

Just below the rapids is the upmarket **Pelagus Resort**, a designer longhouse-style resort, designed by Kuching luminary and architect, Edric Ong. The resort makes a comfortable base for excursions: to longhouses to see Iban women making high-quality *pua kumbu* or ceremonial blankets; to explore waterfalls and jungle trails; or to just laze by the pool, amid beautiful natural surroundings.

Upstream to Belaga

The real last outpost, Belaga has grown larger, due to incessant logging, but visit the town, with its few small but comfortable hotels to see just what a bazaar of the interior looks like. Some of the old wooden buildings remain, although increasingly they are replaced with ubiquitous concrete shophouses. But sit in a coffee shop, sipping on a mug of thick coffee sweetened with spoonfuls of condensed milk, and watch the passing parade of people: Iban women wearing heavy metal decorations in their ears which have stretched to their breasts; young warriors who devote their ferocity to football rather than collecting heads;

BELOW: boats are probably the best means of travel.

children sent down to school to learn the ways of the other world; a collection of traders, hustlers, would-be tour guides on the make, and labourers fresh from the logging camps, money burning in their pockets. It's raw and primitive, with an energy you will never find in the city.

From Belaga, expressboats head upstream when the water is high, but it really is necessary to find a guide or an invitation before venturing afar to visit an upriver longhouse. In spite of their long traditions of hospitality to travellers on the river, most longhouse folk are just not interested in entertaining people they can't talk to and who have little to offer to their lives. Be sure to check on whether the ban of foreigners heading upriver from Belaga is still in force; introduced before the start of construction of the controversial Bakun hydro-electric dam, this forbids non-Malaysians from going beyond Belaga.

Map on page 276

Sojourn with nature

Travelling northeast from Sibu along the main highway to Miri, one passes a few worthwhile stops. A good network of buses, taxis and mini buses makes it quite an easy matter to move east by public transport.

The sleepy Melanau fishing village of **Mukah 6** is a pleasant layover and offers a relaxed respite from jungle life. The traditional wooden houses are stilted and visitors can watch the fascinating process of extracting sago from the thick trunks of the sago palm. An excursion out to sea with the fishermen is another possibility. The town is home to the enigmatic annual Kaul Festival where ancient Melanau rites appease the spirits of the sea and mark the new fishing season as well as give thanks to the fertility spirits. Several towns hold their own Kaul Festival as well as the official one held in the second week of April.

BELOW: performing a religious ritual.

The burgeoning oil town of **Bintulu 7** has developed out of all recognition in the past 10 years. The old wooden bazaar has given way to new shops and hotels, as well as a deep-water port, chemical factories and a massive liquid petroleum gas (LPG) plant to exploit offshore reserves of natural gas.

About 20 km (12 miles) away from Bintulu is the **Similajau National Park 8**. Gazetted in 1976, the 7,067-hectare (17,500-acre) national park is less visited than those closer to Kuching or Miri, but its more difficult access makes it no less attractive. Opened to visitors only in 1991, the long narrow park covers a 32 km by 1.5 km area (20 miles by 1 mile) and is bordered by one of Sarawak's most beautiful stretches of unspoiled beach, with jungle trails running into the forest. Small rivers and rapids on the **Sebulong River** also make for interesting exploration. Similajau is home to saltwater crocodiles, so watch your step when walking close to river inlets. Other, less spectacular inhabitants include gibbons, banded langurs, civet cats, porcupines, wild boar and long-tailed macaques, as well as 185 species of birds, including hornbills. Green turtles come to lay their eggs on the quiet beaches between July and September.

Numerous longhouses can be visited up the Kemana River that runs into Bintulu; some are accessible by road as well as by river. Further upriver are Orang Ulu longhouses of the Kenyah and Penan peoples. ❏

THE LONGHOUSES OF SARAWAK

A visit to an Iban longhouse offers a unique glimpse of an ancient way of life that – although changing fast – is still fascinating for outsiders

Longhouse life is a microcosm of a well-run society, where a close-knit community lives together under one roof with one chief, or *Tuai Rumah*, in charge. Within the structure, a kind of horizontal highrise, each family has its own quarters or *bilek*, where they sleep and eat. The main room is often lined with Chinese ceramic jars much prized by the Ibans. At the rear is the kitchen, where a wood fire provides the heat for cooking, adding a distinctive smokey taste to the food and a dark patina to the surroundings.

CHANGING TIMES

Times are changing in the longhouse. Walls which once held faded photographs of the Brookes and Queen Elizabeth II are now adorned with colour magazine pictures of beauty queens, racing cars and the latest pop icons. Many Dayaks have converted from spirit-sensitive animism to Christianity, and evenings once spent performing tribal chants and sacrificial ceremonies are taken up with prayer meetings. Children who once enjoyed carefree days frolicking in the longhouse and the rice fields are ensconced in schools studying Bahasa Malaysia and physics. Yet still the community spirit lives on.

▷ **LIVING OFF THE LAND**
Longhouse life is hard. Men and women spend long hours working in the fields, planting and tending their crops.

△ **ON THE VERANDAH**
Much longhouse activity takes place on the *tanju* – from drying cocoa beans to socialising.

▷ **COCKFIGHTING**
Cockfighting is a popular male pastime. Animistic beliefs and legendary spirits surround many of the festival cockfights.

◁ MULTI-PURPOSE GALLERY
Winnowing grains on the *ruai*, or gallery – the space used for everything from basket weaving to holding community celebrations.

△ LONGHOUSE STAPLE
Drying rice on the longhouse verandah, or *tanju*. Afterwards, the rice is stored carefully in the different family units.

◁ TRADITIONAL SKILLS
An Iban woman displays her handiwork in a *pua kumbu* – a ceremonial blanket used to decorate longhouse walls.

△ IKAT WEAVING
Preparing to dye the threads for a *pua kumbu*. Intricate pieces can use up to five or six colours, and take months to complete.

FIGHTING COCK OR SACRIFICIAL PET?

Cocks play an important part in Iban culture, and they are kept and cossetted as pets while being prepared for their first big fight. The men of the longhouse play with them regularly, engaging them in mock battles with their neighbours, but without the razor sharp spurs attached to their rear claws. Those are reserved for fighting days and can bring a lesser fighter to its death in minutes. Before the fight, the cocks are sometimes given small shots of *tuak*, rice wine, to keep them energised and slightly aggressive.

The cocks and chickens also play an important part in ceremonial issues. Chicken sacrifices are common and the occult powers of a white cockerel are highly respected, in common with many other cultures around the world.

In many ceremonies – for example, in the case of a sick or possessed person – a cock will be sacrificed, and the blood, valued for its purifying quality, sprinkled over a subject. In milder cases, the live chicken is simply waved over the subject or over the ceremony offering plates.

MIRI AND THE NORTHEAST

*Just over the border from Brunei, the oil boomtown of Miri is the
ideal spot from which to head for the magnificent Mulu caves,
or make a visit to a Sarawakian longhouse*

Map
on page
276

On the northwest coast of Sarawak lies **Miri** , the first town to come to prominence – and win notoriety – with the growth of the oil industry. But gone are its bad old days as a wild cowboy town – a town of oil money and men chasing it. Today, Miri is modern and thriving, with luxurious hotels, including the Rihga Royal and a Holiday Inn, and restaurants and bars catering to the town's new-found wealth. Miri is also the source of bright lights and salubrious entertainments for the inhabitants of nearby **Brunei**, a short drive across the border. Despite all this, the ambience remains decidedly relaxed in this predominantly Chinese oil town.

While Miri offers few attractions apart from food and relaxation, and more recently some excellent diving, it makes an excellent overnight stop before embarking on a trip to the great caves of Mulu, or any of the other interesting spots nearby.

A feast of seafood

Food in Miri is a pleasure. The town has long been known for its seafood, and has several Chinese restaurants specialising in serving up great piles of fresh and delicious delicacies for the most discerning palate. Don't overlook the Miri Café – opened by an Australian couple, this easygoing café cum bar in an open-fronted shophouse offers basic Aussie dishes and a wide selection of drinks.

On top of **Canada Hill** overlooking Miri is Sarawak's first oil well. Constructed by Shell in 1910, the well was the forerunner of a further 623 oil wells drilled in the area known as the Miri Land Field. It also survived longer than most of the other 623. After more than six decades, and an estimated yield of 600,000 barrels, production ceased in the early 1970s.

Just out from Miri are untouched reefs that provide excellent scuba diving, about 90 km (60 miles) off the coast. As the reefs are so far from the coast, they have escaped the destructive dynamiting that has ruined many of the more accessible reefs. Miri is also the starting point for some of Sarawak's most exciting and adventurous upriver trips. Longhouses are scattered from the coast all the way up the Baram River.

The paved road leads as far as **Kuala Baram**, the mouth of the Baram River, and continues towards the Sultanate of **Brunei**. From there, a ferry will take you to the duty-free island of **Labuan**. A road also heads up the northern side of the Baram River to the trading town of **Marudi** ❿.

While most visitors stop just long enough to catch the next expressboat on their rush upriver to Mulu, for a taste of outback Sarawak, Marudi is worth a day or two of exploration by itself. One of the older of

LEFT: bats take flight in Mulu.
BELOW: fish-seller in Miri market.

An elaborate Kenyah headdress.

the Brookes' fort posts and the main supply centre or "bazaar" for the Baram region, Marudi is a fast spreading town which retains the atmosphere of a trading post. Upriver Iban, Kenyah, Kayan and Penan tribal folk come to sell their wares to the Chinese and Indian traders of the town. A lively daily market makes a pleasant diversion and the provision shops stock everything an uplander could need – from chainsaws to chicken feed, plastic buckets to pullovers and even handicrafts. A day or two can be very pleasantly spent wandering about the town, or sitting in a local coffee shop near the expressboat jetty to watch the passing parade of people and produce as boats come and go.

A visit to the Rajah Brooke's **Fort House** is almost mandatory. Erected in 1901 and overlooking the Baram River, the fort was built to control migrations (and wars) up and down river. The fort burned down in the early 1990s, but has been faithfully reconstructed and turned into an interesting little museum.

From Marudi, there are flights to Gunung Mulu National Park and to Bario, in the cool Kelabit Highlands, but book well in advance as seats are scarce.

Marvellous Mulu

BELOW: guides resting at "The Pinnacles", Mulu.

A trip to **Gunung Mulu National Park** ⑪, together with a visit to a longhouse, are two of Sarawak's most memorable experiences. If the trip to or from Mulu follows the old **Headhunters Trail**, using forest paths and longboats, it becomes unforgettable. With the advent of several daily flights to Mulu, getting to the park became much faster and more efficient, but not necessarily more pleasurable, and those with time and a love for travel still prefer to go by boat from Kuala Baram. Flying over part of the park, however, does give you a good idea of its vastness and of the variety of the terrain.

Covering 53,000 hectares (130,600 acres), Mulu is Sarawak's largest park. Gazetted in 1974, it is home to a great variety of flora ranging from flowers and orchids, fungi, mosses and ferns, as well as 10 species of pitcher plants. Ten species of hornbills flourish within the vast park.

A number of tour operators in Miri offer package tours, which include transport as well as meals and accommodation in simple lodges just outside the park boundaries. There is also accommodation within the park – the chalets at the headquarters are ideally located – while nearby, the luxurious Royal Mulu Resort comes complete with a rather incongruous swimming pool. Action sports fans will find new climbing walls, as well as canoeing and rapids shooting.

Be aware that within the park, you are obliged to pay for compulsory guides, many of whom take their job quite seriously, rarely letting their charges out of their sight. Visitors not on a package tour will find themselves paying high prices for boats to get to the caves unless they join forces with others. A trip to Mulu is not necessarily cheap, but it is worthwhile.

World-class caves

For many visitors, the centre of attraction is the magnificent caves. While over 150 km (100 miles) of caves have already been surveyed, specialists estimate that only 20 to 30 percent of this massive system has been documented. The caves are accessible by short longboat rides between the park headquarters and the various sites, and jungle plankwalks make walking easy, freeing your eyes from watching your step and giving you a chance to enjoy the surroundings.

The sheer scale of these caves will please even the most discerning statistician; within their dank confines lies the world's largest natural cave chamber,

> **Maps:**
> **Area 276**
> **Park 299**

Gunung Mulu's primary jungle contains astonishing biodiversity; every scientific expedition that has visited its forests has encountered plant and animal species previously unknown to man.

BELOW: hornbill at Mulu National Park.

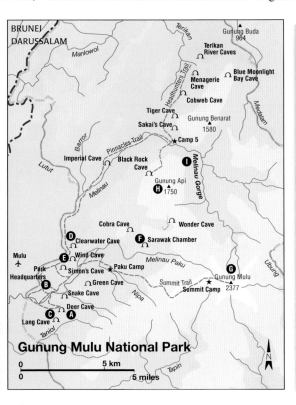

Gunung Mulu National Park

*Subterranean
animals that inhabit
the Mulu caves
include poisonous
cave scorpions,
huntsman spiders,
albino crabs and
snakes which dine on
swiftlets and bats.*

allegedly big enough to hold 16 football fields or 40 jumbo jets and to earn a place in the Guiness Book of Records. Clearwater Cave at 75 km (47 miles), is the longest cave in Southeast Asia.

Exploring the caves

Only four of the 25 caves so far explored are open to public viewing, but this is plenty to gain an idea of the immensity and complexity of this cave system. Most often visited is the **Deer Cave Ⓐ**, named after long vanished deer. The site is accessible by a 3-km (2-mile) plankwalk from the **Park HQ Ⓑ**, passing through a peat swamp forest where orchids thrive and an ancient Punan burial site. This massive hall is 2,160 metres (7,090 ft) long and 220 metres (720 ft) deep. The plankwalk cuts a path over the mounds of guano – a tonne of which is made each day – and leads through to the **Garden of Eden**, an enclosed valley where the vegetation has existed undisturbed for millennia.

It is from near the entrance to Deer Cave that one of the most spectacular sights of Mulu can be enjoyed – the nightly bats' exodus. Around 5.30pm, as the lowering sun turns the limestone walls to gold, the first flutterings can be seen, followed by an ever increasing number of bats circling their way out of the cave, up and over the trees on their nightly forage for food. The dramatic spectacle (which unfortunately does not take place during rainy weather) lasts for a good 20 minutes, and is a sight to awe the most jaded of visitors.

Outside Deer Cave to the left is **Lang Cave Ⓒ**, whose well-lit stalactites and stalagmites make it one of the most beautiful of all the caves.

Clearwater Cave Ⓓ on the way to Camp 5 is located off the main river, a 30-minute boat ride from Park HQ. The 355-metre (1,165-ft) deep cavern is very

BELOW: stunning
Lang Cave in Mulu
National Park.

dark inside, but with a strong torch you'll be able to see the marvellous lime-stone formations, and creatures including scorpions, frogs and centipedes. An exquisitely clear river flows out of the cave from under a sheer rockface, pro-viding a popular spot for bathing. Keep an eye out for beautiful butterflies, including the iridescent green and black Rajah Brooke's Birdwing.

Just a few minutes away, and accessible via a cliff-hugging walkway, is the dramatic **Wind Cave E**, far smaller but filled with limestone stalactites and sta-lagmites with plankwalks passing the most spectacular examples.

Sarawak Chamber F, reputedly the largest cave in the world, is only accessible to scientists, museum experts and special adventure groups, much of it being extremely dangerous. Gaining access to the cavern involves a 4-hour trek through the jungle from the nearest river point, to the small entrance from where you slide into the dank inky blackness. An exciting excursion, but definitely not for the faint of heart.

Map on page 299

Other excursions

Apart from pleasant walks along jungle trails, there are two peaks to be con-quered. **Gunung Mulu G** at 2,377 metres (7,800 ft) and **Gunung Api H**, which at 1,750 metres (5,600 ft) is Malaysia's highest limestone mountain. The stiff ascent of both these mountains is only recommended for very expe-rienced (and very fit) climbers.

The strange limestone spikes, known as **The Pinnacles**, on an alternative path on Gunung Api, can be tackled by anyone of reasonable fitness in about 2 to 3 days. The razor sharp peaks, some standing 45 metres (150 ft) high make a magnificent sight, almost worth the effort of ascending the mountain. The

Caving in Mulu National Park is an unrivalled experience.

BELOW: plankwalk to Deer Cave.

TIP

It is recommended that you wear gloves, long-sleeved shirts and long trousers when climbing the pinnacles; the sharp rocks can cut easily.

journey there begins with a satisfying longboat trip upriver from the National Park HQ, and a short stop-off to visit the Clearwater Cave. A 4-km (2½-mile) walk through lowland forest brings you to the **Melinau River Gorge** ❶ and **Camp 5** – a simple hut shelter and campsite overlooking the Melinau River, and the overnight base camp for the climb to the Pinnacles,

The steep climb, which takes 3 to 6 hours depending on fitness level, starts early morning. This allows enough time to reach the viewpoint by lunch, and to make the descent before dark. The ascent is only to be attempted with experienced guides as the limestone pinnacles are razor sharp. The rough trail passes through the mossy forest where dwarfed trees are festooned with hanging mosses, and numerous pitcher plants, while the often misty environment adds an ethereal air.

The trip to Mulu can be combined with the **Headhunter's Trail**, either starting, or finishing at **Limbang**. The trail, used by Kayan headhunters in the 19th century is a 5- or 6-day journey through the backwoods, either entering or exiting by Camp 5, although leaving from Mulu is the easier option. You'll need a tour company or, at the very least, a guide to arrange the boat transport and longhouse accommodation along the way from Limbang (*see Travel Tips*).

Stone-age secrets

Back in Miri, there are a couple of side-trips which are the main attractions that draw most travellers to Sarawak. **Lambir Hills National Park** ⓬, just south of Miri, makes a pleasant day trip although chalets are available for longer stays. The park's highlights are waterfalls with natural swimming pools and a climb up **Bukit Lambir**.

BELOW: the morning market at Batu Niah.

Much more famous, and with more to offer, is **Niah Caves National Park** ⓭, which while less dramatic than Mulu, offers the freedom for visitors to explore on their own; guides are available if needed.

The limestone caves and their past inhabitants are the attraction here. In the 1870s, animal collector and adventurer, A. Hart Everett, came across the caves – already well-known and protected by the local people – only to dismiss them as "rather dull". It was not until the 1950s that the Sarawak Museum heard of the caves being an archaeologist's gold mine. Sure enough, when the curator dug down 5 metres (16 ft) he found the skull of a young *Homo sapiens* who had lived here possibly up to 40,000 years ago. The Deep Skull, as it was known, was what remained of the earliest known community of modern people in the East. It contradicted the haughty theories which insisted that humanity's true ancestor originated on the west side of the Middle East and only later "wandered" over to this part of the world.

As the archaeologists looked elsewhere, they found haematite paintings, featuring stick figures with strange little boat-like objects. Other discoveries revealed that people living here worked with instruments made from bone and shell, made pottery, cut stone adzes and carved wooden coffins or burial boats. Many agreed that these discoveries were as significant as the unearthing of Java Man. More recent objects, canoe-shaped coffins and paintings found in the cave known as the **Painted Cave**, date from only 1,000 years ago.

When the Iron Age reached Borneo in AD 700, the Niahans were trading hornbill ivory and edible birds' nests for Chinese porcelain and beads. They decorated enormous earthenware urns and placed them beside the graves of special men. Then in 1400, they appear to have entered a tropical Dark Age, which forced them to desert the caves. They then vanished from history.

Maps:
Area 276
Park 299

Local delicacy

The Niahans may have been the forefathers of the nomadic Penan, whose elders still maintain beliefs and rituals that allude to those in the prehistoric grave-yards of the Great Caves. The Penan rediscovered the caves in the 19th century, and found them to be unbelievably rich in edible birds' nests of the millions of swiftlets that inhabit the bowels of the Niah Caves. The glutinous saliva with which they build the nests is believed to be medicinal, and makes the nests the most expensive Chinese delicacy in Borneo. In the markets of Hong Kong and Singapore, the nests can fetch up to US$1,000 per kg (2¼ lbs).

The astronomical cost is almost understandable when you learn the way in which the nests are collected. A typical day's work might entail scurrying up 60 metres (200 ft) on a slender bamboo pole, scraping the nests off rock ceilings and from within deep crevices – and keeping one's balance where any fall could be fatal. You could say that the high cost of nests takes a man's life insurance into consideration.

Naturally, nest collectors guard their trade jealously, and pass their inherited territory on only to their sons. The hundreds of chambers, chimneys and

BELOW: the Niah Caves are thought to have had human inhabitants 40,000 years ago.

Birds' nests, made from the hardened saliva of swiftlets, are treasured by the Chinese for their medicinal and fortifying qualities.

BELOW: entrance to the Great Cave at Niah.

sub-caves where the tiny swiftlets nest are divided into sectors, each privately owned. Some yield but a few hundred nests, others several thousand. The cave owners live in villages and longhouses situated in the park area, and during harvesting – normally two or three times a year, sometimes more – they bring the entire family along to help gather up the riches.

To get to the Niah Caves, you must drive or take a bus or a taxi from either Miri or Bintulu, the former being much closer. From **Batu Niah** village, a short trip along the river brings you to the **Niah Caves Visitor Centre**.

There are several small hotels at Batu Niah, but you'll have to backtrack down the river after you visit the caves – a pleasant boat trip or a 45-minute walk. It is much more convenient to stay at the government-run hostels right in the park if you plan to spend time there. The hostels are friendly and relaxed, providing cooking facilities on request, bedding, toilets and showers with hot water, and electricity. The canteen serves perfectly acceptable, freshly-cooked local food – when you can find the cook.

Walking the planks

The plankwalk to the caves begins from **Pangkalan Lubang**, just across the river from the park accommodation. A museum is located right at the beginning of the walk – entry is free and the information available is not bad. The 3-km (2-miles) long path is built of the mighty *belian* or ironwood, a timber so dense that it will not float. You should get to the caves in about 45 minutes if the planks are dry. Sensible shoes are preferable to sandals both for the plankwalk and the caves. Other necessities include a strong torch (with spare batteries) and some waterproof clothing.

It is well worth stopping during the walk to absorb the atmosphere of the forest and to listen to the jungle chorus. Down one of the forks in the plankwalk, you can visit a collectors' longhouse, although they may charge you to have a look around their home.

Map on page 276

Birds and bats

At the end of the plankwalk you will arrive at a series of steps and the **Trader's Cave**, and a heap of forlorn bamboo scaffoldings where once the traders set up camp during the collecting season. The **Great Cave** is the main area for birds' nest collection – and also for another interesting substance. Besides the three species of swiftlets of which there are said to be around 4 million, there are 12 species of bats, also countable in the millions. The strong-smelling guano lines the cave floor and is collected almost as avidly as the birds' nests – for it is a rich fertiliser. In fact, you may encounter guano collectors on the plankwalk up to the caves, lugging heavy sacks on their backs on their way to Pangkalan Lubang, where it is weighed and then sent down-river to Batu Niah and to the markets beyond.

Eight species of bat live in the Niah Caves. Most common are the horseshoe and fruit bats, but other rare residents include the bearded tomb bat and Cantor's roundleaf horseshoe bat.

With a strong torch you will be able to pick out the creatures that inhabit the caves. Only two of the caves are open to visitors without a guide, and the second, the **Painted Cave**, can only be entered with a permit issued by the National Park Office in Kuching.

The most spectacular sight of all at Niah makes it worth taking camping equipment along. At 6pm, the swiftlets return into the caves to sleep in their nests, while the bats, being nocturnal animals, sweep past them out of the entrance of the cave into the night. While far less spectacular than the great

LEFT: Iban tribesman.
BELOW: guano harvesters in Niah.

Map
on page
276

Mulu exodus, it is quite an experience sitting at the cave mouth, surrounded by dense, green jungle, watching the show. The reverse "shift" takes place at daybreak. It is a sight that humans must have watched and wondered at even 40,000 years ago.

Several other interesting day- or overnight trips can be arranged from Miri. **Bario** ⓮ is the sleepy "capital" of Kelabit country, in the midst of the Bario Highlands, a place right out of time with the industrialised world. A small airstrip, one of a series across the highlands, provides access – when the weather is right – and apart from the daily flights, Bario is remote and untouched. Tom Harrisson described his wartime experiences in the region in his book *The World Within*, and little has changed since. Surrounded by pristine forest, the cool highlands are the perfect place for trekking, stopping at longhouses along the way. One of the best treks is from Bario to **Ba Kelelan** ⓯, a 5-day walk.

Warm welcome

While the culture of the Kelabits has long since given way to the mores of a fundamentalist Christianity, the Kelabits are the kindest and most hospitable people you are ever likely to encounter. The Kelabit community is split across the border between Sarawak and Kalimantan, who are little troubled with the formalities of immigration check points. Visitors are taken to an immigration checkpoint, and the simple formalities are generally ironed out with ease (or a few dollars). From Bario, and with the help of Kelabit guides, it is possible to climb **Gunung Murud**. At 2,423 metres (7,949 ft), this is the highest peak in Sarawak, and you need 5 clear days to ascend and descend the mountain, starting from Bario – a memorable experience. Kelabit guides and porters will also take you on a 6-day walk back to **Long Lallang** ⓰, from where you can fly back to the other, hectic and more hurried world. For the fit and adventurous, one of these expeditions is definitely worth experiencing.

Lawas and **Limbang** are the two forgotten parts of Sarawak, two fingers that are interspersed with the Sultanate of Brunei. **Limbang** is the starting point (or finishing point) for those following the Headhunters Trail to Mulu.

Two hours' drive from Miri, on a turnoff before reaching Niah, is **Loagan Bunut National Park** ⓱. Also known as Bunurung, this very new national park was gazetted only in 1991. The park centres around a mysterious lake that rises and falls with the seasons. In the dry season, it disappears completely, leaving a cracked lake bed and an abundant fish population that hides in the mud. The fish are very easy to catch, a fact that has not escaped the local population of 32 families who are permitted to fish here, or the vast numbers of birds that visit to capitalise on all that fish.

There is little to disturb the peace in this remote place. One old Berawan man tends a guest house that can hold 16 guests, although the government is threatening to put in chalets in a year or two. After arriving by car, the journey can be made into a round trip by taking a longboat and returning via the Baram River and an expressboat to Marudi, then beyond to Kuala Baram and Miri. ❏

BELOW: a soon-to-bloom fern bud.
RIGHT: copper relief of an Iban warrior.

SABAH

Stunningly beautiful, with an air of mystery, Sabah has now become home to a new breed of people seeking adventure

Today's Sabah is a far cry from the romantic days of old. As part of the mysterious Borneo, it inspired visions and wild dreams. It was a land of myth and adventure, of headhunters and strange pagan rites, and the source of buckles of "golden jade" to adorn the imperial belts of Chinese Emperors.

Sabah's ancestors spring from dozens of tribal groups, some deriving from millennia-old migrations from the north of China. Chinese traders sailed to Borneo before the days of Kublai Khan, in quest of kingfisher feathers, hornbill ivory and bezoar stones; others arrived much later, with the British, as coolies and farmers.

Many of today's visitors care less about Sabah's romantic past. They are here to experience excitement and adventure, whether it is diving in unspoilt coastal waters, driving a four-wheel-drive vehicle cross-country, or scaling one of Asia's highest mountains.

Sabah has become a serious adventure destination, whose main attractions glitter bright as stars. It takes a minimum of a 10-day visit to do it any justice at all, and for most visitors, longer is better. The state offers such stellar attractions as Gunung Kinabalu (Mt Kinabalu), one of the highest mountain peaks between the Himalayas and the Andes, primal jungle retreats, wild whitewater rafting, and river cruising to spot wild elephants or the endemic proboscis monkey. Add some of the best diving in Asia – the prime spot, Pulau Sipadan, is rated as one of the world's top five wall dives – and it's no wonder that Sabah is becoming a favoured destination.

And these are only the highlights of this varied state. For those who like to tread more softly, there are secrets to be revealed in the misty jungles and lonely plains.

Remote coral islands are the destination of green turtles, where almost every day of the year, visitors can witness these remarkable creatures laying their eggs in the clean white sands – after making their mysterious odyssey from half-way across the world, following some ancient call of nature.

Sabah may lack the longhouses and diverse tribal communities of Sarawak, but it has remarkable natural assets, with reserves of pristine rainforest and tracts of virgin forest to explore. Places like the untouched Danum Valley exist nowhere else, and the goverment has gone to lengths to preserve this natural heritage, instilling pride in this unique environment into the hearts of the people who live here. ❑

PRECEDING PAGES: Gunung Kinabalu's dramatic rockface framed by swirling clouds.
LEFT: Bajau horsemen of Sabah, "cowboys of the east".

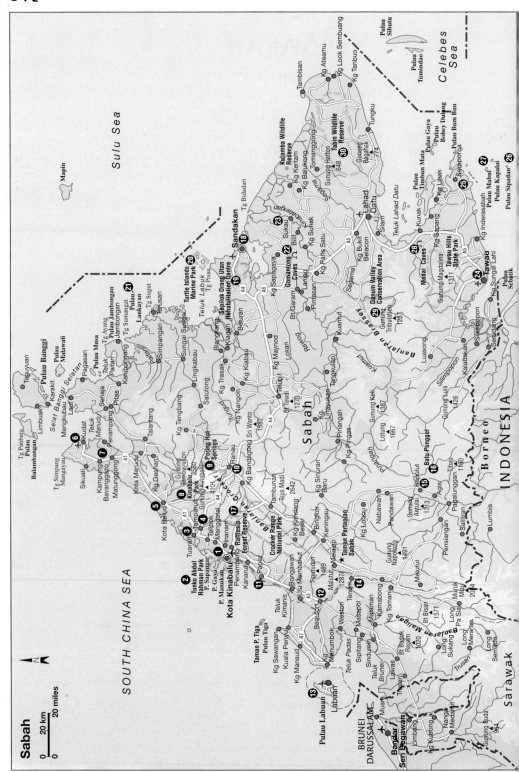

Sabah

0 ——— 20 km
0 ——— 20 miles

N

KOTA KINABALU AND THE WEST

Sabah's capital is dominated by stunning vistas of the towering Gunung Kinabalu. Nearby are burgeoning new beach resorts to try before heading into the interior

Map on page 312

The state capital on the northwest coast, **Kota Kinabalu ❶** is a modern town with little old world charm. Facing the west coast, it affords splendid sunsets over the offshore islands, sunsets which reflect Kota Kinabalu's history – a litany of heated passions, fights and fires – before the town reached its present, easy-going ways.

The British Chartered Company established the first settlement in 1882, on nearby **Pulau Gaya** (Gaya Island) in the bay of the present city, in line with a British colonial penchant for offshore island bases. But it was attacked and burned to the ground by the rebel Bajau prince, Mat Salleh in 1897. Moving to the mainland, the Chartered Company then set up Jesselton, named after the company's vice-chairman, Sir Charles Jessel. The name remained until 1967, when shortly after independence, a new Malaysian consciousness gave the settlement yet another new name.

What's in a name?

The old name for the location of Kota Kinabalu is *Api Api* (literally, "fire, fire"). This does not, however, commemorate bygone arson, but rather the name of a local mangrove tree in which the fireflies twinkle at night. For a short time, the town was called *Singgah Mata* ("Where the Eye Lingers") before becoming Kota Kinabalu, in honour of the great mountain whose craggy peaks lend a magnificent backdrop to the city.

As a trading post, the town grew to be important enough to be bombed to ruins in 1945, in order to prevent the Japanese from setting up a base in this strategic position. Over the following decade, Kota Kinabalu grew into an undistinguished town, occupied with covering up the scars of World War II.

Ever since it was chosen as the site for British North Borneo's west coast base, the town has continued to encroach on the sea. Reclamation was the answer to the shortage of flat land, a process that continues as the need for this precious commodity grows. Even the "coastal highway" was pushed inland by the reclamation of huge areas of shallow sea, and one of the few water villages, known by the generic name of **Kampung Air** (although no one lives there now) can be seen along the seafront towards **Tanjung Aru**.

More recently, Kota Kinabalu has mushroomed. New high rise buildings and a rash of plush hotels are changing its face from the bland, uninspiring sprawl of 1950s concrete shophouses and stilt villages perched over the sea.

BELOW:
Sabahan girls in ceremonial dress.

TIP

Hold on to your bags
in Kota Kinabalu.
Although areas like
the Gaya Street
Sunday Market are
colourful, gangs of
pickpockets roam,
looking for money-
making opportunities.
Be aware.

The most impressive of these new buildings is the gleaming tower of the **Sabah Foundation Ⓐ** (Yayasan Sabah), an institution created with the timber royalties of the state. Situated to the north of the city at Likas Bay, it is one of the few "hanging" structures in the world and this 72-sided polygon rises up some 30 storeys.

Architectural digest

The monumental **Masjid Sabah** (Sabah Mosque) is an example of fine contemporary Islamic architecture, although it is overshadowed by the stunning beauty of the new mosque at Likas, en route to the Sabah Foundation. You can visit at any time other than prayer times, but remove your shoes before entering quietly. Nearby, the new **Sabah Museum Ⓑ** (open Monday–Thursday 10am–6pm; Saturdays and Sundays 9am–6pm), is built in a stylised version of traditional Rungus and Murut tribal architecture. The museum has a good collection of Chinese ceramics and the ethnological and textile sections are growing. The section on Sabah's fascinating flora and fauna helps to make sense of the bewildering variety of wildlife in the state. Within the complex is also a science centre with an exhibition on the oil and petroleum industry, and an art gallery. One of the museum's most striking exhibits is a collection of 10 life-sized traditional houses set in the museum gardens, each depicting the architecture of a different ethnic group. A restaurant, coffee house, an ethno-botanical garden with an artificial lake and a souvenir shop complete the complex.

The town itself is a blend of ultramodern structures and old Chinese shophouses. Walk along **Jalan Gaya Ⓒ** to spot the town's few remaining traditional provision shops, where a delightful jumble of groceries, canned foods and

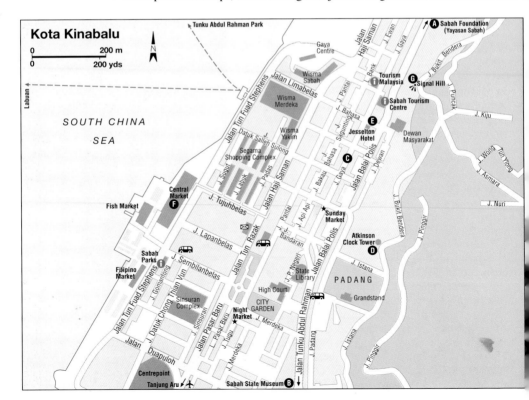

Kota Kinabalu

0   200 m
0   200 yds

SOUTH CHINA
SEA

sacks of rice displayed as artfully as a film set, invite closer inspection. Few older buildings remain in town but take note of the **Atkinson Clock Tower** ⓓ at the end of the Padang, and **Sabah Tourism Centre** (open 9am–5pm) on Jalan Gaya. Once the main post office, its solid white stone walls and colonial architecture make a pleasing contrast to the concrete shophouses. Adjacent, also in Gaya Street, is the renovated **Jesselton Hotel** ⓔ, the town's first hotel which now exudes more old world charm than it ever did before. A charming stop for lunch or dinner, if not overnight.

The bustling **Central Market** ⓕ sits midway along the waterfront, best seen early in the morning as fishermen unload their catch directly onto market tables. Kadazandusun women display their exotic range of fresh fruit and vegetables, some, like young fern leaves, never seen before. One section specialises in tobacco and betel nut products, while yeast tablets for making the local rice wine, *tapai*, hang in strings like big, white beads. Adjacent is the **Filipino Market** (open 9am–6pm) – a casual affair where handicrafts and souvenirs, mostly from the Philippines, are sold in rows of small stalls. Watch your purse as you practise your bargaining skills.

At the other end of the day, Kota Kinabalu's restaurants come alive, and some of the best food in the state is served in small coffee shops dotted around the town. As with towns in Peninsular Malaysia, night markets are ever present, selling clothes and curios, as well as local delicacies. On Sunday mornings, there is the very popular **Gaya Street Fair** (open early morning–12 noon) – a city version of the traditional weekly *tamu* – markets that are held in venues across the state. Cheap clothes, plants, foodstuffs and, occasionally, bargain local handicrafts or antiques can be found.

Map on page 314

Fern tips, lightly stir-fried are a Sabahan delicacy.

BELOW: a Filipino Market vendor.

For a good idea of what Kota Kinabalu looked like in the post-war years, the view from **Signal Hill**  affords a vast expanse of concrete, the only two pre-war buildings still standing being the Tourism Centre and the Clock Tower. Situated at the eastern end of the city, you can reach the hill by foot, or by car, taxi or tour bus. For a more contemporary view, the top floor of the **Pan Pacific Sutera Harbour Hotel**, at the western end of town, looks out to the islands or across the impressive golf course, to stilt villages, the city beyond, and a distant Gunung Kinabalu (Mt Kinabalu).

South of town, past the airport road, is the famous **Tanjung Aru Beach**. The sea here is generally calm, the sand is clean and the coastal food stalls and restaurants offer delicious local seafood. The huge orange-roofed complex at the tip of the cape is the popular **Shangri-la's Tanjung Aru Resort**.

Marine park paradise

Offshore from Kota Kinabalu, surrounded by azure waters, are the five islands of **Tunku Abdul Rahman Park** ❷, a popular destination whether for day trips or longer. The marine park headquarters is on Pulau Gaya, the largest of the islands and home to the **Gayana Resort**, (located outside the park boundaries), with its stilted village-style accommodation.

The other islands that make up the park are **Manukan**, **Mamutik**, **Sapi** and **Sulug**. Snorkelling can be enjoyed on all of these, and is best on remote Sulug. Pulau Manukan, the most developed of the islands, has chalets, a restaurant and swimming pool.

All the islands except Sulug have nature trails. Wildlife can be spotted on occasion, sometimes closer than you'd like; watch out for the thieving macaque

monkeys that proliferate on Pulau Sapi. Pied hornbills, sea eagles and megapode birds can sometimes be seen on Pulau Gaya.

You can camp on any of the islands using your own equipment, but you must obtain a permit from the Kinabalu Gold office on the third floor of the **Kompleks Karamunsing**. Boats to the islands can be chartered from the waterfront and several small jetties in front of the **Hyatt Hotel**. A scheduled service leaves the jetty at 10am.

Heading north

Sabah's long west coast stretches all the way from the Sarawak border to the northern tip at **Kudat** and **Pulau Banggi** in the Sulu Sea, almost meeting the southern Philippines boundary. This area is ideally explored by car, with the freedom to stop at will. Although some areas outside the city may require a four-wheel-drive vehicle, the trunk road linking Kota Kinabalu with **Sandakan** in Sarawak and the east coast is bitumen and a cursory exploration of the state by road presents no difficulty at all.

The road north of Kota Kinabalu leads towards **Tuaran ❸**, passing en route several ceramics factories near Telipok where visitors are welcome to stop for a look and maybe make a purchase or two. At a large roundabout, you can either head north to Tuaran and a couple of beach resorts, or turn right towards **Ranau** and **Gunung Kinabalu**.

Tuaran is a small town known for its colourful Sunday *tamu*. Get there early morning to enjoy the market at its bustling best. It is also noted for a local culinary speciality known as *Tuaran mee* – a delicious mixture of fried noodles, vegetables, pork and pork crackling, and a thick sauce. Enjoy it in one of the shops of the main street before heading to the *tamu*.

Kampung Surusup is about 15 minutes from Tuaran. There, ask for Haji Abdul Samantake, who will take you by motorised canoe to visit **Kampung Penambawan** – a traditional Bajau fishing village.

About 40 minutes north of town are a couple of beach areas with newly developed resorts and golf courses. **Pantai Dalit** – a long strip of white sand backed by forested hills is the location for the popular Shangri-la's Rasa Ria Resort while on nearby **Karambunai Beach** is the plush new Nexus Resort. In the vicinity, by a road just before Tuaran, is the **Mengkabong Water Village**, a rambling Bajau sea gypsy complex of raised stilted pathways and dozens of attap-thatched stilted huts built over an estuary. Transport around the village is by canoe, although many houses are connected to one another by precarious-looking plank walks.

On the road leading towards Ranau is the old world village of **Tamparuli ❹**, where the original shopping area consists of traditional wooden buildings – a sight fast fading across the country. Tamparuli is the site of a Wednesday *tamu* – another colourful traditional market. Beyond Tamparuli is the beautiful **Kiulu River**, a scenic area where the waters run clean. Kiulu is becoming known as a rafting destination, although it offers a more docile ride than the raging waters of the rivers to the south.

Maps:
Area 312
City 314

Bajau men, well-known for their horse riding skills, are mainly found in the Kota Belud area.

BELOW: mosque, Kota Belud.

The Rungus people align their longhouses west to east, and facing Gunung Kinabalu, believing that position to be the most auspicious for good health.

Kota Belud ❺ is a couple of hours' drive north from Kota Kinabalu and has two claims to fame. Firstly, it is renowned for the Bajau "cowboys", famed for their rearing and handling of horses and buffalo. Secondly, it is the scene of one of Sabah's most colourful weekly *tamus*. Bajau and Kadazan-dusun market women, their faces crinkled by the harsh sun, squat beside their wares – tobacco wrappers, piles of fresh vegetables or sugary doughnuts for hours on end, constantly chewing the omnipresent betel nut, which stains their gums and teeth a vivid red. There is always more on sale at the *tamu* than mundane necessities – an entire market row is devoted to the accoutrements of betel nut chewing. These women use the *tamus*, not just to sell their wares, but also for a chance to catch up on the latest news and gossip.

Tourist backwater

From Kota Belud, the road heads north towards Kudat, and **Rungus** country – home to perhaps the most traditional and talented craftspeople in the state. **Kudat ❻** was the state's first capital (albeit for a mere two years), and once an important port in the trade between China and Europe. A British adventurer took advantage of this position and set up a trading post on Balembangan Island in 1773. However, this was plagued by lack of water and continual pirate raids and the area was abandoned for less troubled waters.

Today, Kudat has become the peaceful centre for the northwestern administrative district, and is also an active fishing port. Although the Kudat region has escaped the attention of tourists in the past, the traditional cultures of the Rungus and the long stretches of white sandy beaches, unspoiled and unpopulated, are making it an increasingly popular destination.

BELOW: Rungus woman from Kudat.

The Rungus people are traditional agriculturalists, and a subgroup of the Kadazandusun tribe. Known for their excellent weaving and beadwork, the Rungus live in small communities in simple longhouses, and visiting them is quite a different experience to doing so in Sarawak. The architectural style of their buildings (with their outward-leaning walls) is mirrored in the state museum in Kota Kinabalu.

The Rungus have retained their traditional spiritualistic and animist beliefs, much longer than have the other tribes of Sabah. They are also famous for the long brass coils used by women to decorate their necks, arms and legs. Nowadays, this practice has been discontinued, although you might still see forearm coils on some of the older women. While the women continue to weave shoulder sashes, other woven textiles are rare; these days, people tend to wear decorated black cloth instead. Their excellent beadwork is quite visible in many of the *tamus* in the area.

Rungus life

It is possible to visit a Rungus longhouse and some have been constructed especially for visitors. Built in a green valley, **Kampung Bavanggazo ❼**, not far from the road leading to Kudat, has two purpose-built tourist longhouses where visitors will get to see Rungus women at work, weaving and making handicrafts. In the evening, enjoy a performance of Rungus dance and a chance to sample the local food and rice wine. The Sabah Tourism Centre in town will help with information and bookings.

There is also a large Hakka Chinese community living in Kudat, the first area to be inhabited by the Chinese in the 1880s; many of them are Christians

Map on page 312

Older Rungus women are fond of wearing long brass coils around their necks, arms and legs. The practice, however, is dying out with the younger women.

BELOW:
a Rungus-style longhouse in Kudat.

and farmers by tradition. On the fishing island of **Banggi**, right at Sabah's northern tip, lives a small tribe long thought to be of Dusun extraction, but their dialect contradicts this ancestry. They remain apart, living much as they have done for the last several hundred years. It is possible to visit the island, although tours there are rare.

The ideal way to explore the region is in a four-wheel-drive vehicle, as some of the roads leading to the beaches are little more than dirt tracks. If you don't fancy staying overnight in a longhouse, then modest yet modern, air-conditioned hotels are available in both Kudat and **Kota Marudu**.

If you are looking for the beach while visiting Kudat, you're likely to be directed to the local favourite, **Bak Bak**, which is equipped with toilets and picnic tables. However, much lovelier beaches, some with tiny lagoons, can be found all along the west coast, particularly near the village of **Sikuati**, at Pantai Kelambu and Pantai Terongkongan.

Allied bombers used Gunung Kinabalu's peak as a navigational aid to assist their raids on Japanese targets during World War II.

Highest mountain

Everyone in Malaysia knows about the mysterious **Gunung Kinabalu**, at 4,101 metres (13,455 ft), the highest peak between the Himalayas and New Guinea. The closer one journeys towards its famous jagged profile – which is often wreathed in feathery clouds – the better one understands the meaning the mount has for the local Kadazandusun people. They call it *Aki Nabalu,* or Revered Place of the Dead. It is believed that the spirits of the tribe's dead ancestors dwell among the forbidding peaks, and in the past no one had dared climb to the top for fear of disturbing and angering them.

In spite of the taboos and myths surrounding the mountain, Hugh Low, a young British officer, was still keen to reach the top. Climbing Gunung Kinabalu in 1851, Low was accompanied by a local chief and his guides. Struggling through the intense tangle of vegetation, which covers the lower slopes of the mountain, Low eventually reached the summit plateau, but owing to a faulty barometer, was unable to locate the true summit. He made a second unsuccessful attempt on the summit in 1858. The honour of reaching the small peak of the summit actually ended up going to naturalist John Whitehead, who named it Low's Peak in honour of the earlier climber.

BELOW: sure-footed Kadazandusun women porters

The mountain is said to still be growing, at a rate of half a centimetre a year. Relatively young, its jagged crown was sculpted by the last ice age, about 9,000 years ago. Although Kinabalu's peak is below the snow line, it grows cold enough here in August for ice to form in the rock pool at the base of the summit, and snowflakes sometimes fall. Dropping away 1,800 metres (5,900 ft) straight downwards is the terrifying **Low's Gully**, its name being a typical piece of British understatement.

To get to the top, there is no need to spend days cutting through tropical rain forest just to reach the granite slopes, like Hugh Low's torturous first ascent. Well-laid trails with steps and rails made of wood help today's climber ascend and descend the mountain in just two days.

Accommodation is available both at the park headquarters, and in basic huts on the mountain slopes. Cooking facilities and sleeping bag-hire is available at the latter. However, Laban Rata has a restaurant and centrally-heated rooms. At the headquarters, accommodation ranges from hostels to chalets. There are also two restaurants, and a shop selling basic food supplies for climbers. In the main administration building, there is an exhibit on mountain flora and fauna; in the basement is a film about the park.

The easiest way to reach **Kinabalu Park ❽** from Kota Kinabalu is by mini-bus. From 7am onwards, the bus leaves for Ranau from a spot near the Padang. The trip takes a little under 2 hours and the driver will turn off the main road to drop travellers at the park entrance. A larger bus also leaves for Ranau at 8am daily, but is slower and drops passengers off about 50 metres from the entrance of the park.

Map on page 312

Tips for the top

Before leaving the city, you should book accommodation at Kinabalu Gold Resorts in Kompleks Karamunsing. At certain times of the year, namely July and August and on public holidays, accommodation is tight and bookings need to be made in advance. Alternatively, you can book a package tour through any of Kota Kinabalu's tour operators. Stock up on food if you want to do your own cooking, as the shop at headquarters is limited mainly to noodles and chocolate. Other useful equipment includes a hat and gloves, as it can be extremely cold on the summit, and some kind of waterproof garment to protect you from the frequent rainfall. If possible, leave your luggage at a hotel and take a light pack only, or use the luggage storage area at the headquarters. The air is thinner up

BELOW: looking down at the world from Low's Peak.

*Hardy womenfolk
lugging firewood for
cooking.*

on the mountain, and even the lightest pack can feel heavy after a while. A torch is also useful for the final ascent, which starts long before dawn.

On the way to Kinabalu Park, you will pass by Tamparuli, 50 km (30 miles) north of Kinabalu, (*see page 317*). Less than a kilometre past this town, say goodbye to the level ground as the road begins to ascend the foothills. Although the landscape is often swathed in clouds, the mountain can't be far away because ears begin to pop. Further along, surrounded by the Kinabalu foothills, is the hamlet of **Nabalu**, where a *tamu* is held every Thursday. Kadazandusun women arrive early morning, their goods carried on enormous baskets on their backs. Nabalu is also a popular stop for tour buses, as it is a good place to see genuine native handicrafts and baskets for sale.

On your arrival at reception, Kinabalu Gold staff will confirm bookings, including those for the huts on the mountain. Maps, books, souvenirs and camera films are available at the souvenir store. You might choose not to climb the same day you arrive, so make yourself comfortable in your accommodation, acclimatise to the cool air, check out the exhibition centre with displays on the park and the mountain, and explore the fascinating **Mountain Garden** near the administration building.

Peak of fitness

BELOW: granite
slabs are a sight to
behold near the
summit.

Although Kinabalu is one of the easiest mountains to climb in terms of equipment needs, a certain degree of fitness is required. It would be foolish to head straight from the office, hop onto a plane, and then expect to be able to run up the trail. Some regular exercise is recommended before climbing so that you don't come off the mountain a wreck of cramps, headaches and fatigue.

Map
on page
312

Just before the trail begins, there is a rather forbidding notice placed by the park authorities, listing ailments not recommended for those intending to climb the mountain: hypertension, diabetes, obesity, chronic asthma, heart disease, arthritis, anaemia, ulcers, hepatitis, muscular cramps and epilepsy.

Climbing 1,500 metres (4,950 ft) in one day – from the power station above the headquarters to Panar Laban hut – does take inordinate reserves of strength and zest for those who lead sedentary lives. Although experienced and intrepid climbers have climbed to the summit and back in less than 3 hours in the Kinabalu Climathon, most people have an interest not just in getting to the top, but in fully savouring the views, and the area's flora and fauna.

Attached to the headquarters, but not directly employed by them, are a team of local guides, who for a fee will accompany visitors up the mountain. If interested in the mountain flora, you should be sure that your guide is knowledgeable and also speaks passable English (which is not often the case). Porters can be hired at park headquarters and will carry luggage as far as Panar Laban hut. Here they stop and await for your exhilarated but exhausted faces to appear the following morning before beginning the descent. Fees depend on how heavy your luggage is; anything over 10 kg (22 lbs) will cost more.

From Panar Laban, climbing usually begins at 2am, although you can request your guide to start at 5am to avoid the crowd at the summit. Make sure you have a bar or two of chocolate in your pocket; it's not a luxury but a necessity here, as a provider of instant energy for the climb and the cold. You should also bring some headache tablets; as you will be climbing to a great height very quickly, you may suffer from headaches because of the altitude.

Passing the welcoming gate at the power station (with the slogan *Selamat Mendaki* – "Happy Climbing!" written over the arch), the first steps lead down into a small, lush valley with a waterfall. After the waterfall, the climb begins, at first gently, later steeply through tropical rainforest.

A panoply of habitats

All around you are some of the park's 1,500 species of orchids, clinging to mossy tree trunks and surrounded by swinging vines. Steep and arduous stairs leading ever upwards are happily spaced out between gentler paths. Small rest huts and viewpoints are positioned all the way up the trail to give the out-of-breath climber an excuse to stop and admire the view. Don't bother to bring water, as there is pure mountain water available at all rest stops. At 1,300 metres (4,200 ft), the vegetation on either side of the trail begins to change from lowland rainforest into oak and chestnut forests of more temperate flora, like ferns and flowering plants.

Proceeding up to the next level of vegetation, one has the feeling of growing larger the higher one climbs. The trail began with huge trees towering above; now the trees have shrunk and you are almost the tallest thing in the landscape. At 2,600 metres (8,500 ft), you'll see small gnarled trees, twisted and wrinkled by the mountain air; despite their size, some are more than 100 years old. The soil is poor here, and lichens cling desperately to the little trees.

BELOW: Laban Rata Resthouse, Panar Laban.

TIP

Before you embark on your trek of Gunung Kinabalu, get hold of the intoductory leaflet, *Mount Kinabalu: A Guide to the Summit Trail*, published by Sabah Parks.

BELOW:
the mountain forest takes on a dream-like quality at dawn.

The soil disappears altogether at 3,300 metres (10,800 ft) and the granite body of the mountain reveals itself. Only sedges, grasses and tiny alpine-looking flowers cling to the rocky crevices where a bit of soil might remain.

Just when you thought you'd left all civilisation far below on the trail – now a hazy ribbon in the afternoon mist – you arrive at a series of huts and the resthouse where you will spend the night.

A leisurely climb should get you here by around 2pm. At Panar Laban, you can retreat into the cosy **Laban Rata Resthouse** with its magnificent balcony overlooking the peak. There is a simple restaurant, as well as warm rooms and hot water. A little further up the slope is **Gunting Lagadan Hostel**, which has dormitory rooms, sleeping bags for hire, and a basic kitchen equipped with cooking utensils and electricity. Once you've stopped climbing, you may begin to feel the cold, so even if you don't feel like it, have some hot soup and filling food. You will now be able to rest and think about your achievement so far – but alas! – the path you so strenuously climbed has been lost in the mountain mists.

If it isn't raining, some climbers rest here briefly and then climb for another 1½ hours to Sayat-Sayat Hut, which allows for a later rising time the following morning. Some climbers may find it hard to sleep on the mountain because of the thin air and the headaches caused by the altitude. Yet, you will need to go to sleep extra early to be able to struggle out of bed at 2am (your guide will wake you). Take a hot drink before starting the climb around 3am. If you have a thermos flask, heat some water and fill the flask with sweet tea for a reviving drink at the summit. Don't forget to stuff some chocolate into your pocket and bring your raincoat. Other than cameras, everything else can be left at the hut for retrieval on the way down.

Map on page 312

Rocky mountain high

Soon you will be climbing rock faces of granite in the pitch black as you hold onto the rope systems that guide the way. The steepness of the incline is difficult to gauge in the dark, though, and the granite slopes can be slippery after a night's rain. With an early start, you will be labouring up the slabs of granite with the peak in sight just as the skies begin to lighten. Here the granite rock, bared to the winds, is crumbling and broken, but at last Low's Peak arises.

The sun rises over the horizon in a huge glowing orb, the landscape transformed with the golden hues of the early morning light. On a clear day, the lights of Kota Kinabalu and the coast and then the outlines of the Tunku Abdul Rahman islands are visible.

Venturing a look down into the depths of Low's Gully, the view is awe-inspiring. This does indeed seem a place for spirits, for few mortals could long endure the harsh weather that sweeps away the offerings of sacrificial chickens, eggs, tobacco, betel nut, *sireh* leaves, limes and rice left here by the Kadazandusun. Depending on one's guide and the strength of his beliefs, he may decide to make offerings while you are gushing over the landscape's beauty. The guide may also be carrying personal charms: special pieces of wood, human teeth and other items with protecting properties.

The descent can be more leisurely, especially by climbers still glowing with success of having reached the summit, but appearances can be deceptive. While it is easier on the lungs, the descent is hell to pay on the knees and in the end, can be even more painful than the climb up and the relentless steps leading ever downwards can soon turn even firm legs into jelly!

After collecting your belongings from Panar Laban, you'll continue down through unique vegetation, such as the pitcher plants – some of the eight varieties of *nepenthes* – that were probably missed on the ascent. On your arrival at park headquarters, you can rightfully claim your badge commemorating your ascent, only for sale to those who have made it to the top; this is (your guide can act as witness).

Many climbers leave the park the same day or the day after they have made the climb. But if time permits, stay in the area a couple of days more, both to rest and to explore the jungle around the headquarters, which is neatly laid out in trails for nature lovers.

Amazing species

A guide can introduce you to Kinabalu's magnificent flora and fauna, some of it unique to the region. Among the rare plants found here is the famous Rafflesia, the largest flower in the world, which can measure up to a metre (3 ft) across, and nine species of pitcher plants. In 1858, the explorer Spencer St John chanced upon a huge specimen of the latter that contained approximately 1 gallon (4 litres) of rain water – as well as a dead rat.

The park's 750 sq km (300 sq miles) are unique in the world of flora, containing plants from almost every area on earth: the Himalayas, China, Australia, New Zealand, alpine Europe and even America. There are 1,500 species of orchid, 26 kinds of

BELOW: wild orchids.

Stick insects in the jungles of Sabah are notoriously difficult to spot as they blend so easily against the bark of trees.

rhododendron and 60 types of oak and chestnut, as well as 80 species of fig tree. Animals found here include orang utan, gibbons, leaf monkeys, tarsiers, pangolin (scaly anteaters), wild pig and deer. There is also a whole host of "flying" animals, some rarely found in other parts of Malaysia, including flying squirrels, lemurs, snakes and lizards. Also found here – but seldom seen – is the incredibly rare clouded leopard.

The 518 species of birds include several kinds of hornbills, the scarlet sunbird, the mountain bush warbler, the pale-faced bulbul, the mountain blackeye, and the mountain's own Kinabalu friendly warbler. Around the area's waterfalls, look for the lovely butterflies, some as large as birds, and the less easy-to-see stick insects, well camouflaged to the human eye. You might also catch sight of squirrels, lizards, tree-shrews and bats.

A steaming, hot bath

Although the park holds all these fascinating sights and more besides, many ex-climbers will be too tired to appreciate the beauty of a pleasant stroll through the forest. After perhaps taking a quick look at the exhibition hall and the Mountain Garden, head for **Poring ❾**, 45 km (30 miles) to the east beyond Ranau. The motive? – natural hot sulphur springs to soothe those tired muscles, plus a canopy walkway and butterfly park.

Pleasant chalets with cooking facilities, and a couple of hostels are available, but few visitors rest long before making straight for the baths. There is nothing like a good long soak in the mineral rich waters to ease aching limbs and restore one's sense of well being. To get there, descend some steps and cross a wire-and-wood suspension bridge over the river. The baths themselves are set in park-like

BELOW: a wreathed hornbill.

Map on page 312

grounds with hibiscus bushes and frangipani trees, with the untamed jungle above and beyond. They were originally built during World War II by the Japanese, with their love of communal bathing giving them the impetus to tame the jungle, and channel in both hot and cold water, the latter to temper the heat of the mineral water. Nothing could be nicer than to bathe here at night, with the jungle sounds all around.

Despite aching muscles (if you've climbed the mountain), it is well worth checking out Poring's 140 metre-(460 ft) long canopy walkway strung high above the ground between giant dipterocarp trees, which literally offers a bird's-eye view of the forest. From time to time, a Rafflesia appears in the jungle areas around Poring. Near the baths you'll find the butterfly park, filled with beautiful local species and some remarkable insects.

The area around **Ranau** ❿ is Kadazandusun country and also the market garden of Sabah, situated on Kinabalu's cool foothills. At the weekly *tamu* in Ranau, you'll see rural people dressed in a mix of traditional dress (black sarong and long earrings) and western attire (jeans, or brightly-coloured jogging pants and T-shirts).

About 20 km (12 miles) south of Kota Kinabalu is **Papar** ⓫, situated on the mouth of the Papar River. Paddy fields surround the town and on the coast is a pleasant stretch of sand called **Pantai Manis**, or Sweet Beach. The Sunday *tamu* is a lively scene, as Kadazandusun traders bring their wares from the surrounding hills. Rice wine (*tapai*) is also made here, and if you're lucky enough to get invited to a private home, you will no doubt be offered this potent liquid.

Travelling beyond Papar, there are two choices. Just south of town is the turnoff to a little-travelled highway cutting through the towering Crocker Range to Keningau and Sapulut, and then through a forestry concession to Tawau and Semporna on the east coast of Sabah. The main highway continues on to the town of **Beaufort** ⓬ and beyond to Sipitang, then Sindumin on the Sarawak border.

Beaufort is a busy highway junction, and an important stop on the railway line from Tanjung Aru, in Kota Kinabalu, through to Tenom. It is also the staging point for whitewater rafting trips on the **Padas Gorge** (*see page 328*). A change in train schedules now makes it convenient for rafters to travel right from Tanjung Aru, via Beaufort station where they can change trains.

Offshore millions

Beaufort is on the edge of a swampy peninsula with isolated fishing villages. Just offshore is **Pulau Labuan** ⓭, a burgeoning international banking centre and an island that hopes to give Bermuda, Cayman and the Channel Islands a run for their money. A British naval station was established on the island in the 1870s and the Japanese forces in Borneo surrendered here in 1945, but other than those two events, little of significance transpired on the island.

After independence, Labuan was part of Sabah state until 1984, when it was ceded to the federal government for development. Tax-free status came into effect in 1991 and the Malaysian government is keen to

Sabahian historian K.G. Tregonning referred to Governor P. Beaufort as "the most impotent governor North Borneo ever acquired and who, in the manner of nonentities, had a town named after him".

BELOW:
having a soak at Poring Hot Springs.

If you haven't yet experienced the highly distinctive *durian* fruit, try it while in Tenom; it is reckoned to be the best in Sabah, smell notwithstanding.

attract banks, insurance companies and fund management brokers to Labuan, in addition to offshore holding companies and corporate headquarters. A number of steps have been taken to attract business, including preferential tax laws. The island is also being developed for tourism and a number of wrecks off the coast are said to be worthwhile.

Located right at the end of Borneo's only railway, **Tenom** ⓮ is the centre of Murut country and a rich agricultural centre. The Muruts or "Men of the Hills", have always lived in this region. Young warriors still take their hunting dogs out for a "stroll" in the jungle to catch supper, hunting with a *parang* (large sharp knife) and a shotgun, although no longer with a blowpipe. Although many young people of the tribe have adopted at least the trappings of the fast-encroaching western civilisation creeping in from the capital, some still prefer life in remote areas. Others have turned to cultivating the countryside and growing crops.

A popular festive pastime in the few remaining longhouses is jumping on the *lansaran*, a huge trampoline-like structure supported by a wooden platform. The largest can hold 40 people – perhaps the entire population of the longhouse – the basis for a wild party. The best longhouses can be found around Kamabong, south of Tenom.

Riding the raging river

Tenom is also close to the starting point for the Padas River ride, run by several tour operators out of Kota Kinabalu. After arriving at **Kampung Pangi** on the train from Beaufort, having passed through the dramatic Padas Gorge, rafters disembark. Rafts are carried to the river, there is time for a brief lesson and

BELOW: wild white-water kayaking.

donning of safety gear before taking the plunge. The 1½-hour ride is filled with thrills passing through some hefty waves, deep in the gorge, especially when the river is high. The ride finishes at **Kampung Rayoh** where lunch is served before you catch the train back to Kota Kinabalu.

Tenom is also known for its **Agricultural Research Station**, 18 km (11 miles) northeast of town. The station has grown from its humble beginnings as a centre for cocoa research, to include a full scale agri-park known as **Taman Pertanian Sabah**. The **Tenom Orchid Centre** is also part of the park, where numerous species of orchids can be seen. British botanist Tony Lamb is largely responsible for the success of this growing project. Tenom's one classy hotel, the Perkasa, sits on the hill overlooking the town, although accommodation is also available within the park.

Some 40 km (25 miles) south of Tenom, at **Batu Bunatikan Lumuyu** close to Kampung Tomani, are Sabah's only rock paintings. Strange distorted faces and enigmatic figures are painted on massive boulders. These impressive paintings are thought to be around 1,000 years old.

From Tenom, travel north through Keningau and Tambunan, and from there follow a rough road to Ranau and Gunung Kinabalu or follow the road over the Sinsuron Pass to Kota Kinabalu, thus completing a round trip.

Keningau is the centre of the interior timber industry of west Sabah, with its many sawmills and log-holding depots. The town has prospered from its timber industry, and has several hotels and a sports complex for the management staff visiting their logging sites.

Keningau and beyond

Driving southeast of Keningau, you come first to **Nabawan**, the last outpost of the government administration, and then to the settlement at **Sapulut ⓯**. From here, you can take a rough track to **Agis**, from where a pleasant 4-hour boat ride leads to the border and a fairly easy crossing into Kalimantan at the **Pagalunggan** checkpoint (obtain a visa first) and the traditional longhouse of **Kampung Selungai**, only half-an-hour away. This remote area is well worth exploring, but logging, El Niño and forest fires have taken a toll on the area in the last few years. Traditional longhouses sit along these riverbanks, where boats are built and the women engage in weaving, making intricate rattan mats and elaborate beadwork. Travellers are most welcome to stay the night, and the Muruts are renowned for their hospitality. Remember that it is polite to accept a drink when offered, as it is a host's duty to please guests with a cup of *tapai*. If you don't drink alcohol, simply touch the cup with your lips or the tips of your fingers and ask your guide to explain that you don't wish to partake of the fiery liquid. Gifts of food for the adults and toys for the children are customary, and items from your own country will be even more welcome than a product available in Kota Kinabalu.

Sarawak is not the only state with limestone caves. In Sapulut it is possible to hire a local canoe along the **Sapulut River**, for a 2–3 hour boat journey to

Map on page 312

Orchid blooms at Tenom Orchid Centre.

BELOW: intricate Rungus bead work.

Map on page 312

Batu Punggul , a large limestone outcrop soaring 200 metres (600 ft) upwards from the encircling jungle. A recreated Murut longhouse and a simple resthouse have been constructed opposite, with trails leading to the rock through the forest. Local guides will show you the way to the top of Batu Punggul, a rough climb but well worth it for the spectacular view from the top. Another half-an-hour's walk through the forest leads to the less impressive **Batu Tinahas**, which is almost entirely obscured by the forest. This limestone massif was only recently discovered by a team from the Sabah Museum. Although not as high as Punggul, its cave and tunnel system is enormous and rivals the Gomantong Caves in east Sabah (*see page 336*).

A rough road leads from Keningau to **Tambunan**, passing by an old stone on a grassy plain marking the site of Mat Salleh's last stand. Here, Sabah's most renowned hero built an underground fortress in the middle of the jungle. He might have survived longer than 1900, had not a villager betrayed his location to the British forces, who promptly severed his water supply, and surrounded the fort. Mat Salleh and his followers were massacred when they emerged, ending the rebellion of a native lord who refused to pay tax to foreigners.

The route back to Kota Kinabalu from Tambunan passes through the Crocker Range National Park, with the **Rafflesia Forest Reserve** located not far from the summit at **Sinsuron Pass** which crosses the range at 1,649 metres (5,410 feet). The attractive **Rafflesia Information Centre** (open Monday–Friday 8.45am–12.45pm and 2–5pm; Saturday and Sunday 8am–5pm) has displays on this extraordinary parasitic flower and rangers can advise visitors if any are blooming in the 20 or so identified plots within the reserve.

BELOW: underwater hideout, Sipadan. **RIGHT:** Poring's canopy walkway.

Delirious Diving

Sitting at the southern tip of the Spratley Islands, 250 km (155 miles) northwest of Kota Kinabalu, **Layang Layang** is part of the disputed territory that is being contested by a number of countries in the region – including China, Vietnam, Indonesia and Malaysia. In the meantime, Malaysia is putting the island to good use as a tourist destination – the only country to do so – as well as laying a claim that may become important in future negotiations.

This 7 km by 5 km (4 miles by 3 miles) oceanic reef is as much a draw for migratory seabirds, as it is for the big game fishermen, attracted by the richly-populated waters. Layang Layang is also the site of some of the best diving in Malaysia. Because of the distance from the the main island, the waters are particularly clear and untainted by any amount of pollution, and the divers who come can enjoy spectacular coral walls, which drop down 2,000 metres (6,560 ft) to the coral below. Sharks and pelagic fish are common sights in these unspoiled waters.

Layang Layang has a tiny airport and one small, if basic, resort that stands right next to the Malaysian navy base. However, many people choose to stay aboard the MV Coral Topaz rather than on the atoll. A 45-minute flight from Kota Kinabalu (or 16 hours by boat) covers the journey. A visit to the island can be added on to diving trips to Miri and Sipadan. ❏

SANDAKAN AND THE NORTHEAST

Map on page 312

The lively Chinese trading town of Sandakan is the tourist focus of Sabah's east coast, and the jump off point for Sepilok Orang-utan Rehabilitation Centre

In its heyday, people called the logs bobbing in the Sulu Sea "floating money". Logs were floated down the Segama River from timber concession areas near and far into the hands of Chinese entrepreneurs, who shipped them to Japan. So prosperous was **Sandakan** , that at one time many investors thought the town would become another Hong Kong, but the speed of deforestation of the Sandakan region has quenched that dream. Now the logging centre has moved further south to Tawau, and the derived wealth has been moved to places far beyond. Sandakan remains the same – a medium sized, predominantly Chinese town and the base for tourist exploration of the east.

The capital of North Borneo from 1883, Sandakan was completely razed during the bombings of World War II; the modern town was built on these ruins. The nucleus of the original town began as a gunrunning settlement.

The gunrunners were mostly Germans, although later a Scotsman called William Clarke Cowrie ran guns for the Sultan of Sulu, setting up a camp on Pulau Timbang which he named "Sandakan", the old Sulu name for the area. Later he became the first managing director of the North Borneo Chartered Company, whose main settlement was established here on the fine harbour of Sandakan Bay.

At one time, Sandakan was a major trading centre. Jungle products from the interior – bird's nests, beeswax, rhinoceros horn, hornbill ivory along with marine products like sea cucumber (*trepang*) and pearls were valuable trade items which attracted a cosmopolitan collection of traders from all over the world: Europeans, Arabs, Japanese, Dusun, Javanese, Bugis, Chinese – even Africans came to engage in the wealth-generating business of trade.

Most visitors to the east stay at the Renaissance Hotel just outside town. Built on the site of the town's most historic hotel, it caters to the burgeoning tourist trade. Alternatively, stay at the new Sepilok Nature Resort, or one of the other lodges at Sepilok rather than in the town itself.

Around town

The first Sandakan flight from Kota Kinabalu arrives early morning, allowing ample time for an exploration of the town before heading out. An Asian breakfast can be enjoyed in one of the Chinese *kedai* or coffee shops before a visit to the colourful **Sandakan Central Market**. At its busy best in the early morning, the bustling market is an important source of local vegetables and fresh seafood which is exported across the state and over to Singapore and Hong Kong. Other

LEFT: orang-utan at Sepilok.
BELOW: Sandakan is a major logging centre.

TIP

Pulau Selingan, the largest of the Turtle Islands, has everything you could ask for: coconut palms, sandy beaches, with chalets nearby. However, accommodation is limited and must be booked in advance. See Travel Tips.

BELOW: Sepilok is the largest of three orang-utan sanctuaries in the world.

town sights include an obligatory stop at the observation point on Bukit Merah for an overall perspective of the town. Once, the most vivid sight from this spot was the sea pens filled with the wealth of the forest; thousands of logs from felled timber giants, awaiting shipment to foreign parts.

Several Chinese temples are dotted around – the most spectacular being the huge modern **Puu Jih Shih Buddhist Temple** on a hilltop south of town. Outside Sandakan, the **Australian Memorial** is built on the site of a Japanese prisoner-of-war camp, and commemorates the Allied soldiers who lost their lives during World War II.

Sandakan's main source of tourist fame is the **Sepilok Orang-utan Rehabilitation Centre** ⑲, a 20-minute drive westwards from town. In 1964, 4,000 hectares (9,880 acres) were designated a reserve for these lovable and intelligent creatures. It takes but a little interaction to fall in love with these most "human" of primates. The orang-utan shares 96 percent of its genes with a human being, while its intelligence level can reach that of a six-year-old child. The centre assists orphaned orang-utans, or those who have been forced to live in captivity, to adjust gradually to jungle life and a return to the wild. Instruction to the animals includes encouraging them to climb, building nests in trees (something wild orang-utans do each night) and foraging for food in the jungle. Gradually they are weaned from the milk and bananas provided, and taught to fend for themselves.

Those who stay longer than the obligatory hour-long feeding stop will find nature trails set around the park, where the stunning vegetation is the main feature, although you may spot birds, squirrels and macaques. Visit the nature centre and watch a video show on orang-utans in the wild. Adjacent to the cen-

tre are several lodges of various standards. Right next to the Sepilok Forest Reserve is the tasteful Sepilok Nature Resort, where trekking tours, birding and visits to the rehabilitation centre can be arranged. The Sepilok Jungle Lodge provides a pleasant, cheaper alternative.

Map on page 312

Life of the turtle

Pulau Selingan, Pulau Bakkungan and Pulau Gulisan are the islands which make up the **Turtle Islands Marine Park ⑳**, a 1,740-hectare (4,300-acre) tropical paradise in the Sulu Sea, about 40 km (25 miles) north of Sandakan. Green (*Chelonia Mydas*) and Hawksbill turtles (*Eretmochelys imbricata*) or *sisik,* as the locals call them, come here to lay eggs nearly every night of the year, but the best time to watch is between July and September. Rangers will take you out to the beaches where you can observe female turtles after they have commenced laying their eggs. Later, the eggs are scooped into plastic buckets and reburied at a nearby turtle hatchery, where they are safe from predators. Earlier in the evening, if you are lucky and a previous batch of eggs has hatched, you can witness their release and watch them begin their struggle for life as they make their way down the beach to the sanctity of the sea. Only some 3 percent of these turtles will reach maturity.

The best time to visit Turtle Islands Marine Park is between April and October when green turtles converge on the island to hatch their eggs.

Another 40 km (25 miles) due north is the exclusive and reclusive tropical retreat known as **Pulau Lankayan ㉑**, a previously uninhabited coral island. The Lankayan Island Resort is a tranquil place of white sand beaches that provides a wonderful escape – and utter peace. It is particularly good for divers, with accessible wrecks to explore, and vivid marine life of hard and soft corals. One dive resort is established on the island.

BELOW: an endangered turtle in motion.

Map on page 312

Bats galore can be seen in **Gomantong ㉒**, where some of Sabah's largest caves are found. These caves are also home to one million swiftlets, whose nests are collected to furnish the tables of Cantonese restaurants both in town and abroad. Collectors scale the hanging *rotan* (cane) and bamboo ladders which hang from the cave roof up to heights of 90 metres (300 ft) above the bat guano-covered ground, to collect these treasures in the vast caves. The bats are only in evidence at dusk, as they make their nightly flight out to forage for food, just as the swiftlets return home. The huge, odorous guano pile is gradually raising the cave floor level. At one time the guano was harvested for use as fertiliser, but the cave's swift population declined so quickly that the guano now stays in an ever-mounting carpet, alive with cockroaches and other tiny cave dwellers. A wooden boardwalk makes is possible to tour the main **Simud Hitam** cave with ease. If visiting these caves, bring a flashlight and mosquito repellent. The fastidious might wish to bring a pair of gloves.

River journey

An enjoyable excursion is a trip up the **Kinabatangan River**. Now one of Sabah's most popular tours, it is dominated by tour operators who bus guests to **Sukau ㉓**, stopping off at Sepilok Orang-utan Rehabilitation Centre and Gomantong Caves along the way. It is also possible however, to charter a boat and explore the river starting from **Sandakan Bay**.

After crossing Sandakan Bay, the first stage of the journey is dominated by mangrove swamps and twisting waterways of the lowland floodplain. The occasional Orang Sungei (river people) settlement of stilted houses can be seen along the banks. It is these low-lying flood plains, and the lack of commercial timbers that have saved the Kinabatangan area from the large-scale exploitation prevalent in other parts of the state. Its role as an important wetlands area – the biggest in Malaysia – has been recognised by the WWF. Plans are in the pipeline to have it gazetted as a Wetlands Conservation Area.

The Kinabatangan and its tributaries are famed for the wildlife, not least of which is the long-nosed, pot-bellied proboscis monkey. The best places for close up sightings of these unique animals is the swampy forest along the small Menanggol River, a tributary of the Kinabatangan, just upstream from Sukau. Boats leave in the cool of the afternoon (around 3.30pm to 4pm) in time to catch the monkeys as they crash through the trees, making their way to the riverside, for their nightly sojourn.

Even more exciting to many visitors are the wild elephants that roam thorough the Kinabatangan area. Sightings of elephants along the river are not uncommon and recently, some pleasing encounters with a group of 40 or so elephants were reported by some very happy tourists.

The ox bow lakes, formed as the river has changed its slow course over the years, are exceptionally rich sources of birdlife, and you're likely to find a visit particularly rewarding. More than 100 species of bird live in these habitats, including waterfowl, snake birds and hornbills. ❏

BELOW: Gomantang Caves near Sukau.
RIGHT: Kadazan girls all dolled up for a concert.

TAWAU AND THE SOUTHEAST

Right in the southeast tip of Sabah, near the border with Indonesia, the regional centre of Tawau provides an access point to world-class diving and some beautiful jungle habitats

Map
on page
312

F lights from Kota Kinabalu and Sandakan arrive at **Tawau ㉔**, Sabah's main town of the southeast. As well as being the hub of an important timber and cocoa growing area, this busy little town has a very mixed population, where Muslim Filipinos from Mindanao and Indonesian estate workers have helped create a different atmosphere to the towns of the west coast. As well as the present timber capital of the state, Tawau is also the home of a reforestation programme situated at **Kalabakan**, where 30,000 hectares (70,000 acres) have been planted with fast-growing trees such as *Albizia facalaria*; the fastest is said to have soared 30 metres (100 ft) in just five years.

However, Tawau's real pride is the cocoa plant, which thrives in the region's volcanically-rich soils, making Sabah the largest cocoa-producing state in Malaysia; oil palm is grown, too, in huge quantities, in estates that stretch mile after mile across the country. Tawau also boasts an international-standard hotel, and **Tawau Hills State Park**, a nature reserve where hot springs and waterfalls can be found.

Stilts and seafood

Tawau's main interest to the thousands of scuba divers who pass through each year is its proximity to **Semporna ㉕**, the gateway to Pulau Sipadan – Malaysia's only oceanic island and famous with the international diving fraternity as one of the world's five best dive sites. A 1½-hour drive east of Tawau brings visitors to the small settlement, where Bajau sea gypsies, Suluk tribespeople, and Chinese traders lend a village atmosphere and a far-flung feel. Fringing the town are numerous settlements built on stilts over the water, an architectural style utilised by many of the newer resorts being built in the vicinity. One hotel, the Dragon Inn known locally as the "Floating" because of its stilted style, is part of the Semporna Ocean Tourism Centre. The rich marine life around Semporna yields delicious seafood, which can be bought (often live) at the inn's restaurant. Prepared by Chinese chefs in any style you wish and served with fresh, locally-grown vegetables, it is among the best seafood found in Malaysia.

Pulau Sipadan ㉖ is Malaysia's only true oceanic island, rising up 600 metres (2,000 ft) from the seabed. The first dive tourists to Sipadan in the late 1980s slept in tents, disturbed at night by nesting turtles burrowing in the sand. Today, the turtles are disturbed by the tourists as valuable space has been encroached upon by an ever-increasing number of chalets and support facilities.

This oceanic island, praised by the late marine ecologist and diver, Jacques Cousteau, for its magnificent

LEFT: wild ginger bloom.
BELOW: keeping sentry at Kapalai.

Moray eels can turn out to be vicious creatures if you stick your arm too far up their resting holes.

array of marine life, is the tip of a pinnacle of limestone and coral which rises up 2,000 metres (6,560 ft) from the bed of the Celebes Sea. The clear waters, where visibility can be anything between 18 metres and 36 metres (60 ft to 120 ft), are a wonderland of caverns and caves, home to marine species that range from green turtles, barracudas, wrasse, tuna, mackerel, sailfish, whitetip sharks, to pelagics and colourful live corals.

A local company, Borneo Divers, built simple huts to accommodate scuba divers in 1989, and other operators have followed suit to the effect that the tiny island is now in danger of ecological overload. Efforts are being made to protect the reefs and island from over-exploitation, to say nothing of the numerous green turtles that come to lay their eggs in the clean coral sands.

Eco-aware development

Fortunately, some far-sighted developers have been establishing new, ecologically responsible resorts on reefs and islands close to Sipadan to lighten the load on the tiny island. In addition, the federal government has placed restrictions on the numbers of divers who can now visit Sipadan. Kapalai Resort, built on a submerged reef, is an example of the new, ecologically conscious resorts. With its own water processing plants and sewerage treatment facilities, it is less damaging to the fragile environment. There are also several resorts on the nearby **Pulau Mabul** ㉗, built in the style of stilt villages. One of these, the Sipadan Water Village Resort, is of international standard and is particularly popular with Japanese divers.

BELOW: snorkelling in Sipadan.

North of Semporna, **Pulau Bohey Dulang** (once the site of a Japanese pearl farm) and other surrounding islands have been designated as marine

park, but tourist facilities are not expected to be developed for some time to come. One company located on the Semporna jetty, Pulau Bajau, organises diving and snorkelling day trips, or camping on the Semporna islands, as well as visits to seaweed farms.

Map on page 312

Subterranean settlements

An hour's drive north from Tawau and Semporna towards **Lahad Datu**, leads to the **Madai Caves** ㉓, where you'll find a limestone outcrop with large caves just 2 km (1½ miles) off the main road. Outside the caves is a village that may be deserted except for a small nucleus of caretakers, but will be packed twice a year when harvesters come to gather the valuable edible nests built by swiflets in the caves.

A flashlight is necessary for exploring the caves; although sunlight filters down through crevices in the limestone roof of some caves, many of the deeper caves are pitch black. Remains found at Madai prove that people lived in the area as long as 15,000 years ago.

Further evidence of ancient settlement in the region – in this case going back some 20,000 years – can be found 18 km (11 miles) west of Madai. **Baturong** is another limestone outcrop, situated near what was once a lake known as Tingkayu, which drained away 16,000 years ago. With a guide from Lahad Datu or Kunak, you can visit this fascinating massif. The journey involves an hour's drive through cocoa and oil palm plantations to a mud volcano.

Lahad Datu is another of Sabah's "cowboy towns", known for its lawlessness. Situated close to the Sulu Islands of the Philippines it is, like the Semporna area, subject to occasional pirate attacks on shipping.

BELOW:
aerial walkway
at Danum Valley.

Map
on page
312

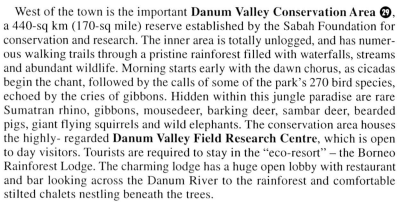

West of the town is the important **Danum Valley Conservation Area ㉙**, a 440-sq km (170-sq mile) reserve established by the Sabah Foundation for conservation and research. The inner area is totally unlogged, and has numerous walking trails through a pristine rainforest filled with waterfalls, streams and abundant wildlife. Morning starts early with the dawn chorus, as cicadas begin the chant, followed by the calls of some of the park's 270 bird species, echoed by the cries of gibbons. Hidden within this jungle paradise are rare Sumatran rhino, gibbons, mousedeer, barking deer, sambar deer, bearded pigs, giant flying squirrels and wild elephants. The conservation area houses the highly- regarded **Danum Valley Field Research Centre**, which is open to day visitors. Tourists are required to stay in the "eco-resort" – the Borneo Rainforest Lodge. The charming lodge has a huge open lobby with restaurant and bar looking across the Danum River to the rainforest and comfortable stilted chalets nestling beneath the trees.

Local guides, with an intimate knowledge of their subject, can take guests on nature walks; if you are lucky, they can show you how to call the different animals, and pick out a bird hidden in the jungle at a hundred paces. Many guides grew up in the region and have turned their well-honed hunting skills to better use, tracking down animals to photograph. But you'll need plenty of time and patience, standing silently, hoping to catch a glimpse. On the more remote trails, a total disregard for leeches is also an advantage during the wet months.

One of the most popular short excursions is an early morning walk to the canopy walkway, strung high between giant dipterocarps. It can be a rewarding experience to sit for an hour or so and watch for hornbills and honeyeaters, and possibly even the Asian paradise flycatcher – one of Danum's most exotic inhabitants. Night drives in an open jeep will often reveal deer, bearded pigs and other creatures, caught in the beam of the strong spotlight.

BELOW: wild
elephants at Tabin.
RIGHT: waterfall in
the Danum Valley.

More wildlife

To the east of Lahad Datu is the **Tabin Wildlife Reserve ㉚**. Although logging encroached on the area in the 1970s and 1980s, the re-growth has provided a home for larger mammals such as the elephant, rhino and banteng. There is no accommodation within the reserve, but a wildlife lodge is in the process of being built on the perimeter.

From the Tawau district, the north coast can be reached by road via Keningau (over the Crocker Range), and via Sapulut in the interior, travelling close to the Indonesian border along logging tracks passing by the **Maliau Basin**. Four-wheel-drive vehicles, which have obtained permission to carry passengers through the logging concessions, make the trip daily. The drive from Tawau to Keningau takes between 8 and 10 hours, depending on the condition of the tracks. The road north to Sandakan is easy and open, passing through mile after mile of oil palm plantations on what was once rainforest. Buses – which travel north almost to Sandakan before heading west across the Crocker Range – take 12 hours to Kota Kinabalu, and cost half the price of the airfare, although the flight takes just 40 minutes. ❏

INSIGHT GUIDES

Travel Tips

A.D.

Your specially tailored
Royal Orchid Holidays begin
the moment you board
when you fly with THAI,
official carrier to
Amazing Thailand.

Insight Guides portray destinations in depth, providing the complete picture and the top photography

Insight Pocket Guides focus on the best choices for places to see and things to do and include large fold-out maps

Insight Compact Guides' portability makes them the perfect books to carry with you for on-the-spot reference

Three types of guide for all types of travel

INSIGHT GUIDES Different people need different kinds of information. Some want *background information* to help them prepare for the trip. Others seek *personal recommendations* from someone who knows the destination well. And others look for *compactly presented data* for on-the-spot reference. With three carefully designed series, Insight Guides offer readers the perfect choice. Insight Guides will turn your visit into an experience.

The world's largest collection of visual travel guides

CONTENTS

Getting Acquainted

The Place

Area 342,000 sq. km. (132,000 sq. miles) comprising Peninsular Malaysia, and Sabah and Sarawak on Borneo island.

Situation North of the equator, with the peninsula bordered by Singapore in the south and Thailand in the north. Sabah and Sarawak border Indonesia (Kalimantan).

Time Zone Malaysia's standard time is 8 hours ahead of Greenwich Mean Time.

Population 21 million.

Language The official language is Bahasa Malaysia (Malay), but English is the language of business and technology. The Chinese also use Mandarin and various Chinese dialects, while the Indians use Tamil and other Indian languages. The native people retain their own languages.

Currency Ringgit and sen. RM1=100 sen. Coins come in denominations of 5, 10, 20, and 50 sen, and RM1, and notes in RM1, RM2, RM5, RM10, RM50, RM100, and RM500.

Weights and Measures Malaysia follows the metric system, but people in rural areas might still use miles (*batu*) rather than kilometres for distance.

Electricity 220 volts, 50 cycles. American products do not work here, but most supermarkets stock adapters. Major hotels can supply an adapter for 110–120 volt, 60 Hz appliances.

International Dialling Code To call Malaysia from abroad, dial 00 60 followed by the local code, omitting the initial zero, then the number you want. (*For local dialling codes see Practical Tips, page 353*).

Climate

Malaysia's weather is generally warm and sunny all year round, with temperatures wavering between 32°C during the day and 24°C at night. Humidity is high at 80 percent. The temperature in the highlands is much lower.

The onset of the monsoon season from May to September brings with it rain to the west coast of Peninsular Malaysia. The east coast of the peninsula and Sabah and Sarawak experience their monsoon season between November and February.

The inter-monsoon periods experience the heaviest rainfalls. Otherwise, light showers come and go, helping to relieve the heat from the sun.

Public Holidays and Festivals

Malaysia has the greatest number of public holidays in the world. Many relate to cultural festivals, and are not fixed, but follow the lunar or Muslim calendar. Some are observed only in certain states; for example, the birthday of the respective sultans. If a public holiday falls on a Saturday or Sunday, the following Monday is an "off-day"; likewise if a holiday falls on a Thursday or Friday in the states that follow the Muslim week, the following Saturday is an off-day. Check with Tourism Malaysia. School holidays start on a Saturday closest to these dates: January 16–24, February 13–20, May 22–June 6, September 4–12, November 20–31.

- **January** New Year's Day (1); Hari Raya Puasa, the main Muslim festival, a 2-day holiday celebrating the end of the Muslim fasting month of Ramadhan; Thaipusam (31), the Hindu festival of penance, celebrated most colourfully in Kuala Lumpur and Penang.
- **February** Chinese New Year (16, 17), 2-day holiday for main Chinese festival celebrated over a 15-day period.

People

A blend of the great Asian cultures of the world, Malaysians comprise Malays and the indigenous tribes, which make up some 60 percent of the population, Chinese fewer than 30 percent, Indians fewer than 10 percent, and a potpourri of other ethnic groups.

The main and official religion is Islam, adopted by the Malays, but religious tolerance sees the open practice of Buddhism and Taoism among the Chinese, Hinduism among the Indians and Christianity among non-Malays. Some indigenous people retain their animist beliefs.

This diversity has seen the flowering of Malaysia's places of worship, colourful festivals, variety

- **March** Hari Raya Haji (28), celebrating the annual Muslim pilgrimage season.
- **April** Pesta Kaul (8–15), a Melanau festival celebrated in the fishing communities around Mukah on Sarawak's north coast. Awal Muharam (17), Muslim New Year that is low-key and pious.
- **May** Labour Day (1); Vesak Day (18), temple celebrations to mark Buddha's birth, enlightenment and nirvana; Harvest Festival (30), 2-day holiday, the main festival for the different tribal groups of the state of Sabah.
- **June** Gawai, a 2-day holiday that is the main official festival for the different tribal groups of Sarawak; Birthday of the Yang Dipertuan Agung (king) (5); Birthday of Prophet Muhammad (26), prayers and Quran recitals at mosques.
- **August** National Day (31), with nationalistic parades.
- **November** Deepavali (7), Hindu festival of lights.
- **December** Christmas (25), midnight mass, celebrated in churches.

of food, and their particular brand of English. A Malaysian custom during major festivals is the "open house", whereby practitioners of the various religions open their doors to visitors all day. This is when people of different races visit each other to wish each other *Gong Xi Fa Cai* during Chinese New Year, *Selamat Hari Raya* during the Muslim New Year, and *Happy Deepavali* during the Hindu Festival of Lights.

Economy

Electrical and electronic goods, manufactured goods, textiles, clothing and footwear, palm oil, natural gas, petroleum, timber and rubber are the main exports. Malaysia's main trading partners are the United States, Singapore and Japan. Tourism also ranks among the top three contributors to the economy.

Despite the economic crisis that began in 1997, employment stands at 95 percent. The stabilisation of the ringgit and stimulation of domestic demand are expected to help resuscitate the economy.

The government's ambitious information technology-based Multimedia Super Corridor (MSC) project, is also viewed as an important springboard in helping the country to achieve developed nation status by 2020.

Government

Malaysia is a constitutional monarchy comprising 13 states and a federal territory. Independent from British colonial rule since 1957, the Malaysian government is regulated by the Parliament comprising the Yang di-Pertuan Agung (king), who is elected for a five-year term from among the sultans of the states, and two houses: the House of Representatives, to which members are elected once every five years, and the Senate, to which members are nominated.

The executive functions of the government are carried out by the cabinet, led by the prime minister. The longest serving prime minister, both in Malaysia and Southeast Asia, is Dato' Seri Dr Mahathir Mohamad, who came into office in 1981. The political entity which has been in power since Independence is the Barisan Nasional (National Front) coalition representing numerous race-based parties.

Business Hours

In an Islamic nation with a British colonial past, the definition of the "working week" varies. In the former British Federated States, it runs from Monday–Friday and Saturday morning. However, the formerly semi-autonomous states of Johor, Kedah, Perlis, Terengganu and Kelantan retain the traditional half-day on Thursday and are closed on Friday, not Sunday.

The working day begins at 8am and ends at 4.30pm with time off on Friday from noon–2.30pm for communal prayers at the mosque. Most private businesses stick to the nine-to-five routine. Shops start to close at 6pm, but large supermarkets and department stores are open 10am–10pm.

Planning the Trip

Malaysia's tourism industry is well-established and caters to both the individual traveller as well as groups. While the major peninsula destinations could be covered in a fortnight, distances in Sabah and Sarawak are far greater, and attractions more remote, therefore requiring a little more planning.

Finding accommodation and transport is generally not a problem, except during school holidays and public holidays when it is best to book ahead. In places that are popular with Singaporeans, you should take into account Singaporean holidays, too, when these places can be crowded. Local favourites such as waterfalls near towns can also be crowded with picnickers at the weekend.

Packages are popular with locals, and are usually a better deal than making separate arrangements for accommodation and transport, although they are less flexible. Packages usually include a guided tour, and can be booked through tour agents in the major towns.

The peninsula's west coast is good to visit all year round, although temperatures can be uncomfortably high at the end of January and beginning of February.

The peninsula's east coast usually experiences heavy rain between November and February, and, apart from Chinese-run eateries, food is almost impossible to obtain during the day in the Muslim fasting month of Ramadhan.

Sabah and Sarawak are fine to travel in all year round, although they can be wet during the October–February monsoon period.

A good time to visit the country

is during the major festivals when towns and people get prettied up, unusual goodies are on sale, and tradition flaunts itself.

Passports & Visas

Valid passports or internationally-recognised travel documents are required to enter Malaysia. Immigration requests that your passport be valid for at least 6 months. Remember that Sabah and Sarawak are treated like separate countries, and you will have to go through customs again there, both from Peninsular Malaysia and between the two states.

A social single-entry visa is valid for 3 months. Visas can be applied for at Malaysian diplomatic missions overseas. Citizens of Commonwealth countries (except India), Ireland, Switzerland, Netherlands, San Marino and Liechtenstein do not need a visa to visit. The following countries do not need a visa for a visit not exceeding 3 months: Austria, Italy, Japan, South Korea, Tunisia, United States, Germany, France, Norway, Sweden, Denmark, Belgium, Finland, Luxembourg and Iceland. You are not allowed to be employed with this visa.

Extensions may be applied for at any *Pejabat Imigresen* (Immigration Office):

Kuala Lumpur
Headquarters Office,
Pusat Bandar Damansara
Tel: 03-255 5077
Alor Setar
Kedah, Wisma Persekutuan,
Jalan Kampung Baru
Tel: 04-733 3302
Ipoh
Perak, Bangunan Sri Kinta,
Jalan Sultan Idris Shah
Tel: 05-241 5233
Johor Bahru
Johor, Wisma Persekutuan,
Jalan Air Molek
Tel: 07-224 4253
Kangar
Perlis, Menara Kemajuan PKNP,
Jalan Bukit Lagi
Tel: 04-976 2636

Kota Bharu
Kelantan, Wisma Persekutuan,
Jalan Bayam
Tel: 09-748 2120/748 2644
Kota Kinabalu
Sabah, Bangunan Penerangan
Tel: 088-216 711
Kuala Terengganu
Terengganu, Wisma Persekutuan,
Jalan Paya Bunya
Tel: 09-622 1424
Kuantan
Pahang, Wisma Persekutuan,
Jalan Gambut
Tel: 09-514 2155
Kuching
Sarawak, Bangunan Sultan Iskandar,
Jalan Simpang Tiga
Tel: 082-245 661
Labuan
Sabah, Jalan Tanjung Kobang
Tel: 087-412 298
Melaka
Wisma Persekutuan,
Jalan Hang Tuah
Tel: 06-282 4955
Pulau Pinang (Penang)
Jalan Lebuh Pantai
Tel: 04-261 5122
Seremban
Negeri Sembilan,
Wisma Persekutuan,
Jalan Dato' Abdul Kadir
Tel: 06-762 0000
Shah Alam
Selangor, Kompleks PKNS
Tel: 03-559 0653

Customs

Import duties seldom affect the average traveller, who may bring in 250 g (½ lb) of tobacco, 50 cigars, or 200 cigarettes, and a 1-litre bottle of liquor duty-free as well as personal cameras, watches, cassette players, cosmetics, etc.

On rare occasions, visitors may be asked to pay a deposit for temporary importation of dutiable goods (up to 50 percent of the value) which is refundable upon departure. Be sure to get an official receipt for any tax or deposit paid.

Pornography, weapons and walkie-talkies are strictly prohibited. Exporting antiques requires a licence from the Museum Department. The duty-free

guidelines do not apply on domestic flights, or from Singapore.

Non-residents also have to declare how much cash they are bringing into the country. Due to currency control regulations imposed in 1998, you are only allowed to bring in and out of the country RM1,000 in cash and travellers' cheques. In terms of foreign currency, you are not allowed to take out more than you brought in.

Note Possession of narcotics and other illegal drugs carries the death sentence.

What to Bring

There is very little need to worry about leaving something important behind when you visit Malaysia. Toiletries, medicines, clothes, film, suntan lotion and straw hats are all readily available in most towns, and definitely in the large cities. So, travel lightly.

If you are planning to visit the hill stations, a light sweater would be a good idea for the cooler evenings. In more remote areas, you will not have the luxury of a shaving point, but disposable razors are widely available, or you can buy a battery-operated razor. Sanitary products for women are also available, but tampons are not easily obtainable.

In Malaysia's tropical climate, think cotton. Malaysians are fairly informal but they do dress up for dinner or a night out, especially in the cities. In fact, the fancier establishments have a dress code. Moreover, since this is a predominantly Muslim and conservative country, observance of local customs is important. T-shirts and longish shorts are fine, except in rural areas and especially if you go off the beaten tourist track, in which case, keep your legs and upper arms covered. Check the required attire before entering any house of religious worship.

Cheap clothes are everywhere – colourful batik shirts and "I was here" T-shirts make good souvenirs, too. Large shoe sizes could be a problem though.

Toilet paper is still not widely available, even in cities, so unless you are "handy" with the local pail or hose-and-water method, pack a roll, or carry tissue paper with you.

Health and Insurance

Travellers have little to worry about in a country where the health standards are ranked among the highest in Asia. Water in cities is generally safe for drinking, but it is safest to drink it boiled. Bottled drinks are also widely available. Avoid drinking iced water from roadside stalls. It is important to drink sufficiently to avoid dehydration; drink more than you would normally if you're from a temperate country. Cooked stall food is generally safe to eat.

The sun is deceptively strong in Malaysia: one hour of sunbathing a day for the first few days will get you a lasting tan without giving you sunstroke.

If you are visiting remote rainforest areas, it is advisable to take protection against malaria. See your doctor before leaving home. Malaria tablets are only available on prescription in Malaysia. To keep mosquitoes at bay, use insect repellents, mosquito coils and mosquito nets at night.

Treat open cuts and scratches immediately as infection in humid climates can delay healing, and at worst, cause tropical ulcers. It is advisable to read up about which rainforest and marine creatures to be wary of.

Medical supplies and treatment are readily available in Malaysia, in pharmacies and hospitals as well as at 24-hour private clinics.

It is advisable to buy travel and health insurance before arriving in the country.

Emergencies

For ambulance, fire or police services, the free emergency number to call is 999.

Money Matters

Carry a combination of cash and travellers' cheques and/or a credit card. Cash is imperative in rural areas, but you can change travellers' cheques and use credit cards in urban areas and established tourist areas.

Most currencies can be exchanged for ringgit, but the popular ones are US dollars (to which the ringgit is pegged), British sterling and Singapore dollars. Licensed money changers (open from early morning until late at night) offer better rates than banks, while hotels and shopping centres levy a service charge (usually 2–4 percent).

Local and international banks handle the gamut of transactions, and automated teller machines, from which you can use your credit card to withdraw cash, are widespread in towns.

In the more flashy quarters of the larger towns, in department stores, shops, first-class restaurants and hotels, travellers' cheques can be exchanged easily. Have your passport ready when changing cheques.

Banking Hours

Banking hours are Monday–Friday 10am–3pm, Saturday 9.30–11.30am. In Kedah, Perlis, Kelantan and Terengganu, banking hours are Saturday–Wednesday 10am–3pm, Thursday 9.30–11.30am.

Credit cards

The most widely used credit cards are Visa and MasterCard. Diners Club and American Express are less welcome, but accepted, too. Make sure you have enough cash before you leave a city.

Taxes

There is no general sales tax on purchases, but there is a government tax of 10 percent and service tax of 5 percent that is levied on services in the bigger establishments. Hotels are obliged to list net prices, but restaurants generally do not.

Dressing for the Jungle

Going into the rainforest requires extra preparation. It is much more humid in the rainforest, so packing light is even more imperative, as you could find yourself getting tired easily. Be prepared to get wet, so a light raincoat is a must. A rainpack could be useful, but line your backpack with a plastic bag anyway, and check that everything is waterproof, because river-crossings are almost inevitable. Long-sleeved cotton shirts and cotton trousers are comfortable and protect you from thorny rattan and insects.

Leave your heavy-duty leather boots behind – after a river-crossing, your feet will feel like lead. Sports sandals or light sneakers with a good grip are a better bet.

Temperatures can drop to 0°C on the mountain peaks, such as Mount Kinabalu and Mount Mulu, so warmer clothing and even gloves are a good idea.

Also, pack a water bottle, purifying tablets (or boil all your water), insect repellent, sunscreen, a cap, small towel or sarong, and your own energy supplements such as chocolate and sweets – these can double as goodwill gifts to any children you might meet. Leech socks come in handy, too.

If you travel with a tour company, everything else will be provided. Otherwise, tents, sleeping bags and cooking utensils can be hired in places such as Taman Negara, but book beforehand.

Note that while bikinis might be fine in the beach resorts, they are considered offensive in the more remote areas, particularly in the presence of Orang Asli or native guides, who consider some of their places sacred. So, you can also forget about going starkers.

Tourist Offices

Tourism Malaysia (TM) and Malaysia Airlines (MAS) have offices throughout the world. For information in each country, contact:

Australia
Tourism Malaysia
65 York Street, Sydney, NSW 2000
Tel: 02-9299 4441/2/3
Fax: 02-9262 2926
e-mail: Amir@iaccess.com.au/
Ishak@iaccess.com.au
Malaysia Airlines
16 Spring Street, Sydney,
NSW 2000
Tel: 02-364 3500

Canada
Tourism Malaysia
830 Burrard Street, Vancouver, BC,
Canada V6Z 2K4
Tel: 604-689 8899
Fax: 604-689 8804
e-mail: mtpb-yvr@msn.com
Malaysia Airlines
9th Floor, Hong Kong Bank Building,
885, West Georgia Street,
Vancouver V6C, 3E8
Tel: 604-6817741

Germany
Tourism Malaysia
Rossmarkt 11,
60311 Frankfurt Am Main
Tel: 069-283 782/3
Fax: 069-285 215
Malaysia Airlines
An Der Hauptwache 7,
60313 Frankfurt
Fax: 069-1387 1910

Singapore
Tourism Malaysia
10, Collyer Quay, #01-06 #18-02,
Ocean Building, Singapore 049315
Tel: 65-532 6321
Fax: 65-535 6650
e-mail:
mtpbmail@mbox3.singnet.com.sg
Malaysia Airlines
190, Clemenceau Avenue, #02-
09/11, Singapore Shopping Centre,
Singapore 239924
Tel: 65-336 6566

South Africa
Tourism Malaysia
1st Floor, Hutton Court, corner of
Jan Smuts Avenue and Summit
Road, Hyde Park 2196,
Johannesburg

Tel: 011-327 0400/1
Fax: 011-327 0205
Malaysia Airlines
1st Floor, Barclay House,
261 Oxford Road, Illovo,
Johannesburg 2196
Tel: 011-881 2792

Thailand
Tourism Malaysia
Unit 1001, Liberty Square, 287
Silom Road, Bangkok 10500
Tel: 02-631 1994
Fax: 02-631 1998
Malaysia Airlines
20th Floor, Ploenchitr Tower, 898,
Ploenchitr Road, Bangkok 10300
Tel: 02-263 0520

United Kingdom
Tourism Malaysia
57, Trafalgar Square,
London WC2N 5DU
Tel: 020-7930 7932
Fax: 020-7930 9015
e-mail: info@malaysia.org.uk
Malaysia Airlines
247/249, Cromwell Road,
London SW5 9GA
Tel: 020-7341 2000

United States
Tourism Malaysia
595, Madison Avenue, Suite 1800,
New York, NY 10022
Tel: 212-754 1113/4/5
Fax: 212-754 1116
Malaysia Airlines
2, Grand Central Tower, 140 East,
45th Street, 42nd Floor,
New York 10017
Tel: 1-212-697 8994
Tourism Malaysia
818, Suite 804, West 7th Street,
Los Angeles, CA 90017-3432
Tel: 213-689 9702
Fax: 213-689 1530
e-mail: malinfo@aol.com
Malaysia Airlines
100, North Spulveda Boulevard,
Suite 400, El Segundo, CA 90234
Tel: 1-800-552 9264

Photography

Professionals working in the tropics have one tip for good results: beware of the heat. Exposure of film or camera equipment to hot sun causes changes in the chemical emulsions of the film, which detract from natural colour.

Whenever possible, store your camera and film in a cool place; if not in an air-conditioned room, at least in the shade. Also, buy film in the cities, or where you can see that film is properly stored.

Get your films processed as soon as possible. You can do this everywhere in Malaysia where it is cheaper than in Western countries, with fairly good to excellent results. All outlets will process colour print film, sometimes in as little as half an hour. Bigger shops handle slides and APS-processing, too, while black-and-white takes approximately 48 hours.

Only photography shops in the bigger cities stock accessories, but those that do offer a good gamut, from tripods to the latest types of film and cameras.

Note that rainforest trips are camera-killers because of the humidity. Bring a plastic bag for your camera; likewise wrap film tightly in a plastic bag. Pack a dry, non-lint cloth. When you reach your campsite, wipe your camera dry, and leave it out to air. If you can, bring silica gel to absorb moisture.

For rich colours, snap your shots before 10.30am or after 3pm. At noon, the light is too strong. Early morning or late afternoon sidelights give softer contrasts and deeper colour density. And you perspire less as well.

Most Malaysians are more than amiable about having their pictures taken. It usually takes a gang of schoolchildren about 15 seconds before they merrily begin jabbing peace signs in front of your 20 mm lens. Mosques and temples are rightly more reserved about photographers posing their subjects in front of altars. Whatever the situation, you should always ask for permission. This is imperative during religious ceremonies, where you should keep a respectful distance. Likewise with tribal people, ask your tour guide. You should also ask if you should pay – this is controversial, but don't be surprised if payment is demanded.

Carry sweets (without wrappers) for the children. If you can bear to carry one, a zoom lens is a solution, ensuring your slideshows back home comprise your best memories.

Getting There

Malaysia is served by a large number of airlines. It can be reached by road from Singapore and Thailand, and ferries and boats connect the coastal towns.

BY AIR

Malaysia is well connected by about 50 airlines to all continents. Besides Kuala Lumpur International Airport (KLIA) at Sepang, one of the most advanced airports in the world, the other international airports are at Penang, Langkawi, Johor Bahru, Kuching, Kota Kinabalu and Labuan.

Direct flights from Singapore connect with Kuala Lumpur, Kuantan, Tioman and Kuching in the peninsula, and Kota Kinabalu in Sabah. Likewise, direct flights from Bangkok (Thailand) and Bandar Seri Begawan (Brunei) connect with Kuala Lumpur and other cities.

Malaysia Airlines (MAS), the national airline, handles international (about 120 destinations worldwide) and domestic routes. MAS and Singapore Airlines run shuttle services between Kuala Lumpur and Singapore about every half an hour – just go to the airport and

take a number and you will be put on the first available flight. This is cheaper than confirmed seats, however, early-morning and late-night flights are popular.

Note If you are coming into the country to any city via Kuala Lumpur, your plane will depart from KLIA. All other domestic flights from Kuala Lumpur are from the old airport at Subang (Sultan Abdul Aziz Shah Airport – SZB).

Enquire about special multi-sector air passes in your own country – these apply only if you purchase your ticket there. The peak season is over Christmas when overseas students flock home for the holidays. Summertime in Europe and the United States are also busy periods. Make sure you confirm your return ticket. You will have to pay airport tax.

International airlines
Malaysia Airlines
Tel: 03-746 3000 (24 hours)
Air New Zealand
Tel: 03-242 5577
Air Lanka
Tel: 03-274 0211
Air Nippon
Tel: 03-244 1331
British Airways
Tel: 03-232 5797
Cathay Pacific
Tel: 03-238 3377
China Airlines
Tel: 03-242 7344
Emirates Air
Tel: 03-244 3288

Eva Air
Tel: 03-262 2981
Garuda
Tel: 03-262 2811
Gulf Air
Tel: 03-242 4311
Japan Air
Tel: 03-261 1722
KLM
Tel: 03-242 7011
Korean Airlines
Tel: 03-242 8311
Lufthansa
Tel: 03-261 4666
Philippine Airlines
Tel: 03-242 9040
Qantas
Tel: 03-238 9133
Royal Brunei Air
Tel: 03-230 7166
SAS
Tel: 03-242 6044
Saudi Airlines
Tel: 03-201 7788
Singapore Airlines
Tel: 03-292 3122
South African Air
Tel: 03-241 7456
Thai International
Tel: 03-293 7100
Northwest Airlines
Tel: 03-336 3371
United Airlines
Tel: 03-261 1433

BY RAIL

The railway runs north from Singapore through Malaysia to Bangkok. Malaysian KTM trains operate night and day services from Singapore to Kuala Lumpur and to Tumpat near Kota Bharu on the east coast. The journey to Kuala Lumpur takes 7–10 hours; 12–15 hours to Tumpat.

From Bangkok, the Thai-owned International Express leaves daily for Butterworth (Penang) where you change trains for Kuala Lumpur. From Haadyai in southern Thailand you can travel all the way south. This journey takes about 2 days. Trains from Haadyai connect to Malaysia's east coast line. You can travel in a first-class air-conditioned sleeper, a second-class non-air-conditioned sleeper, or in upright

From Airport to Town

Kuala Lumpur International Airport (KLIA) is about 80 km (50 miles) from Kuala Lumpur city centre. Prices of airport limousines are based on a zone coupon system, and cost more than double the price of a coach ticket. To travel between the airport and town, tel: 1-800 880 733 (freephone).

Coaches for the 1-hour trip to the Hentian Duta bus stop depart from the airport basement every 15 minutes 6.45–12.30am

(5.30am–10.30pm from Hentian Duta). From Hentian Duta you can catch a bus or taxi for the 10-minute ride into town.

Buses go from the airport to the Subang Jaya (every hour) and Nilai (every 30 minutes) KTM commuter train stations where you can catch a train into town. The 90-minute journey is inexpensive; it departs from KLIA 8am–10pm. The Subang Jaya bus also goes to the domestic airport at Subang.

seats, third class. For reservations, contact the station in Bangkok (Hualamphong), or any KTM station (Kuala Lumpur, tel: 03-273 8000).

Sabah has only one railway that runs from Kota Kinabalu to Beaufort in the interior.

BY ROAD

There are two road links to the peninsula from Singapore and a plethora from Thailand, just as numerous points link Sabah and Sarawak with Kalimantan in Indonesia. From Singapore, there are links across the Causeway from Woodlands to Johor Bahru, and Linke Dua (Second Link) from Tuas to Tanjung Kupang. In Singapore, buses to Peninsular Malaysia depart from Ban San Street (tel: 65-292 8151) and Queen Street. If you opt for long-distance taxis, take the bus to Johor Bahru and get a taxi from there.

The main routes from Bangkok or Haadyai in Thailand are across the border at Padang Besar (Perlis), Bukit Kayu Hitam (Kedah) and Rantau Panjang (Kelantan). Buses and taxis serve these routes.

From Pontianak in Kalimantan regular buses go to Kuching, Sarawak (10 hours). Miri is the jump-off point to Brunei's Bandar Seri Begawan. In Sarawak there is a road from Kuching to Kalimantan (Pontianak) and a long coast road joins Miri with the Brunei capital of Bandar Seri Begawan.

BY SEA

Malaysia has a number of authorised entry points by sea. Singapore has ferry links to Tanjung Belungkor and Kukup in Johor, and a high-speed catamaran to Tioman. Satun in south Thailand has a regular ferry or longboat service to Langkawi. Penang connects to Medan in Sumatra, Indonesia and Melaka connects to Dumai further south on the same island.

In Sabah, Tawau connects to Tarakan in Kalimantan, Indonesia;

Brunei is linked to Labuan, and Limbang and Lawas in Sarawak. Sabah has ferry services from Kota Kinabalu to Labuan from where a boat can be taken across to the Sarawak side.

Tour Operators

Kuoni Travel Ltd
Kuoni House, Dorking,
Surrey RH5 4AZ
Tel: 01-306 740 888
Fax: 01-306 740 328
e-mail: fareastsales@kuoni.co.uk
Winner of the Tourism Malaysia Travel Awards 1998 for the "Best Overall Tour Programme to Malaysia". Tailor-made service also available.

Travelbag Plc
12 High Street, Alton
Hampshire GU34 1BN
Tel: 01-420 808 28
Fax: 01-420 821 33
e-mail: freequotes@travelbag.co.uk
Specialist in providing tailor-made service, with single or multicentre-holidays to Malaysia.

Trailfinders Ltd
42–50 Earls Court Road,
London W8 6FT
Tel: 0207-938 3366
Fax: 0207-937 9294
Long-established operator offering tailor-made holidays to Malaysia, including Sabah and Sarawak.

Specialist Holidays

Golden Days in Malaysia
10 Barley Mow Passage, Chiswick
London W4 4PH
Tel: 0208-994 7788
Fax: 0208-831 9844
e-mail: tours@goldendays.co.uk
Tailor-made arrangements for the independent traveller to Peninsular Malaysia, Sabah and Sarawak.

Footprint Adventures
5 Malham Drive, Lakelands
Lincoln LN6 0XD
Tel: 01-522 804 929
Fax: 01-522 804 928
e-mail: sales@footprint-adventures.co.uk
Specialist in jungle trekking, birdwatching trips, and butterfly and wildlife safari holidays.

Practical Tips

Media

Newspapers and Magazines

The main daily newspapers are in Bahasa Malaysia and English. There are also Chinese and Tamil language newspapers. The *New Straits Times* is the voice of the government, but it is difficult to be otherwise when all media have to apply annually to renew their operating licence under the Printing and Presses Act. The other big English language national daily is *The Star*. Business papers include *The Edge* and *Business Times*. The *Malay Mail* is an afternoon tabloid with a more chatty, local slant. Sabah and Sarawak have their own papers, including *The Sabah Times*, *Sabah Daily News*, *Daily Express*, *People's Mirror*, *Sarawak Tribune* and *Borneo Post* .

Most of these papers have online editions; *The Star Online* is one of the most popular websites for Malaysian news. With the growing popularity of the Internet, online publications have sprung up by the dozen, some of them the equivalent of community papers, while others concentrate on speciality topics. There is also a large number of local magazines, from leisure to entertainment and business. Foreign newspapers and magazines can be purchased in large cities.

Radio and Television

The radio can be heard everywhere, blaring out a wild assortment of different sounds; a flick of the dial will tune you to Malay rock or heavy metal, Tamil numbers or Western classical music, Canto-pop or the latest hits from Britain or the United States. The main national English language radio stations are: Hitz FM, Mix FM, Light & Easy (format radio stations which play a mix of local and international numbers), Time Highway Radio, which specialises in traffic updates, and the government-run Radio Four, which caters for older listeners.

Television is the most popular medium in Malaysia, watched in international hotel rooms and longhouses with the same enthusiasm. Programmes are cosmopolitan and American sit-coms and documentaries are shown alongside Indonesia's hottest films and Koran reading competitions. Sports are given generous amounts of air-time.

The government television stations are RTM1 and 2, the private operators are TV3 and NTV7, while the subscription-only satellite TV broadcaster, Astro, offers 18 channels, including MTV and CNN. The news in English is broadcast at 8pm on RTM2 (also known as TV2) and 11pm on TV3 and NTV7. Most hotels offer an in-house cable station as well as selected Astro satellite channels.

Check the local newspaper for programme details.

Postal Services

Malaysian postal services are reliable, and there are post offices everywhere. Post offices are open Monday–Saturday, 8am–5pm, while a handful in large housing estates are open until 10pm. The full range of services is available, including PosLaju courier and overnight Pos Ekspres services.

Most large hotels provide postal services; and stamps and aerogrammes are often sold at the small Indian sweet and tobacco stalls on street corners.

Telecommunications

Three telephone companies operate coin-operated public phone services. These also accept credit cards and/or telephone cards, which are sold at many small shops. Telekom Malaysia is the only national operator. Home country direct calls can also be made from public phones. Off-peak periods for inter-state calls are 7pm–7am.

Faxes can be sent through Kedai Telekom Bureaufax centres and Pos 2020 outlets in the major towns.

Medium to luxury hotels provide in-room telephones with local and international connection as well as public telephones in the foyer.

In Sarawak and Sabah two companies operate the phones, Telekom and Uniphone, so it is a bit of a lottery whether your card will be the correct one, or indeed if you can find a public phone that works.

Telephone Codes

Malaysia country code 60
Johor 07
Kedah 04
Kelanan 09
Kota Kinabalu 088
Kuala Lumpur 03
Kuching 082
Labuan 087
Melaka 06
Miri 085
Negeri Sembilan 06
Pahang 09
Penang 04
Perak 05
Perlis 04
Selangor 03
Terengganu 09
Singapore from Malaysia 02

Internet

Cybercafés can be found in all the capitals and some towns and tourist areas, including several in Kuching and Kota Kinabalu. Many are in the large shopping centres. Backpacker hotels seem to be more advanced in providing this service than some of the medium-class ones. Major hotels offer an Internet service at a high cost in their business centres, and business-class international hotels offer it in the room.

Tourist Information

Tourism Malaysia has offices in every state. Offices vary in the amount of literature available, but there are usually comprehensive brochures on each state and sometimes local places of interest, and the officers are informed and helpful. The regional offices can also be contacted for information on reliable tour and travel operators, who have to be registered with them.

Tourist Offices
Head Office
24–27th & 30th Floor, Menara Dato' Onn, Putra World Trade Centre, 45 Jalan Tun Ismail, KL
Tel: 03-293 5188
Malaysia Tourist Information Complex (MATIC)
109 Jalan Ampang, KL
Tel: 03-264 3929
East Coast Region
2243 Ground Floor, Wisma MCIS
Jalan Sultan Zainal Abidin,
Kuala Terengganu, Terengganu
Tel: 09-622 1433
Northern Region
10 Jalan Tun Syed Sheh Barakbah
Penang
Tel: 04-261 9067
Southern Region
1 Fourth Floor, Tun Abdul Razak Complex, Jalan Wong Ah Fook
Johor Bahru, Johor
Tel: 07-222 3591
Sabah
Ground Floor, Wisma Wing Onn Life
1 Jalan Sagunting, Kota Kinabalu
Tel: 088-248 698
Sarawak
2nd Floor, Rugayah Building, Jalan Song Thian Cheok, Kuching, Sarawak
Tel: 082-246 575

Embassies and Consulates

Australia
3 Jalan Semantan 2
Damansara Heights
Tel: 03-255 0176
Canada
7th Floor MBF Plaza
172 Jalan Ampang
Tel: 03-261 2000
China
229 Jalan Ampang
Tel: 03-242 8495
Denmark
22nd Floor Bangunan Angkasa Raya, 123 Jalan Ampang
Tel: 03-241 6088

France
192–196 Jalan Ampang
Tel: 03-248 4122

Germany
3 Jalan U Thant
Tel: 03-242 9666

India
Jalan Taman Duta
off Jalan Duta
Tel: 03-353 3510

Indonesia
233 Jalan Tun Razak
Tel: 03-984 2011

Iran
1 Lorong U Thant 1
Tel: 03-451 4824

Iraq
2 Jalan Langgak Golf
off Jalan Tun Razak
Tel: 03-248 0555

Italy
99 Jalan U Thant
Tel: 03-456 5122

Japan
Wisma AIA, 47 Jalan Tun Razak
Tel: 03-242 7044

Kuwait
229 Jalan Tun Razak
Tel: 03-984 6033

Libya
6 Jalan Madge, off Jalan U Thant
Tel: 03-248 2122

Myanmar
5 Taman U Thant I
Tel: 03-242 3863

Netherlands
4 Jalan Mesra, off Jalan Damai
Tel: 03-248 5151

New Zealand
193 Jalan Tun Razak
Tel: 03-248 6422

Norway
11th Floor Bangunan Angkasa Raya
Jalan Ampang
Tel: 03-243 0144

Oman
24 Lingkunan U Thant, off Jalan Ru
Tel: 03-475 011

Pakistan
132 Jalan Ampang
Tel: 03-241 8877

Papua New Guinea
1 Lorong Ru Kedua
off Jalan Ampang
Tel: 03-457 4202

Philippines
1 Changkat Kia Peng
Tel: 03-248 4233

Saudi Arabia
7 Jalan Kedondong
off Jalan Ampang Hilir
Tel: 03-457 9433

Singapore
209 Jalan Tun Razak
Tel: 03-261 6277

South Korea
422 Jalan Tun Razak
Tel: 03-984 2177

Sri Lanka
2A Jalan Ampang Hilir
Tel: 03-456 0917

Sweden
6th Floor Wisma Angkasa Raya
Jalan Ampang
Tel: 03-245 5981

Switzerland
16 Persiaran Madge
Tel: 03-248 0622

Thailand
206 Jalan Ampang
Tel: 03-248 8222

United Kingdom
186 Jalan Ampang
Tel: 03-248 2122

United States
376 Jalan Tun Razak
Tel: 03-248 9011

Old Customs – New Lifestyles

Leisure and tourism are relatively new concepts to Malaysians. As an industry, tourism was established only in the 1960s, which was also when Malaysians started travelling on holiday. Today, tourism is one of the top three revenue-earners for the country, and the industry comes under a federal ministry which spends millions on infrastructure and promotions. This investment is most evident in ease of access and range of accommodation.

The industry's Achilles' heel is service. Therefore, sometimes, a complaint might receive a less than satisfactory response, or staff at a three-star resort might be slow or ignorant. The key is to be patient and firm – often, making a joke out of a situation gets a quicker response than anger.

Punctuality, or the lack thereof, is the other point to note. Malaysians follow "Malaysian time", which translates to anything from a few minutes to hours late. Rarely does a bus or boat leave ahead of schedule, and almost never without a passenger. Have a cuppa and wait. Detailed information about an area is also scarce, although it is improving; but locals are always happy to regale you with a local legend, or point out "must-sees".

Because of the incipience of tourism, particularly in the rural areas, great is the danger of cultural pollution. Satellite television notwithstanding, age-old traditions, lifestyles, and morals are crumbling before the holy grail of the so-called better life. Tourism can rent the fragile social fabric of a family and community through something as simple as what a foreigner wears (or often, does not), to more direct interaction and infusion of ideas.

Visitors to the country are also, more and more, encountering another breed of locals: the Malaysian on holiday. To many Malaysians, spending money on leisure is still anathema to their frugal, Asian work-based ethos. Malaysian Chinese, in particular, holiday only once a year during Chinese New Year, and often go overseas; otherwise, those running their own businesses in particular, work 7 days a week. On the other hand, leisure is important to the city-bred, middle-income baby-boomers of the 1990s, and especially those exposed to Western norms.

Malaysians generally like to travel in big groups and thus tend to be noisy – it is a cultural trait. They like crowds, and will try to replicate home by bringing along their stereos, card games and mahjong sets. They also enjoy karaoke, even in a rainforest or cave. On the other hand, Malaysians do not generally sunbathe in the nude or wander about drunk, yelling obscenities – generally, nor do tourists.

Vietnam
4 Persiaran Stonor
Tel: 03-248 4036

Women Travellers

Travelling alone is fairly safe for women, but no thanks to Hollywood. Western women do have the image of being "easy", so a wedding ring helps, or a "Yes, I'm married" to the inevitable query. Ignore wolf whistles and catcalls. If you are approached, be polite but firm. Mostly people are just being friendly, even if some might be hoping for something more; if you start feeling uneasy, walk away. Be careful about being over-friendly with your tour guide.

Malaysians stare – both men and women – but wearing revealing clothes in areas that are newer to tourism will invite harassment. In Malaysia's rural societies, young women rarely approach or speak to male strangers, and travel is virtually unheard of, let alone travelling alone. Topless and nude sunbathing is prohibited.

Travelling with Kids

There are enough attractions to keep children occupied when travelling in Malaysia. However, children might be more susceptible to heat and food-and-water related ailments. Food could be a problem off the beaten track. Malaysian infrastructure is not at all baby-friendly, even in the cities. There are no mother's rooms or nappy-changing tables in toilets, and it can be difficult to buy infant products in rural areas. Public transport and public areas are unsympathetic to pushchairs. Yet Malaysians love children, so a helping hand is never far away.

Tipping

In most hotels and large restaurants, a 10 percent service charge is added to the bill along with a 5 percent government tax, so tipping is not obligatory. However, it is appreciated and is common, but only in the cities and major tourist spots. In large hotels, bellboys and porters usually receive tips from RM2 to RM5 depending on the service rendered. In smart restaurants you can just leave behind the loose change. Tourist guides expect a tip. Otherwise, a simple thank you (*terima kasih*) and a smile will do.

Religious Services

Minarets, spires, domes and steeples adorning the skylines reflect a rich diversity of faiths in Malaysia. However, churches might be difficult to locate outside urban centres and in the predominantly Muslim east coast of Peninsular Malaysia. Check with your hotel.

Security and Crime

Like anywhere else, pickpockets will be your biggest worry. Unless you are in a luxury hotel, do not leave valuables in your room, even in a safe. Carry your passport and money with you at all times – even for a bout of sunbathing – or keep them in the main hotel safe. Sling your camera around your body, and make sure your backpack is firmly strapped on. If you are going diving or snorkelling or taking part in any other adventure sport, put valuables in a small backpack which you can leave with the operators. Travelling on public transport is safe – just keep an eye on the luggage that is taken out whenever your interstate coach stops. Walking around at night is safe; women should be a little more careful, especially in tourist areas, but groups are fine.

Hitch-hiking is uncommon and hence can be frustrating and dangerous. Public transport, if slow and erratic in some places, is cheap and plentiful.

Etiquette

The customs, religions and social norms of many nations converge in Malaysia. But they have one common thread, Malaysians smile a lot, and are more often than not polite and helpful. Visitors behaving courteously stand little chance of unintentionally giving offence. Cities and entrenched tourist areas have a more liberal atmosphere, but if visiting rural areas, and especially someone's private home, it helps to know something of local norms.

Seniority is much respected. The oldest male member of a family is greeted first, often sits in the best and highest seat, and is consulted first on any matter.

If you are a man, greet the men first, then the women. Women usually greet other women first. It is not uncommon for women not to shake hands with male strangers. Although handshakes are common, particularly in the cities, do not be offended by what is a limp handshake by Western standards. The Malay style of greeting is to touch the other's palm and then his heart, "I am pleased to meet you from the bottom of my heart."

Hugging and kissing are foreign among non-family members, so except for children, refrain from doing so, no matter how fond you become of someone, especially someone of the opposite sex. Necking or fondling each other in public is a no-no, too, particularly in rural areas. In traditional homes, it is rude to cross your legs when you sit down in front of the host, particularly for women.

Drinks and snacks are always served to guests. Never refuse. At the very least, take a nominal sip or one biscuit. Use the right hand to pass or accept anything. The left is traditionally "dirty" because of its washroom connections.

Pointing with the finger is considered very rude and a whole hand is used to indicate a direction, but never a person. To point to a person, close the right hand into a fist with the thumb on top and then aim it at the subject.

Malaysians remove their shoes at the door to keep the house free from dirt. You can always tell if there is some kind of get-together at someone's house by the number of shoes and sandals scattered around the front door.

Getting Around

Towns in pre-independence Malaysia were called "stations", hence the term "outstation", meaning "inter-state". "Outstation", however, has stuck and going outstation by public transport today is easy and cheap.

Two points to remember: the air-conditioning is often such that it can make an Eskimo reach for his blanket; and movies in Chinese or English are usually shown, the norm being mindless gore, explosions and *kung fu*, which helps since the sound system is usually less than adequate.

On land, buses are the cheapest mode of transport; outstation taxis the quickest, and trains the most scenic. In Sabah and Sarawak, expressboats are an exciting and novel means of transport for the landlocked.

On Arrival

Buses, public and private, taxis and limousines operate from major airports in Malaysia. Many airports have a taxi desk, where you purchase a coupon; the price is fixed. Kuala Lumpur's railway

Touting for Business

The airport is where you are likely to meet your first tout. Unlicensed taxi operators, called *teksi sapu* or *kereta sapu*, hang around airport, train, bus and boat terminals, and will charge a flat rate, usually higher than official rates. They sometimes go round gathering a few passengers before they depart. Opt for a licensed cab if you can.

station also uses a coupon system. Tolls are paid by the passenger. Elsewhere, inquire about fares at the information desk. Taxi fares from airports are higher than around the town.

Sarawak and Sabah

Please note that although Sarawak and Sabah are part of Malaysia, it is necessary for both Malaysian and foreign visitors, whether coming from other parts of Malaysia or from another country, to go through immigration procedures on arrival.

By Air

Travelling by air is the best way to cover the great distances in Sabah and Sarawak, and in some cases, the only way – other than days of walking – to access the high hills and deep rainforests. Locals hop on and off planes like they do buses.

The most extensive network of flights is operated by Malaysia Airlines (MAS). In the more remote areas, its Fokker 50s and Twin Otters are the fastest link to capitals. Airport tax (RMS) for domestic flights is collected at all airports. Check in 30–45 minutes before departure. You may check baggage through to your final destination. All flights are non-smoking.

MAS has a night tourist fare which is 30 percent cheaper on Kuala Lumpur sectors to Alor Setar, Penang, Kota Bharu, Johor Bahru, Kuching and Kota Kinabalu. Other discounts on selected routes (mainly from Johor Bahru, Kuala Lumpur, Kuching and Kota Kinabalu) include a special one-way fare (less 20 percent) if you pay up 7 days' in advance; a special round-trip fare (less 30 percent) if you stay between 3 and 30 days; and a group fare (less 50 percent) for travel between the peninsula and Sabah or Sarawak if you are in a group of three, pay up 7 days' in advance, and remain in the destination between 3 and 30 days; other restrictions apply. There is also a special rate for families. Enquire at the nearest MAS office.

Note that a competitor, Air Asia, runs regular scheduled services from Kuala Lumpur to Kuching (Sarawak) and Kota Kinabalu (Sabah) at lower prices than MAS.

Malaysia Airlines Offices

(T=ticketing, R=reservations):
Alor Setar Lot 180, Kompleks Alor Setar, Lebuhraya Darulaman, Kedah
Tel: 04-731 1106 (T)
04-731 1186 (R)
Ipoh Lot G-01 Bangunan Seri Kinta, Jalan Sultan Idris Shah, Perak
Tel: 05-312 2460 (T)
05-241 4886(R)
Johor Bahru Suite 1.1, Level 1, Menara Pelangi, Jalan Kuning, Taman Pelangi, Johor
Tel: 07-331 0035 (T)
07-334 1001 (R)
Kota Bharu Ground Floor, Komplek Yakin, Jalan Gajah Mati, Kelantan
Tel: 09-748 3477 (T)
09-744 7000 (R)
Kota Kinabalu 10th Floor, Blk C, Kompleks Karamunsing, Sabah
Tel: 088-239 310 (T)
088-213 555 (R)
Kuala Lumpur Bangunan MAS, Jalan Sultan Ismail
Tel: 03-261 0555 (T);
Lot 157, 1st floor, Complex Dayabumi Jalan Sultan Hishamuddin
Tel: 03-274 8734; and
Shop Lot No. 15/16 Menara Majlis Perbandaran Petaling Jaya, Jalan Tengah, Petaling Jaya, Selangor
Tel: 03-755 0770; reservations (24 hours), tel: 03-746 3000
Kuala Terengganu 13 Jalan Sultan Omar, Terengganu
Tel: 09-622 2266
Kuantan 7 Ground Floor, Wisma Persatuan Bolasepak Pahang, Jalan Gambut, Pahang
Tel: 09-515 7055
Kuching, Lot 215, Jalan Song Thian Cheok, Sarawak
Tel: 082-244 144 (T)
082-216 622 (R)
Labuan Lot No. 1, Wisma Kee Chia Jalan Bunga Kesuma, Sabah
Tel: 087-412 263
Langkawi GF5/GF44, Langkawi Fair Shopping Mall, Jalan Persiaran Putra, Kedah
Tel: 04-966 8611 (T)

Melaka 1st floor, Hotel Shopping
Arcade, City Bayview Hotel,
Jalan Bendahara, Melaka
Tel: 06-283 5722 (T)
06-283 5723 (R)
Miri Lot 239, Beautiful Jade Centre,
Sarawak
Tel: 085-414 144, 414 155
Penang 4th floor, KOMTAR,
Penang Road, Penang
Tel: 04-262 1403 (T)
04-262 0011 (R)
Sandakan Mezzanine Floor, Sabah
Building, Jalan Pelabuhan, Sabah
Tel: 089-273 907 (T)
089-273 966 (R)
Sibu 61 Jalan Tuanku Osman,
Sarawak
Tel: 084-321 055 (T)
084-326 166 (R)
Tawau First and Ground Floor, TB
319 Block 38, Jalan Haji Sahabudin
Fajar Complex, Sabah
Tel: 089-765 533

Border Shuttle Service

MAS operates a coach shuttle
service between Johor's Senai
Airport, Johor Bahru, and Novotel
Hotel in Singapore, tel: 02-250
3333 (Singapore), 07-223 3333
(Senai), 07-599 4737 (airport).

Tours

MAS's subsidiary, MAS Golden
Holidays, offers a range of holiday
packages including flights,
transfers, accommodation, meals,
and guided tours. There are options
of fly-drive and coach holiday
packages, as well as golf, scuba
diving, and adventure packages.
Tel: 03-265 5124, 03-746 3000
(24-hours); fax: 03-263 5003.

By Rail

Malaysian Railways (KTM Berhad)
runs right from Singapore through
the peninsula and into Thailand in
the north. Express services call
only at major towns; the others stop
everywhere. Malaysian trains are
comfortable and equipped with
restaurant cars. There are
extremely cold air-conditioned first-
and second-class coaches and
bunks on the night trains. Third-

class coaches are fan-cooled. Book
in advance during peak periods.
  The west coast line goes through
Kuala Lumpur to Butterworth
(Penang) and joins Thailand at
Padang Besar, Kedah. The Ekspres
Rakyat (ER) departs every morning
from Singapore to Butterworth and
vice-versa. Ekspres Sinaran (XSP) is
the other morning service and links
Kuala Lumpur and Butterworth.
  The night trains are the
Senandung Malam sleepers (SM)
servicing Kuala Lumpur–Singapore
and Kuala Lumpur–Butterworth,
and Ekspres Langkawi (EL) Kuala
Lumpur–Haadyai.
  The east coast line branches off
at Gemas in Johor, plunges through
the central forests and emerges at
Tumpat in Kelantan, near the border
to Thailand. Only night trains do this
route, the Ekspres Timuran (XST)
Singapore–Tumpat and Ekspres
Wau (XW) Kuala Lumpur–Tumpat
(via Gemas).
  For foreign tourists, KTM offers a
railpass which entitles the holder to
unlimited travel in any class and to
any destination for a period of 10 or
30 days. Sleeping berths are extra.

Good Deals

Two smaller airlines service
limited destinations and offer
cheaper rates. However, service
can be erratic.
Pelangi Air (tel: 03-755 5557;
fax: 03-755 3355, or travel
agents) has Fokker 50s that fly
to Penang, Ipoh, Johor Bahru,
Kuantan, Tioman and Kerteh
(Terengganu), as well as to
Sumatra in Indonesia, and
affordable packages to Kijal
(near Kerteh), Redang, Tioman
and Pangkor. There are special
fares for families and groups of
three, as well as flight and
accommodation packages.
Air Asia (tel: 03-745 7777) flies
to Langkawi, Kuching and Kota
Kinabalu. Tickets are only valid
for 30 days and payment must
be made 7 days before the flight.
Three-day/two-night packages
are also available.

For more information, call KTM:
Tel: 03-273 8000/275 7267
Fax: 03-273 6527
e-mail: passenger@ktmb.com.my
http://www.ktmb.com.my

Touring by Train

KTM offers good value rail packages
to various destinations in Malaysia,
which include train tickets,
transfers, accommodation, some
meals and tours. Try the Gunung
Jerai package, which includes a visit
to the archaeological Lembah
Bujang (Bujang Valley) site, or
Kelantan, which includes a city tour
of Kota Bharu and Rantau Abang
turtle beach. Tel: 03-275 7267;
fax: 03-273 6527.
  The Eastern & Oriental Express
is the ultimate in luxury rail travel,
complete with mahogany marquetry
and Burmese rosewood inspired by
the 1932 Marlene Dietrich film
Shanghai Express. The 132-
passenger train travels 2,000 km
(1,260 miles) over 2 nights from
Singapore through Kuala Lumpur to
Bangkok (or vice versa) with side
trips to Penang and Kanchanaburi.
For reservations, tel: 03-781 1337
(Malaysia), 65-323 4390
(Singapore), 662-216 5939
(Thailand).

By Boat

On the peninsula, boats are the
chief means of travel to the islands
and in the interiors. Regular ferries
service the islands of Pangkor
(6.30am–7pm), Penang (24 hours)
and Langkawi (8am–6pm). Boats
out to islands on the east coast
generally do not follow schedules,
and in the monsoon season
(November–February), services may
stop altogether. Note that the sea
can be choppy just before and after
the monsoon period.
  In the north, services run from
8.30–9am and stop between
2–2.30pm. Other than during public
and school holidays, it is generally
fine to arrive on the Perhentian
Islands (from Kuala Besut) and
Kapas (from Marang) without having
booked accommodation, but safer

to pre-book accommodation and therefore boats at Redang and Tenggol (from Merang).

In the south, Mersing services the bulk of the Johor islands and Tioman, while Tanjung Leman is the staging point for the Sibu isles. Scheduled ferries depart Mersing only to Tioman (arrive at Mersing as early as possible) and Rawa (one service at midday). Other services can be a little confusing (see chapter on Mersing and Isles, page 241). Tioman can also be accessed from Tanjong Gemok and Singapore. The Tanjung Leman boats depart daily at 11am, 1.15pm and 4.30pm.

In the interior, Taman Negara is the only destination with scheduled boats (9am and 2pm). It is generally all right to arrive at Kenyir, Kenong and Cini without booking, but Temenggor (for Belum) and Bera must be pre-booked.

SARAWAK

There are no scheduled shipping lines to Sarawak, but within the country express boats and local river craft are still the main form of transport to the interior.

In recent years logging companies have opened up previously inaccessible areas. There is a lot of traffic on the rivers inland throughout most of the year as roads are still few and far between and are generally in poor condition.

On the Rejang River, regular boats run between Sibu and Kapit, and if the waters are high enough, they go on to Belaga and beyond to longhouse territory. Expressboats travel to many of the smaller rivers stopping at remote longhouses along the way. Chartered boats can be fearfully expensive.

Bigger boat services operate between Kuching and Sibu – daily departures with a three- to four-hour ride. Regular ferry services also connect Kota Kinabalu in Sabah with the tax-haven island of Labuan and then on to Brunei and the Sarawak divisions of Lawas and Limbang.

Cruises

Short-term cruises on the peninsula have been a hit with a niche market, mainly because of on-board gambling in international waters. Besides casinos, ships are usually equipped with a swimming pool, cinema, disco and karaoke. There is usually a live band or cabaret-style shows, ballroom dancing classes and other activities, and packages are full-board. The 450-passenger ship Empress offers dinner, theatre and 2-day/1-night packages to Penang and a "cruise to nowhere". It also goes to Langkawi and Phuket in south Thailand.

The luxurious 800-passenger ship Gemini offers 3-day/2-night to 6-day/5-night packages to those destinations as well as Pangkor, Melaka and Singapore. From Singapore, this ship and sister ships sail along the east coast to Thailand, stopping at Kijal and Perhentian Kecil in Terengganu.

Travel agencies offer better rates than the cruise companies. Try Mansfield Travels in Kuala Lumpur, which also handles international liners, tel: 03-242 8980; fax: 03-242 8992; Penang, tel: 04-262 1233; fax: 04-262 1835.

By Road

Malaysia's inter-state (outstation) buses and taxis are a fairly comfortable and convenient way of covering the country. Both the roads and public transport are better in the peninsula than Sabah and Sarawak, but good networks link capital cities and major towns. Sarawak's road system is pleasant enough to explore the areas surrounding Kuching and up to the Kalimantan border. The longer northern road to Miri is driveable, but not yet in perfect condition.

Outstation Buses

Three types of outstation buses operate in Malaysia: the non-air-conditioned buses plying between the states, the air-conditioned express buses connecting major towns, and the non-air-conditioned buses that provide services within each state. With the exception of the express buses, the others seldom adhere to the schedule, but are frequent between 9am–6pm.

Express buses usually connect two or three major towns, and will break the journey for a toilet stop at a restaurant (serving fairly inedible local food with the occasional burger stall) for half an hour – even in the early morning. Driving on the highway is not so bad, but the single-lane trunk roads bring out the devil in people and you would need to steel yourself for dicey overtaking, taking corners too quickly, and other such tricks.

There are several classes of buses: the VIP or business-class coaches have the most legroom, and do not cost that much more (recommended for longer journeys). At bus stations, you will inevitably be accosted by touts selling tickets for unlicensed operators. Tickets might be cheaper but these buses do not depart until enough passengers are rounded up; they also make numerous stops.

Different operators handle different towns – information and fares are displayed at the counter window. Outside public holidays, you don't need to purchase your ticket beforehand (bookings are rarely taken). The popular routes are serviced hourly.

There are three bus terminals in Kuala Lumpur. North and southbound services are at the old and bustling Puduraya bus station and the Kuala Lumpur railway station; coaches to the east coast and Tasik Kenyir depart from the Putra bus station (opposite the Putra World Trade Centre); and the interior destinations such as Kuala Lipis are serviced from Hentian Pekeliling, at the ring road off Jalan Tun Razak.

A luxury executive coach service is operated by Mara Holdings, Bangunan Mara, Jalan Raja Laut, tel: 03-291 8113. At double the price, you get plush aeroplane-style seats, a blanket, velvet drapes, a toilet, and an on-board telephone. Snacks are served by a hostess. It

Trishaws

Trishaws are found in Kota Bharu, Kuala Terengganu, Georgetown, Penang and Melaka. These three-wheeled contraptions are a memorable way to cover a city as their slow pace allows you to see points of interest along the way, providing more photographic opportunities. The bicycle is usually at the side of the carriage, except in Penang, where the two passengers sit in a sun-hooded carriage in front of the cyclist. Trishaw drivers will warn you to hold on to your bags firmly for fear of snatch-thieves on motorcycles. Incidences of this kind, however, are rare. Fix the price before you get on. You could try renting the trishaw for a time, say, half-a-day.

is non-stop and services Kuala Lumpur, Johor Bahru, Singapore, Butterworth and Penang.

SARAWAK

Sarawak has no main bus station, but there are small bus terminals in Kuching, close to the river, and each bus company has its own operating area. For southwest Sarawak, the Sarawak Transport Company can take you to Semonggoh and other points west. The distinctive green and yellow buses leave from Leboh Jawa. Petra Jaya Transport buses go to Damai, Santubong and Kampung Bako and leave from the bus area near the open-air market.

SABAH

A network of buses and mini buses operate in Sabah. In Kota Kinabalu the buses to the Kinabalu National Park leave from a shaded spot near the Padang. In rural areas, mini-buses operate effectively and transport you much faster than the larger yellow town buses.

Outstation Taxis

These "share" taxis go to any destination and are quicker than buses. They are old Mercedes Benz vehicles and some are air-conditioned. However, you have to wait until there are four passengers, unless you want to pay for the whole cab – remember, you do not have to charter the whole taxi. So turn up early and be prepared to wait; you wait longer in the afternoon. If you book a cab to yourself, the driver will pick you up from your hotel for free if you are close to town.

Note that there is a quota for how many taxis can ply a route. During public holidays, this quota could be full, in which case you would be asked to pay extra for non-quota taxis because the driver would not be allowed to pick up passengers on the return leg. Sometimes, if the traffic is heavy, particularly on the busy Karak Highway, you might have to pay more, so make sure you sort all this out with your driver. Night journeys have a surcharge. Long distance taxi stands are usually near the inter-state bus stations. In Kuala Lumpur, the stand is at the Puduraya bus station.

City Transport

All towns have public buses and taxis. Buses usually charge according to distance except in Kuala Lumpur, where the fare is standard. Timetables are a mystery, and listings of stops and routes elusive, except for the signs on the front of each vehicle. However, buses are a great way to rub shoulders with the locals. Of course, nerves of steel are required to take on the Kuala Lumpur bus ride, thanks to the driver's daredevil attempts to meet his quotas irrespective of traffic laws and other road users.

Taxis can be hailed at taxi stands or by the roadside. Bargain to agree your price before you get in. Meters are installed in Kuala Lumpur's cabs and you should insist on using

them. There is a surcharge for traffic jams, a 50 percent surcharge for trips between midnight and 6am and a small additional charge for more than two passengers. You can book a cab by telephone, which incurs a surcharge. There is usually a fixed rate to go to the airport – ask at your hotel. For taxi complaints, tel: 03-255 4444.

Light Rail Transport

Kuala Lumpur is the only city with monorail and commuter train services. These are air-conditioned and very convenient. Day and weekly passes are available. The Light Rail Transport (LRT) operates 6am–midnight and covers Kuala Lumpur and Petaling Jaya; the Komuter goes to Seremban, Port Klang, Kajang and Rawang.

Tour Companies

The whole gamut of tours is available in Malaysia, from city and night tours to week-long packages that cover several destinations, and any combination of fly, drive and coach choices with accommodation and sometimes transfers and food. Ask at your hotel, the tourism information centre, or check newspapers for the latest listings.

Large reputable companies in Kuala Lumpur usually have branches in several states. Try:
Mayflower Acme Tours
Tel: 03-622 1888
Fax: 03-627 0416
http://www.mayflower.com.my
SA Tours
Tel: 03-242 9155
Fax: 03-242 9420
http://www.mol.net.mt/-satours/
Sferas Tours and Travel
Tel: 03-243 2022
Fax: 03-243 1022.
Asia Overland Services
Tel: 03-452 9100
Fax: 03-452 9800
http://www.aostt.com
Ping Anchorage
Tel: 09-626 2020
Fax: 09-622 8093
e-mail: patrvl@tm.net.my
http://www.pinganchorage.com.my
This is your best bet for the east

coast, especially Terengganu, offering innovation and variety.

The Asia Travel Network
Tel: 03-966 8000
Fax: 03-966 800
e-mail: info@asiatravelnet.com.my
Has developed a secure online reservation system at http://asiatravelnet.com/ where you can book hotels, tours and rental cars throughout Malaysia.

SARAWAK

In Sarawak, tour companies are very helpful when it comes to longhouse visits and trekking tours. Unless one speaks at least a little Malay, it is not recommended to visit longhouses without a guide, who will make a trip far more enjoyable and meaningful. Ask around until you find a company that fulfils your requirements.

Borneo Adventure
55 Main Bazaar, Kuching
Tel: 082-245 175
Fax: 082-422 626
e-mail: bakch@po.jaring.my
Known for its eco-tourism specialities, although it handles almost every type of tour.

Borneo Transverse
15 Ground Floor, Jalan Greenhill
Kuching
Tel: 082-257784
Fax: 082-421 419
e-mail: btt@po.jaring.my

Tropical Adventure
1st Floor, 17 Main Bazaar, Kuching
Tel: 082-413 088
Fax: 082-413 104
e-mail: hthee@pc.jaring.my
Adventure specialist with its main office in Miri and a subsidiary office in Kuching. It is recommended for trekking in Bario, and for Mulu excursions.

Ibanika
Lot 435, Ground Floor, Section 62
Loring 9, Jalan Ang Cheng Ho
Kuching
Tel: 082-424 022
Fax: 082-424 021
e-mail: ibanika@ace.cdc.abu.com
Offers longhouse and general tours and can tailor a tour to suit your requirements.

Interworld Travel Service
161–162 Temple Street, Kuching
Tel: 082-252 344
Fax: 082-424 515
Specialist Sarawak operators.

SABAH

Many excursions in Sabah are almost impossible without the help of a tour company, or at least a guide, and destinations are often geared to tour groups.

Discovery Tours
Wisma, Sabah
Tel: 088-221 244
Fax: 088-221 600
e-mail: distour@po.jaring.my
An energetic company with many interesting tours. It also has offices at the Shangri La Tanjung Aru Resort and the Rasa Ria Resort.

Wildlife Expeditions
3rd Floor, Wisma, Sabah
Tel: 088-260 701
Fax: 088-259 701;
Room 903, 9th Floor, Wisma Khoo Siak Chiew, Sandakan
Tel: 089-219 616
Fax: 089-214 570;
331B, 3rd floor, Wisma Sabah
Kota Kinabalu
Tel: 088-254 300
Fax: 088-231 758;
Tour desk at Tanjung Aru Resort
Tel: 088-246 000
Fax: 088-231 758
The most experienced operator on Sabah's east coast. Tours to most Sabah destinations.

Nature Society

The Malaysian Nature Society (MNS) has chapters in every state, and a very active Selangor branch, which organises trips for members in caving, hiking, etc. MNS also runs nature education courses in Kuala Lumpur, Cameron Highlands, Kuala Selangor and Endau-Rompin in Johor.
Tel: 03-287 9422
Fax: 03-287 8773
e-mail: natsoc@po.jaring.my
http://www.mns.org.my/mns

Borneo Eco Tours
Block J, 1st Floor, Lot 74
Bandar Pasar Raya
Jalan Labuk Mile 4, Sandakan
Tel: 089-220 210
Fax: 089-213 614;
2nd Floor, Shop Lot 12a, Lorong Bernam 3, Taman Soon Kiong, 88300 Kota Kinabalu
Tel: 088-234 009
Fax: 088-233 688
e-mail: betsb1@po.jaring.my
Run by one of the leading tour operators in Sabah, this company specialises in environmentally oriented tourism, with trips focusing on the flora and fauna of Sabah. The company also runs a lodge at Sukau on the Kinabatangan River.

Borneo Expeditions
3rd Floor, Unit 306 Wisma, Sabah
Tel: 088-222 721
Fax: 088-222 720;
Tanjung Aru Resort, Shangri-la, Shopping Arcade, Shop Lot No: 7
Jalan Aru, 88000 Kota Kinabalu
Tel: 088-222 721
Fax: 088-222 720;
10th floor, Wisma Gaya
Tel: 088-238 731
Fax: 088-238 730
Personalised service from thoroughly professional company with head office in Kuching, Sarawak.

Eco-tours

The term "eco-tourism" is bandied about with abandon by tour agencies and resorts, but the reality often falls short. Nonetheless, a few small companies do a good job, keeping groups small, offering trained interpretive guides, hiring locals, especially natives, and paying villages which host their guests. Most are site-specific and resort-based.

Kuala Lumpur
Kuala Lumpur-based operators include:

Asia Overland Services
Tel: 03-452 9100
Fax: 03-452 9800
http://www.aostt.com
A nationwide pioneer, which started

with nature/adventure tours 20 years ago. It has broadened its scope to incorporate leisure, sightseeing, and other tour packages. Solid philosophy, trained guides, innovative ideas, tailor-made itineraries covering the whole country, good for long-haul journeys.

Try Adventure
Tel: 03-617 9221
Fax: 03-636 8801
e-mail: tryadventure@netlane.com
Soft and hard nature and adventure packages. Offers off-the-beaten track areas such as Belum, Kenong, Endau-Rompin, Gunung Tahan (from Merapoh), Stong (Kelantan) and Kuala Gula (Perak). It is run by an interesting German- and Norwegian-speaking tour guide.

Kembara Station
Tel: 03-706 4752/9
Fax: 03-706 4753
http://www.kembarastation.com
Offers a variety of tours, including adventure sports. Of note are its day tours to an elephant sanctuary in Pahang where you can interact with the animals, and to Sumatran Rhino, which has a breeding programme for this endangered species.

Kingfisher Tours
Tel: 03-242 1454
Fax: 03-242 9827
A naturalist-run operation specialising in birdwatching. It also offers botanical, wildlife and general nature tours, covering Fraser's Hill, Taman Negara, Kuala Selangor, and a 3-week Malaysia traverse.

Meranti Nature Tours
Tel/fax: 03-405 6492
e-mail: mikechn@pc.jaring.my
Specialises in birdwatching tours, also wildlife, ecology and nature photography and documentaries, in Kuala Selangor, Fraser's Hill, Gombak Forest Reserve and Ulu Kali Mountain. Manned by an ornithologist/naturalist.

Sabah and Sarawak

In Sabah and Sarawak most of the companies listed under *Tour Companies, left*, provide ecologically-sound tours as well as more commercially minded ones.

Driving

Driving is the best way to see Peninsular Malaysia, which has an excellent network of trunk roads and a dual-carriageway highway on the west coast. Driving is also enjoyable in Sabah and Sarawak, but you need a stauncher vehicle or even a four-wheel drive and lots more time.

Having your own transport gives you the freedom to go off the beaten track at your leisure. Visitors need an international driving licence and it is advisable to buy travel insurance. Local car hire firms are found in major cities in both the peninsula, Sabah and Sarawak.

Driving is on the left-hand side of the road. The speed limit is 50 kph (30 mph) in towns, 80 kph (50 mph) outside towns, and 110 kph (68 mph) on highways. Slow down when you go through a *kampung* – keep your eye out for children, livestock and bicycles, especially at night. Keep left unless overtaking. The wearing of seat belts in the front is compulsory. Breaking traffic rules incurs a flat-rate fine.

International traffic signs apply along with local ones (*see box, above right*). Local drivers have developed a few signals; there are individual variations so watch what other motorists do. If the driver in front flashes his right indicator, he is signalling to you not to overtake. This is usually because of an oncoming vehicle or a bend in the road, or he himself might be about to overtake the vehicle in front of him. If he flashes the left indicator, this means to overtake with caution. A driver flashing his headlamps at you is claiming the right of way. At roundabouts or traffic circles, the driver on the right has the right of way.

Malaysian drivers can be speed maniacs and bullies – the bigger the vehicle, the more so. Give way. In towns, motorcyclists can shoot out from nowhere or hog the road. Don't lose your cool: count to 10 instead. Heavy rain can be hazardous, so switch on your lights, drive slowly and be prepared for delays on smaller roads as entire roads are sometimes washed away. At worst, pull over until the downpour lightens up.

Petrol Stations

Petrol can be found in or around the fringes of towns and along the highway, where there are also eateries and toilets. Many operate 24 hours (24 *jam*) and accept credit cards. Stations in Kuala Lumpur, Johor and Langkawi are self-service.

Maps

Road maps are becoming more accurate, but road signs can be frustratingly misleading, and asking for directions even more so – be patient. The names of tourist attractions are highlighted in green writing on signs, while the highway is illustrated with a little picture.

Breakdown Services

The Automobile Association of Malaysia (AAM) is the national motoring organisation and has offices in most states – it has a prompt breakdown service, tel: 03-242 5777.

Main Routes

Peninsular Malaysia's North-South Highway starts at the causeway connecting to Singapore and runs north along the west coast to the Thai border. The old trunk road runs roughly parallel to that through small towns, and branches off to interesting nooks and corners, but you could be stuck behind a long queue waiting to overtake a series of rattling lorries.

Several main routes link the east and west coasts through the spectacular Main Range. From Kuala Lumpur, the busy Karak Highway goes to Kuantan (4 hours), the dual carriageway ending midway at Karak town. A fork at Bentong heads north through Kuala Lipis to Kota Bharu on the Gia Musang road (9 hours). Kota Bharu is also linked to Penang via the East-West Highway (5 hours), and Kuala Kangsar in Perak at the Grik fork.

From Johor Bahru, the Segamat Highway goes to Kuantan (4 hours), but the more scenic and much longer route hugs the east coast north from Desaru all the way to the Thai border. A parallel inland road with less traffic runs from Kuantan to Kota Bharu.

SABAH AND SARAWAK

In Sabah and Sarawak, motorways run along the coast connecting major towns. Roads leading to more remote areas inland are often unpaved or rough, and a four-wheel drive is advisable for these interior routes; unless you want to explore jungle tracks and logging routes, a little Suzuki Jimny or the equivalent can handle most conditions with ease. For day trips to Santubong, Damai, or west towards Lundu and beyond along the coast, a normal saloon car can be used. In Sabah, too, most of the main destinations along the coast are trouble free, as

is the road to Kinabalu Park and northwest to Kudat.

Car Rental

Car rental firms have branches in the main towns throughout Malaysia and at big airports. Rentals are usually based on time rather than mileage and most allow you to pick up a car from one place and drop it off at another. Credit cards are preferred; a large deposit is required if you pay cash.

Kuala Lumpur
Avis Rent A Car
Tel: 03-242 3500
(Freephone: 1-800 881 054)
Fax: 03-242 9650
KLIA
Tel: 03-8787 4087
Pacific Rent A Car
Tel: 03-245 4119
(Freephone: 1-800 886 155)
Fax: 03-245 1125
KLIA
Tel: 03-8787 4393
Hertz Rent A Car
Tel: 03-248 6433
Fax: 03-242 8481
KLIA
Tel: 03-8787 4572
Subang Airport
Tel: 03-746 7721
National Car Rental
Tel: 03-248 0522
Fax: 03-248 2823
KLIA
Tel: 03-8787 3890

SARAWAK

Kuching
Mayflower Car Rental
Lot 4, 24A
4th Floor Bangunan Satok
Jalan Satok
Kuching International Airport
Tel: 082-410 110/410 117
Pronto Car Rental
1st floor
98 Jalan Padungan
Tel: 082-236 889/237 889
Fax: 082-236 889
A wide range of vehicles, including Landcruisers, Mercedes and Hondas.

SABAH

Kota Kinabalu
Padas Jaya Rent A Car
Lot 1, 28B 1st Floor, Block B,
Karamunsing Complex
Tel: 088-233 239, 239 936
Fax: 088-239 937
e-mail: pta@tm.net. my
Kinabalu Rent A Car
3rd Floor, Karamunsing Complex
Tel: 088-232 602/3
(Hyatt Tour Desk), 088-217 643
(Shangri-La's Tanjung Aru Resort)
Fax: 088-242 512
e-mail: krc@sabah.com.my
http://www.sabah.com.my/krc

Where to Stay

Choosing a Hotel

The economic meltdown and glut of hotels means that high-quality accommodation has become remarkably affordable. This has unfortunately pushed some medium-priced accommodation out of the market, but there is always plenty of budget accommodation.

Choose your location then the price category. Always enquire about packages, which include a buffet or local breakfast with the room, and if you stay more than one night, you can try bargaining for better rates. Most hotels are fine with triple-share. Hotels are supposed to display net rates (including the 10 percent service and 5 percent government tax).

Cities and main tourist destinations offer the range. At the lowest end are dormitories at RM15–40 depending on location and whether the room has air-conditioning, or a ceiling fan.

Then come the simple Chinese-run Rumah Tumpangan motels which you can find in almost every town, and beachside Malay kampung-type chalets; these go for RM40 to more than RM100 and are sometimes equipped with TV, air-conditioning and hot showers.

Medium-class hotels come in traditional hotel blocks or chalets, and are popular with locals (RM100–300). The higher end ones in this category generally have full room facilities and services, including air-conditioning, ensuite baths with hot showers, colour TV, IDD telephones, laundry, mini bar, coffee-making facilities, room service, and a restaurant and/or coffee house. The world's top hotel chains and resorts are also here, complete with the usual full room facilities and services, saunas and gourmet restaurants (RM200–400, luxury hotels can be upwards of RM800). Incidentally there is local

Price Guide

Prices are for a standard double room during peak periods.
$$$$: more than RM400
$$$: RM200–400
$$: RM100–200
$: less than RM100

and international accreditation (five-star, four-star, etc.). Options in the medium to upper range are the condotels or apartment hotels, although rarely is cooking allowed.

Check-in times are between 1–3pm, check-out 11am–noon, late checkout requests until 2pm; some hotels do not accept guests

Government Resthouses

Government resthouses were established during the colonial era for travelling administrators. They can be found almost anywhere, particularly in small towns, are cheap, but not new. Some have a reputation for being haunted.

More recently, the government set up the Seri Malaysia chain to fill the void in quality medium-class hotels. These are in prime locations, close to transport or attractions. Like the resthouses, management is contracted out, but the buildings are newer. They have air-conditioning, attached baths, hot showers and a restaurant. Look for the red roofs.
Central reservation number:
03-243 2376 (Kuala Lumpur)
e-mail:
central@serimalaysia.com.my
http://www.serimalaysia.com.my
Alor Setar
Jalan Stadium
Tel: 04-730 8737
Fax: 04-730 7594

Genting Highlands
Tel: 03-210 2525
Fax: 03-210 1125
Ipoh
Jalan Sturrock, off Jalan Ipoh
Tel: 05-241 2936
Fax: 05-241 2946
Johor Bahru
Jalan Langkasuka
Tel: 07-221 1002
Fax: 07-221 1004
Kuala Terengganu
Jalan Hiliran (Balik Bukuit)
Tel: 09-623 6454
Fax: 09-623 8344
Kuantan
Jalan Telok Sisek
Tel: 09-555 3688
Fax: 09-555 3118
Marang
Kampung Paya
Tel: 09-618 2889
Fax: 09-618 1285
Mersing
Jalan Ismail
Tel: 09-799 1876
Fax: 09-799 1886

Port Dickson
Jalan Pantai Batu 4
Tel: 06-647 6070
Fax: 06-647 6028
Penang
7 Jalan Mayang Pasir, Bayan Baru
Tel: 04-642 2723
Fax: 04-6442 9461
Rompin
Tanjung Gemok
Tel: 09-413 2723
Fax: 09-413 2732
Seremban
Jalan Sungai Ujong
Tel: 06-764 4181
Fax: 06-764 4179
Sungai Petani
Seksyen 21, Jalan Pasar
Tel: 04-423 4060
Fax: 04-423 4106
Taiping
4 Jalan Sultan Mansor
Tel: 05-806 9502
Fax: 05-806 9495
Temerloh, Jalan Hamzah
Tel: 09-296 5776
Fax: 09-296 5711

between midnight and 7am. Sometimes, a 50 percent deposit is needed to secure bookings, rooms are held up to 6pm.

Hotel Listing

KUALA LUMPUR AND ENVIRONS

Kuala Lumpur

Kuala Lumpur's budget hotels are in Chinatown and Jalan Tunku Abdul Rahman, while the medium-class to luxury accommodation is in the business and shopping areas along Jalan Sultan Ismail and Jalan Bukit Bintang.

Carcosa Seri Negara
Taman Tasik Perdana
Tel: 03-282 1888
Fax: 03-282 7888
e-mail: carcosa@mol.net.my
For a taste of colonial splendour, the 13 extravagant suites in this former British governor's residence have butlers, a gorgeous restaurant overlooking huge landscaped gardens, and a bar. The "in thing" is to have high tea and curry tiffin on the terrace. **$$$$**

Hotel Istana
73 Jalan Raja Chulan
Tel: 03-244 1444
Fax: 03-244 0111
http://www.pernas.com
Right in the heart of the Golden Triangle, this extravagantly "palatial" hotel has 516 rooms, an excellent Italian restaurant, lounge overlooking a pretty garden, huge disco with karaoke, and a health centre. **$$$$**

KL Hilton
Jalan Sultan Ismail
Tel: 03-242 2222
Fax: 03-244 2157
e-mail: klhilton@tm.net.my
http://www.hilton.com
This is situated within walking distance of the Bukit Bintang shops, the hotel has 581 rooms, a grill, tennis and squash courts, health centre, a disco which is popular among the jet-set, and a commitment towards the environment. Art exhibitions are often held in the lower basement. **$$$$**

Mandarin Oriental
Kuala Lumpur City Centre
Tel: 03-380 8888
Fax: 03-380 8833
e-mail: reserve-mokulmohg.com
http://www.mandarin-oriental.com
Set within the office/shopping complex featuring the world's tallest twin buildings, this hotel has 643 luxurious rooms and executive apartments, six restaurants featuring sumptuous buffets, a grill and bar, and a Cantonese restaurant specialising in seafood. **$$$$**

Regent of Kuala Lumpur
160 Jalan Bukit Bintang
Tel: 03-241 8000
Fax: 03-242 1441
e-mail: regentkl@tm.net.my
KL's most elegant hotel sits on the fringes of bustling Bukit Bintang, and is well-known for its service and opulence. Classical music welcomes you in the lovely lounge; the gym has Roman baths; and the 469 rooms are tastefully furnished. **$$$$**

Rennaisance Hotel
Corner Jalan Sultan Ismail
Jalan Ampang
Tel: 03-262 2233
Fax: 03-263 1122
This hotel tries to capture decadent European splendour with plush decor of black marble and crystal chandeliers, but targets the business sector. It has a Mediterranean restaurant and shares the car park and pool with the slightly more modest New World Hotel, which has a disco specialising in techno. **$$$$**

Shangri-La Hotel
Jalan Sultan Ismail
Tel: 03-232 2388
Fax: 03-230 1514
e-mail: bc@po.jaring.my
http://www.shangrila.com
Busy hotel with 721 rooms, fairly good French restaurant and grill, well-stocked deli that is packed at lunchtime, English-style bar, tennis, squash, health centre, and a disco that's popular with the trendy. **$$$$**

Concorde Hotel
Jalan Sultan Ismail
Tel: 03-244 2200
Fax: 03-244 1628

e-mail: chlk@ppp.nasionet.net
Central, busy hotel close to nightlife and trendy eateries. It has 673 rooms, and an oldish, popular coffee shop and lounge attracting spill-over weekend crowds from the nearby Hard Rock Café. **$$$**

Crown Princess
City Square Complex
Jalan Tun Razak
Tel: 03-262 5522
Freephone: 1-800 883 886
Fax: 03-262 4687
e-mail: cprinces@tm.net.my
At the far end of Jalan Ampang, this was probably the original hotel-in-a-shopping-and-business-complex and targets business travellers. It has 528 rooms and an award-winning Indian restaurant with great ambience. **$$$**

Federal Hotel
35 Jalan Bukit Bintang
Tel: 03-248 9166
Fax: 03-248 2877
e-mail: fedhot@po.jaring.my
Hotel shares the same age as Malaysia with a colourful history, situated right on Bukit Bintang. It has 450 rooms, a revolving lounge, decent Chinese restaurant, full-window café that is great for people-watching, supper club showcasing golden oldies stars such as Engelbert Humperdinck, and an 18-lane bowling alley. **$$$**

Nikko
165 Jalan Ampang
Tel: 03-261 1111
Fax: 03-261 1122
e-mail: guests@hotelnikko.com.my
http://www.hotelnikko.com.my
Japanese-style hotel with 470 rooms at the end of Jalan Ampang, opposite Ampang Plaza, and with access to KLCC. Popular Japanese restaurant and pub that occasionally feature interesting acts. **$$$**

Pan Pacific Kuala Lumpur
Jalan Putra
Tel: 03-442 5555
Fax: 03-443 8717
e-mail: bc@ppkl.po.my
Oldish hotel opposite the Mall and next to the Putra World Trade Centre with all-glass elevators on the exterior providing good views of this part of the city. It has 571

rooms, and is busy during conventions. **$$$**

Park Royal Hotel
Jalan Sultan Ismail
Tel: 03-242 5588
Fax: 03-241 4281
A fairly old hotel in the heart of the Bukit Bintang shopping district, with 337 rooms and a rather bewildering layout to navigate before reaching the car park and entertainment outlets. British Airways dinner-theatre is a feature. **$$$**

Swiss Garden Hotel
117 Jalan Pudu
Tel: 03-241 3333
Fax: 03-241 5555
e-mail: sghkl@sgihotels.com.my
http://www.sgihotels.com.my
Situated on the busy Jalan Pudu, within walking distance to Puduraya and Bukit Bintang without being in the thick of it. This is a small but pleasant hotel, with 306 rooms and a Chinese restaurant that serves good *dim sum*. **$$$**

Hotel Capitol
Jalan Bukit Bintang
Tel: 03-243 7000
Fax: 03-243 0000
Part of the Federal group, this 240-room hotel is smack in the middle of Bukit Bintang, with no car park and a faceless lobby, but it has a one-stop service to answer all guests' needs; good restaurant and a café with gourmet sandwiches and coffee. **$$**

Century Hotel
Jalan Bukit Bintang
Tel: 03-243 9898
Fax: 03-468 0880
http://www.centuryhotels.com/century
New hotel in the heart of the Bukit Bintang shopping area with 418 rooms, and a restaurant of Mediterranean and local fare that features full- and "half"-lunch and dinner buffets. **$$**

Heritage Station Hotel
Tel: 03-273 5588
Fax: 03-273 2842
Sitting among the graceful cupolas of the Kuala Lumpur Railway Station, this hotel has been extensively renovated. Although the rooms are smaller now, some of the old-style charm is retained in the

furnishings and furniture, including its restaurants. **$$**

Ming Court Vista Hotel
Lot 2, Jalan Ampang
Tel: 03-261 8888
Fax: 03-261 2393/262 3428
Opposite the KLCC, which some of its 447 rooms overlook, the hotel offers tennis, squash and a swimming pool. It is popular with the business sector. **$$**

Price Guide

Prices are for a standard double room during peak periods.
$$$$: more than RM400
$$$: RM200–400
$$: RM100–200
$: less than RM100

Swiss Inn
Jalan Sultan
Tel: 03-232 3333
Fax: 03-201 6699
e-mail: sikl@sgihotels.com.my
http://www.sgihotels.com.my
Decent, busy hotel in the heart of Chinatown. It is popular with foreigners who people-watch from its sidewalk café, which has quite a good variety on its international menu. **$$**

Backpackers' Travellers' Inn
2nd Floor, 60, Jalan Sultan
(opposite Furama Hotel)
Tel: 03-238 2473
Right in Chinatown, close to food and transport, some air-conditioned rooms with own bathrooms, laundry, kitchen, left luggage facilities. **$**

Chamtan
62 Jalan Masjid India
Tel: 03-293 0144
Fax: 03-293 2422
In bustling Little India with its *sari* shops and curry smells, this hotel has 44 rooms with air-conditioning and hot showers, and a restaurant with cheap and tasty – if spicy – local fare. **$**

Coliseum Hotel
Jalan Tunku Abdul Rahman
Tiny and very old 10-room hotel with shared baths, it is mentioned in every guidebook because of its historical importance. The café is

popular for its good steaks and infamously bad service; bar patrons are determined to keep up its colourful character. **$**

The Travellers Station
Kuala Lumpur Railway Station
Tel: 03-273 5588 (ext 3070)
e-mail: station1@tm.net.my
Decent backpackers' accommodation among the station's beautiful minarets, with hot showers, kitchen, laundry, Internet facilities, air-conditioned dormitories and rooms, and useful "diaries" with latest input by travellers. **$**

YWCA
12, Jalan Hang Jebat
Tel: 03-238 3225
Small, clean, 12-roomed facility for women, couples and families only. It has a small restaurant, and is within walking distance of the heart of Chinatown. **$**

Selangor

The Mines Beach Resort
Jalan Dulang, Sri Kembangan
Tel: 03-943 6688
Fax: 03-943 5555
e-mail: sales@mbr.com.my
http://www.signature.com.my
Part of The Mines rehabilitated mining pond theme park and development, this classy 481-roomed hotel has an artificial beach, ferries to the Wonderland theme park, and a shopping and conference centre. It has six restaurants, but a rather stuffy lounge. **$$$$**

Palace of the Golden Horses
Jalan Kuda Emas
Mines Resort City
Sri Kembangan, Selangor
Tel: 03-943 2333
Fax: 03-943 2666
e-mail: helen@signature.com.my
This opulent Indian-influenced hotel at which heads of governments reside and meet, has 481 rooms and seven restaurants, and lovely gardens; it's a pity the same attention is not extended to the car park. **$$$$**

Sunway Lagoon Resort Hotel
Persiaran Lagoon
Bandar Sunway
Petaling Jaya

Tel: 03-582 8000
Fax: 03-582 8001
e-mail: sunway@po.jaring.my
Malaysianised version of the
palatial South African Sun City
resort, this plush hotel is next to
the Sunway Lagoon theme park, the
country's most successful
rehabilitated mining pond, as well
as the Egyptian-themed Sunway
Pyramid shopping centre, complete
with sphynx. The hotel's 439 rooms
are underground, and there's a
large and popular disco and
excellent American-Italian
restaurant. **$$$**
Jungle Lodge
Alang Sedayu (Gombak)
Tel: 03-452 9100 (Asia Overland
Services)
Fax: 03-452 9800
About half an hour from Kuala
Lumpur, this large timber lodge sits
in 2 hectares (5 acres) of green
grounds with streams and ponds.
There are two river-fed swimming
pools, treks, canoes, old war
tunnels nearby and supervised
outdoor activities. There is also a
hostel for 60. **$$**
Kuala Selangor Nature Park
Kuala Selangor
Tel: 03-889 2403/2294
Wake up to the sound of birds:
these new budget chalets and
dormitories at the park entrance
have hours of trails on the
doorstep; booked out at weekends.
Food is available at Kuala Selangor
town a short walk away. **$**

NORTHWESTERN PENINSULA

HILL STATIONS
Maxwell Hill (Bukit Larut)
(accessible from Perak state)
All accommodation and transport
come under the Bukit Larut Hill
Resort, tel: 05-807 7241/3. Book
in advance. The bungalows have to
be booked in their entirety: Beringin
(two rooms or eight people),
Cendana (three rooms or eight
people) and Tempinis (four rooms or
10 people, highest point). **$$**
  Double rooms are available at
the Maxwell Hill Resthouse and

Gunung Hijau (four rooms each). **$**
Meals have to be pre-arranged – no
dogs, pork or unmarried Muslim
couples sharing a room.

Cameron Highlands
(accessible from Perak state)
If you get stuck for the night in
Tapah, you could try the Rest House
Tapah (tel: 05-401 1190) or N.H.
Hotel (tel: 05-401 7288), both
close to the train station. **$**
The Concorde Lakehouse
30th Mile
Ringlet
Tel: 05-495 6152
Fax: 05-495 6123
e-mail: cameron@concorde.net
http://www.concorde.net
The first hotel on the Cameron's
road, 1 hour from the toll gate,
opposite the Sultan Abu Bakar lake.
It features Tudor architecture, cosy,
English antique furnishings, 18
rooms/suites with four-poster beds,
a restaurant overlooking the lake,
fishing and jungle walks. Isolated
from towns. **$$$**
Heritage Hotel
Jalan Gereja
Tanah Rata
Tel: 05-491 3888
Fax: 05-491 5666
This boxy, 170-room hilltop hotel is
the first when you reach Tanah Rata.
Ask for a room with a view of the
charming little garden. Cantonese
restaurant, coffee house, bar, and a
health centre. **$$$**
The Smokehouse Hotel
Tanah Rata
Tel: 05-491 1215
03-263 3136 (KL)
Fax: 05-491 1214
03-261 2044 (KL)
e-mail: smokel@tm.net.my
Built in 1937, this is a beautiful
replica of an English Tudor inn
complete with lush English country
garden, log fires, antique
furnishings, 13 family suites (most
overlooking the golf course), dining
and tea rooms, two bars and a
restaurant; packed sandwiches and
pies are available for your jungle
walk. **$$$**
Strawberry Park Resort
Tanah Rata
Tel: 05-491 1166

Fax: 05-491 1949
Mock-Tudor blocks at the top of a
steep, windy road, with great views
from the hotel's 127 rooms and
apartments (no cooking). It has an
indoor heated pool, Chinese
restaurant, coffee house, grill, bar,
disco, racquet sports, horse-riding,
travel service, and is popular with
locals and Singaporeans. **$$$**
Equatorial Hill Resort
Brinchang
Tel: 05-496 1777
Fax: 05-496 1333
Monstrosity perched precariously on
carved hill, up from Brinchang town.
It has a good tour agency. **$$**
Merlin Inn Resort
Tanah Rata
Tel: 05-491 1211
Fax: 05-491 1178
Once *the* place to stay in
Camerons, it may be old but it is
still decent. Golfers favour this
resort for easy access to the golf
course opposite. It has 64 rooms,
full room facilities, restaurant and
bar, karaoke, disco, pool tables and
tennis. Enquire about golf
packages. **$$**
Rosa Passadena
Brinchang town
Tel: 05-491 2288
Fax: 05-491 2688/902
Right in town next to the bank and
bakery. This is an average, no-frills
hotel with 120 rooms, a restaurant
with big city prices, karaoke,
lounge, laundry, tours, babysitting
by arrangement, basement parking,
sports facilities. **$$**
Bala's Holiday Chalet
Lot 55
Tanah Rata
Tel: 05-491 1660
Fax: 05-491 4500
http//balasch@hotmail.com
Former backpackers' hotel in an
English cottage which has gone
upmarket. The hotel is set in a
lovely green location 10 minutes
from Tanah Rata (free shuttles),
close to walks. Recently renovated,
re-carpeted and newly-furnished, the
hotel has 25 different types of
rooms – some with balconies – a
lounge, restaurant, laundry and it
offers tours. Advance bookings
receive a 20 percent discount. **$**

The Cool Point
891 Persiaran Dayang Endah
Tanah Rata
Tel: 05-491 4914
Fax: 05-491 4070
Next to a garden, small and
unassuming but secluded. The
hotel has 44 rooms, restaurant,
and Internet. **$**
Twin Pines Chalet
2 Jalan Mentigi
Tanah Rata
Tel: 05-491 2169
Fax: 05-491 5007
e-mail: firhill@tm.net.my
This friendly and clean
backpackers' hotel is located
behind new town development,
offering hot showers, laundry,
tours, travel arrangements,
telephones and Internet. There are
free kitchen facilities, a spacious
lounge area with TV and videos, a
restaurant, travellers' notebooks,
free book exchange, indoor games,
a safe for valuables; free pickup. **$**

Fraser's Hill
Accessible from Selangor and
Pahang.
Silver Park Holiday Resort
Tel: 09-362 2888
Fax: 09-362 2185
Large blocks of apartments that fail
to blend with the surroundings. **$$$**
Fraser's Hill Bungalows & Chalets
Tel: 09-362 2248, 03-262 8561
(KL, MATIC)
Fax: 09-362 2273
Run by the Fraser's Hill
Development Corporation, there are
about 60 rooms in old stone
bungalows, with 3–4 rooms each,
all with ensuite bathrooms. Make
arrangements with the caretaker for
food; day-use available. **$$**

Genting Highlands
Accessible from Kuala Lumpur.
Awana Golf and Country Resort
Tel: 03-261 9888
Freephone: 1-800 881 328
Fax: 03-261 6611
e-mail: roomrsv@genting.po.my
http://www.awana.com.my
Much quieter surroundings, 10 km
(6 miles) down the hill, with an 18-
hole golf course, nice views, full
room facilities including jacuzzis,

and outdoor activities. Packages
include rides and use of facilities.
$$$
Genting Highlands Resort
Tel: 03-262 3555
Freephone: 1-800 888 228
Fax: 03-261 6611
e-mail: roomrsv@genting.po.my
http://www.genting.com.my
A conglomerate of large hotels on
the hilltop, including Genting Hotel,
Highlands Hotel, Theme Park Hotel,
and Resort Hotel. There are also
apartments. Full room facilities, but
rooms are cheap, especially off-
peak. Restaurants of every variety,
including buffet, dinner theatre and
excellent Western fare at the Sails
Grill. Health centre with jacuzzi and
sauna, bowling alley, disco.
Packages include rides and use of
facilities. **$–$$$**
Gunung Jerai Resort
Gunung Jerai
Tel: 04-421 3345/411
Fax: 04-732 9788/422 3059
This 1920s building has 30 rooms,
including two-bedroom chalet-suites
with cooking facilities. Good views,
landscaped gardens; quiet. **$**

PERAK
Ipoh
Casuarina Parkroyal Hotel
24 Jalan Gopeng
Tel: 05-255 5555
Fax: 05-255 8177
A little out of town, this is Ipoh's
swankiest hotel with 217 luxurious
rooms, full room facilities and an
Italian restaurant. **$$$**
Excelsior Hotel
Jalan Clarke
Tel: 05-253 6666
Fax: 05-253 6908
Rather old, but central and close to
good food. Popular with the
business sector, the hotel has 181
rooms, a coffee house, bar, and
sauna. **$$$**
The Syuen
88, Jalan Sultan Abdul Jalil
Tel: 05-264 1105
Fax: 05-264 0580
Central hotel, reminiscent of an
enormous white wedding cake, with
290 rooms, Cantonese restaurant,
spa facilities and Shiatsu massage,
popular disco, and poolside bar. **$$$**

Heritage Hotel
Jalan Raja Dihilir
Tel: 05-242 8888
Fax: 05-241 5299
Pleasant new hotel, overlooking the
Turf Club, with 270 rooms,
Continental grill, Japanese
restaurant, a branch of a famous
Chinese restaurant chain, and a
health club. **$$**
Seri Malaysia
Lot 10406
Jalan Sturrock
off Jalan Tambun
Tel: 05-241 2936
Fax: 05-241 2946
Not central, but this hotel has a
restaurant serving reasonably good
food; 100 rooms. **$$**
Majestic Ipoh Station Hotel
Ipoh Railway Station
Tel: 05-255 5605
Fax: 05-255 3393
Famous colonial hotel in the best
tradition of railway station hotels,
with huge verandahs, original lights,
and an old-style restaurant. **$$**
Rega Lodge
131 Jalan Raja Ekram
Tel: 05-242 5555
Fax: 05-241 1555
On the fringes of the town centre,
but secluded. It has 93 rooms, a
restaurant-cum-pub with Italian and
local cuisine, and air-conditioned
rooms with ensuite baths. **$**
YMCA
211 Jalan Raja Musa Aziz
Tel: 05-254 0809
Fax: 05-241 2093
Fringes of town next to park. Clean
budget-class rooms with air-
conditioning and ensuite baths and
hot showers; basic canteen. **$**

Pasir Salak
Sri Bayu Riverine Village Resort
Pasir Salak Historical Complex
Tel: 05-443 8930

Fax: 05-442 3450
New *kampung*-style, all-suite chalets lining the Perak River, within charming *kampung* and orchards. A traditional Malay palace welcome is held for groups by handmaidens and drummers. There are 50 single- and double-storey two-roomers, a restaurant, bar, karaoke, cultural shows, swimming pool, Malay massage, watersports, and tours to the village, traditional industries and plantations. **$$**

Pulau Pangkor

Accommodation is on the west coast, with clusters at Pasir Bogak and Teluk Nipah. Tour companies and taxi drivers receive a commission for recommending accommodation, so unless it is peak period, the best bet would be to pick a beach, get dropped off on the main road and walk around until something catches your fancy. However, some tour agents can offer better prices – select from their photograph albums. At Teluk Nipah, the chalets are virtually identical and so are the prices; many do not offer food during the low season. During the busy periods, go for a room further back from the beach – it's quieter.

Coral Bay Resort
Lot 34
Pasir Bogak
Tel: 05-685 5111
Fax: 05-685 5666
Its name belies the ordinariness of this town-style hotel with 190 rooms and apartments; facilities, but no beach. **$$$**

Pan Pacific Pangkor
Teluk Belanga (Golden Sands)
Tel: 05-685 1399
03-441 3757 (KL)
Freephone: 1-800 887 777
Fax: 05-685 1095
03-441 5559 (KL)
e-mail: sales@pprp.po.my
http://www.panpac.com
Oldish, isolated hotel, with great private beach and lush forest, and its own ferry from Lumut. There are 240 rooms (top floor has nice views), bungalows and chalets, watersports, restaurants, bars, barbecue on beach, children's

activities, traditional massage, tours. Day-trippers are allowed to use the beach and facilities. **$$$**

Sri Bayu Beach Resort
Pantai Pasir Bogak
Tel: 05-685 1929/1035
03-443 6939 (KL)
Fax: 05-685 1050
03-442 3450 (KL)
Pleasant resort with 60 chalets spread out in a landscaped *kampung* setting, with an additional 80-room hotel block on the horizon. It is popular with local tour groups and has Internet access, karaoke, disco, a local and Western buffet in an open air restaurant; tours. Nothing fancy about the beach. **$$**

Teluk Dalam Resort
Pulau Pangkor
Tel: 05-685 5000
Fax: 05-685 4000
Lovely setting, with 163 chalets, bungalows and luxury villas sprawled over 16 hectares (40 acres) of beachside and forested land. There are cute seashell showers at the swimming pool, restaurants, pubs, special jungle trails, and tours. The beach is only suitable for swimming at high tide. **$$**

Pangkor Holiday Resort
Lot 41 Pasir Bogak
Tel: 05-685 3321/685 3626
Fax: 05-685 3627
Unassuming but clean, with a beautiful jungle and orchard backdrop, 62 air-conditioned chalets and rooms and 30 quads; no beach. Cafeteria offers local fare and DIY BBQ. Popular for group retreats, especially churches. **$**

Pulau Pangkor Laut
Pangkor Laut Resort
Tel: 05-699 1100
03-926 8000 (KL)

Fax: 05-699 1200
03-925 7012 (KL)
One of the country's poshest luxury hotels sits on its own island and has its own ferry from Lumut. It has the gorgeous Emerald Bay beach to itself. There are 178 luxurious rooms in hillside or beachfront Malay-style villas as well as suites on stilts over the sea (a concept it pioneered), swimming pools, six restaurants, a library of books and CDs, and a watersports centre. **$$$$**

Lumut
Orient Star
Lot 203 & 366
Jalan Iskandar Shah
Tel: 05-683 4199
Fax: 05-683 4223
Lumbering facility at the edge of town with traditional Malay house entrance; 150 recently upgraded rooms (odd numbers are sea-facing), restaurants, lounge, swimming pool with bar; mainly Navy patronage. Also manages the Lumut International Yacht Club with its five small but fully-equipped cabins (**$**). **$$$**

Swiss-Garden Resort
Damai Laut
101–107, Jalan Titi Panjang
Tel: 05-618 3333
Freephone: 1-800 883 093
Fax: 05-618 3388
e-mail: sgrdl@sgihotels.com.my
http://www.sgihotels.com.my
Isolated in enormous grounds with ocean, mangrove, river, rainforest and oil palm surrounds, the resort is 20 minutes by ferry from Lumut, or over 1 hour by road. It features a beautiful pool overlooking the sea, 300 rooms, 18-hole golf course, disco, karaoke, and every sort of resort facility, including children's activities. Ask about a golf package with unlimited rounds; day-trippers are allowed use of facilities. **$$**

Blue Bay Resort
Jalan Titi Panjang
Tel: 05-683 6939
Fax: 05-683 6239
Block-ish accommodation with 35 decent rooms, swimming pool, garden and esplanade at the back, seafood restaurant. **$**

Lumut Country Resort
331 Jalan Titi Panjang
Tel: 05-683 5109
Fax: 05-683 5396
Built in the 1980s with colonial-inspired architecture and now fraying at the edges, but still decent. The 44 motel-style rooms surround the swimming pool. A bistro serves so-called "country fare", such as Beef Stroganoff and Chicken Maryland. **$**

Kuala Kangsar
Seri Temenggong Resthouse
Jalan Istana
Tel: 05-776 3872
One of Malaysia's prettiest resthouses, with views of the Perak River and rooms of various sizes with ensuite baths and hot water. An open-air restaurant, serving local and Western meals, overlooks the lake. The resthouse is within walking distance of attractions, so is very popular; make sure you book ahead. **$**

Temenggor/Belum
Banding Island Resort
36 km (22 miles)
Grik/East-West Highway
Tel: 011-329 027/05-791 2273
Fax: 05-791 2273
Lakeside motel that is very quiet unless there's a fishing competition, with 28 spacious rooms, a restaurant overlooking the lake, karaoke, fishing, boating, and jungle trekking; camping permitted. **$**
Rumah Rehat Gerik
682, Jalan Haji Meor Yahya
Tel: 05-791 1454/791 2305
Fax: 05-791 2288
Basic and old hotel, but with clean and spacious rooms, some air-conditioned, for 50 guests. Restaurant serves traditional Malay, Thai and Western fare. **$**

Taiping
Legend Inn
2 Jalan Long Jaafar
Tel: 05-806 0000
Fax: 05-806 6666
Close to the bus station, this is the best hotel in town, set against Bukit Larut, with 88 rooms with

bathrooms, hot showers and TV, and a café with a view. **$**
Hotel Panorama
61–79 Jalan Kota
Tel: 05-834 111
Centrally located, next to a large supermarket, with 70 rooms, baths and hot showers; car rental. **$**

PENANG
The city's powerful preservation lobby has seen some of Penang's older buildings preserved as "nostalgia" and boutique hotels. Georgetown's bigger hotels cater to the business sector, while budget and backpackers' accommodation is along Lebuh Leith and Lebuh Chulia. These are mainly Chinese hotels that need facelifts, but many have great atmosphere, and sit amid eateries, travel and tour agencies, and motorbike and bicycle rental firms.
Equatorial Penang
1 Jalan Bukit Jambul
Bayan Lepas
Tel: 04-643 8111
Fax: 04-644 8000
e-mail: eqp@md.com.my
Catering to the Free Trade Zone industrialists, this beautiful hotel with its impressively high-ceilinged lobby and lovely landscaping has 460 rooms, restaurants, and sports facilities, including an 18-hole golf course. **$$$$**
The Northam
55 Jalan Sultan Ahmad Shah
Tel: 04-370 1111
Fax: 04-370 2222
e-mail: northam@po.jaring.my
The town's fanciest business hotel with a resort feel, towering 38 floors high, with all business and non-business mod-cons, such as jacuzzis with a view of the ocean in its 233 suites, including a whopping 96 presidential suites, in-suite massage, and fine dining in Italian, Indian and Chinese restaurants. Aptly situated on "Millionaires' Row", it assumes the colonial road name. Small swimming pool, gymnasium, spa. **$$$$**
Shangri-La Inn
Jalan Magazine
Tel: 04-262 2622
Fax: 04-262 6526

http://www.shangri-la.com
Next to KOMTAR, therefore its top floors offer some of the same great views of Georgetown rooftops, this mainly business sector hotel has 442 rooms, a decent Chinese restaurant, disco, car rental. **$$$$**
Sheraton Penang
126 Jalan Burmah
Tel: 04-226 7888
Fax: 04-226 7257
e-mail: res649penang@ittsheraton.com
Smack in the centre of the shopping district, with 295 rooms, grill, coffee house, bars, swimming pool, health centre, disco. **$$$**
Bellevue Hotel
Penang Hill
Tel: 04-892 9600
This is Penang Hill's only hotel with fine views of Georgetown; built in the colonial style with a garden terrace. Quiet and cool because of

Penang on a Budget

Lebuh Chulia in Penang is chock-a-block with backpackers' accommodation, from dilapidated to decent. Most are basic and fan-cooled, with coffee house downstairs serving breakfast and snacks, and offering some help with travel arrangements. Best bet is to walk around and check them out. Among the established ones are:

Tye Ann Hotel
No. 282
Tel: 04-261 4871
With English breakfasts downstairs.
Eng Aun Hotel
No. 380
Tel: 04-261 2333
Set back from the road.
Swiss Hotel
No. 431F
Tel: 04-262 0133
Set back from the street and kept in better shape than most.
Hang Chow Hotel
No. 511
Tel: 04-610 810
With a money-changer and restaurant. **All $**

Penang's Beach Hotels

The beach hotels in Penang are the country's oldest seaside resorts. Many have been refurbished, but some are a little worn. Sea-view rooms are pricey during peak season; otherwise stiff competition makes them absolutely affordable.

Mutiara Beach Resort
1 Jalan Teluk Bahang
Tel: 04-885 2828
Fax: 04-885 2829
e-mail: pmr@po.jaring.my
http://asiatravel.com/
penangmutiara
Luxurious, large, and the last resort on the stretch, with tasteful use of local motifs; 440 rooms, full resort facilities. **$$$$**

Lone Pine Hotel
97 Batu Ferringhi
Tel: 04-881 1511/1512
Fax: 04-881 1282
Feringghi's first hotel is now a boutique hotel, refurbished for a 1970s feel. There are verandahs for all 50 rooms, some of which have Balinese-style courtyards. Hainanese and Western cuisine. **$$$**

Penang Parkroyal
Batu Ferringhi Beach
Tel: 04-881 1133
Fax: 04-881 2233
Austere exterior, beautiful swimming pool and beach, and 333 good-sized rooms, deli, children's facilities, disco. **$$$**

Rasa Sayang Hotel
Batu Ferringhi Beach
Tel: 04-881 1611
Fax: 04-881 1180
http://www.Shangri-la.com
The most famous of Penang's beach resorts, its *Minangkabau* roofs cap 536 rooms which spread out in mature gardens; pools; popular disco. **$$$**

Casuarina Beach Hotel
Tanjung Bungah
Tel: 04-881 1711
Fax: 04-881 2155
Pleasant hotel, sea-view rooms. Excellent Italian restaurant. **$$**

Copthorne Orchid
Tanjung Bungah

Tel: 04-890 3333
Fax:04-890 3303
One of the first hotels on the stretch, beautifully breezy, 318 sea-view rooms with balconies, Cantonese and Szechuan restaurant; no beach. **$$**

Ferringhi Beach Hotel
Jalan Low Yat
Tel: 04-890 5999
Fax: 04-890 5100
e-mail: ferringhi@po.jaring.my
http://interconti.com
Bridge links the hotel to a nice beach, windy lounge, 350 rooms with sea view, grill. **$$**

Golden Sands Hotel
Batu Ferringhi Beach
Tel: 04-881 1911
Fax: 04-881 1880
http://www.Shangri-la.com
Adjoining Rasa Sayang, an old hotel with pool, 395 rooms, sea views, Italian restaurant. **$$**

Holiday Inn Penang
Batu Ferringhi Beach
Tel: 04-881 1611
Fax: 04-881 1601
e-mail: hirp@tm.net.my
Beach hotel with 352 rooms, good steakhouse. **$$**

Paradise Sandy Bay
527 Jalan Tanjung Bungah
Tel: 04-899 9999
Freephone: 1-800 888 248
Fax: 04-899 0000
e-mail: sandbay@po.jaring.my
http://www.paradisehotels.com
Pleasant all-suite hotel with 333 sea-facing rooms; popular nightspot, good Italian fare. **$$**

Ali's Guest House & Restaurant
53 Batu Ferringhi
Tel: 04-881 1316
Friendly accommodation on the beachfront near Parkroyal. Nice restaurant/pub in the garden. Fan and shared facilities, some rooms air-conditioned with own bath. **$**

Shalini's Guesthouse
56 Batu Feringgi
Tel: 04-881 1859
Budget accommodation with homestay feel. Shared bathrooms. Fans, good local meals, kitchen, self-service laundry. **$**

the altitude, with an aviary at entrance. **$$**

City Bayview Hotel
25A Lebuh Farquhar
Tel: 04-263 3161
Fax: 04-263 4124/160
e-mail: cbvpg@tm.net.my
Fringing the main shopping area, within walking distance of Leith Street pubs, the hotel has a new wing, good Malay restaurant, a charming café serving hawker fare, and a revolving restaurant. **$$**

Hotel 1926
Jalan Imigresen
Tel: 04-228 1334
Fax: 04-227 7926
Saved from demolition (and the erection of yet another modern shopping complex), this former government quarters has been conserved as a medium-budget boutique hotel with Penang's longest corridor, which also doubles as a sort of art gallery. The 94 rooms come in different sizes, but are all air-conditioned and have ensuite baths. Café, Malay restaurant, and lounge. **$$**

MidTowne Hotel
101 Macalister Road
Tel: 04-226 9999
Fax: 04-229 5149
e-mail: midtown@po.jaring.my
http://www.MidtowneHotel.com
Aggressively-marketed business hotel with 96 decent rooms, coffee house with specials, including pick-up for meals. **$$**

Sunway Hotel
No. 33 New Lane
Tel: 04-229 9988
03-731 6077 (KL)
Fax: 04-228 8899
e-mail: sunway@swhtlpg.po.my
Another business hotel in a quiet area near good hawker stalls and a shopping centre; 262 rooms with city and sea views, swimming pool with jacuzzi. Packages sometimes include voucher to Kuala Lumpur's Sunway Lagoon. **$$**

Traverse Inn
53 Kampung Malabar Road
Tel/fax: 04-261 9858
Clean and central in a colourful location within walking distance of major food stalls, shopping centres and historical sites. **$**

Butterworth

An uninteresting place, stay the night only if you're stuck here. Try Butterworth Travel Lodge, 1 Lorong Bagan Luar, tel: 04-333 3399 (**$$**) or Hotel Kuala Lumpur, 4488 Lorong Bagan Luar, tel: 04-332 6199 (**$**)

KEDAH
Alor Setar
Grand Continental Hotel
134 Jalan Sultan Badlishah
Tel: 04-733 5917
Fax: 04-733 5161
The town's fanciest hotel, central, with 130 rooms. Restaurant serves good local fare. **$$**
Hotel Grand Crystal
40 Jalan Kampung Perak
Tel: 04-731 3333
Fax: 04-731 6368
Good value in central location, 145 rooms, swimming pool, sauna and coffee house. **$**

Sungai Petani
Swiss-Inn Sungai Petani
1 Jalan Pahlawan
Tel: 04-422 3333
03-241 5333 (KL)
Fax: 04-422 4473
e-mail: sisp@sgihotels.com.my
http://www.sgihotels.com.my
Lovely hotel with 101 rooms. Restaurant overlooks nice landscaped pool. **$**

Tasik Pedu
Desa Utara Pedu Lake
Dejabat Pos
KB 2 Kuala Nerang
Kedah
KB2 Kuala Nerang
Tel: 04-732 8888
Fax: 04-732 4999
Kampung-style two- and three-room chalets with balconies, some with views of the lake, well spread out in forested area. **$$$**
Holiday Inn Pedu Lake Resort
KB1 Kuala Nerang
Tel: 04-730 4888
03-348 1242 (KL)
Fax: 04-730 4488
Located on two islands and accessible only by boat, there are 200 Kedah-Thai style chalets and a pleasant restaurant. **$$$**

Pulau Langkawi

Everything is here, from some of the most impressive hotels in the country, to budget accommodation. Kuah is very built-up, so the beach hotels are certainly more pleasant, but the town has more eateries and shops. Book ahead during the peak season and especially in December when the *Lima Maritime* exhibition takes place.

The Andaman Datai Bay
Jalan Teluk Datai
Tel: 04-959 1088
Fax: 04-959 1168
e-mail: anda@po.jaring.my
Exclusive luxury resort in gorgeous surroundings, 188 rooms with five restaurants, including Mediterranean and Japanese cuisine. Close to 18-hole golf course; children's activities. **$$$$**
The Datai
Jalan Teluk Datai
Tel: 04-959 2500
Fax: 04-959 2600
e-mail: datai@ghmhotels.com
Award-winning Balinese-inspired luxury resort in isolated lush surroundings, with a beautiful private beach. It has 108 villas and rooms, three restaurants, and an adjacent 18-hole golf course. **$$$$**
Pelangi Beach Resort
Pantai Cenang
Tel: 04-955 1011
Fax: 04-955 1122
e-mail: pbrl@tm.net.my
At a splendid curve of the beach, with a gracious lobby, these 350 traditional-style bungalows and chalets are best known for having housed the Commonwealth heads of government, including Britain's Queen Elizabeth. **$$$$**
Radisson Tanjung Rhu Resort
Tanjung Rhu
Tel: 04-959 1033
Freephone: 1-800 885 164
Fax: 04-959 1899
e-mail: radtr@tm.net.my
http://www.tanjungrhu.com.my
This is peacefully situated on a secluded northern beach in lush mangrove forest, with classy landscaping and intelligent use of space. There is a 2.5-km (1½-mile) private beach. Luxury cars for hire. **$$$$**

Sheraton Langkawi Beach Resort
Teluk Nibong
Tel: 04-955 1901
Freephone: 1800-801 001
Fax: 04-955 1968
Older resort with 264 rooms, including chalets with ocean views. A cascade of stairs lead down to the swimming pool. The sea-facing Captain's Grill serves seafood; popular disco. **$$$$**

Price Guide

Prices are for a standard double room during peak periods.
$$$$: more than RM400
$$$: RM200–400
$$: RM100–200
$: less than RM100

Sheraton Perdana Resort
Jalan Pantai Dato' Syed Omar
Tel: 04-966 2020
Fax: 04-966 3097
Isolated from other hotels, the resort is situated just past the yacht club within walking distance of the jetty. There are 204 rooms. Although there is not much of a beach, the sports facilities are excellent, including salt and freshwater swimming pools, watersports, jogging track, bicycles, top-class gym, and squash. **$$$$**
Awana Porto Malai Langkawi
Teluk Baru
Tel: 04-955 5111
Fax: 04-955 5222
http://www.awana.com.my
Built on reclaimed land with a marina, the hotel has 175 sea-facing rooms, a nice boardwalk café and casual fine dining. Next door is a gruesome 16-lane bowling alley. Cruise liners unleash thousands of passengers here regularly. Package tours are available. **$$$**
Burau Bay Resort
Pantai Kok
Tel: 04-955 1061
Fax: 04-955 1001
On one of the island's loveliest beaches and close to lush forest, the resort has 150 rooms in tent-style cabins, karaoke, and traditional massage. The restaurant, however, is uninspiring. **$$$**

The Paloma Boutique Resort
Lot 2605–2606
Pantai Cenang
Tel: 04-955 6789
Fax: 04-955 6889/955 7988
Charming hotel across the road
from the beach, with restaurant and
lounge, classy furnishings and a
wrought-iron staircase. **$$$**

Tiara Langkawi Hotel
Persiaran Mutiara
Kuah
Tel: 04-966 2566
Fax: 04-966 2600
e-mail: tiaralgk@tm.net.my
http://www.tiaralgkhotel.com
Castle-like towers in 18th-century
French-style are noticeable from
afar. The colonial-looking hotel has
238 rooms and apartments and
wrought iron balconies. There is a
hawker centre on the Esplanade.
$$$

Beach Garden Resort
Pantai Cenang
Tel: 04-955 1363
Fax: 04-955 1221
Small, pretty 13-room outfit with
thatched roofs, run by a German
couple and popular with foreigners.

Kuah on a Budget

Budget and backpackers'
accommodation can be found at
Kuah and Pantai Cenang/Pantai
Tengah. In Kuah, try the family-
owned basic **Gaya**, tel: 04-966
7704, or the friendly **Iska
Travellers Guesthouse**, Taman
Seri Pelang, tel: 04-966 8879.
One of the original budget places
at Cenang is **Langkawi Sandy
Beach Motel**, tel: 04-955 1308,
which now offers air-conditioned
chalets alongside the original A-
frames; other popular ones
include **Semarak Langkawi
Beach Resort**, tel: 04-955 1377,
and **Grand Beach Motel**, tel: 04-
955 1457. Right at the end of
Pantai Tengah are **Charlie's**,
small but clean, with a popular
bar, tel: 04-955 1200, **Sunset
Beach Resort**, popular bar and
restaurant, tel: 04-955 1751 and
Tanjung Mail Beach Resort,
tel: 04-955 1891.

Beachfront eateries, including good
Italian fare and margaritas. **$$**

Bonton
Pantai Cenang
Tel: 04-955 3643
Fax: 04-955 6790
Charming, authentic thatched
Indonesian-style *kampung* houses
reconstructed from old wood, with
verandahs, basic bathrooms and
fans-only. They are next to a famous
and very good restaurant, which
unfortunately now faces a golf
course rather than a beach; good
Asian curio shop. **$$**

The City Bayview Hotel
Jalan Pandak Mayah 1
Pusat Bandar Kuah
Tel: 04-966 1818
Fax: 04-966 3888
Like a white monolith, this 282-
room city hotel rises from among
the roofs of the market, catering
mainly to groups. The top floors
have sea view, swimming pool,
sauna, and a gym. **$$**

The Gates Langkawi Resort
Jalan Persiaran Putra
Kuah
Tel: 04-966 8466
Fax: 04-966 8443
Close to Kuah, opposite the jetty. It
doesn't have a beach but there are
great views from its hilly location.
Kampung chalets, 177 rooms,
decent restaurants with good local,
Thai western and Italian fare, and a
shuttle to town. **$$**

Delima Resort
Kuala Muda (near the airport)
Tel: 04-955 1801
Fax: 04-955 1811
In the best of Malaysian
superlatives, this was built in the
fastest time, and is the country's
largest hotel, with 1,400 rooms in
longhouse-style chalets that go on
forever. Not surprisingly, it caters
mainly to groups. **$$**

Tanjung Sanctuary
Jalan Pantai Kok
Tel: 04-955 2977
Fax: 04-955 3978
Quiet, 32-room, all-suite wooden
chalets with balconies, well spread
out among the trees; some are
beach-fronting. Restaurant has
beautiful 270-degree view of the
sea. **$$**

Perlis

Kangar Travelodge
Persiaran Jubli Emas, Kangar
Tel: 04-976 7755
Fax: 04-976 1049
e-mail: kgtrl@po.jaring.my
The state's fanciest hotel with 146
rooms and standard facilities; good
fine-dining Chinese restaurant. **$$$**

Pens Hotel
Jalan Kuala Perlis
Tel: 04-985 4122
Fax: 04-985 4131
A short walk from the Pulau
Langkawi jetty, useful in case you
need to spend a night en route
to/from Langkawi. **$**

SOUTHERN PENINSULA

MELAKA
Melaka City
Room prices are lower by 30
percent on weekdays. Hotels are
located in a so-called "hotel zone"
in the Jalan Bendahara area, just
outside the historic hub, and in the
Old Town across the bridge.
    Backpackers' accommodation is
on Jalan Parameswara and the
Taman Melaka Raya, but be careful
about these, especially if there are
girls hanging around downstairs.
You'll also find some lovely
renovated accommodation that
successfully maintains a degree of
old-world charm.

Century Mahkota Hotel
Jalan Mahkota
Tel: 06-281 282
03-262 2999 (KL)
Fax: 06-281 232
03-262 8644 (KL)
Sitting on reclaimed coastal land
near the historic centre and the
Mahkota Parade shopping mall, this
massive 617-room hotel has
beautifully-landscaped swimming
pools and a host of activities.
Linked to the Tiara Melaka Golf
Club. **$$$$**

Renaissance Melaka Hotel
Jalan Bendahara
Tel: 06-248 8888
Fax: 06-284 9269
Towering over the city, this 295-
room luxury hotel is beautifully-
furnished, centrally located and has

great views of the town, Melaka River and the sea. Swimming pool on the 9th floor, Chinese restaurant, coffee house, lounge-cum-library, fun pub, disco. **$$$$**

City Bayview Hotel
Jalan Bendahara
Tel: 06-283 9888
Fax: 06-283 6699
e-mail: cbviewmk@tm.net.my
http://www.staymalaysia.com/malacca/
Situated near St Peter's Church, this hotel has good views, 182 rooms, swimming pool, a Chinese restaurant and a coffee house. **$$$**

Emperor Hotel
123 Jalan Munshi Abdullah
Tel: 06-284 0777
Fax: 06-283 8989
Decent and central, the hotel has 240 rooms, some with views of the sea, a Chinese restaurant with good *dim sum*, a coffee house, a swimming pool and sauna. **$$**

Heeren House
1 Jalan Tun Tan Cheng Lock
Tel: 06-281 4241
Fax: 06-281 4239
Lovely, cosy six-room restored shophouse in the Old Town overlooking the Melaka River and facing the historic centre. It has air-conditioned rooms with ensuite baths, and a café offering Peranakan and Portuguese fare. **$$**

Straits Heritage Lodge
591-A Taman Melaka Raya
Tel: 06-282 3950
Fax: 06-282 3957
Beautifully-renovated Peranakan interior that belies its boring facade; 20 minutes' walk from the historic hub. There is a lovely open-air fountain courtyard which serves as a reading area. Rooms are air-conditioned with ensuite baths. The Portuguese pub downstairs serves food and wine. **$$**

Hotel Portugis
12–20 Jalan Melaka Raya 20
Tel: 06-292 4100
Fax: 06-292 9300
Loud and heavy on the kitsch, but decent standard rooms and wonderfully-decorated VIP rooms which are nontheless still affordable. Portuguese restaurant, 24-hour food court, karaoke. **$–$$**

Baba House
125–7 Jalan Tun Tan Cheng Lock
Tel: 06-281 1216
Fax: 06-281 1217
Pretty Peranakan house in the Old Town serving as backpackers' accommodation, with clean simple rooms, some with air-conditioning and ensuite baths, few with views, no restaurant. **$**

Hotel Puri
118 Jalan Tun Tan Cheng Lock
Tel: 06-282 5588
Fax: 06-281 5588
e-mail: enquiries@hotelpuri.com
http://www.hotelpuri.com
Carefully restored 1819 Peranakan house in the quaint "Millionaires' Row", which belonged to an eminent philanthropist. Marble and wood abound. There are 50 rooms, a decorated original airwell, beer garden and L-shaped new wing; near the Kochee Café. **$**

Coast

Riviera Bay Resort
10 km (6 miles)
Jalan Tanjung Kling
Tel: 06-315 1111
Fax: 06-315 3333
e-mail: rivbr@po.jaring.my
Showy Roman gateway, 450 sea-facing suites, three restaurants, pub, swimming pool that is a better bet than the sea, and lots of facilities. **$$$$**

Tanjung Bidara Resort
Tanjung Bidara Masjid Tanah
Tel: 06-542 990
Fax: 06-542 995
Beachside resort of ocean-facing chalets (85 rooms), restaurant, lounge, swimming pool, but no public transport. **$$**

Ayer Keroh

Air Keroh Country Resort
Tel: 06-336 4126
Fax: 06-232 0422
A green and secluded chalet resort next door to Mini Malaysia, with swimming pool and restaurant; jungle-trekking and car hire can be arranged. **$$**

Air Keroh d'Village Melaka
Tel: 06-328 000
Fax: 06-327 541
Oldish resort with 274 motel

rooms/chalets, seafood restaurant, coffee house, pool, terrace, sports facilities, bicycle hire. **$$**

Paradise Malacca Village
Tel: 06-232 3600
Freephone: 1-800 888 797
Fax: 06-232 5955
Imposing 510-room chain hotel across from the zoo, with Malay-style chalets and modern apartments (no cooking) in landscaped grounds. Swimming pools, tennis courts, golf, Malaysian, Chinese and Japanese restaurants. **$$**

Price Guide

Prices are for a standard double room during peak periods.
$$$$: more than RM400
$$$: RM200–400
$$: RM100–200
$: less than RM100

NEGERI SEMBILAN
Seremban
Allson Klana Resort
Jalan Penghulu Cantik
Taman Tasek
Tel: 06-762 9600
Fax: 06-763 9218
Facing the pretty lake, this is the town's only upmarket hotel, with 223 rooms, full room facilities and service, Japanese and Chinese restaurants, coffee house, bars, business centre, fitness centre, swimming pool. **$$$**

Carlton Hotel
47 Jalan Dato' Sheikh Ahmad
Tel: 06-762 5336
Fax: 06-762 0040
Central location near the bus and taxi station as well as food stalls, with 34 rooms, air-conditioning, Chinese restaurant, coffee house. **$$**

JOHOR
Johor Bahru
Hyatt Regency
Jalan Sungai Chat
Tel: 07-222 1234
Fax: 07-222 0159
Luxurious hotel with 406 rooms, some with views of the Straits of Johor and Singapore, two-tier

swimming pool, Roman spa. Within walking distance of town. **$$$$**

Holiday Inn Crown Plaza
Jalan Dato Sulaiman
Tel: 07-332 3800
Fax: 07-331 8884
Out of town hotel with 200 rooms, disco, and Italian and Szechuan restaurants. **$$$**

Puteri Pan Pacific
Jalan Salim
Tel: 07-223 3333
Fax: 07-223 6622
e-mail: panpjjb@po.jaring.my
Massive, central hotel, close to shopping malls, with 500 rooms, some with views of the straits and Singapore, Italian restaurant. **$$$**

Straits View Hotel
1-D Jalan Skudai
Tel: 07-721 4000
Fax: 07-242 6989
Out of town hotel with upstairs rooms overlooking the straits; 76 air-conditioned rooms, open-air seafood restaurant. **$**

Wadi Hassan Traveller's Home
52E Jalan Wadi Hassan
Clean backpackers' hotel with dormitories and family rooms, fan-cooled, laundry, tours and information. **$**

Kota Tinggi

Kota Tinggi Resort
Km 16, Jalan Lombong
Tel: 07-883 1753
Fax: 07-883 1146
Resort comprising 63 chalets and rooms by the waterfalls with air-conditioning and ensuite baths; mostly Singaporean clientele. Weekday rate 20 percent cheaper, also much quieter. **$$**

Desaru

Accommodation here is classy, and expensive because of the mostly-Singaporean clientele. Weekend rates are about 20 percent higher. All eateries are in the hotels or the coastal villages a drive away. Seaview rooms are at a premium. All resorts have swimming pools, sea-sport facilities and bicycles.

Desaru Impian Resort
Tanjung Penawar
Tel: 07-838 9911
Fax: 07-828 9922
Like Disney's Sleeping Beauty's castle whose towers are topped by flags that don't flutter, this gigantic theme-park hotel at the entrance to Desaru has staff dressed as pirates, a water park surrounded by 16 blocks of 356 well-furnished all-suite family apartments (cooking allowed), two swimming pools – one in a Taj Mahal clubhouse on the beach – mini zoo and sports facilities. Day use allowed. **$$$**

Desaru Perdana
Tanjung Penawar
Tel: 07-223 2157
Fax: 07-223 1673
Blocks harbouring 200 rooms around beautiful pool with waterfall; nice landscaping. **$$$**

Sebana Golf and Marina Resort
Tanjung Penawar
Tel: 07-825 2411
Fax: 07-825 2413
The approach road winds through an 18-hole golf course, past the yacht clubhouse and the beautiful marina which is overlooked by the resort's tavern. There are 60 rather small rooms, some with marina views. Pub lunches at the bar,

nominal fee for recreational facilities, river cruises. Ask about packages. **$$$**

Desaru Garden Beach Resort
Tanjung Penawar
Tel: 07-822 1240
Fax: 07-822 1221
Oldie resort with 1970s feel, but decent; 220 rooms and chalets, including newer sea-fronting villas. The famous golf course is just down the road. **$$**

Desaru Leisure Camp
Tanjung Penawar
Tel: 07-822 1211
Fax: 07-822 1937
Most basic offering but not good value, with rooms and tiny chalets with mattress. Camping permitted with equipment for rent; friendly staff, food on request only, popular with groups. Mountain biking pit nearby; day use allowed. **$**

Tanjung Balau Fishing Village
Tanjung Balau
Tel: 07-822 1601, 010-7183524
Next to a modern fishing village, this new government venture has 115 family and double rooms and 20 triple-share dormitories, and a local restaurant. Traditional fishing is seasonal only, but there's a good fishing museum and nice uncrowded beach. **$**

Endau-Rompin National Park (Johor)

Staging Point and campsites
Tel: 07-223 7471 (Johor Park Corporation in Johor Bahru)
Fax: 07-223 7472
The Staging Point at Endau-Rompin National Park has chalets (20 people) and dormitories (100 people – men and women separate), otherwise there are campsites: Kuala Jasin, Kuala Marong, Upih Guling, and Batu

Hampar (maximum 200 visitors) with some shelters and basic toilets. Booking ahead is imperative. Bring everything in, including food and cooking gas. Limited equipment may be hired. The area is accessible by boat from Felda Nitar (jump-off point Mersing or Kahang). Permits are required (and for cameras). A guide can be arranged.

Nature Education and Research Centre (NERC)
Tel: 03-287 9422 (Malaysian Nature Society in Kuala Lumpur)
Fax: 03-287 8773
e-mail: natsoc@po.jaring.my
The centre offers 4-day/3-night nature courses (minimum groups of 10, maximum 40), including full board and excellent meals (student concessions available).

PENINSULA'S EAST COAST

MERSING AND ISLANDS
Mersing
Hotel Timotel
839 Jalan Endau
Tel: 07-799 5888
Fax: 07-799 5333
e-mail: timotel@tm.net.my
Situated past the bridge north but within walking distance of the jetty, the hotel is clean with 44 rooms, local and Western food. **$$**
The Cuckoo's Nest
9–1 Jalan Dato Timur
Tel/fax: 07-799 1060
Newer backpackers' hostel with dormitories, library, breakfast. **$**
Kali's Guest House
12 E Kampung Sri Lalang
Tel/fax: 07-799 3613
Beautiful Balinese-style accommodation 1 km (½ mile) north of town on the outer coastal road. Among thick foliage sit 13 traditional thatched huts of different architecture and size, in a peaceful landscaped garden complete with koi pond and gazebo with scatter cushions. Gamelan music and open restaurant. Some rooms have ensuite bathrooms, all are fan-cooled; mosquitoes can be nasty. **$**
Mersing Inn
38 Jalan Ismail
Tel/fax: 07-799 1919
Next to a supermarket in a central location with clean, air-conditioned rooms, ensuite baths and hot water. **$**
Omar's Backpackers' Hostel
Jalan Abu Bakar
Tel: 07-799 5096, 019-774 4268
Opposite the post office is Mersing's arguably best-established backpackers' hostel. Situated on the first floor with dormitories for 10 only; kitchen, tours, walking distance of jetty. **$**

Pulau Besar
D'Coconut Island Resort
Tel: 07-271 4531,
010-272 9306/019
Fax: 03- 491 1808
e-mail: dcoconut@tm.net.my
http://www.geocities.com/The
Tropics/Cabana/1441

New, *kampung* environment with 20 air-conditioned chalets with ensuite baths, satellite TV and mini fridge, mountain bikes, watersports, dive shop. **$$**
Nirwana Beach Resort
Tel: 07-799 5979
Fax: 07-799 5978
Basic chalets, some air-conditioned, all with ensuite baths, dormitories for 6–10 people, bar. **$$**
Radin Resort and Safaris
Tel: 07-799 4152,
03-242 1033 (KL)
Fax: 07-799 1413, 03-242 5621
Smartest hotel with 50 beach-fronting (premium) and hill-view coconut-framed chalets arranged in clusters for *kampung* feel, with hot showers, lush grounds, 24-hour electricity, bar, sea-sports, a 45-minute cross-isle jungle trek from back of huts; no TV, no karaoke, or dive shop. **$$**
White Sand Beach Resort
Tel: 07-799 4995
Established outfit with beach-fronting chalets, dive packages. **$$**

Pulau Rawa
Rawa Safaris Island Resort
Tel: 07-799 1204
Fax: 07-799 3848
One-island-one-resort tagline, with 53 wood-and-attap A-frames, chalets and bungalows on beach and hill, some with air-conditioning and ensuite bathroom. A quiet spot with a lovely beach, electricity until midnight (lanterns provided), bar, sea-sports, scuba gear for hire but no dive master. **$$**

Pulau Tinggi
Nadia's Comfort Inn
Tel: 03-242 9506, 011-333 656
Fax: 03-242 9325
Big resort, with 110 rooms (premium for sea view), swimming pool and jacuzzi, karaoke, sea-sports, diving. **$$$**
Cahaya Beach Chalet
Tel: 011-764 084
One 11-room longhouse, four to a room, very basic. **$**

Pulau Pemanggil
Basic accommodation and only packages are available, usually for

groups of 10 or more. Enquire at the travel agencies. The biggest operation is **Pemanggil Holiday Heaven** with 13 chalets and a 10-room longhouse; **Ranting Resort** is fairly big; other smaller operators with chalets and dormitories are **Pemanggil Baru Chalet** and **Pulau Pemanggil Mini Resort**. **$$$**

Johor Islands

Accommodation on the islands is divided into what are termed resorts – the bigger air-conditioned and hot-shower operations – and chalets, which can be dormitory-style. All have restaurants and snorkelling facilities. Some are diver-friendly. Operations have a habit of changing management and ownership. Some have their own offices or agents in town, but tour agencies can book you into any of the islands – they receive a commission, so be firm. Ask to see their photo album of resorts and boats. Enquire about 3-day/2-night packages, which include boat transfers, accommodation, all meals and a snorkelling trip.

Pulau Aur/Dayang
Another packages-only destination, the prettiest beaches are on Pulau Dayang: chalets and longhouses available at **Blue Water Holiday Resort**, tel: 07-799 5696; **Dayang Blues**, tel: 07-799 4558; and on Aur, **Mahmood's Chalet**, tel: 07-799 4217. Enquire about the smaller operations at tour agencies; packages. **$$$**

Pulau Tioman
Years of tourism have seen an upgrading in the class of accommodation from basic A-frame huts to fairly decent beach-fronting chalets with ensuite baths and hot showers, some air-conditioned, all with restaurants.
Tekek beach is lined with small virtually indistinguishable resorts – you can check out each one until you find something you like. At the

end of the stretch is **Berjaya Tioman Beach Resort**, tel: 09-419 1000; fax: 09-419 1718, the largest – and only luxury – resort, with 400 rooms and suites, golf and all the facilities expected of a resort. **$$$**

  Peladang is well-kept, *kampung*-style accommodation with roomy chalets in pretty gardens, but sits across the road near the mini market and has no beach. **$**

  Air Batang (ABC) and Juara are backpacker and A-frame beaches, Salang also has budget accommodation as does Mukut, while Paya and Genting cater to locals and Singaporeans and have more up-market accommodation.

  There are dive shops at Tekek (Tioman Reef Divers and Scuba Point), ABC (B&J Dive Centre), Salang (Dive Asia and Fishermen Dive Centre), Penuba (Bali Hai Divers).

Price Guide

Prices are for a standard double room during peak periods.
$$$$: more than RM400
$$$: RM200–400
$$: RM100–200
$: less than RM100

Pulau Sibu Besar
(accessible from Tanjung Leman)
Sea Gypsy Village Resort
Tel: 07-222 8642
Fax: 07-238 7305
Lovely resort set in a 5-acre coconut-fringed site with 23 sea-facing Malay chalets with ensuite baths and verandahs. Bar, barbeque on Saturdays, dive shop, full-board. **$$**
Sibu Island Cabanas
Tel: 07-331 7216
Comfortable, 18 fan-cooled chalets with ensuite baths, dive shop, full-board. **$$**
  There is plenty of basic accommodation, mainly A-frames and huts. **O&H Kampung Huts** (tel: 07-799 5096, 011-354 322) is an established backpackers' haunt; **Twin Beach Resort** (tel: 07-243 144, 011-331 896) commandeers

the middle of the island, and therefore two beaches.

Pulau Sibu Tengah
Sibu Island Resort
Tel: 07-223 1188, 799 5555
Fax: 07-223 1199, 799 4455
Fancy resort and the island's only one with 121 air-conditioned chalets and a host of facilities and activities including batik-making classes, tennis courts, sunken pool bar; *teh tarik* stall in the shape of a boat, selling Indian breads and tea at night.

PAHANG, TERENGGANU AND KELANTAN
Resorts are usually open all year round, but during the monsoon season, some offer a free stay if it rains during your visit. Sea-view rooms are premium; weekends and public holidays are 20–30 percent more pricey. Transfers from airports can be arranged by the bigger hotels.

PAHANG
Kuantan
All the town hotels are medium range, clustered around the centre and cater to the business sector, offering the same facilities; air-conditioning, TV, IDD phones, hot-water baths and breakfast. Among them are **M.S. Garden Hotel**, Lorong Gambut, tel: 09-515 5899 (202 rooms), **Vistana**, Jalan Telok Sisek (en route to Teluk Cempedak), tel: 09-568 8000, **Classic Hotel**, Jalan Besar, tel: 09-515 4599 (33 rooms), **Hotel Pacific**, Jalan Bukit Ubi, tel: 09-514 1980 (60 rooms), **Mega View**, Jalan Besar, tel: 09-555 1888 (105 rooms), **Citiview**, Jalan Haji Abdul Aziz, tel: 09-555 3888.

Teluk Chempedak Beach
Hyatt Kuantan
Tel: 09-513 1234
Fax: 09-513 7577
Grand old lady of the beach, with 353 rooms, restaurant with commanding ocean view, pizzas by the pool or on the beach, fun pub, tours. **$$$$**
Hotel Kuantan
Tel/fax: 09-568 0026

Distinct 1960s feel with high ceilings, colonial fan-cooled restaurant and bar, tiled floors, some rooms with air-conditioning and hot showers, tiny bathrooms, upstairs rooms with balcony and bathroom. Friendly, family-owned. **$**

Beserah
Le Village Beach Resort
Lot 1260 Sungai Karang
Tel: 09-544 7900, 03-283 6204
Fax: 09-544 7999
e-mail:
tancoholidays@ppp.nasionet.net
Mature is the word for this resort 14 km (9 miles) north of Kuantan, with wooden chalets and blocks of rooms amid lush foliage. Water sports, tours and car rental available. **$$**
Swiss-Garden Resort
2656–7 Sungai Karang
Tel: 09-544 7333
03-263 1333 (KL)
Fax: 09-544 9555
e-mail: sgrk@sgihotels.com.my
http://www.sgihotels.com.my
This new 306-room hotel 13 km (8 miles) from the Kuantan airport has a beautifully breezy lounge area and lovely garden terrace. **$$**
De Rhu Beach Resort
152 Sungai Karang
Tel: 09-557 9000
Fax: 09-557 9002
e-mail: derhunch@derhu.com.my
Oldish hotel that has changed hands several times, with a beautiful beach beneath the casuarinas, large grounds, huge pool with sundeck, disco. **$**

Cherating
Club Med
Batu 29
Jalan Kuantan/Kemaman
Tel: 09-581 9133
03-261 4599 (KL)
Fax: 09-581 9172
03-261 7229 (Reservation)
Just north of Kampung Cherating is Asia's first Club Med, spread out in carefully preserved forested surroundings, with a lovely private beach, the usual organised activities, including racquet sports, circus acts, rock-climbing, archery and watersports in non-monsoon

period. Wide range of international food from Japanese to French, Rio-type carnival with live band every weekend. Day visitors from 10am–12pm, 2–6pm. **$$$$**

Impiana Resort Cherating
Jalan Kuantan-Kemaman
Tel: 09-581 9000
Fax: 09-581 9090
Situated just beyond Cukai, this is a graceful and tasteful adaptation of traditional Malay architecture, with an interesting pond design merging into a lounge and 121 rooms. Outdoor jacuzzi, lessons in arts and craft, full sports facilities. **$$$**

Legend Resort
Lot 1290, Sungai Karang
Tel: 09-581 9439
Fax: 09-581 9400
Regular hotel whose brochures are much more impressive than the reality, with 152 rooms. **$$$**

Cherating Holiday Villa
Sungai Karang
Tel: 09-581 9500
03-262 2922 (KL)
Fax: 09-581 9178
e-mail: anthol@po.jaring.my
http://www.hijau.com.my/HolidayVilla
The first resort north from Beserah to Cherating. Established, lovely ambience with 138 rooms, including a unique *kampung* section with a chalet cluster based on architecture from each state, two open-air jacuzzis, steak house, full watersports facilities. **$$**

For budget travellers, there are many cheap and cheerful chalets for rent along the entire stretch of Cherating beach. The price varies with the duration of the stay – bargaining is expected and advised.

Kampung Cherating

There is a host of accommodation here, now also called Cherating Lama ("old Cherating"). Many are still backpackers' hostels and budget-class hotels, but upmarket developers are gradually moving in. Walk around until you see something you like.

Residence Inn
Tel: 09-581 9333
Fax: 09-581 9252

Upmarket, with 74 rooms in chalets and normal hotel blocks around a swimming pool; 5 minutes' walk to the beach. **$$**

Cherating Cottage
Tel: 09-581 9273
Fax: 09-581 9279
Classy chalets and double-storey block around a lotus pond, some rooms with air-conditioning and TV, open-air bar. **$**

Ranting Resort
Tel/fax: 09-581 9068
Tel: 012-322 6474
Chalets in beautiful, clean *kampung* setting, complete with chickens and goats, lotus pond at the back; great value set dinners in charming restaurant with different nightly themes; friendly management. **$**

Turtle-watching

At Rantau Abang, prices are higher by about 30 percent during the turtle season of May–September.

Awang's Beach Bungalows & Restaurant
Tel: 09-844 3500
Long-time "turtle tourism" resort near Turtle Information Centre, it has 37 bungalows with terraces, and dormitories, and a self-service laundry. **$**

Dahimah's Guest House & Restaurant
Tel: 09-983 5057/09-845 2843
Clean, different-sized *kampung*-style chalets with verandahs, a little away from the beach. The river-fronting huts are nice. Restaurant open only during turtle season. **$**

Ismail Beach Resort
Tel: 09-845 4202
Right in front of the Turtle Museum, similar to Awang's, with choice of fan or air-conditioning. **$**

Rantau Abang Visitor's Centre
Batu 13 Jalan Dungun
Tel: 09-844 1533
Fax: 09-844 2653
Minimum quad-share traditional huts and chalets overlooking the lagoon, some air-conditioned. **$**

The Shadow of the Moon
Tel: 09-581 9186
At the northern entrance, this is an established backpackers' hostel with attitude. Rustic fan-cooled and, imperatively, mosquito-netted, chalets are set amid much greenery on a hillside, all with baths. There is a wonderful restaurant/bar/reading area that is completely open – bring insect repellent. **$**

TERENGGANU
Kuala Terengganu

Permai Park Inn
Jalan Sultan Mahmud
Tel: 09-622 2122
Fax: 09-622 2121
Within walking distance of Batu Buruk beach, comfortable, pleasant hotel with 150 rooms, and a nice pool. **$$$**

Primula Park Royal
Jalan Persinggahan
Tel: 09-622 2100/623 3722
Fax: 09-623 3360
e-mail: primula@po.jaring.my
Town's fanciest hotel, renovated, with a sandy beach; 249 rooms, some with sea view; grill, cosy Italian restaurant, tours. **$$$**

Grand Continental
Jalan Sultan Zainal Abidin
Tel: 09-615 1888
Fax: 09-625 1999
Beachside but close to the town centre, 200 pleasant rooms, swimming pool, pastries and cakes, live bands. **$$**

Hotel YT Midtown
Jalan Tok Lam
Tel: 09-623 5288
Fax: 09-623 4399
Right in the heart of town, a decent new hotel with 144 air-conditioned rooms with ensuite baths, good value set lunch and dinner; supper special of local bread, *roti jala*, with curry. **$$**

Motel Desa
Bukit Pak Apil
Tel: 09-622 3438
Fax: 09-622 3443
Established and well-kept hilltop establishment with town views, but not central, with 20 air-conditioned, good-sized rooms with ensuite baths. Swimming pool, restaurant, bar. **$$**

KT Mutiara
67 Jalan Sultan Ismail
Tel: 09-622 0527
Fax: 03-623 6895
Centrally located with 39 clean, decent-sized rooms arranged around a central airwell with koi pond that looks better at night; hot water. **$**

Ping Anchorage
77A Jalan Dato' Isaacs
Tel: 09-623 2141
Fax: 09-622 0851
Central, small, clean backpackers' hostel with rooms and dormitories atop the town's best travel agency; sunny rooftop café and bar. **$**

Dungun

Tanjong Jara Resort
8th Mile off Jalan Dungun
Tel: 03-926 8000 (KL)
Fax: 03-925 7012 (KL)
Award-winning traditional Malay all-timber resort located 13 km (8 miles) north of Dungun on a 17-hectare (42-acre) site. There are 100 beach cottages and sea-facing hotel rooms (great views from second floor rooms) with 1.5 km (1 mile) of private beach. Restaurants, two swimming pools, hot spa, library, "well-being" centre with stress-release programmes, massages. **$$$$**

Awana Kijal Golf & Beach Resort
Km 28, Jalan Kemaman-Dungun
Tel: 09-864 1188
Fax: 09-864 1688
http://www.awana.com.my
Only one word for this place; huge. There are 364 rooms, nine food and beverage outlets, a massive swimming pool and nine holes of golf fairways on either side. Cruise ships unload passengers here. **$$$**

Marang

Anguilla Beach House Resort
Kampung Tanjung Rhu
Tel/fax: 09-618 1322
Opposite beach with 52 clean chalets in 2 hectares (5 acres) of well-kept grounds facing Pulau Kapas. Garden shelters, set meals, laundry, boat service. **$$**

Marang Resort & Safaris
Batu 17 Jalan Dungun/Marang
Tel: 09-618 2588

Fax: 09-618 2334
Difficult to reach without transport, this is a beautiful 100-room resort in thickly-vegetated surrounds. *Kampung*-style houses with ensuite baths and hot water are thinly scattered along the beach and river. River cruises, tours. **$$**

Kamal's
Kampung Tanjung Rhu
Tel: 09-618 2181
Facing the lagoon is the original backpackers' hostel and therefore entrenched as the place to stay; dormitories and chalets in a pleasant garden. **$**

Pulau Gemia

Gem Isles Resort
As there are no scheduled boats and the resort takes people booked on packages only, book through a travel agent such as Ping Anchorage, tel: 09-622 0851. The 52 air-conditioned chalets have views of the alcove and Pulau Kapas. Snorkelling, diving, non-motorised watersports, deep-sea fishing and squid fishing (*candat sotong*) all available. Small turtle hatchery. **$$$**

Merang

Aryani Resort
Jalan Rhu Tapai-Merang
Tel: 09-624 1111
Fax: 09-624 8007
Wonderful, and very exclusive heritage Terengganu house-suites by the same architect as the Floating Mosque; each house has a courtyard and an outside bath. **$$$$**

Sutra Beach Resort
Kampung Rhu Tapai
Tel: 09-623 1111
Fax: 09-626 96410
Traditional-style chalets gathered together in *kampung* clusters overlooking the islands; nice gardens. **$$**

Pulau Redang

There are no scheduled boats to Redang, so resorts offer packages which include boat transfers from Marang jetty, accommodation, meals and snorkelling trips and gear. Dive packages are available.

Pickups from airports can be arranged. Book with the resort or tour agency. Resorts listed are in Pasir Panjang unless stated otherwise.

Berjaya Redang Beach Resort
Tel: 03-242 9611
Fax: 03-248 8249
Luxury hotel in Teluk Dalam with 152 rooms and all the mod-cons. **$$$**

Coral Redang Island Resort
Tel: 09-623 6200/011-972 174
Fax: 09-623 6300/669 6270
e-mail: coral@tm.net.my
The nicest hotel on Pasir Panjang, with 40 chalets and standard rooms with air-conditioning and hot water, around swimming pool with bar. Local and continental dishes, dive shop. **$$$**

Redang Bay Resort
Tel: 09-623 6048
Fax: 09-622 8190
Austere cement room blocks and small chalets near noisy generator. Excellent food served in a breezy restaurant; beautiful beach and very cheap diving. **$$$**

Redang Beach Resort
Tel: 09-623 8188,
03-201 5079 (KL)
Fax: 09-623 0225, 03-201 5075
Rooms in two-storey wooden block, nice breakfasts, deck chairs, DIY batik, jungle-trekking, fishing and *candat sotong* (squid fishing), dive shop. **$$$**

Redangkalong Resort
Tel: 09-622 1591/09-622 3537
Fax: 09-622 8186/09-622 3537
Beach-facing rooms in a longhouse with air-conditioning and hot

Diving Camps

Fun camping tours for groups (20 or more) of snorkellers and divers, as well as dive instruction are offered by **Camping Holiday**, tel: 03-717 8935; fax: 03-716 8470, e-mail: campholiday@ yahoo.com, and **Redang Aquatic Adventures**, tel: 09-623 8188; fax: 09-623 0225, which also ties up with Redang Beach Resort and arranges outings to Lang Tengah and Perhentian.

showers as well as ensuite baths, but this beach is rather corally. Dive shop. **$$$**

Redang Reef Resort
Tel: 09-626 2020
Fax: 09-622 8093
Perched on rocks, this hotel has 24 air-conditioned rooms in a two-storey block with ensuite baths. Large wooden deck for dining overlooks the bay, also used for karaoke. Dive shop. **$$$**

Pulau Lang Tengah
Blue Coral Island Resort
Tel: 03-705 2577 (KL)
Fax: 03-705 2579
Facing a lovely quiet beach are 70 rooms with air-conditioning, hot water and verandah, swimming pool, library, movies, karaoke and grocery shop. Fishing and diving tours and instruction available; house reef good for snorkelling. **$$$**

Square Point Redang Resort
Tel/fax: 09-623 5333
http://www.terengganu.net/square point
Peaceful and basic, this resort has 48 rooms in longhouses, all air-conditioned and with ensuite baths; snorkelling, house reef good at high tide. Dive shop. **$$$**

Pulau Perhentian
Facilities notwithstanding, these islands have never outgrown their original backpacker mentality. The smaller outfits have no proper reception area or management as such, so do not be surprised to be faced with grumpy and/or ignorant staff. Water is also a problem during the dry months. Just focus on the islands' amazing beauty.

Perhentian Besar
Perhentian Island Resort
Tel: 09-691 0946
03-244 8530 (KL)
Fax: 09-697 7562
e-mail: pir@po.jaring.my
http://www.jaring.my/perhentian
The island's only three-star resort with 104 beautifully-furnished chalets and bungalows with ensuite bath and air-conditioning, some on the private beach. No problem with water. Excellent fresh grilled fish

and dinner buffet, but food here is on the pricey side; dive shop, non-motorised sea-sports, tennis and swimming pool, circular jungle trek behind the resort, tours. Cheaper rates from tour agencies. **$$$**

Coral View Island Resort
Tel: 09-695 6943
Fax: 09-691 0943
The next upmarket resort to PIR, it has 75 pretty chalets on two beaches, though only the rockier one is good for swimming. Some chalets are air-conditioned. Breezy restaurant, dive operation pioneer. **$$$**

Perhentian Kecil
Impiani Tropical Island Resort
One of the loveliest resorts in the Perhentians, this sits alone, beautifully camouflaged among trees, and comprises 25 large hexagonal sea-facing chalets with woven mat walls and verandahs that sit on boulders and which are linked by a wooden walkway and stairs; unfortunately, water is a problem. **$$**

The rest of the island is backpacker haven, both at Teluk Aur and Pasir Panjang. Around the jetty at Teluk Aur where the best picture-postcard sunset scenes are, sit six chalet operators, including **Rajawali's** (tel: 010-984 7200) on the headland in the north, with A-frames and great views of the bay.

There are eight operators fronting the famous Pasir Panjang (Long Beach), where it all began. There is no jetty so you have to wade in, or

small boats will charge to bring you in if you have not decided on a resort. The original **Pasir Panjang Chalet** (tel: 010-985 3589) has been upgraded to chalets with ensuite baths (11 chalets), some with air-conditioning; local food and nightly BBQ.

Mohsin Chalet
Tel/fax: 010-333 8897
03-463 9950 (KL)
e-mail: marhms@pc.jaring.my
Newer accommodation, set back from the beach with 30 hillside chalets with ensuite baths, great views from the restaurant which serves local and Western fare, use of telephones and Internet, friendly staff. **$**

The Perhentian Dive Centre and Turtle Bay Divers are at this beach. The snorkelling site of D'Lagoon in the northeast has some budget accommodation, including **D'Lagoon Chalet and Restaurant**, tel: 011-970 631, 010-212 9943 with chalets, A-frames and dorm rooms.

KELANTAN
Kota Bharu
Perdana Hotel
Jalan Mahmud

Perhentian Besar on a Budget

Budget accommodation at Perhentian Besar is found south of Coral View. Among the established hostels is **Mama's Chalet & Restaurant**, tel: 010-984 0232, with basic chalets, some with ensuite baths, a turtle-egg adoption scheme, and a dive shop. There is more accommodation on Teluk Dalam, the southern beach over the headland – get off at the jetty at Ibi Chalet and walk around. Among

operations here are the pretty **Flora Bay**, tel: 011-977 266, with chalets, some air-conditioned, money changing, 20 hours of electricity a day, dive shop. Smaller operators include **Coco Hut's A-frames**, tel: 010-982 7546; **Rosli Chalets, Dormitories and Rooms**, tel: 09-691 0155; and **Cozy Chalet**, tel: 011-326 822, 010-330 9717. **Seahorse Divers** are beside the basic ABC Chalet.

Tel: 09-748 5000
Fax: 09-744 7621
Close to the Cultural Centre, within walking distance of the Central Market, the hotel has 136 rooms, restaurants, coffee house, swimming pool, sports facilities, and car rental. **$$**

Perdana Resort
Pantai Cahaya Bulan
Tel: 09-773 3000
Freephone: 1-800 888 844
Fax: 09-773 9980
Nicest hotel in town, with chalets well spread out along the beach, great sunsets, decent Chinese and Western restaurants. **$$**

Budget accommodation in the form of dormitories and rooms is offered by: **City**, 2nd Floor, Jalan Pintu Pong; **Ideal Traveller's Guest House**, Jalan Padang Garong, tel: 09-744 2246 (52 rooms); **Rebana Hostel**, 1218, Jalan Sultanah Zainab (40 rooms).

Kuala Besut
Primula Besut Beach Resort
Tel: 09-697 1563
Very run-down hotel on the quiet beachfront with large rooms, swimming pool, restaurant and disinterested staff. **$**

Putra Inn
Tel: 09-695 6919,
019-981 2919
A 20-minute walk from the Kuala Besut jetty. New adaptation of lovely wooden handicraft centre that didn't take off; 10 air-conditioned rooms with *kampung* furnishings, ensuite bathrooms and hot water, free transport to jetty, friendly management.

EASTERN INTERIOR
Tasik Kenyir
Each resort is close to a waterfall and trek routes and is pretty much isolated from the others. Most are very basic floating chalets moored to the mainland, which means that if a group comes along and decides to make merry, there isn't much you can do about claiming back peace and quiet on the deck or in your room. Otherwise, the setting is truly tranquil. Meals are Chinese-

style and buffet. Generators are usually switched on only at night.
Duta Lakes Resort
Tel: 010-276 8646
Tel/fax: 03-284 6606 (KL)
e-mail:
tancoholidays@ppp.nasionet.net
Six-year-old resort 15 minutes from the jetty, which was given a facelift in 1999. There are 20 floating chalets around a 4-hectare (9-acre) island, on which there are 15 two-layer giant tents with beds, communal baths and cooking area; and 15 caravans with baths and cooking facilities. Normal camping is allowed on the island, too. You can trek up Sungai Kiang/Siput, or take a trip to Saok Waterfall. **$$$**

Kenyir Lake Resort
Tel: 09-514 6002
011-950 609
Fax: 09-513 5687
Chalets with ensuite bathrooms and hot water in an upmarket setup, which is developing animal viewing hides. A free-form swimming pool is fed by continuously flowing natural springs; there is a fish farm for anglers and a wide range of activities. **$$$**

Kenyir Outdoor Leadership Academy (KOLA)
Tel: 010-983 6105
Fax: 010-934 0999
Right across the jetty, this former upmarket resort that went bust is now an outward bound/leadership camp, which accounts for its fancy reception area and 40 deluxe chalets. The entire island has been turned into an adventure playground with campsites, artificial rock-climbing wall, rope course, and sea-sports, all supervised by instructors. **$$$**

Lake Land Resort
Tel: 010-278 2939,
03-774 7913 (KL)
e-mail:
enquiry@lakelandmalaysia.com
http://lakelandmalaysia.com
Recently upgraded, this remote resort comprises 20 green-roofed chalets (4–6 people per chalet) on an island. There is basic accommodation on a floating deck, 24-hour electricity, satellite TV, karaoke, 3-hour trail to Ulu Terang.

Camping is sometimes available. Two dining halls, ice and bar. **$$$**
**The Little Traveller
(Uncle John's Resort)**
Tel: 09-622 9564,
010-984 2085
Fax: 09-622 9596
Small floating concern close to Lasir Waterfall, with lovely design of varnished split bamboo and open deck, 12 rooms, karaoke, videos, accessible from main dam jetty. **$$**

Tasik Kenyir Golf Resort
Tel: 09-666 8888/6249 1150
Fax: 09-666 8316
Upmarket mainland venue of 150 chalets with golf course. **$$$**

Price Guide

Prices are for a standard double room during peak periods.
$$$$: more than RM400
$$$: RM200–400
$$: RM100–200
$: less than RM100

Tasik Cini
Kijang Mas Gumum Resort
Kampung Orang Asli Gumum
Tel: 011-950 700
Tel/fax: 03-424 9396 (KL)
Basic lakeside chalet outfit run by the Orang Asli co-operative, set within the modern village of Kampung Gumum and accessible by road and boat. There are 10 chalets and dormitories for 32; shared facilities, tours. **$**

Rimba Resort Tasik Cini
Tel: 09-477 8037
Fax: 09-477 8036
Rather run-down government-owned 13-year-old resort on the banks of a lake that is lotus-covered from June to September. Decent-sized chalets with balconies, some with air-conditioning; dormitories and campsite. Jungle-trekking (two guides) and boat trips by arrangement. Decent restaurant, karaoke, TV in lounge. Walkway leads to jetty of private boat operators. **$**

Tasik Bera
Persona Lake Resort
Kompleks Pelancungan Tasik Bera

Tel: 09-276 2505
Fax: 09-255 3386
Set in the wilderness of oil palms, this simple lakeside resort has 50 rooms, dormitories for 40, and a campsite for 200, including eight riverine huts. Interesting Orang Asli homestay programme is among the numerous tours led by trained guides. **$$$**

TAMAN NEGARA
Kuala Tahan
Taman Negara Resort
Tel: 09-266 3500
03-245 5585 (KL)
Fax: 09-266 1500
03-245 5430 (KL)
e-mail: tnresort@tm.net.my
Fancy resort that is somehow a little too civilised for a wild jungle reserve. Malaysian-styled wooden chalets with balconies, 110 rooms, dormitories, nice camping ground with limited equipment for hire, pricey restaurant and cafeteria, tours, guides, helpful information desk. Also, there are 10 lodges upriver in Keniam and Terengganu respectively, but they're not very well maintained and have a small restaurant. **$$**
Department of Wildlife and National Parks
Tel: 09-296 1267
03-905 2872 (KL)
Accommodation at camp sites, fishing lodges at Berkoh and Perkai (maximum eight people each), and five jungle hides (maximum eight each). Bring your own sleeping bag and food. Permits required. **$**
Nusa Camp
Tel: 09-266 2369
266 1832
Comprising 36 hectares (90 acres) of park buffer zone across the river; located upriver, with its own trails. Basic accommodation at 20 chalets and A-frames, dormitories for 40, and a camping ground (tents supplied). Restaurant with a great view of the river, and babbling brook; guided tours. **$**

Kampung Kuala Tahan
The tiny village opposite the Park Headquarters outside the park has been invaded by a host of budget accommodation, some with dubious sewerage facilities and management; the village is accessible by boat or by dirt road from Jerantut. Among the accommodation on offer is: **Ekoton Chalet**, tel/fax: 09-266 9897, air-conditioned chalets and dormitories in pretty *kampung* set-up with laundry, safe deposit box; pioneer **Tembeling Lodge** overlooks the river, and has dormitories with bamboo walls that open at the top and useful mosquito nets, table and chair outside, lawn on which to hang out, complete with hammock; **Teresek View Motel**, tel: 09-266 7839/9177, consisting of A-frames and basic chalets in a quiet location away from the river. **$**

Jerantut
Hotel Jelai
6 Tingkat Atas, Jalan Besar
Tel/fax: 09-266 7412
019-328 3468
Catering mainly to travelling salesmen, this is a small but decent, clean hotel above a chicken-rice restaurant. **$**
Jerantut Rest House
Jalan Benta
Tel: 09-268 6200
Fax: 09-266 6200
This basic motel, which also has dormitories, sits 500 metres (550 yds) from the bus/taxi station, and operates free pick-ups within town. It also handles Taman Negara bookings. Food is available from 7am–11pm. **$**
Hotel Sri Emas Jerantut Guest House
Bangunan MUIP
Jalan Besar
Tel: 09-266 4499/88/77
Fax: 09-266 4801
Doubles as pro-active travel agency offering nightly briefings on Taman Negara; agent for some resorts in the village. Dormitories and restaurant. Foreigner-only hotel. **$**

Kenong
Persona Rimba Resort
Kenong Rimba Park
Tel: 09-312 5032
Fax: 09-312 1421
Basic chalets on stilts among trees

Hilton Batang Ai Resort
Batang Ai Dam
Tel: 083-584 388
Fax: 083-584 399
A longhouse-styled resort with standard Hilton facilities, 4½ hours from Kuching. It offers a gentle introduction to longhouse living. Close enough to real longhouses for excursions. **$$$**
Bukit Saban Resort
Paku River, Betong
Tel: 082-423 167
Fax: 082-245 551
About 4½ hours from Kuching with excursions to local plantations, longhouses and nature treks. **$$**
Pelagus Resort
Rejang River
Tel: 082-238 033
Fax: 082-238 050
A resort situated just below the treacherous Pelagus Rapids in an untouched area of longhouses. Offers river safaris and nature excursions. **$$$**

accommodating 32 people. Activities include jungle trekking, mountain climbing, river activities, cave exploration; guides available; packages only. **$$**

SARAWAK

Kuching
Kuching abounds with accommodation on all levels. We have chosen the best – most have been personally tried or recommended by others.
Crowne Plaza Riverside Kuching
Jalan Tunku Abdul Rahman
Tel: 082-247 777
Fax: 082-425 858
e-mail: cprk@tm.net.my
Ritzy new addition to Kuching's hotel scene situated between the Hilton and the Holiday Inn. **$$$**
Hotel Grand Continental
Jalan Ban Hock
Tel: 082-230 399
Fax: 082-255 099
A newer hotel a little out of the old

centre, popular with local businessmen; good facilities. **$$$**

Holiday Inn Kuching
Jalan Tunku Abdul Rahman
Tel: 082-423 111
Fax: 082-426 169
e-mail: hikrsv@po.jaring.my
Popular hotel that looks out over the Kuching River. Good facilities. **$$$**

Kuching Hilton Hotel
Jalan Tunku Abdul Rahman
Tel; 082-248 200
Fax: 082-428 984
The imposing white facade of Kuching's best hotel looks out across the Kuching River and magnificent sunsets over the old trading town. Facilities and service are as good as might be expected. **$$$**

Borneo Hotel
Jalan Tabuan
Tel: 082-244 122
Fax: 082-254 848
Kuching's oldest established hotel with a friendly staff but small rooms, just behind the main bazaar area. **$$**

Telang Usan Hotel
Jalan Ban Hock
Tel: 082-244 122
Fax: 082-254 848
A friendly, comfortable hotel owned and run by Orang Ulu with traditional Kenyah decor and good advice for upriver trips. **$$**

Green Mountain Lodging House
Jalan Green Hill
Tel: 082-416 320
Fax: 082-246 342
Popular with backpackers and travellers, situated in a convenient location. Rooms are air-conditioned with hot water. **$**

Damai Beach

Holiday Inn Resort Damai Beach
Teluk Bandung Santubong
Tel: 082-846 999
Fax: 082-846 777
e-mail: hirdb@po.jaring.my
Long-standing popular resort with comfortable atmosphere. The newer hilltop chalets overlook panoramas of the sea and mountains; has a scenic pool. **$$$**

Holiday Inn Resort Damai Lagoon
Teluk Penyu Santubong

Tel: 082-846 900
Fax: 082-846 901
Big hotel blocks near the sea with full range of watersports and facilities. **$$$**

Santubong Kuching Resort
Santubong
Tel: 082-846 888
Fax: 082-846 666
A smaller family-style resort with watersports and activities. **$$$**

Damai Rainforest Resort
Pantai Damai Santubong
An outdoor activity centre with camping facilities and a rainforest location. **$$**

Lundu

Lundu Gading Hotel
Lundu
Tel: 082-735 199
Fax: 082-735 299
Small hotel with air-conditioned rooms and bathrooms – a fine base to explore the Lundu area. **$$**

Sibu

Sibu is usually a stopover on the way upriver, but most visitors stay overnight and visit the colourful morning market near the river.

Kingwood Hotel
12 Lorong Lanang 4
Tel: 084-335 888
Fax: 084-334 559
Sibu's biggest hotel complete with plush granite tiles and views of the Rejang River. **$$$**

Tanahmas Hotel
Jalan Kampung Nyabor
Tel: 084-333 188
Fax: 084-333 288
One of Sibu's best hotels, well run and popular with local businessmen; good restaurant. **$$$**

Hotel Capitol 88
19 Jalan Wong Nai Siong
Tel: 084-336 444
Fax: 084-311 706
Clean rooms and a 10-minute walk from the expressboat jetty. Good for early morning departures upriver. **$$**

Hotel Ria
21 Jalan Channel
Tel: 084-326 622
This budget hotel is close to the expressboat jetty. **$**

Homestays

Homestay in a Sarawak longhouse or Orang Asli village are popular options in the rainforest. These are usually "tourist-friendly", but if you are lucky, your hospitable Malaysian guide might just invite you home for the real thing – however, be especially mindful that this is someone's home, and respect local mores. Longhouse visits are arranged though a tour company, so it's worth asking around first to find a suitably interesting one.

Sarawak Fishing Village Homestays allows guests to stay with Malay families fluent in English, giving a taste of genuine *kampung* life. For more information, tel: 082-245 481; fax: 082-256 871; e-mail: gazul@tm.net.my

Kapit

The first upriver town, Kapit has an array of accommodation, mostly small hotels. This is the last chance for pizza or ice cream.

Greenland Inn
463 Jalan Teo Chow Beng
Tel: 084-796 388
Fax: 084-796 708
A small hotel with comfortable clean rooms and ensuite bathrooms – especially welcome after a journey upriver. **$$**

Ark Hill Inn
Jalan Penghulu Geridang
Tel: 085-796 168
Fax: 085-797 168
Small friendly hotel with clean, reasonably-priced rooms. **$**

Belaga

This upriver bazaar town has a few simple hotels.

Bee Lian Hotel
Belaga Bazaar
Tel: 085-461 416
Small hotel with air-conditioned rooms of an adequate standard. **$**

Belaga Hotel
Belaga Bazaar
Tel: 085-461 244

A friendly hotel with restaurant downstairs and some air-conditioned rooms. **$**

Mukah
An idyllic little fishing community with well-preserved fishing villages on the way to Bintulu, about 2 hours from Sibu.

King Ing Hotel
Mukah River
Tel: 084-871 400
Located near the town's colourful old bazaar and a Chinese temple. For character and local flavour it is the best place to stay. **$**

Pantai Harmonie Beach Resort
4 km Jalan Mukah Oya
Tel: 084-872 566
Fax: 084-871 010
Pleasant resort by the beach with some facilities. **$**

Bintulu
Mainly known for its fame as an oil town, Bintulu is close to Similajau National Park, the spectacular caves of Niah National Park and some decent beaches.

Plaza Hotel
Jalan Abang Galau
Tel: 086-335 111
Fax: 086-332 742
Bintulu's best hotel with swimming pool, nice restaurant with Western food and good value rooms. **$$$**

Hoover Inn
Jalan Abang Galau
Tel: 086-335 111
Fax: 086-332 742
A popular moderate hotel. **$$**

My House
Jalan Taman Sri Dagong
Tel: 085-336 339
Fax: 085-332 050
Small, friendly hotel with clean rooms and air-conditioning. **$**

Miri
This former oil town is becoming increasingly green and pleasant, and makes a fine base between visits to Mulu, Niah and Loagan Bunut national parks. Restaurants and nightlife make it a good stopover.

Holiday Inn Miri
Jalan Temenggong Datuk Oyong Lawai
Tel: 085-418 888
Fax: 085-419 999
Well-run Holiday Inn with excellent food; by the sea. **$$$**

Mega Hotel
Jalan Maju
Tel: 085-432 432
Fax: 085-433 433
New hotel with good facilities. **$$$**

Rihga Royal Hotel
Jalan Temenggong Datuk Oyong Lawai
Tel: 085-421 121
Fax: 085-421 099
Comfortable and popular, with good facilities and a large swimming pool next to the sea. **$$$**

Brooke Inn
Jalan Brooke
Tel: 085-421 111
Fax: 085-422 222
This is a good location for budget travellers, close to the bus station and visitor information; friendly staff. **$**

Marudi
This little trading town is worth at least a night's stopover and a visit to the morning market. It's also a good place to arrange upriver trips.

Grand Hotel
Lot 350 Backlane, Marudi
Tel: 085-755 711/755 712
Fax: 085-755 293
A good hotel with some air-conditioned rooms, close to the boat jetty. Useful source of information for upriver journeys. **$–$$**

Mulu
Royal Mulu Lodge
Mulu National Park
Tel: 085-421 121
Fax: 085-425 057
Comfortable, with friendly staff and close to all the rainforest attractions; by the river. The hotel can arrange trips and sporting activities. **$$$**

Ba Kelalan
Apple Lodge
Ba Kelalan
Tel: 085-436 566
Fax: 085-414 146
This little lodging house near the airport is clean and simple, providing adequate and friendly accommodation. **$**

Bario
This highland valley is close to many longhouses and has the perfect climate for trekking.

Tarawe's Lodge
Bario
This small lodge, close to the airport and main bazaar, provides friendly service and big older-style rooms. No phone or fax and only accessible by plane or on foot. **$**

SABAH

Kota Kinabalu
Kota Kinabalu (KK) is burgeoning with big new hotels, catering to the high end of the tourist market. Action-adventure and packaged nature tours are Sabah's big new draw, as well as the already well known Mount Kinabalu.

Staying in Sarawak's National Parks

For accommodation in the national parks, bookings can be made at the Visitors Information Centre in Kuching, or for Mulu and Niah, in Miri. Prices for park chalets and hostels vary between **$–$$**.

On arrival at the park, registration is required and the payment of additional fees of a nominal sum for entrance and for cameras.

Bookings for Bako, Kubah, Gunung Gading national parks and the Matang Wildlife Centre can all be made at the Visitor's Information Centre, Lot 31, Jalan Masjid, Kuching, tel: 082-248 088; fax: 082-416 700.

In Miri, bookings for Mulu, Niah, Lambir Hills, Similajau and Loagan Bunut national parks can be made at the Visitor's Information Centre, Lot 452, Jalan Melayu (close to Miri Bus Station), tel: 085-434 184; fax: 085-434 179; e-mail: stb@po.jaring.my

Berjaya Palace Hotel
Jalan Tanki Karamunsing
Tel: 088-211 911
Fax: 088-211 600
Located in a quiet part of town, a short taxi ride away from the centre. **$$$**

Hyatt Kinabalu International
Jalan Datuk Saleh Sulong
Tel: 088-221 234
Fax: 088-225 972
This is a long-established, always pleasing hotel. Rooms enjoy magnificent sunset views over the waterfront and out to the nearby islands. **$$$**

Jesselton Hotel
Gaya Street
Tel: 088-223 333
Fax: 088-241 401
A delightful recreated nostalgic hotel offering gracious service and good Western food in a formal dining room, as well as an informal coffeeshop. **$$$**

Pan Pacific Sutera Harbour
Sutera Harbour Boulevard
Tel: 088-318 888
Fax: 088-317 777
A big new complex of two hotels, yacht marina, 27-hole championship golf course and sports facilities, overlooking the islands of the Tunku Abdul Rahman Marine Park with sunsets across the South China Sea. **$$$**

ShangriLa Tanjung Aru Resort
Tanjung Aru
Tel: 088-241 800
Fax: 088-217 155
A very popular and well regarded resort that has grown in popularity and size over the last 10 years. **$$$–$**

City Inn
Jalan Pantai
Tel: 088-218 933
Fax: 088-218 937
A popular small hotel, which is often full; good value **$$**

Town Inn
Jalan Pantai
Tel: 088-225 823
Fax: 088-217 762
Convenient location, clean with good facilities and good value. **$$**

Backpacker Lodge
Lorong Dewan, Australia Place
Tel: 088-261 495

Fax: 088-261 495
A basic backpackers' lodge with dormitories, in a convenient location in the city, close to everything you need before heading into the interior. **$**

Trekker's Lodge
Jalan Pantai
Tel: 088-213 888
Fax: 088-262 818
Clean air-conditioned dormitories and a wealth of travel information; good location. **$**

Pantai Dalit

Pantai Dalit is a 40-minute drive from Kota Kinabalu. A pristine beach area backed by rainforested hills.

ShangriLa Rasa Ria Resort
Pantai Dalit
Tuaran
Tel: 088-792 888
Fax: 088-792 777/792 000
e-mail: rrr@po.jaring.my
This is a big modern resort, perfect for holiday makers, including families. Activities include crabbing and fishing along the shore as well as the more traditional watersports and beach activities. Situated about 40 minutes from Kota Kinabalu. **$$$–$**

Nexus Golf Resort Karambunai
Menggatal
Tel: 088-411 222/411 030
Fax: 088-411 020/412 028
e-mail: nexushtl@tm.net.my
This luxurious new resort is about 30 minutes from Kota Kinabalu by road. Situated on a pristine beach with adjacent golf course.

Tunku Abdul Rahman Park

These offshore islands just outside Kota Kinabalu have attractive chalet accommodation on Pulau Manukan, with one restaurant serving continental and Asian dishes. Prices are in the **$–$$** category.

For bookings, contact Kinabalu Gold Resorts Block C, Karamunsing Complex in Kota Kinabalu; tel: 088-243 629/245 742; fax: 088-242 861.

Gaya Island has a privately-run resort and some snorkelling and diving.

Mt Kinabalu NP

Accommodation both in the park and outside has been privatised, making it necessary to book through Kinabalu Gold Resorts, Block C, Karamunsing Complex, Kota Kinabalu, tel: 088-243 629/245 742; fax: 088-242 861.

Within Kinabalu Park, the company manages a variety of lodges and chalets with prices ranging from **$$–$$$**. Large dormitories with shared kitchen facilities also have budget-priced rooms.

Laban Rata Resthouse can also be booked through Kinabalu Gold Resorts, with prices in the **$** range. The company also arranges porter hire and climbing permits. Slightly higher up are the **Waras Hut** and **Gunting Lagadan Hostel** with very basic facilities **$**. Poring Hot Springs has accommodation prices from **$–$$$**.

Located just outside the park limits, the **Mesilau Nature Resort** has chalets and lodges with prices ranging from **$$–$$$**.

Rina Ria Lodge
Mile 36, Ranau Road
Tel: 088-889 282
Within walking distance of the park entrance, this hotel is very convenient when the park is full. Hostel and more luxurious accommodation available. **$–$$$**

Kundasang

Some 3 km (2 miles) from Kinabalu National Park, Kundasang is the location for a rash of new hotels and chalets for park visitors.

Hotel Perkasa
Mt Kinabalu, Kundasang
Tel: 088-889 511
Fax: 088-889 101
The rooms enjoy great views of Mt Kinabalu. Good facilities including tennis and shops. The hotel is also a handy 20-minute drive from Mt Kinabalu Golf Course. **$$–$$$**

Gayana Resort
Pulau Gaya
Tel: 088-264 461
Fax: 088-264 460
A water resort with stilted chalets built over the sea, backed by rainforest. Watersports facilities and jungle walks. **$$$**

Tambunan
Gunung Mas Highland Resort
Kota Kinabalu Road
Tel: 011-811 562
A small highland resort with tree-top cabins, as well as dormitory accommodation and suites. The resort is close to Tambunan and Tenom – the starting point for white-water rafting trips – and is also near both the Keningau Golf Club and the Crocker Range Rafflesia Centre. **$–$$**
Tambunan Resthouse
Tambunan
Tel: 087-774 331
Located on a hilltop, this pleasant resthouse has great views, and a comfortable bar and dining facilities. Each of the six rooms has an ensuite bathroom. **$**

Tenom
A highland town in the centre of Murut country. It is close to the Agricultural Research Station and the new agro-tourism park lies within the boundaries of the research station, as does the magnificent orchid park.

Perkasa Hotel Tenom
Tel: 087-735 811/736 166
Fax: 087-736 134
Overlooking Tenom town, on top of a hill, the seven-storey hotel has full facilities and great views. You can call to be picked up from the railway station and staff are eager to help with local knowledge. **$$$**
Antanom Hotel
Tomani Road
Tel: 087-736 381
Cute, characterful and on the main street. **$**
Lagud Sebrang Resthouse
Agricultural Research Station
Tel: 087-737 952
Fax: 087-737 571
Located within the grounds of the

research station, this resthouse is out of town and transport (or a tour) is needed. It has three double rooms, outdoor dining, views and beautiful gardens. **$**

Labuan
This tax haven island is a popular stop-off for those wanting to buy duty-free goods or simply to see Malaysia's own slice of offshore economics in action. There is also a well-kept war cemetery.
Hotel Sheraton Labuan
Jalan Merdeka
Tel: 087-422 000
Fax: 087-422 222
Situated opposite the financial park, the Sheraton offers the best in service and cuisine. **$$$**
Hotel Global
Jalan OKK Aawang Besar
Tel: 087-425 201
Fax: 087-425 180
A new hotel with good facilities; good value. **$$**
Victoria Hotel
Jalan Bungah Kasuma
Tel: 087-412 411
Fax: 087-412 550
Old hotel that retains some character; private bathrooms. **$$**

Sandakan
Sandakan is the base for visitors embarking on tours to east Sabah. Many people choose to stay outside the town itself, at the Renaissance Hotel, or further afield at Sepilok, where it is quieter and probably safer.
Sandakan Renaissance Hotel
Jalan Utara Km 1
Tel: 089-213 299
Fax: 089-271 271
This one-time colonial governor's house has been rebuilt and upgraded so that the old architecture has all but

disappeared. Located slightly out of town in a pleasant hilly location. **$$$**
Uncle Tan's Bed & Breakfast
Km 29 Labuk Road
(5 km/3 miles past the Sepilok turnoff)
Tel: 089-531 917
Fax: 089-531 639
This friendly guest house is popular with budget travellers. It also has a simple wildlife camp lodge on the Kinabatangan. **$**

Pulau Lankayan
Pulau Lankayan is located north of Sandakan, past the Turtle Islands. The remote coral island has one luxurious dive resort making it a unique hideaway.
Lankayan Dive Resort
Langkayan Island
Tel: 089-765 200
Fax: 089-763 575/763 563
e-mail: psrt@po.jaring.my
A luxurious resort on its own coral island in the Sulu Seas north of Sandakan. Good wreck dives and corals nearby. Dives conducted by divers from the resort's dive centre.

Sepilok
This orang-utan rehabilitation centre, located in the jungle, has several standards of accommodation nearby.
Sepilok Nature Resort
2.5 km (1½ miles) Sepilok Road
Tel: 089-535 001
Fax: 089-535 002
An upmarket resort adjacent to the

The Turtle Islands

Located north of Sandakan, the Turtle Islands have egg-laying turtles arriving almost every day of the year. Chalets to accommodate 20 guests are available on the island. **$**
To visit the islands, contact the Assistant Park Warden, Turtle Islands Park, 9th Floor, Wisma Khoo Saik Chiew, Sandakan, tel: 089-273 453; fax: 089-274 718. Permits and accommodation can also be arranged through a tour operator in Sandakan (*see list of Sightseeing Tours, page 360*).

orang-utan centre, in a garden setting. It has timber air-conditioned chalets with private verandahs overlooking the gardens. **$$$**

Wildlife Lodge
Sepilok Jungle Resort
Sepilok Road
Tel: 089-533 031
Fax: 089-533 029
The lodge is the handiwork of owners John and Judy Lim. It offers a range of accommodation, from campsites to air-conditioned luxury chalets, set amid gardens filled with exotic native birds and butterflies. **$$–$$$**

Sepilok B&B
Jalan Sepilok
Tel: 089-532 288/216 912
Fax: 089-217 668
The lodge offers budget accommodation with both dormitories and double rooms with ensuite bathrooms. **$**

Kinabatangan River, Sukau
Many of the tour operators to Sukau run their own lodges. However, it is possible to stay without booking, if they are not full. Two lodges are right by the end of the road, while the others are a 5-minute boat ride upstream.

Sukau Rainforest Lodge
Sukau
Tel: 089-220 210
Fax: 089-213 614
Run by Borneo Eco Tours, this eco-friendly lodge has accommodation for 40 guests and is located right at the banks of the Kinabatangan River. Solar-powered fans cool the room and ensuite bathrooms have hot water. **$$**

Sukau River Lodge
Sukau
Tel: 089-219 616
Fax: 089-214 570
Operated by Wildlife Expeditions, the lodge accommodates around 40 guests. The food offered at the buffet meals is both delicious and plentiful. **$$**

Lahad Datu
The gateway to Danum Valley, Lahad Datu has an airport with daily flights to Kota Kinabalu. A good road connects it to Sandakan and

Tawau and Semporna to the south.
Executive Hotel
Jalan Teratai
Tel: 089-881 333
Fax: 089-881 777
This hotel is nothing special, but it is fine for an overnight stop in Lahad Datu. **$$**

Silam Lodge
10 km (6 miles) Lahad Datu/ Tawau Road
Tel: 088-243 245
Fax: 088-254 227
Managed by Borneo Nature Tours, the lodge was built by an American timber company and offers a good alternative for those who want to make day visits to the Danum Valley. **$$**

Price Guide

Prices are for a standard double room during peak periods.
$$$$: more than RM400
$$$: RM200–400
$$: RM100–200
$: less than RM100

Danum Valley
Sabah's hidden Danum Valley of 483 sq. km (186 sq. miles) of pristine rainforest has a sole upmarket resort to accommodate visitors. There is a field study centre available only to serious bona fide researchers. The rainforest is teeming with wildlife, although it can be difficult to see it; you'll need plenty of time and patience.

Borneo Rainforest Lodge
Danum Valley
Tel: 089-880 206/7
Fax: 089-885 051
Based on Tiger Tops in Nepal, this pleasing nature resort is located beside the Segama River facing a misty and untrammelled jungle. Built on elevated plank-walks, the chalets are comfortable with good facilities. Guides and talks are available for visitors. **$$$**

Tawau
This airport town is the easiest access point to Semporna and Pulau Sipadan.

Marco Polo Hotel
Jalan Clinic
Tel: 089-777 988
Fax: 089-763 739
Popular with tourists as well as businessmen, it is the best hotel in town and has a good bar. **$$**

Pan Sabah Hotel
Jalan Stephen Tan
Tel: 089-762 488
Good value, and a convenient location close to the bus station. **$**

Semporna
The gateway to Pulau Sipadan and the other offshore islands, Semporna is a fine overnight stopover.

Dragon Inn
Semporna Tourist Jetty
Tel: 089-781 088
Fax: 089-781 088
This stilted hotel over the sea has a great location and adequate facilities, including a seafood restaurant. **$$**

Pulau Sipadan
The lure of Sipadan's out-of-this-world-class diving has created a kind of eco-nightmare on the island, with too many people crammed into too small a space in confined resorts. The surrounding islands of Kapalai and Mabul offer excellent alternative and spacious accommodation which eases the overcrowding on Sipadan.

Sipadan Island Resort
Sipadan Island
Tel: 089-765 200
Fax: 089-763 575/763 563
One of the better resorts located on Sipadan Island with its own well-run dive centre. **$$**

Borneo Divers Resort
Tel: 088-222 226
Fax: 088-221 550
e-mail: bdivers@po.jaring.my
Borneo Divers' own resort on Sipadan.

Pulau Kapalai
Kapalai Dive Resort
Kapalai Island
Tel: 089-782 322/765 200
Fax: 089-763 575/763 653
e-mail: psrt@po.jaring.my
An upmarket stilt village built over a reef with comfortable rooms and

verandahs looking towards a distant horizon of sea and sky, 10 minutes from Pulau Sipadan. **$$$**

Pulau Mabul

Mabul island is about 10 minutes from Sipadan. While Sipadan has the best diving, alternative accommodation on the other nearby islands is recommended.

Sipadan Mabul Resort
Mabul Island
Tel: 088-230 006/7
e-mail: mabul@po.jaring.my
Located on the island itself, the resort consists of beach chalets that look across to Pulau Sipadan. The all-inclusive price covers diving, watersports and meals. **$$$$**

Sipadan Water Village Resort
Mabul Island
Tel: 088-221 221
Fax: 088-219 233
e-mail: panborn@po.jaring.my
A stylised water village built on stilts which reaches out over shallow reefs from the main island. Comfortable and quiet with few distractions and a good restaurant and dive shop. **$$$**

Permits can be obtained from the Sabah Parks (east coast office), 9th Floor, Wisma Khoo Saik Chiew, Sandakan, tel: 089-273 453; fax: 089-274 718.

Where to Eat

All of Malaysia's medium-class hotels have decent eateries, the higher-class ones have good restaurants, while hotels at the very top of the range will probably have at least one Western outlet – but these are not listed here unless they are outstanding.

Hotels also usually offer high-tea at the weekend, and their coffee houses would have the usual buffet breakfast, lunch and sometimes dinner, to cater to value-for-money demand. Western fast food chains such as McDonald's, KFC, and A&W are everywhere, for those who cannot possibly stomach another scorcher of a curry. There are also fairly decent burger stalls, run by Malay boys.

Otherwise, try the local fare, which are not only different according to where you are, but subdivide into regional varieties, too. The best often comes as hawker food, sold at street stalls or in coffeeshops; sometimes you can get authentic preparations in restaurants, but you miss out on the atmosphere of the roadside stalls. Restaurants charge a 10 percent government tax and 5 percent service tax.

Breakfast is served from about 6am, lunch 11.30am–2.30pm, and dinner 6.30–11pm, although some places open until 2am; supper joints close at 3.30–4am.

Restaurant Listing

Restaurants are listed in the same order as they appear in the Places section, but focus on the main tourist destinations. The restaurants are in alphabetical order within price categories, with hawker food at the bottom.

KUALA LUMPUR & ENVIRONS

Kuala Lumpur

Malay

Restoran Rasa Utara
Bukit Bintang Plaza
Tel: 03-248 8369
This chain serves Malay specialities, including satay, and spicy *sambal* and *rendang*; fully air-conditioned. **$$**

Restoran Seri Melayu
1 Jalan Conlay
Tel: 03-245 1833
A tourist-targeted outfit complete with Minangkabau roof and nightly cultural performances, but the food is decent; buffet available. **$$**

Hawker Food

The best Malay fare is in Kampung Bahru, from satay to rice porridge, curries and soups, and a chance to sample the cooking styles of the different states. Head towards the stalls at Jalan Raja Mahadi. You'll find good *nasi lemak* at the Benteng stalls by the Klang River in Masjid India, particularly Nasi Lemak Benteng Utama; these stalls are, however, open only at night. **$**

Chinese

Fortune Palace
Melia Kuala Lumpur, Jalan Imbi
Tel: 03-242 8333
Cantonese and Szechuan specialities, with *dim sum* served both for breakfast and lunch. Open from 7am. **$$**

Hakka Restaurant
Jalan Bukit Bintang
Tel: 03-985 8492
Serves superb Chinese Hakka food. **$$**

Kapitan's Club
Jalan Ampang
(opposite Standard Chartered)
Tel: 03-201 0242
A charming restored shophouse with antique furnishing and good Nonya house specials such as the curried Kapitan Chicken. **$$**

Lee Ho Fook Restaurant
Jalan Sultan Ismail
Tel: 03-264 3391
Famous chain with Cantonese specialities such as spare ribs,

sharksfin soup, and abalone concoctions. **$$**

Lee Wong Kee
Jalan Tunku Abdul Rahman
Chinese specialities such as fried sharksfin with salad leaf appetiser and lemon chicken. **$$**

Esquire Kitchen
Level 1 Sungei Wang Plaza
Jalan Bukit Bintang

Tel: 03-248 4506
A variety of Chinese delicacies such as noodles fried Chinese style; well known for its *woh tieh* or fried dumplings. **$**

Hawker Food
All sorts of Chinese fare can be found from morning until the wee hours in Chinatown, while the night

stalls are on Jalan Alor, and behind Jalan Imbi (especially for *bah kut teh* pork rib soup). **$**

Indian
Bombay Palace
388 Jalan Tun Razak
Tel: 03-245 4241/7220
Fine Indian food in a beautiful setting; with large variety of spicy

Fruits of the Land

Though seasonal, there is fruit all year round, cheapest and freshest at a *pasar tani* (farmer's market), *pasar malam* (night market), or rural roadside stalls. Malaysian fruit also features in local *kuih* (cakes) and desserts.

Durian, the football-sized "king of the fruits", emanates a distinct smell that evokes either love or disgust. Passionate Malaysians will travel miles for the best and spend a week's salary on one fruit. Although available all year round, the prime season is June to August. A spiked green casing encompasses a sweet, creamy yellow flesh.

Mangosteens are a traditional accompaniment to the durian, as they are believed to "neutralise" the potent, "heaty" properties of the latter. The size of a small orange, the mangosteen's thick, dark purple skin is squeezed open to reveal five to eight snowy-white segments. The flesh is perfectly astringent and sweet, but mind the rind's staining purple juice.

Rambutan is an egg-shaped red fruit covered in dark thin hair and grows in bunches. A relative of the lychee, the rambutan's translucent white flesh, hugging a flat seed, is extremely succulent and sugary sweet. Open the rambutan by inserting a thumbnail into the thin rind. Rambutans are also canned.

Pomelos are a large sweet grapefruit that the Chinese consider auspicious because it resembles an orange (*kum* meaning "gold"). Beneath the green rind and a thick layer of spongey pith, are the large

segments which are gently prised apart. Perak has indisputedly the sweetest and juiciest pomelos in Malaysia.

Papayas were introduced into Southeast Asia in the 16th century, and today, local varieties abound. Hailed for its digestion-aiding properties, the local papaya is about 30 cm (1 ft) long with a yellow skin. In the fruit's hollow centre lies a mass of slippery, round black seeds. The orange flesh is smooth and slightly sweet.

Starfruit is pale yellow fruit with a waxy edible skin covering a translucent watery flesh. Eaten raw, or juiced for an acidic, slightly sweet thirst-quencher.

Jackfruit (*nangka*) is a large fruit that grows all year round. It is often seen on trees covered with sacks or plastic bags to keep away birds and insects. Averaging 50 by 25 cm (18 by 9 in), its thick rind is bumpy and greenish yellow. Inside are 20–30 oval seeds encased by thick sweet and fragrant flesh, with a firm, plasticky texture. A relative is the **chempedak**, which is smaller, with sweeter, creamier-textured and stronger-smelling flesh. Battered and deep-fried, they make a delicious snack.

Pineapples are grown in the southern state of Johor, while a sweet variety is a Sarawak signature. Locals sprinkle salt onto slices of the fruit – fresh pineapples are said to "cut the tongue", probably an enzymatic process, and salt supposedly counteracts this painful effect.

Ciku (pronounced "chickoo") looks like a hairless kiwi fruit. Its light

brown flesh is unmistakably sweet and smooth, with a pear-like, gritty texture. Flat, black seeds are found in the centre of each fruit.

Guava (*jambu*) comes in two varieties: a smaller, softer pink, or larger, harder white with an edible green casing. Generally, the former are sweeter and juicier, while the latter are crisp and milder-tasting. Locals eat the fruit with various condiments such as a sweet-sour plum powder. The best come from Perak.

Duku is about the size of a golf ball, and is available from August to September. Its leathery light-brown rind is peeled off to reach the small segments of transparent tangy-sweet flesh around a hard small green seed. **Langsat** is a relative, but with a much thinner, lighter-coloured skin. Also available is *duku langsat*, a hybrid.

Buah susu, literally "milk fruit"; this passion fruit comes in many delicious varieties: crisp-skinned orange from Indonesia, purple from Australia and California, and local ones with soft, velvety yellow skins. The translucent seeds are sweet and juicy.

Custard apples are not apples at all. About the size of a fist, the knobby green skin encloses black seeds wrapped by delicate sweet flesh, which is custardy smooth and fragrant.

Mangoes come in different varieties in Malaysia: small, hard and fragrant jungle types, eaten with salt or a spicy soy sauce dip; sweet, bright orange varieties dripping with juice; and pale yellow, milder-tasting ones of Thai origin.

and non-spicy meat and vegetable dishes, including North Indian breads. **$$$**

The Taj
Crown Princess Hotel
Jalan Tun Razak
Tel: 03-262 5522
Award-winning restaurant with an excellent menu, including vindaloo, tandoori and Goanese dishes in an authentic Indian setting and often with live music. **$$$**

The Bangles
60A Jalan Tuanku Abdul Rahman
Tel: 03-298 6770
Kuala Lumpur's oldest Indian restaurant; serving authentic, fragrant North Indian Mughlai cuisine for 25 years. **$$**

Hawker Food
The *teh tarik* tea stall with *roti canai* bread and *dhall* curry is literally round every corner, and a stall somewhere is bound to be open no matter the time. There are bigger shops which also sell rice accompanied by an array of spicy curries on banana leaves behind Istana Hotel, on Jalan Tunku Abdul Rahman, Masjid India, and Brickfields. **$**

Local/Fusion
Be Be's
Hotel Capitol
Jalan Bukit Bintang
Tel: 03-243 7000
Affordable East-West meals in a lovely contemporary setting; good selection of wines and beer. **$$**

Bon Ton
Jalan Kia Peng
Tel: 03-241 3614
A gorgeous old bungalow behind the nightspots, with excellent Malay, Peranakan and Western fusion fare such as the Nonya *pie tee* pastry, chicken and mushroom pie, and grilled rack of lamb; set meals are good; so book ahead. **$$**

Sakura
Jalan Imbi
Tel: 03-242 2319
Hawker fare in a restaurant setting, although the air-conditioning is at sub-zero temperatures. Good *nasi lemak*, curry *laksa* and desserts; also steak and other Western fare.

There are hawker stalls round the corner and a famous beef noodle eatery down the road. **$$**

Malayan Aroma
City Square Centre
Jalan Tun Razak
Tel: 03-262 1566 ext. 250
Serves a wide range of locally-grown coffees and teas. Limited but interesting menu; a special is its gratinated spinach *popia* (a local version of Mexican *fajitas*). **$**

Other Asian
Chikuyo-Tei
Plaza See Hoy Chan
Jalan Raja Chulan
Tel: 03-230 0729
Good-value Japanese set meals for lunch and dinner. **$$**

Korean BBQ
Life Centre, Jalan Sultan Ismail
Tel: 03-242 0425
Good, self-cooking hot plate-type lunch buffet with variety of meats, seafood and vegetables in open area, but you still leave smelling smoky. **$$**

Restoran Sri Thai
42 Jalan Sultan Ismail
Tel: 03-248 1284, 03-248 1282
Traditional Thai cuisine at its best. **$$**

Western
Lafite
Shangri-La Hotel
Jalan Sultan Ismail
Tel: 03-232 2388
Fine French fare in classical continental setting. **$$$$**

Ciao
Jalan Tun Razak
Tel: 03-985 4827
Authentic Italian pasta and pizza in a candlelit bungalow; has some good wines. **$$$**

Marche Mediterranean Restaurant
Rennaisance Kuala Lumpur
Jalan Sultan Ismail/Jalan Ampang
Tel: 03-262 2233
Buffet of antipasti, *mezze* and tapas, breads and salads; interesting bar and open-grill and wood-oven kitchen; wines. **$$$**

Coliseum Cafe
Jalan Tunku Abdul Rahman
Tel: 03-292 6270
Lamb and beef steaks with fries in

a colonial setting so real it is easy to imagine bushy-moustached white planters at the bar complaining about the heat. **$$**

Le Coq D'Or
Jalan Ampang
Tel: 03-242 9732
Chops and fish-and-chips in a beautiful colonial bungalow with a romantic history; only the downstairs dining area and massive bathrooms are open to patrons. **$$**

T.G.I. Friday's
Life Centre, Jalan Sultan Ismail
Tel: 03-263 7761
Good Western dishes in large portions with an array of alcoholic and non-alcoholic drinks; American paraphernalia on the walls; good music and friendly waiters. **$$**

NORTHWESTERN PENINSULA

Cameron Highlands
The Smokehouse Hotel
Tanah Rata
Tel: 05-491 1215
Delectable cream teas, lunch and afternoon teas on the terrace, which on a fine day offers a peaceful view of the hills. Fine dining of English fare including steaks, pies, seafood; light meals all day long in the conservatory. **$$$$**

Bala's Holiday Chalet
Lot 55 Tanah Rata
Tel: 05-491 1660
Old English cottage restaurant, well-known for its homestyle cooking, especially its Indian curries; Western fare also available. **$$**

Fern Restaurant
Rosa Passadena Hotel
Brinchang

Tel: 05-491 2288
Decent Western meals, including steaks and chops, but at KL prices. Chinese meals, steamboat at lunch and dinner; high tea. **$$**

Kafe Palm Leaf
Brinchang
In front of Rosa Pasadena, dishes up good Thai, Western and local dishes at reasonable prices. **$**

Tanah Rata's famous Indian fare outlets sit in a row opposite the bus station. Try **Suria's** banana leaf rice and Indian breads. Opposite are Malay hawker stalls. Western set lunches are at **Cafe Downtown** and the **Highlander's Grill**. **Brinchang's** hawker fare is found at the bus terminal and Food Court, and there are stalls throughout town selling Indian breads and curry. Good Chinese at **Kowloon Hotel** and, down the road, Indian fare at **Shal's Curry House**. **$**

Frasers Hill
The Smokehouse Hotel
Jalan Jeriau
Tel: 03-362 2226
Excellent high-tea of scones or apple pie on the garden patio or in the cosy tea room. English meals by candlelight in a beautiful dining room. **$$$$**

Price Guide

These are the prices of meals for two people, including drinks, but excluding alcohol such as wine, which is expensive.
$$$$: more than RM200.
$$$: RM100–200.
$$: RM50–100.
$: less than RM50.

Ipoh
FMS Bar
Jalan Sultan Yusof
Tel: 05-254 0591
This rather worn-down colonial gem by the Padang serves Western-style meals; its bar has hardly changed since British administrators sipped at its counters. **$$**

Restoran Yum Yum
5 Persiaran Green Hill
Tel: 05-253 7686

The new gourmet lane of Ipoh is on this stretch perpendicular to Excelsior Hotel, whose eateries are more upmarket than Jalan Leech (*see below*). Among them is this excellent outlet with great Chinese-Nonya ambience; it serves an excellent grouper in basil, and Yum Yum fried chicken. **$$**

Ipoh Tandoori House
135F Jalan Dato Lau Pak Kuan
Tel: 05-548 0806
Opposite Fatimah Hospital in the Ipoh Garden suburb; good North Indian fare in an air-conditioned restaurant; try the breads. **$**

Ming Court
36 Jalan Leong Sin Nam
Tel: 05-255 7134
This popular and good *dim sum* venue near Excelsior Hotel is packed during breakfast. **$**

Sin Yoon Loong
Jalan Bandar Timah
(near Jalan Silang)
This is the original Ipoh coffeeshop, where a fragrant local brew tastes its best. Watch the regulars at breakfast, and try the excellent home-made coconut jam (*kaya*) and toast. **$**

Hawker Food
Chinese hawker fare is found in old Chinese coffeeshops around Jalan Leech (Jalan Bandar Timah). Kedai Kopi Nam Heong has a good range, particularly the Ipoh speciality of chicken *kway teow* (noodle) soup; also available at the crowded and rather airless Kedai Kopi Kong Meng, which offers good *popiah* (fresh springrolls), satay, and the sour-spicy Turf Club *laksa*. A little out of town is Wooley Food Centre and the adjoining Gourmet Square in Ipoh Garden. The Stadium has good Chinese and Malay food. More Malay fare is available at the late-night Pusat Penjaja Padang Kanak Kanak, Jalan Raja Musa Aziz.

Pulau Pangkor
Pan-Pacific Resort
Teluk Belanga
Tel: 05-685 1399
Western dinners at the Pacific Terrace, happy hour cocktails at the bar, seafood BBQ on Wednesday

and Saturday, buffet with daily themes at poolside Hornbill Terrace Restaurant. You can also dine and watch the sun set on a beautiful beach (upon request). **$$$$**

Guan Guan
Pangkor town (near jetty)
Chinese seafood eatery that is good but pricey. **$$**

Yee Lin Seafood Garden
Pasir Bogak
Next to Coral Bay Hotel, established seafood restaurant with typical Chinese decor; serves fresh fish, shellfish and crabs. **$**

Hawker Food
Next to Sri Bayu Hotel in Pasir Bogak, open till the wee hours of the morning, serves excellent Indian *roti* bread and *teh tarik* at night. **$**

Taiping
Bismillah Restoran
(opposite the Town Market)
Enjoy hot, fresh *roti canai* with tea for breakfast and for lunch try Indian *briyani istimewa* (rice and curries). **$**

Jalan Kota
Any number of Chinese seafood restaurants line this road, with fresh produce from the Kuala Sepetang fishing area. **$**

Hawker Stalls
Jalan Panggung Wayang
A multi-ethnic food centre beneath the Fajar Supermarket with delicacies such as *popiah*, satay, *rojak sotong* (squid salad with peanut sauce) and fresh ginger tea. **$**

Penang
The Northam
55 Jalan Sultan Ahmad Shah
Tel: 04-370 1111
Fine Western dining in beautiful plush decor with lovely views. One section is devoted to Italian, and the other to Indian. Signature dishes include Sardinia Roast Lamb, Salmon Carpaccio and Lobster Spaghetti. Good selection of wines. **$$$$**

Eliza Malay Restaurant
City Bayview Hotel
Lebuh Farquhar

Tel: 04-263 3161

Award-winning restaurant serving *kampung*-style buffet meals. Live traditional music and great views of Georgetown. **$$**

Hai Chu Hooi

338 Jalan Tanjung Tokong

Sitting on rocks by the seaside, this secluded basic open-air Chinese restaurant serves superb crabs (try the chilli crabs) and giant prawns. **$$**

Hot Wok

Tanjung Tokong

Tel: 04-899 0858

One of the best places for Peranakan fare; cosy atmosphere with antiques and tiles, and all the traditional dishes. Close to the Island Shopping Plaza. **$$**

Il Ritrovo

Casuarina Beach Hotel

Tanjung Bungah

Tel: 04-881 1711

The most popular Italian restaurant, with a good selection of wines and a lovely setting. **$$**

Modesto's By the Sea

Sandy Bay Paradise Hotel

Tanjung Bungah

Tel: 04-899 8406

Excellent thin-crust pizza in a snazzy pub atmosphere. **$$**

B.M. Sagars Restaurant

Lebuh Bishop

Specialises in North Indian vegetarian food. **$**

Coca Steamboat

Level 3 Island Plaza

Tanjung Tokong

Tel: 04-890 6808

Steaming hot soup-based meal. Cook your own food at the table and order from a large selection of meat, seafood, vegetables and soya products. Air-conditioned. **$**

Dawood Restoran

63 Lebuh Queen (opposite the Sri Mariamman Temple)

Tel: 04-261 1633

Good *roti canai* Indian bread served with *dhall* (lentil curry) and the restaurant's famous Indian-Muslim *nasi kandar*. **$**

Pot Bless Restaurant

Hutton Lane

Tel: 04-263 7984

Made its name with its tasty rich soups like the self-cooking

Food Notes

Eat	Makan
Drink	*Minum*
Bread	*Roti*
Beef	*Daging lembu*
Chicken	*Ayam*
(pronounced "ah-yarm")	
Fish	*Ikan*
(pronounced "ee-karn")	
Vegetables	*Sayur*
Fried noodles	*Mee goreng*
Fried rice	*Nasi goreng*
Salt	*Garam*
Spicy	*Pedas*
Delicious	*Sedap*
A cup of coffee	*Kopi satu*
A cup of tea	*Teh satu*
Water	*Air*
(pronounced "ah-yayr")	
Less sweet	*Kurang manis*
Without sugar	*Tanpa gula*
Without milk	*Tanpa susu*
Without ice	*Tanpa ais*
(pronounced "ice")	
Not enough	*Tak cukup*
Not hot/cold	*Tak cukup*
enough	*panas/sejuk*
Add	*Tambah*
Big	*Besar*
Small	*Kecil*

steamboat, with a large variety of meats, seafood and vegetables. For those who can take it, there is also glutinous rice or bread with durian-flavoured coconut jam. **$**

Hawker Centres

The entire stretch of Persiaran Gurney (Gurney Drive) has the most famous of Penang's foodstalls, selling all of the island's favourites from spicy prawn-based *hokkien mee* to *jiu hoo eng chai* (squid with spinach). They are open from sunset to the wee hours of the morning. Hawker food is also good (and cheaper) at the coffeeshops at Jalan Penang and Jalan Macalister, Pengkalan Weld, and Jalan Burma, up to Pulau Tikus. Fatty Loh's Chicken Rice at Tanjung Bungah has the island's most famous chicken rice, with moist, succulent meat and "oily rice". The Chowrasta stalls off Jalan Penang are a must for *nasi kandar*. **$**

Pulau Langkawi

Beach Garden Resort

Pantai Cenang

Tel: 04-955 1363

Worth the splurge for an evening meal on the beach. Steaks, buttered potatoes, herbed salad, waffles and cream and coffee, not to mention the excellent margaritas; the menu changes nightly. **$$$**

Bon Ton

Pantai Cenang

Tel: 04-955 3643

Charming Balinese-inspired setting; limited menu but wonderful traditional Malay cooking in Western packaging, such as the seafood platter with baked fish in banana leaf, and prawn ravioli in spicy *tom yam* broth. **$$$**

Charlie's Place

Langkawi Yacht Club

Kuah

Tel: 04-966 4978

Great breezy ambience; best place for coffee as the sun sets over the boats, followed by succulent steaks and lamb chops. **$$$**

Prawn Village

Kuah

Typical Chinese restaurant set-up with very bright lights, well-known for its seafood, and signature prawn dishes – try the buttered prawns, sweet and sour, or simply steamed. **$$**

Sari Seafood Restaurant

Kuah

Tel: 04-966 6192

Great sunsets from the wooden deck which sits on stilts over the sea; local Malay fare, specialising in seafood. **$$**

The Barn Thai Jazzaraunt

Kampung Belangga Pecah

Tel: 04-966 1001

Long lamp-lit plank-walk through mangrove forest leads to a lovely wooden cabin that serves excellent Thai food with jazz music in the background and sometimes live bands. Great desserts. **$$**

Restoran Haji Ramli

Pantai Cenang

At the Pantai Tengah end is a simple open-air Malay restaurant with blinking Christmas tree lights, where you choose your seafood from a boat; raw delectable grilled fish, and Thai-style chilli crab; no alcohol sold. **$**

Hawker food
There are Chinese coffeeshops all over Kuah town offering the usual noodle and rice dishes; Malay fare is in the basement of the Lada building and at night, by the taxi stand. **$**

SOUTHERN PENINSULA

Melaka
Ole Sayang Restaurant
198/199 Taman Melaka Raya
Tel: 06-283 1966
Excellent authentic Peranakan cooking and great traditional decor, just ignore the morose staff. It is popular with large groups, so go early for lunch or dinner. **$$**
Restoran de Lisbon
Portuguese Square
Tel: 06-284 8067
Good Malaysian-Portuguese fare, such as devil curry, complete with Portuguese brew; on Saturday evenings there are cultural performances. **$$**
Restoran Peranakan Town House
107 Jalan Tun Tan Cheng Lock
Tel: 06-284 5001
Another gorgeous Peranakan showpiece. All the well-known Nonya dishes are on the menu and there is a nightly cultural show. The same management runs another heritage restaurant, Nam Hoe Villa, in the coastal town of Klebang Besar. **$$**
San Pedro
Portuguese Settlement Ujong Pasir
Tel: 06-245 734
Home-cooked style Portuguese fare, including spicy baked fish in banana leaf. **$$**
Heeren House
1 Jalan Tun Tan Cheng Lock
Tel: 06-281 4241
Set lunches in a cosy and old-world environment, with Western, Peranakan and Portuguese dishes, and delicious cakes. **$**
Hoe Kee Chicken Rice
4 Jalan Hang Jebat
Located just near the bridge and open only from around mid-morning

to lunch, it has remained low key despite the fame won by its delicious Hainanese chicken and billiard ball-sized rice balls; good home-made barley drink. **$**
Madame Fatso's Restoran
Bunga Raya Glutton's Square (facing Melaka Parade)
Famous baked crab and Chinese-style soup-based steamboat. Set in open-air row of hawker stalls where you can gawk at cars that drive past. **$**
Hawker Food
Anuar Catering in Jalan Taman next to the food stalls, dishes up spicy Malay *nasi briyani* rice with chicken

---

Price Guide

These are the prices of meals for two people, including drinks, but excluding alcohol such as wine, which is expensive.
$$$$: more than RM200.
$$$: RM100–200.
$$: RM50–100.
$: less than RM50.

---

or mutton, and accompanied by pickles and *rojak*, a spicy fruit salad. For Melaka-style Malay home-cooking, particularly in the very spicy-sour *asam pedas* style, head for 35 Jalan Merdeka. A hawker centre sits all the way out at Klebang Besar, with goodies such as satay and Malay baked fish (*ikan bakar*) and tables facing the Straits of Melaka. **$**

Johor Bahru
Eden Floating Palace
Johor Bahru Duty Free Zone
Jalan Ibrahim Sultan
Tel: 07-221 9999
This has the final word on big – a converted passenger ferry with three restaurants on four air-conditioned decks, seating 600 diners and serving duty-free wines. Part of the huge Eden seafood chain, Chinese/Western menu. **$$$**
Jaws 5
Straits View Hotel
Jalan Skudai
Tel: 07-223 6062

Very popular, and therefore pricey, but excellent Chinese style seafood in a glitzy over-lit environment – good for Drunken Prawns and Chilli Crab. **$$**
Manhattan Grill
Level 5 Plaza Kota Raya
Tel: 07-224 7946
Famous Western food outlet that does prime rib, stews, steaks, salads; check out the desserts. **$$**
Briyani House
Jalan Kebun Teh
Dishes up the Johor speciality of *briyani gam*, a rice dish served with spicy mutton or chicken and pickles. **$**
Capati Corner
Jalan Kolam Air
Home-made *capati* – Indian bread, served with *dhall* (lentils) or curries and vegetables of your choice. **$**
Prawn House
Jalan Kebun Teh
This seafood joint sits along the same road as the Briyani House, with fresh fish cooked in various styles; a speciality is the yam cake dessert. **$**
Tepian Tebrau Food Centre
Jalan Abu Bakar
A favourite among locals for its seafood steamboat, *nasi briyani* spiced rice with mutton or chicken, *ikan bakar* grilled fish, and the delectable Wahid family recipe *mee rebus* with fat noodles. **$**

Hawker food
Go for Johor favourites, *laksa Johor*, noodles in thick fishy coconut gravy, *ikan bakar* grilled fish and *lontong*, rice cubes in a creamy coconut sauce, at the big hawker centres at Lido Beach and Stulang Laut.

PENINSULA'S EAST COAST

Pulau Tioman
Babura Sea View Chinese Restaurant
Babura Sea View
Kampung Tekek
Breezy beachside Chinese restaurant with excellent seafood. **$**
Liza Restaurant
Kampung Tekek

Good selection of Malay and Western dishes. **$**

Mekong Restaurant
Kampung Paya
Good Chinese-style seafood. **$**

Sunset Boulevard
Kampung Salang
Built on stilts over the sea. You can jump off your boat onto the restaurant itself. Great for a beer and good seafood. **$**

Kuantan

Kampong Restaurant
Hyatt Regency Kuantan
Teluk Cempedak
Tel: 09-566 1234
Built on stilts over the sea, this restaurant serves good Malay and Continental food, and excellent pizzas. **$$**

Pak Su Seafood Restaurant
Batu 6 (6th mile)
Kuantan-Beserah Road
About half-an-hour north of Kuantan, just before De Rhu Beach Resort, sits a breezy Chinese restaurant overlooking the sea, that is well-known for its stuffed crab, salad lobster and spicy-sour *asam* steamed fish. Air-conditioned. **$$**

Cherating

Ranting Resort
Cherating Lama
Tel: 09-581 9068
This may be tiny, but it has great tropical ambience with candles and flowers, and wonderful home-cooked meals; a different, good-value set menu of Western and local fare nightly. **$**

Kuala Terengganu

Good Luck Restaurant
11Y & Z Jalan Kota Lama
Tel: 09-622 7573
Popularly known as Lucky Restaurant, it is centrally located, next to a *bah kut teh* (pork ribs herbal soup) eatery, and serves seafood specialities and frogs legs *à la* Cantonese, as well as one-dish noodle and rice dishes. Air-conditioned upstairs. **$**

Restoran Meka
66/16 Taman Seri Intan
Tel: 09-623 1831
Traditional Terengganu Malay cooking with mainly fish dishes in various spicy coconut concoctions and *ulam*, traditional salads eaten with a prawn paste-based chilli condiment called *sambal belacan*. The dishes are laid out in trays. **$**

Hawker Food
The traditional Malay breakfast of *nasi dagang*, glutinous rice and curry fish is best at Cendering, slightly south of town, but the Batu Buruk beach stalls also cook up a decent meal. There are Chinese hawker stalls behind The Store departmental store.

Kota Bharu

Azam
Jalan Padang Garong
North Indian fare, including breads and *dhall* (lentil curry). **$**

Central Market
The bustling first floor is packed with foodstalls selling local Malay rice and curries – try the *nasi kunyit*

glutinous rice concoction; also there is a large variety of local *kuih* (cakes), which cannot be bought outside Kelantan. **$**

Kedai Kopi White House
Jalan Sultanah Zainab
Located opposite the State Mosque, it is the best place to enjoy *nasi dagang* – unbleached rice with sweet curry sauce. **$**

Kow Lun
Jalan Kebun Sultan
Chinese set-up with meat and vegetable dishes; piping hot noodles, as well as beer. **$**

Hawker Food
Opposite Central Market next to the bus station, stalls are set up at a night bazaar. You can buy satay and other spicy Malay delectables, including Thai-style spicy-sour noodles. **$**

SARAWAK

Kuching

Recommended

Hornbill's Corner Café
Jalan Ban Hock
Tel: 082-252 670
Both a bar and a restaurant, the Hornbill has the best barbeque steamboat in town with an inexpensive all-you-can-eat buffet. The bar has a friendly clientele; cold draught beer and the satellite TV soccer attracts a lot of foreign visitors. **$**

Waterfront Café
Hilton Hotel
Tel: 082-428 200
Gaze out across the Kuching River in air-conditioned comfort as you enjoy excellent espresso, fresh baked bread, salads and delicious food. The café features different food promotions each day. **$**

River Café
Kuching Waterfront, opposite the Chinese Museum
Enjoy local snacks like *popiah* and *laksa* in the evening. Open from 3–11 pm daily.

Western

Beccari's Ristorante
Merdeka Palace Hotel

Eating Out in Kuching

Good food abounds in Kuching, whether it is such typical Malaysian favourites as *roti canai*, chicken rice, or chilli crab, or the usual Western fare often found in the big hotels. Kuching has its own specialities as well – with influences deriving from Malay, Indian, Chinese and Dayak heritages. The slightly sour-ish Sarawak *laksa* is a big favourite, a noodle dish cooked in chicken stock with coconut cream and

spices, as is *umei* – a Melanau dish of raw, marinated fish blended with limes, chilli and shallots. There are the jungle vegetables like *midin* and *paku* – baby fern served boiled or fried with the spicy addition of *belacan* paste and garlic and perhaps a hint of oyster sauce. Fresh seafood, venison, wild boar, *pansoh manok* – an Iban chicken dish cooked in bamboo tubes with rice wine – are not to be missed.

Authentic Italian fare from an authentic Italian chef, plus the best pizzas in town. Sensible prices. **$–$$**

The San Francisco Grill
Jalan Ban Hock
Good service and good steaks make for a pleasant experience. **$–$$**

The Steak House
Hilton Hotel
Tel: 082-428 200
Probably the best steaks in town, plus other excellent dishes with an Italian touch in elegant surroundings. Try the set meal for extraordinarily good value. **$–$$**

Price Guide

These are the prices of meals for two people, including drinks, but excluding alcohol such as wine, which is expensive.
$$$$: more than RM200.
$$$: RM100–200.
$$: RM50–100.
$: less than RM50.

Indian

Several Muslim shops in Jalan Carpenter serve *roti canai* – the delicious fried Indian pancake served with a curry sauce; or equally delicious eaten with sugar. *Murtabak* (meat-filled *roti canai*) is also available, as well as curries and fried chicken. Look out for the National Islamic Café and the Green Restaurant in the Main Bazaar.

Green Vegetarian Restaurant
16 Main Bazaar
Serves all the south Indian favourites and vegetarian food. **$**

Lyn's Tandoori
Lot 62 No 10G
Lorong 4,
Nanas Road
Just a short taxi ride from town. Serves genuine North Indian *tandoori* dishes and *naan*. **$**

Japanese

Kikyo-Tei
Jalan Crookshank (in front of Government Rest House)
Tel: 082-257 886
Japanese, and also Chinese and Western food with a Japanese

touch. Teppanyaki and and Tatami rooms available. **$–$$**

Ten-Ichi
Bangunan Bee San
Jalan Padungan
Tel: 082-331 310/335 042
Serves elegant Japanese food. Book in advance for the weekend. **$–$$**

Chinese

The quaint old streets of Chinatown are lined with *kedai kopi* (coffeeshops) serving fresh Chinese noodle dishes and specialities like roast chicken or pork rice. Wander about until you see a restaurant that looks attractive, find a seat and order up.

Golden Phoenix Restaurant
Ban Hock Road
Tel: 082-415 588
Reasonably priced and eclectic menu with Vietnamese and Thai specialities included. **$–$$**

Meisan
Holiday Inn
Tel: 082-423 111. **$–$$**

River Palace
Crowne Plaza Riverside
Tel: 082-247 777
All the above serve very excellent Chinese cuisine in elegant and cool surroundings. **$–$$**

Toh Yuen
Hilton Hotel. **$–$$**

Seafood

Fresh seafood abounds in Kuching. Look out for *ambal* (bamboo clam), a local speciality. Served steamed or cooked in a mild curry, it tastes far more delicious than it looks.

Benson's Seafood
49 Jalan Abell
Popular spot by the river for fresh seafood, this relaxed place is just past the Holiday Inn. Simply point to the vegetables and fish, crabs, prawns, etc. of your choice and say how you'd like them cooked. **$**

See Good Food Centre
53 Ban Hock Road
Excellent seafood, fresh and affordable. Delicious noodle dishes are served between main meal times. **$**

Top Spot Food Centre
5th Floor, Jalan Bukit Mata Kuching

An open-air seafood plaza where half-a-dozen eating outlets vie for business with tempting displays of fresh seafood on ice. **$**

Hawker Centres
Most of the hawker centres serve excellent local Malay and Chinese favourites at reasonable prices. Try eating the way the locals do – wander about until you see a dish that strikes your fancy and simply order it. **Petanak Central Market** above the Kuching wet market is an early-opener with plenty of local favourites seasoned with local colour. Try it at 4am as the market awakens. A covered market near the Electra House in Jalan Market is good for seafood and noodle dishes and especially the beef noodles. **$**

Sibu

The food in Sibu is as good as elsewhere in Malaysia with plenty of seafood and Chinese restaurants. The strong Chinese population means a variety of Chinese cuisines like Foochow, Szechuan, Cantonese and Teochew.

Golden Palace
Tanahmas Hotel
Jalan Kampung Nyabor
Tel: 084-33 188
Cantonese and Szechuan dishes and plenty of seafood. **$–$$**

Jhong Kuo
13 Jalan Wong Nai Siong
Foochow food of a good standard. **$–$$**

Hock Cho Lau Restaurant
Jalan Blacksmith
A popular Chinese restaurant; good for Foochow duck and fried noodle dishes. **$**

Hawker Centres
These provide a good source of cheap eating. The Rex Food Centre on Jalan Cross has a good selection of outlets as does the hawker centre in Jalan Market. Close to the expressboat jetty, the Gerai Makanan Muslim offers delicious Malay dishes.

Western

Pepper's Café
Tanahmas Hotel

Jalan Kampung Nyabor
Tel: 084-333 188
Good for both Western and local
dishes. **$–$$**
Villa By The Grand
2nd Floor Grand Meridien Building
Jalan Kampung Nyabor
Canadian-run restaurant serving
Western food. **$–$$**

Miri

With a large Western population
and an affluent Chinese community,
Miri has an assortment of eateries
and excellent, reasonably-priced
seafood. In the old part of town,
there are good coffeeshops with
hawkers selling an array of
delicious fried noodle dishes.
Western
Golden Steak Garden
Gloria Hotel, Jalan Brooke
Good steaks. **$–$$**
Holiday Inn
Jalan Temenggong Datuk Oyong
Lawai
Tel: 085-418 888
Serves the best Western food in
town. **$–$$**
Chatterbox Coffee House
Mega Hotel, Jalan Maju
Tel: 085-432 432
Good Western and local food. **$**
Miri Café
Taman Yakin Shopping Centre
Jalan Miri Pujut
Tel: 425 122
A few kilometres from the town
centre, a relaxed café run by an
Australian Chinese man and his
wife. Great array of drinks and
plenty of Australian specialities. **$**

Seafood
Apollo
Lot 394
Jalan Yu Seng Selatan
(close to Gloria Hotel)

Take a walk through the old part
of Miri where the tour guides
never take you – down to the fish
market and an old Chinese
temple. The Jalan Oleander Food
Stalls on the left serve excellent
and authentic Malay food.

Popular seafood restaurant, run on
a similar basis to Maxims. **$–$$**
Maxims
Jalan Pujut
Lutong (next to Bintang Plaza)
Open-air evening eatery. Choose
your fish from the iced fresh
seafood on display and specify the
style of cooking. Informal and good
value. **$–$$**

SABAH

Sabah dining is, generally speaking,
casual, in coffeeshops and hawker
stalls. In Kota Kinabalu there are
several notable restaurants.

Kota Kinabalu
Peppino's
Shangri La Tanjung Aru Resort
Tel: 088-225 800
Italian food with a Filipino band.
$$–$$$
Gardenia Grill Room
Jesselton Hotel
Jalan Gaya
Tel: 088-223 333
Nostalgic and slightly formal, the
Gardenia offers a high standard of
Western cuisine. **$$**

East-West
Café Boleh
Pan Pacific Sutera Hotel
Tel: 088-318 888
24-hour coffee house with delicious
Eastern and Western dishes. **$–$$**
Wishbone Café
Jesselton Hotel
Jalan Gaya
A pleasant air-conditioned
coffeehouse in the downtown area
with local and Western specialities.
$–$$

Chinese
Silk Garden
Pan Pacific Sutera Hotel
High standard Chinese eatery with
great views of the gardens and
marina. **$$–$$$**
Phoenix Court
Hyatt Hotel
Tel: 088-221 234
Excellent *dim sum* served from
7am–2pm daily. Also at the
Poolside Hawker Centre try a

Sabah has its own specialties,
especially vegetable dishes. Best
of all is *sayur manis*, a green
leafy vegetable with a slightly
crunchy stem and sweet green
leaves. Try it in oyster sauce, or
for the Asiaphile, in a spicy
sauce of *sambal belacan* which
has a heady, fishy tang that
takes time to get used to.

Chinese steamboat (minimum two
people).

Japanese
Azuma
2rd Floor Wisma Merdeka
Jalan Tun Razak
Tel: 088-225 533
$$$
Nishiki
On the corner of Jalan Gaya and
Jalan Segunting
Tel: 088-230 582
Good Japanese food. **$$**

Indian
Jothy's Restaurant
Block 1, Lot 9
Api Api Centre
Lebuh Raya Pantai
Clean and air-conditioned, this is
the place for South Indian
specialities including vegetarian
dishes and good fish curries. **$**

Seafood
Port View
Jalan Haji Saman
Tel: 088-242 875
Opposite the old Custom's House
This huge seafood palace has a
good selection of fresh and live
seafood in glass tanks. Great chilli
crab. Popular with locals who know
their seafood. **$–$$**
100% Seafood Restaurant
Jalan Aru
Tanjung Aru
Choose from the fresh iced fish
display and say how you would like
it cooked. **$**
Chuan Hin
Jalan Kolam (next to Cottage Pub)
Luyang
Tel: 088-235 960

Barbequed sting-ray and other delicacies, as well as Chinese specialities such as fried *woh tieh* dumplings (delicious) and fried *kway teow* noodles. A casual open-fronted place whose looks belie the quality of the food. **$**

Singapore Chicken Rice
Gaya Street
Tel: 088-216 982
Chicken Rice, Singapore-style in air-conditioned comfort, at reasonable prices. **$**

Sandakan

This one-time Hong Kong of Malaysia has numerous coffee-shops serving excellent noodle and seafood dishes. Overlooking the town atop Trig Hill are several excellent seafood restaurants.

Golden Palace
Trig Hill
Tel: 089-211 878
Superb seafood and a sumptuous variety. The restaurant offers lifts back to town in the evening. **$–$$**

Ming Restaurant
Renaissance Hotel
Sandakan
Tel: 089-213 299
Just out of town, the Ming serves *dim sum* breakfast and delicious lunches and dinners. **$$**

Semporna

Dragon Inn Restaurant
Semporna Jetty
Tel: 089-781 088
Excellent fresh seafood. The fish and prawns are kept in nets in the sea. **$–$$**

Drinking

Alcohol is expensive in Malaysia. A glass of wine may cost as much as a tot of brandy, but the full range is available. Wine bars are becoming increasingly popular, and also sell cigars. Although alcohol is forbidden to Muslims, it is freely available at pubs, hotels, restaurants and in Chinese eateries, as well as in supermarkets in towns and tourist areas. Tiger and Anchor beers and Guinness Stout are the most popular. Don't be surprised if a bucket of ice is served with your

beer – this is the way many locals enjoy their brews.

Fruit juices are available everywhere – make sure you stipulate that you want yours freshly squeezed, not from a can. If you don't want sugar, ask the waiter not to add the sugar syrup; in Kelantan, salt is often added to cut fruits and juices, so ask for plain fruit or juice.

Young coconuts produce a refreshing clear juice which can be drunk straight from the coconut with ice added and a straw stuck into a hole in the top.

Try soya bean milk, barley or Chinese herbal teas (*leong char*). Mineral water is widely available.

Local coffee and tea pack a punch, and are served with condensed milk and sugar. You can also ask for Nescafé. Decaffeinated and flavoured teas are available only in higher-class restaurants.

American coffee-bar chains are opening up in the cities, which serve finger food, too.

Culture

Museums

All museums in Malaysia are documented in the Places section. Most are open 9am–5pm daily. They close noon–2.30pm on Friday and a half-day on Thursday or Saturday. Admission to museums is free or at a nominal fee. Tours are rare, and information is usually in English and Bahasa Malaysia.

Art Galleries

Malaysia's serious art gained credence only in the 1960s after independence. Art is becoming a popular collectable locally, particularly in Kuala Lumpur, with the increase in number of exhibitions and galleries.

Other than subject matter, there is nothing really to define Malaysian art in terms of style; the diversity is staggering from Chinese brush painting to abstract art and sculpture, although batik would come closest – the artist who pioneered this style, Chuah Thean Teng, has a gallery in Penang.

The best place to see the range of established Malaysian art is at the National Art Gallery, Jalan Temerloh, Kuala Lumpur (tel: 03-274 0157). Newer artists are featured in smaller galleries throughout the country, with many congregating in the trendy Bangsar suburb in Kuala Lumpur. Check dailies for exhibition listings and art spaces.

Music Venue

World-class international music performances are held at the Dewan Filharmonik Petronas in Kuala Lumpur, tel: 03-207 7007.

Galeri Petronas
KLCC, Kuala Lumpur
Tel: 03-207 7770
This circular gallery surrounding a cube of offices is Malaysia's first international museum-quality display space. It also contains an experimental area.

Theatre

Malaysian

Authentic cultural performances are difficult to catch these days. National Day and Malaysia Fest parades in Kuala Lumpur provide some glimpses, while a handful of hotels stage performances, as does Kuala Lumpur's Central Market.

For Malaysian culture, Kota Bharu's Gelanggang Seni (Cultural Centre) is probably the only venue where cultural performances are staged regularly. Competitions held in villages are the best places to watch traditional pastimes and *wayang kulit* (shadow puppetry).

A professional dance troupe has scheduled performances in the Dewan Filharmonik Petronas in Kuala Lumpur, while the Suasana Dance Company is the sole purveyor of the Malay dance-drama.

For traditional Borneo Malaysian native performances, the Sarawak Cultural Village in Kuching has regular shows, but the best performances are in longhouses, the further into the interior the better; the local people are always ready for an excuse to break into music, song and dance. Likewise in the more remote areas in Sabah. The harvest festival in June is the best time to catch the action.

Chinese

Traditional Chinese opera is staged on temporary platforms in the suburbs during special Buddhist and Taoist festivals. Based on mainland Chinese myths and old tales, this sees the use of traditional Chinese costumes and heavy make-up.

Chinese dances are performed only during official functions, but there are many dance groups who use this as a base for modern work.

There are a few classical Chinese orchestras, with Dama being the most professional and creative.

Indian

Classical Indian artforms are well and truly alive, with dance, vocal and instrumental performances held regularly, particularly in temples. The most famous troupe is the Kuala Lumpur-based Temple of Fine Arts, known for its epic productions. It also incorporates contemporary and Malaysian elements in its shows.

Contemporary Arts

The contemporary arts scene is centred in Kuala Lumpur, with some productions in Penang and Ipoh.

Contemporary dancers have small companies and some are quite good, training and performing internationally. The most popular contemporary theatre is the comedy revue, attracting trendy urbanites, although drama, some locally written, is also staged.

The established companies are the Instant Café Theatre, particularly for its revues, the Five Arts Centre which pursues the alternative and Malaysian themes, and the Actors' Studio. For listings, check dailies and the arts website http://www.artseefartsee.com, or call The Actors' Studio, tel: 03-294 5400.

Cinemas

Subtle drama never stays on the billboards long, although *Titanic* wove its magic in Malaysia, too, and the movie that scored as longest-playing was a classic Hindi tear-jerker in the 1970s. Nonetheless, local box-office hits are invariably the action movies, preferably with violence and explosions.

American movies do the circuit in the big urban cinema chains, as well as the odd Hong Kong hit. Otherwise, Bahasa Malaysia, Chinese and Indian language films are screened in the smaller cinemas; English language hits rarely make it to the small towns.

In deference to the official religion of the country, Islam, nude, semi-nude and even kissing scenes between unmarried people are diligently, but not always professionally censored, so that sometimes, vital dialogue disappears, too.

However, the same concern does not always apply to very violent scenes, particularly Hong Kong ghost-story and mafia flicks.

The chain that revived cinema-going and made it fashionable in the early 1990s is Tanjung Golden Village, with its plush multiplexes and prime locations in large shopping complexes. The KLCC also has two THX cinemas.

Other chains are upgrading slowly, but for a taste of the original movie theatre, head for Rex, Cathay and Ruby in Kuala Lumpur, where there is first- and second-class seating, groundnut shells under your feet as well as the occasional rat.

Nightlife

Pubs, discos and karaoke dens are how Malaysians party at night. The best nightlife is in the capital. Elsewhere, the action concentrates in hotel lounges and discos. Other than Kuala Lumpur, people tend not to dress up, but shorts and sandals are definite no-nos.

Nightclubs/Discos

Kuala Lumpur

Nightlife has tended to congregate in specific areas. Clubs and discos may be the trendsetters, but they have a shorter shelf-life and pubs stick around longer, particularly the neighbourhood ones. Generally, club crowds swell after 11pm or even midnight, and there is a cover charge on Friday and Saturday, which includes one drink from a limited menu. In most places, jeans, shorts, collarless T-shirts and sandals are not allowed, and yuppies dress to kill.

Live bands are popular and usually play three sets from 10pm onwards. Almost all the larger hotels have bars featuring live music. This is usually broad-appeal, middle-of-the-road music, so hotel lounges are not listed here unless they have a reputation for something different.

Pub- or disco-hopping has long been happening in the Jalan Sultan Ismail/Jalan Ampang area. The Rennaisance Hotel's basement **Roxy** plays techno and features dancers. Across the road is the **Hard Rock Café** at Concorde Hotel, with great local and international live acts and a small dance floor. Long queues form at the weekend, so go early or book a table for a meal. Concord also has a popular lounge with good acts. Down Jalan Sultan Ismail and into Jalan P. Ramlee under the Petronas Twin Towers are a host of sidewalk coffeeshops and eateries, including **Benson & Hedges Bistro, T.G.I. Fridays**, and **Coffee Bean and Tea Leaf**.

The discos are the **Emporium**, a jazz/pop place, **Brannigan's** with its large beer garden, the ever-yuppie **Modestos'** and **Heaven** upstairs, and **Rio's** down the road. In **Wall Street**, drink prices go up when demand increases (like stocks); the prices are on a screen.

The Backroom behind Shangri-La plays techno and house at the front section, and jungle/rave at the back, and has a young crowd. At KL Hilton, the older, more sophisticated crowd grooves to live 1980s sounds at the **TM2 Fun Bar & Nite Club**. A similar crowd hangs out at Istana Hotel's **Musictheque**, with its huge dance floor, karaoke rooms and huge video walls – and a high cover charge.

The Bukit Bintang area has the open-air relaxed, café-type **Blues Café** at the bottom of Lot 10, which sometimes has good live acts. **Sydney Two Thousand** at Jalan Bukit Bintang is a converted movie theatre that reverberates with non-stop techno. **The Baze** is an established basement joint in Wisma Central, Jalan Ampang, which spins R&B, funk and hip-hop. Elsewhere, Latin rules at **El Nino**, off Jalan Yap Kwan Seng.

Head out to the Bukit Damansara suburb for the country's top jazz act at a basement place called **All That Jazz at Grubz**, where local and international personalities perform with the resident band. There is a huge **Modesto's** too with a very young crowd.

Penang

This is not really a town with a sizzling nightlife. Most of the action tends to centre on the beach hotels, such as the ever-trendy **Modesto's** at Paradise Sandy Bay or **Beers** at Parkroyal Hotel, which is a sports bar with styrofoam figures, boutique beers and a genuine Wurlitzer jukebox. It also has a ceiling of personalised banknotes.

In town, **20 Leith Street**, housed in a beautifully renovated colonial mansion and its walls adorned with scenes by Penang artists and antique clocks, has a beer garden in front and a cosy bar that spins out some great music. Elsewhere in Georgetown's backpacker alley, there are little Chinese watering holes. Bear in mind, however, that some of these are of dubious nature.

Pulau Langkawi

Nightlife concentrates in Pantai Cenang and Tengah, at the little restaurants such as **Beach Garden**, **Champor-Champor** and the beachside, coconut-tree strewn **Charlie Bar's** at the end. There is a disco at **Holiday Villa**, while for good jazz and a great atmosphere, visit **Barn Thai**. Sheraton Langkawi Beach Resort's **Black Henry**, with its regular live acts, remains a favourite.

Bangsar – the Place to Party

The most "happening" place in Kuala Lumpur is a suburb south of the city centre called Bangsar, where the young and not-so-young but totally trendy hang out. Here, neck-to-neck are bars, coffee bars, restaurants and art galleries, whose names you don't bother remembering because the sky-high rents ensure they don't last anyway. This is where the expatriates hang out, and like bees to the honey pot, the so-called *sarong* party girls, whom they pick up (or vice-versa). There's always no parking here, and lots of partying. At one end is a huge all-night hawker centre with Malay and Indian fare, to which the bleary-eyed and not-so-sober retire when the party ends anywhere around town.

Cherating

The action focuses on Kampung Cherating, and usually starts at **Pop Inn** at the northern end, where a live band plays from Thursday to the weekend, moves on to the dimly-lit **La Pippin** down the road, and usually ends up in the wee hours at **Nan's Beach Bar**, behind Coconut Inn. **Club Med's** guest relations officers come in for a taste of – or to add to – the action. The **Moon's Deadly Nightshade** is a tiny hillside bar-restaurant in a rough *attap*-roofed open setting with great ambience.

Kuching

Kuching is a relaxed town where the friendly inhabitants like to enjoy themselves. A popular stop off point for visitors is the **De Tavern** opposite the Hilton. This is a place to try Iban hospitality where the girls are pretty and chatty and the atmosphere is informal. **Hornbill's Cafe and Corner Pub** is also a popular meeting place with both locals and visitors on Jalan Ban Hock. Pubs, discos and karaoke bars abound, from the more upmarket venues in the big hotels like the Hilton to small, dimly-lit places that hide between bigger buildings.

Kota Kinabalu

In Kota Kinabalu try **The Cottage** on Jalan Bukit Pandang, a popular gathering place for both locals and visitors, or the lively pub at the **Pan Pacific Hotel**.

Shopping

General

Shopping malls are found in every city and comprise a supermarket, department store (the big chains sell branded goods), and lots of little shops, including boutiques, shoe-stores, and stores selling watches, electrical goods, computers, mobile phones, music shops, bookshops and/or stationery/magazine stores, sometimes with money changers and tour agencies, cinemas and video-arcades. Some malls specialise in certain items. They usually have eateries, too, including hawker fare-type food courts, Western fast food chains, or restaurants.

Kuala Lumpur

From branded goods to rustic handicrafts, foodstuffs to software, Kuala Lumpur's shops have it all. The shopping area is Bukit Bintang around Jalan Bukit Bintang and Jalan Sultan Ismail. Here you'll find Bukit Bintang Plaza (BB Plaza), which is joined to Sungei Wang Plaza, well-known for its electrical items and photographic equipment. The more upmarket Lot 10 is across the road from Sungei Wang Plaza with mid- to high-priced items and branded goods in the top floor; there's a good bookshop, too. Down the road is the even more upmarket Starhill Centre, with its international shops. Next door at KL Plaza is the American Tower Records, Kuala Lumpur's largest music store. Along Jalan Imbi, Imbi Plaza is the place for computer goods, including software and peripherals.

Central Market is probably the best place for souvenirs, with its two levels offering Malaysiana, Asian hand-crafted goods and souvenirs, and artwork. Kuala Lumpur's glitziest shopping mall to date is the modernistic Suria KLCC at the base of the Petronas Twin Towers, which houses all the big chains as well as interesting boutique shops, international cuisine and cosy cafés as well as cinemas.

Sogo Kuala Lumpur on Jalan Raja Laut is one of the largest department stores in Southeast Asia with eight floors, a waterfall on the top floor where the restaurants are, and good sales.

Down the road, Pertama Complex sells cheaper goods, but is good for shoes. The Mall on Jalan Putra opposite the Putra World Trade Centre is still popular for *haute couture* and specialist shops; there is a stuffy hawker centre on the top floor and souvenir stalls.

Jalan Tuanku Abdul Rahman has small interesting shops selling Asianware such as Chinese embroidery and antiques. The Globe Silk Store along this road has affordable clothes and textiles. Jalan Tuanku Abdul Rahman is closed to traffic every Saturday 5–10pm and transformed into a *pasar malam* (night market) with bargain goods hawked in stalls.

Jewellery, Indian saris and comfy cotton *kurta*-pyjamas are found behind this road in Masjid India. The famous and crowded Petaling Street *pasar malam* comes to life 5–11pm every evening, with a variety of stalls offering textiles, clothes, leather goods, jewellery, and "designer watches".

Melaka

The best place to shop is undeniably Jonker Street (now Jalan Hang Jebat), a haven for antique-collectors and bargain-hunters. Authentic artefacts and relics, some 300 years old, can be found among a host of interesting collectables, each with its own history and mystery.

Check out Wah Aik Shoemaker Shop at No. 92 for its tiny shoes made for Chinese women with bound feet, an ancient tradition of beauty that is dying out. Amid the history are the trendy modern and creative handicraft shops such as the Orang Utan House at No. 59, run by an artist whose humorous T-shirts and artwork make great souvenirs.

Handicraft stalls are at Taman Merdeka, and there is a *pasar malam* on Sunday at Jalan Parameswara.

The city's biggest shopping mall is the Mahkota Parade at Jalan Merdeka, which also has an Asian antique and handicraft centre.

Penang
Georgetown's maze of little shops around Jalan Penang are great for antiques and curios, such as antique clocks, old bronze and brassware, chinaware, Dutch ceiling lamps, old phonographs and Chinese embroideries and porcelain and batik. Saw Joo Aun at 139 Jalan Pintai Tali has a large range of antique furniture.

Elsewhere in Penang, Little India on Lebuh King and Lebuh Queen has brightly-coloured saris and *kurta*, brassware and jewellery. Chulia Street has good second-hand bookshops.

Chowrasta Market specialises in all kinds of cotton, silk and other materials, as well as dried local foods such as nutmeg and preserved fruits.

More bargain-price Chinese

Night Markets

Open-air *pasar malam* (night markets) are good to soak in the local atmosphere and find bargain-price items, including clothes (which you try on in the open), shoes, trinkets, CDs and VCDs (often pirated) and household items. You can usually buy fresh produce, including fruit, and delicious local street food and titbits. The traders are itinerant, so check locations in the local press or at your hotel.

souvenirs are at the Kek Lok Si Temple in Ayer Itam. Batu Ferringhi and Teluk Bahang have brightly-coloured, hand-painted batik sarongs and T-shirt souvenirs; the night market at the former sells fake but decent quality designer clothes and watches.

Modern shopping malls are at KOMTAR, Yaohan and Gama on Jalan Penang, the Midlands Shopping Mall on Jalan Kelawei, the suburban Sunshine Square in Bayan Baru and Bukit Jambul Complex, which also has an ice-skating rink.

Johor Bahru
Like KL, Johor Bahru is home to giant shopping malls, the biggest of which is the 440-unit Holiday Plaza on Jalan Dato Suleiman. Another popular spot is the Plaza Pelangi in Taman Pelangi.

The new Johor Bahru Duty Free Complex on Jalan Ibrahim Sultan (Stulang Laut) which comprises multiple facilities, sits on a 160-metre (540-ft) waterfront, and includes 180 of the usual kind of shops over four floors.

Bargain-hunters head for Kompleks Lien Hoe, just off Jalan Tebrau, which has a bazaar on the ground floor.

JARP (Johor Area Rehabilitation Organisation) on Jalan Sungai Chat has a showroom and workshop where handicapped people produce cane furniture, soft toys, rattan baskets as well as bind books. Commercialised handicrafts are at Mawar House on the same road.

There is a *pasar malam* (night market) on Jalan Tebrau every Monday.

Terengganu
Jalan Bandar is the place to head for, with the Central Market selling batik and local handicraft.

Teratai Arts and Craft, at No. 151, is a lovely gallery/shop owned by renowned artist Chang Fee Ming. It showcases his depictions of local life, as well as curios from all over Asia, including coconut shell craft and textiles.

The Batik Gallery next to the Chinese temple has contemporary hand-printed batik cotton material and souvenirs as well as interesting clothing designs beyond the usual *kaftan* and shapeless shirts.

Antiques and Curios in Kuching

Shopping is a Kuching speciality. Antiques, Iban textiles, handicrafts, and quality collectables as well as pretty and interesting handcrafted souvenirs are readily available in what is perhaps the best antique market in Malaysia.

Walking down the Main Bazaar can take all day for a shopping enthusiast. Old trading houses and shophouses have been converted and restored into galleries and shops selling a range of goods.

Look out for Fabriko, with Edric Ong's fine range of silk woven *pua*

blankets, and scarves with authentic Iban motifs using natural dyes. Nelson's Gallery offers an eclectic collection – even if you don't buy, a meeting with this local character is a must. Margaret Tan's Galeri M in the Hilton Lobby has a fine collection of antique *pua*, jewellery and numerous collectables. Lucas Goh's Atelier opposite the Chinese museum is also filled with fine textiles and collectables, while Arts of Asia, in the Main Bazaar, has beautifully crafted wooden bowls, statues,

and woodcarvings among its treasures. Richard Yong's Sarawak House has fine top-end pieces.

In addition there are several air-conditioned malls with lots of shops selling food, adventure gear and fashion items.

Don't miss Kuching's Sunday market which starts on Saturday afternoon. Held at Jalan Satok, the market is filled with Bidayuh vegetable sellers, Chinese and Malay stalls selling all manner of handicrafts, jungle products, wild honey, pets, snacks and plants.

Kelantan

Like Terengganu, Kota Bharu's Central Market has copious amounts of batik and foodstuffs. The ultimate handicraft heaven is the road to PCB (Pantai Cahaya Bulan), along which certain *kampung* are renowned for their particular handicraft – grab a Tourism Malaysia brochure.

Kota Kinabalu

Kota Kinabalu is more orientated towards adventure and relaxation than shopping. Several air-conditioned plazas have an array of shops selling locally-made clothes and some international brands.

Some handicraft shops can be found in the Wisma Karamunsing and the Wisma Merdeka where Borneo Books has the best range of books on the country. Borneo Handicraft has plenty of handicrafts but purists will find that most come from Bali.

The Filipino Market offers an interesting excursion into the more colourful side of Kota Kinabalu – pearls (some genuine), Filipino handicrafts, basketware and shell crafts abound. But beware of pickpockets; there have been reports of bag-snatching and worse.

Sport

The country's national sport is football (soccer), but favourites include badminton, basketball, hockey, netball, table-tennis, tennis, squash, *sepak takraw* (a local game), fishing, bowling, volleyball, martial arts and golf. In regional and international competitions, Malaysia has tended to shine in badminton and bowling, with squash being a rising star. Sports development falls under voluntary organisations, many affiliated to the Olympic Council of Malaysia.

Fishing

Malaysia offers good fishing but the sport is not regulated or organised. Boats range from bare basics to converted trawlers, and unless you go with a tour, you have to bring your own equipment. Shops stock the range, but do not rent. Malaysia is a manufacturer of rods and reels and is, in fact, a good and relatively cheap place to buy fishing equipment. Fishing tackle shops are plentiful in all major towns.

Freshwater Fishing

Malaysia's fast-flowing rivers offer good fishing upstream, with smaller fish, but a more pristine rainforest environment, usually accessible via four-wheel drive and some walking. Good spots include upper Sungai Endau in Johor, and the higher reaches of rivers that flow into Kenyir (Terengganu) and Temenggor (Perak). Here, you get the *kelah* (Malaysia Mahseer), a good fighter with which locals usually practise catch-and-release, and *tengas*, which also make fun fishing. Bigger-sized *kelah* are found in the middle river, as are *kaloi* (giant gouramey), *belida* (giant featherback) and the

powerful *toman* (giant snakehead), the so-called shark of Malaysian freshwater fish.

Rivers in Sarawak and Sabah are excellent fishing grounds, particularly near the Kalimantan border, but the distances are great, and they are difficult to get to.

Besides artificial lures, live and dead bait are used for *toman* while fruits such as oil palm and rubber seeds are used as *kelah* bait.

Lakes and reservoirs are where the other big freshwater fishing opportunities are. Since Malaysia has few natural ponds, anglers head for dammed lakes such as Kenyir and Temenggor. However, these are relatively "young", in that the eco-system is still not developed. The best fishing is where the rivers flow into the lakes bringing *toman* and *seberau*. The natural lakes of Cini and Bera in Pahang are shallow, but good for *toman*.

Saltwater Fishing

There are plenty of boats for hire on the coast. Most are basic, but a handful offer reasonable facilities. Nonetheless, some anglers find this primitiveness an attraction. Minimum numbers are needed before a boat will set off.

Deep-sea bottom fishing is expensive, but compared to other countries in the region, relatively affordable. This involves going out with a rod and line with one or two hooks, using bait such as small fish and prawns, and fishing at depths of 50–100 metres (150–300 ft).

Some locations could be up to 4 hours away. A 2-day/1-night trip can be arranged, including boat, ice and bait. Meals can also be arranged.

Anywhere along the peninsula's west coast is good for fishing all year round, including Bagan Datoh and Pangkor (Perak), and Langkawi (Kedah). Table fish are the norm, including *kerapu* (grouper) and *ikan merah* (red snapper). Sarawakian locations include Miri and Tanjung Datu near Kuching.

The peninsula's east coast is good for blue-water game fishing. A popular centre is Mersing, the jumping-off point to the islands of Aur, Dayang and Pemanggil. Here you get black marlin, mackerel, sailfish, baraccuda, and giant trevally. Redang is another good location. In Sarawak, Miri is a centre; in Sabah, Labuan is good for bill fish, and Semporna and Sipadan are the spots for yellow fin tuna, great fighters that go up to 100 kg (220 lb). The best times for this sport are March–September.

For more information, contact:
Persaturan Memancing Malaysia (Malaysian Angler's Association)
Tel: 03-738 8864
Fax: 03-733 8213
Hook, Line & Sinker
Tel: 03-274 5921
Fax: 03-274 1392
e-mail: rnc@pc.jaring.my
Fook Soon
Tel: 03-774 3066
Fish Hunters
Tel: 03-656 6275
It's also worth checking out the *Malay Mail* and angling magazines.

Martial Arts

Silat is the Malay equivalent of *kungfu*. Its origin is accredited to the famous Hang Tuah of old Melaka, who did not hesitate to draw his sword, and even to strike to kill, for the sake of justice. Though mystical and requiring fasting and meditation, youths today regard it as exercise in an artistic form. Demonstrations at weddings and other feasts are given to the rhythmic beat of gongs and drums. It is also part of the school curriculum for boys.

Tai chi is widely practised among older Chinese as a form of exercise, and dawn sees entire fields of people doing various forms of the art. Young Chinese, and indeed, urban Malaysians, favour *tae kwon do* and *karate*, and competitions are held regularly. The Indian traditional martial art form is *silamban*, which sees the use of long sticks.

Remember to ask about group sizes and facilities.

Golf

The golf boom in the late 1980s has made Malaysia a golfer's paradise, especially on the peninsula's west and south coasts. The courses are designed to exploit the natural landscape and offer something for all levels of golfers, amateur or professional.

Generally, clubs are private. However, the so-called "resort clubs" are open to anyone, especially in holiday destinations, where the playing traffic is low. Courses are generally of international standard and are well-maintained; equal care is taken in the design and facilities of club houses. Equipment of every brand can be hired, and bought at affordable prices. Updated lists of golf clubs and resorts plus descriptions can be found in the monthly *Golf Times* magazine; http://www.golftimes.com.my; and http://www.geocities.com/Augusta/4411/

Peninsular Malaysia
Staffield Country Resort
Selangor
Tel: 03-816 6177
Regarded as one of the country's best, this 27-hole course sits on 136 hectares (335 acres) of transformed rubber estate, with 82 bunkers and seven lakes. The Tudor-style club house offers food and a wide range of sports facilities.
Damai Laut Golf and Country Club
Perak
Tel: 05-618 3333
This 18-holer is a challenging course on an isolated landscaped coast, designed by the golf course architect Ronald Fream. There is a club house, and a professional golf trainer is available. The club has links with the Swiss Garden Resort, across from Pulau Pangkor.
Datai Bay Golf Club
Langkawi
Tel: 04-959 2700
A scenic, but tight 18-hole course

between the Andaman Sea and the lush rainforest of Gunung Matcincang. The course lies uphill and downhill with some flat terrain. There is a club house and watersports facilities.
Desaru Golf and Country Resort
Johor
Tel: 07-822 2333
Famous old 18-hole course designed by Robert Trent Jones Jr, sitting in 120 hectares (300 acres) of forest along the coast; lovely all-wood club house with good views. It is linked to the Desaru Golden Beach Hotel.
Awana Golf and Country Resort
Pahang
Tel: 09-211 3222
At a cool 1,000 metres (3,000 ft) up in the Genting Highlands, this scenic 18-hole course is fairly demanding but enjoyable. Bunkers, ponds and streams add to the challenge. There is a three-tiered driving range.

Sarawak
Kelab Golf Sarawak
Kuching
Tel: 082-440 966
This championship 18-hole course is situated on converted secondary forest and swampland in Kuching, with ponds, sand traps and water hazards around the course's total of 36 undulating holes. The club house's terrace bar has a fine view of the course.
Damai Golf Course
Santubong
Tel: 082-440 966
A popular and accessible course with full facilities adjacent to Damai beach and the resort hotels.

Sabah
Sabah Golf and Country Club
Kota Kinabalu
Tel: 088-247 533
A tricky 18-hole course with wide fairways and fast greens. The wind makes play even more interesting, especially during the monsoon months. Facilities include a swimming pool, gymnasium and karaoke lounge. Panoramic views.
Kinabalu Golf Club
Kota Kinabalu

Horse Racing

Meetings are held at the weekend and on Wednesday, rotating between Kuala Lumpur, Ipoh, Penang and Singapore. There are at least eight races a day between 1.30pm and 6pm. A minimum bet is RM5. A racing guide book can be purchased at the entrance of the race course. Off-course betting is also available, where you watch the horses on TV.

Tel: 088-817 396
The 18-hole course is set high on the slopes of Mt Kinabalu with magnificent views and the greater comfort of cooler air.
Bongawan
Kota Kinabalu
Tel: 088-232 350
The two Nicklaus-designed courses at Bongawan, an hour's drive from Kota Kinabalu, offer excellent golf.
Pan Pacific Rasa Ria Resort and **Sutera Harbour**
Kota Kinabalu
Tel: 088-318 888
The new course at Rasa Ria, an hour's drive north along the coast from Kota Kinabalu and the Sutera Harbour course, right on the outskirts of Kota Kinabalu, offer smooth greens and sea views.

Adventure Sports

Sport Diving
Dive operators are divided into on-site operators and those which arrange scheduled trips.
The most popular dive certification in Malaysia is PADI, although some schools offer NAUI and SSI; BSAC is offered only by East Marine in Langkawi (tel: 966 5805), a dive centre with multilingual dive masters which also offers deep-sea fishing.
Most operations are dive shops with dive masters and instructors; a few are certified dive centres offering the full range, from retail to rental and equipment servicing. Retail outlets are usually in the city rather than on the beach.

Peninsular Malaysia
Kembara Station
Tel: 03-706 4752/9
e-mail: enquiries@ kembarastation.com
Focuses on peninsula diving.
Dive Connection
Tel: 03-241 0031
e-mail: simrr@pd.jaring.my
Operates anywhere in Malaysia. It has a dive shop in Redang.
Scuba Point
Tel: 03-774 7288
Operating on the peninsula's east coast, it has a dive shop in Tioman.

Sabah
Among operators for scheduled trips, including instruction, are:
Borneo Divers
Tel: 03-717 3066 (Kuala Lumpur), 088-222 226 (Kota Kinabalu)
e-mail: bdivers@po.jaring.my
Dive pioneer specialising in Sipadan (where it has a dive centre), nearby Pulau Mabul and the Labuan wrecks. It can also handle trips to the peninsula's east coast (including underwater photography trips).
Pulau Sipadan Resorts
Tel: 089-765 200
Fax: 089-763 575
e-mail: psrt@po.jaring.my
These resorts run their own excellent dive centres on Sipadan, Pulau Kalapai (close to Sipadan) and on beautiful Pulau Lankayan situated to the northwest of Sandakan.

Sarawak
Although diving is not a sport normally associated with Sarawak, there is excellent diving off the coast of Miri.
Scuba Sarawak
Royal Righa Hotel
Tel: 085-423 975
Operates a dive boat that takes divers to untouched offshore oceanic shoals, reefs and drop-offs, as well as out to Layang Layang and Labuan.

Mountain Biking
Mountain Biking is a popular new sport to hit both Sabah and Sarawak.

Sarawak
Trails around the rural areas outside Kuching are popular with local groups. Damai Beach is home to the annual Rainforest Cup bike racing event, an increasingly prestigious regional event, and trails here are popular, too.
Contact **Best Systems** for details; tel: 082-255 5000;
e-mail: mtbbike@pl.jaring.my

Sabah
Popular trails include rural areas around Kota Kinabalu. A good route is to bike down from Park headquarters on Mt Kinabalu to Tamparuli, passing through magnificent verdant vistas and undiscovered villages.
Contact **Borneo Expeditions** tel: 088-210 393/222 721.

Rock-climbing
Nomad Adventure
Tel: 03-724 5152
http://www.nomadadventure.freese rver.com
This new indoor rock climbing gym at a shopping centre in Kuala Lumpur organises trips to popular sites, runs special classes for women, and offers equipment for rent and sale.
Tracks Outdoor
Tel: 03-777 8363
e-mail: Tracks@mol.net.my
This operator has a 12-metre (39-ft) featured wall at Kuala Kubu Bahru with a slight overhang, suitable for all levels. Abseiling is conducted from 20–40-metre (60–120 ft) cliffs around its whitewater centre. Equipment can be hired and mountain bike trips arranged, too.

Whitewater Rafting
Minimum numbers are required for whitewater rafting trips. Some companies also arrange transport from the city. The whitewater rafting centre at Kuala Kubu Bahru is under threat from a controversial new dam to be built, but as of end 1999, the following are based there:
Khersonese Expeditions
Tel: 03-784 9040
Experienced adventure guides

offering river-rafting and sea-canoeing in various peninsula locations, including multi-day trips; they can also arrange insurance.

Nomad Adventure
Tel: 03-724 5152
Weekend trips on Sungai Selangor using one- and two-person kayaks.

Tracks Outdoor
Tel: 03-777 8363
e-mail: Tracks@mol.net.my
Arranges daily and multi-day river-rafting trips for all levels in the peninsula, Sumatra and Indonesia with certified river guides. It also has one-person kayaks and holds courses for all levels.

Sabah
Sabah has some of the country's best white-water with trips available to the well known, wild Padas River. Contact **Borneo Expeditions**; tel: 088-210 393/222 721.

See Eco Tours, page 360, for more operators

Language

General

Bahasa Malaysia or BM (Malay) is spoken by all Malaysians, and although dialects differ regionally, the basic structure is the same. Adjectives always follow the noun. *Rumah* (house) and *besar* (big) together as *rumah besar* means "a big house" and so on.

When constructing a sentence, the order is subject-verb-subject: *Dia* (he) *makan* (eats) *nasi* (rice) *goreng* (fried). *Dia makan nasi goreng* = He eats fried rice.

The traditional greeting is *Apa khabar?* – literally "What news?" but is the equivalent of "How are you?" to which the reply is *Khabar baik* – "I'm fine." Today, the ubiquitous "Hello!" or "Hi!" serve the same purpose. Here are some general pronunciation guidelines.

a as in car. *apa* – what; *makan* – eat
ai as in aisle. *kedai* – shop; *sungai* – river
au as in how. *pulau* – island; *jauh* – far
c as in chat. *capal* – sandal; *cinta* – love
e as in early. *membeli* – to buy; *besar* – big
g as in go, and not gem. *pergi* – go; *guru* – teacher
gg as in single. *ringgit* – Malaysian dollar; *tetangga* – household
h as in halt. *mahal* – expensive; *murah* – cheap
i as in feet. *minum* – to drink; *lagi* – again
j as in judge. *jalan* – street; *juta* – million
ng as in singing. *sangat* – very; *bunga* – flower
ny as in onion. *minyak* – petrol/oil; *banyak* – a lot

o as in hop. *orang* – people; *tolong* – help
u as in pool. *ukiran* – carving; *minum* – to drink

Although nearly all syllables are given equal stress, sometimes the final syllable of a word is emphasised, especially the last word in an utterance. This has led to the widespread use of the appendage *-lah* to the important word, whose purpose is purely emphatic. However, *-lah* is also liberally used in English; for instance, you could get thrown a "*Cannot-lah!*", when you are trying to bargain.

Useful Phrases

Good morning *Selamat pagi*
Good afternoon *Selamat tengah hari*
Good evening *Selamat petang*
Good-bye *Selamat tinggal*
Yes *Ya*
No *Tidak*
Thank you *Terima kasih*
Please come in *Sila masuk*
Please sit down *Sila duduk*
Thank you very much *Terima kasih banyak-banyak*
You're welcome *Sama-sama*
Where do you come from? *Asal dari mana?*
I come from… *Saya datang dari…*
What is your name? *Siapa nama anda?*
My name is… *Nama saya…*
Can you speak Bahasa Malaysia? *Boleh anda bercakap Bahasa Malaysia?*
Only a little *Sedikit sahaja*
Do you like Malaysia? *Suka tak Malaysia?*
I like it here *Saya suka berada di sini*
Where are you going? *(Pergi) ke mana?*
I am going to… *Saya pergi ke…*
Turn right *Belok (ke) kanan*
Turn left *Belok (ke) kiri*
Go straight *Jalan terus*
Please stop here *Sila berhenti di sini*
How much? *Berapa harga?*
That's too expensive *Mahal sangat*

Can you reduce the price? *Boleh kurang?*
Wait a minute *Tunggu sekejap*
I would like to change money *Saya hendak tukar duit*
Excuse me *Maafkan saya/Maaf*
Could I make an enquiry? *Tumpang tanya?*
Where is the toilet? *Di mana tandas?*
In the back *Di belakang*
Over there *Di sana*
Over here *Di sini*
What time is it? *Jam berapa?*
One-thirty or half-one *Pukul satu setengah*
What time does the bus leave? *Pukul berapa bas bertolak?*

Useful words

Mr *Encik, Tuan*
Mrs *Puan*
Miss *Cik*
(When you address an older Malay man, you may call him *pakcik*, and a lady, *makcik*. Non-Malays may be addressed as "Uncle" and "Auntie" respectively. Someone obviously younger and children are addressed as *adik*)
I *saya*
you (to someone the same age or younger) *awak, anda* or *kita* (in Borneo Malaysia only)
you (formal) *encik*
he, she *dia*
we *kami* (excluding the speaker), *kita* (including the speaker)
they *mereka*
what? *apa?*
who? *siapa?*
where (place) *di mana?*
where (direction) *ke mana?*
when? *bila?*
how? *bagaimana?*
why? *mengapa?*
which? *yang mana?*

to eat *makan*
to drink *minum*
to sleep *tidur*
to bathe *mandi*
to come *datang*
to go *pergi*
to stop *berhenti*
to buy *beli* (*membeli*)
to sell *jual* (*menjual*)
road, walk *jalan*

airport *lapangan terbang*
post office *pejabat pos*
shop *kedai*
coffeeshop *kedai kopi*
money *wang, duit*
minute *minit*
hour *jam*
day *hari*
week *minggu*
Monday *Isnin*
Tuesday *Selasa*
Wednesday *Rabu*
Thursday *Khamis*
Friday *Jumaat*
Saturday *Sabtu*
Sunday *Ahad*

Numbers

1 *satu*
2 *dua*
3 *tiga*
4 *empat*
5 *lima*
6 *enam*
7 *tujuh*
8 *lapan*
9 *sembilan*
10 *sepuluh*
11 *sebelas*
12 *dua belas*
13 *tiga belas*
20 *dua puluh*
21 *dua puluh satu*
22 *dua puluh dua*

30 *tiga puluh*
40 *empat puluh*

100 *seratus*
263 *dua ratus enam puluh tiga*
1,000 *seribu*

Further Reading

Bookshops

The major book chains in Malaysia are Times, MPH and Popular, while specialist bookstores are found mainly in Kuala Lumpur. Worthy of note are Kinokuniya in the Sogo Departmental Store, and Page One in Lot 10. Skoobs in Brickfields has a good collection of second-hand titles.

Dewan Bahasa dan Pustaka, the language and literature body responsible for developing literature in the national language, has published some fine work on culture and tradition, some of which is available in English translation.

A rich repository of Sarawakian, Borneon and Asian published work is the Sarawak Museum in Kuching. Another excellent bookshop sits within the Holiday Inn Kuching. Small but good collections of nature books, including specialist titles, can be bought at the Kuala Lumpur headquarters of the Malaysian Nature Society (MNS) (tel: 03-287 9422) and the World Wide Fund for Nature (WWF) Malaysia (tel: 03-703 3772).

There are decent maps of the country, including road maps, for sale in Kuala Lumpur; more detailed state maps can be found in the respective states.

Day & Night is a weekly information magazine with useful "what's-happening" listings, while *Vision KL* focuses on the Klang Valley.

History/Political

A History of Malaya, by Barbara Watson Andaya and Leonard Andaya, Macmillan London (1982). Non-colonial objective interpretation of the country's development.
The Golden Chersonese: the Malayan Travels of Victorian Lady,

by Isabella Bird, Oxford University Press Singapore (1883), reprinted. Lyrical 19th-century impressions of the experiences of this intrepid traveller.

Government and Society In Malaysia, by Harold Crouch, Allen & Unwin Australia (1996). An insider's view from an outsider on Malaysian politics, founding his analysis on the fact that Malaysian politics and society operates essentially on the basis of a "moving equilibrium".

The Malay Dilemma, by Mahathir Mohamad, Malaysia (1970). Important text that outlines the prime minister's thoughts on the country's racial politics and economics; recent books by him have been compilations of his speeches and policies.

Malaysia's Political Economy, by Edmund Terence Gomez & Jomo K.S., Cambridge University Press (1997). An insightful and accessible analysis of contemporary Malaysian business and politics, examining through detailed case studies political patronage on wealth accumulation, and policies and their consequences.

Malaysian Journey, by Rehman Rashid, Malaysia (1993). A witty, sharp treatise on contemporary Malaysia, though somewhat dogmatic.

Malay Society: Transformation and Democratisation, by Khoo Kay Kim, Malaysia (1992). The study of Malay society from the Melaka Sultanate to the 1990s, by one of the country's most prominent historians.

Paradoxes of Mahathirism: An Intellectual Biography of Mahathir Mohamad, by Khoo Boo Teik, Oxford University Press (1995). Like all books on the prime minister, this takes an academic approach to his ideas on nationalism, capitalism, Islam, populism, and authoritarianism – the core of Mahathirism.

Sejarah Melayu (The Malay Annals), translated by C.C. Brown, The Royal Asiatic Society (1953), reprinted. The best and most important Malay historical account on the Melaka Sultanate.

General

The Crafts of Malaysia, Dato' Haji Sulaiman Othman, Yeoh Jin Leng, etc, Archipelago Press, Singapore (1994). A beautiful documentary of the development of the Malay arts in a changing society, with pictures of the best craft from museums and private collections.

Cuzinhia Cristang: A Malacca-Portuguese Cookbook, by Celine J. Marbeck, Tropical Press, Malaysia. A lovely collection of six centuries of the food of the Melaka-Portuguese Cristang people.

The Encyclopedia of Malaysia, Editions Didier Millet, Singapore (1998). A five-volume highly-illustrative effort on the environment, plants, animals, early history and architecture.

The Food of Malaysia, edited by Wendy Hutton, Periplus Editions, Singapore (1995). Handy-sized collection of local recipes with nice background information and lovely colour photographs.

Kuala Lumpur – A Sketchbook, by Chin Kon Yit, and Chen Voon Fee, Archipelago Press, Singapore (1998). Beautiful watercolour paintings of old Kuala Lumpur with suitably brief captions.

Lat, Malaysia, Times Publishing. Compilations of the work of the country's sharpest and funniest cartoonist; hilarious depictions of Malaysian life and psyche.

Rasa Malaysia, by Betty Yew, Times Publishing, Malaysia. A collection of Malaysia's best-loved recipes by a leading chef and writer of cookbooks.

Culture Shock! Malaysia, by Heidi Munan, Graphic Arts Center Pub Co. (1991). A witty and invaluable treatise on Malaysian customs, can-do's and absolutely-nots.

Natural History

Beaches of Malaysia, The Department of Irrigation and Drainage, Malaysia and Design Dimension Sdn Bhd, (1997). The first comprehensive photographic record of more than 168 beaches, illustrating their moods and beauty.

National Parks of Malaysia, by WWF Malaysia, New Holland, Malaysia (1998). Pictorial, tourist-market coffee-table book, with an excellent bibliography.

Photographic Guide to the Birds of Peninsular Malaysia and Singapore, by M. Strange, and A. Jeyarajasingham, Malaysia (1993).

Pocket Guide to the Birds of Borneo, by Sabah Society with WWF Malaysia, Malaysia (1995).

Wild Malaysia: The Wildlife and Scenery of Peninsular Malaysia, Sarawak and Sabah by Junaidi Payne, Gerald Cubitt (photographer), MIT Press (1990), World Wide Fund for Nature. A pictorial introduction containing 400 colour photographs of animals and habitats. The text, by a leading Malaysian environmentalist, examines conservation and development, as well as peoples and natural history.

Fiction/Biography

Lord Jim, by Joseph Conrad, Penguin, London (1900). The tale of an Englishman who abandons his ship and hides in Malaya eventually becoming a Lord. Conrad set many other stories in the Malay Archipelago, including *Victory: an Island Tale* and *The Rescue.*

Maugham's Malaysian Stories, by Somerset Maugham (1933, reprinted 1986). Masterful story-telling of British colonial life in the country.

Among the White Moon Faces: An Asian-American Memoir of Homelands (Cross-Cultural Memoir Series) by Shirley Geok-Lin Lim, Feminist Press (1996). A biographical recount of a Malaysian childhood and later life in the United States; the author has also published short stories.

Borneo

Travel

Into The Heart Of Borneo, by Redmond O' Hanlon, The Salamander Press (1984). A heartwarmingly and laugh-aloud treatise on O'Hanlon's hilarious expedition to Borneo, told with great sympathy and style.

Stranger In The Forest, by Eric Hanson (*out of print*). A gripping and sometimes chilling tale of one man's adventures as he learns the ways of the tribal folk during his solitary wander through the forest.

World Within, by Tom Harrisson, Oxford University Press Singapore (1986). A classic story by the man who later became curator of Sarawak Museum tells of Bario's Kelabit Highlands during the Japanese occupation years of World War II.

History/Culture

Sarawak Crafts – Methods and Motifs, by Heidi Munan, Oxford University Press (1989). Written by a Sarawak expert, this small book is filled with a wealth of information.

Sarawak Style, by Edric Ong, Times Editions Singapore (1996). Well-photographed book examining style in the Sarawak way.

Natural Man, by Charles Hose, Oxford University Press Singapore (1988). A reprint of a 1912 study by one of Sarawak's colonial administrators under Rajah Charles Brooke.

Enchanted Gardens of Kinabalu, by Susan M. Phillipps, Natural History Publications (Borneo), Malaysia (1995). A beautiful book of botanical paintings that include coral gardens, too.

The Malay Archipelago, by Alfred Russell Wallace (1869). A classic tale of a Victorian naturalist who spent several years wandering through the archipelago. He was also instrumental in assisting in the setting up of Sarawak Museum and his theories on evolution coincided with those of Darwin.

Online

For newsgroups, there's nothing like soc.culture.Malaysia, although you will have to wade through the usual diarrhoea. There are numerous discussion, news- and travel-sites on Malaysia. Try Malaysian search engine Malaysia

Search: http://www.cari.com.my

Useful Websites

News: *The Star*, http://www.thestar.com.my
Malaysiana: Malaysia Homepage, http://www.mymalaysia.net.my
Tourism: Tourism Malaysia, http://tourism.gov.my
Sarawak Tourism: http://www.sarawaktourism.com
Sabah Tourism: http://www.jaring.my/sabah/eclipse.htm

ART & PHOTO CREDITS

Picture Spreads

INSIGHT GUIDE
Malaysia

Cartographic Editor **Zoë Goodwin**
Production **Caroline Low**
Design Consultants
Carlotta Junger, Graham Mitchener
Picture Research **Hilary Genin**

Index

Numbers in italics refer to photographs

The Insight Approach

The book you are holding is part of the world's largest range of guidebooks. Its purpose is to help you have the most valuable travel experience possible, and we try to achieve this by providing not only information about countries, regions and cities but also genuine insight into their history, culture, institutions and people.

Since the first Insight Guide – to Bali – was published in 1970, the series has been dedicated to the proposition that, with insight into a country's people and culture, visitors can both enhance their own experience and be accepted more easily by their hosts. Now, in a world where ethnic hostilities and nationalist conflicts are all too common, such attempts to increase understanding between peoples are more important than ever.

Insight Guides:
Essentials for understanding

Because a nation's past holds the key to its present, each Insight Guide kicks off with lively history chapters. These are followed by magazine-style essays on culture and daily life. This essential background information gives readers the necessary context for using the main Places section, with its comprehensive run-down on things worth seeing and doing.

Finally, a listings section contains all the information you'll need on travel, hotels, restaurants and opening times.

As far as possible, we rely on local writers and specialists to ensure that information is authoritative. The pictures, for which Insight Guides have become so celebrated, are just as important. Our photojournalistic approach aims not only to illustrate a destination but also to communicate visually and directly to readers life as it is lived by the locals. The series has grown to almost 200 titles.

Compact Guides:
The "great little guides"

As invaluable as such background information is, it isn't always fun to carry an Insight Guide through a crowded souk or up a church tower. Could we, readers asked, distil the key reference material into a slim volume for on-the-spot use?

Our response was to design Compact Guides as an entirely new series, with original text carefully cross-referenced to detailed maps and more than 200 photographs. In essence, they're miniature encyclopedias, concise and comprehensive, displaying reliable and up-to-date information in an accessible way. There are almost 100 titles.

Pocket Guides:
A local host in book form

However wide-ranging the information in a book, human beings still value the personal touch. Our editors are often asked the same questions. Where do *you* go to eat? What do *you* think is the best beach? What would *you* recommend if I have only three days? We invited our local correspondents to act as "substitute hosts" by revealing their preferred walks and trips, listing the restaurants they go to and structuring a visit into a series of timed itineraries.

The result: our Pocket Guides, complete with full-size fold-out maps. These 100-plus titles help readers plan a trip precisely, particularly if their time is short.

Exploring with Insight:
A valuable travel experience

In conjunction with co-publishers all over the world, we print in up to 10 languages, from German to Chinese, from Danish to Russian. But our aim remains simple: to enhance your travel experience by combining our expertise in guidebook publishing with the on-the-spot knowledge of our correspondents.

66 I was first drawn to the Insight Guides by the excellent "Nepal" volume. I can think of no book which so effectively captures the essence of a country. Out of these pages leaped the Nepal I know – the captivating charm of a people and their culture. I've since discovered and enjoyed the entire Insight Guide series. Each volume deals with a country in the same sensitive depth, which is nowhere more evident than in the superb photography. 99

Sir Edmund Hillary

The World of Insight Guides

400 books in three complementary series cover every major destination in every continent.